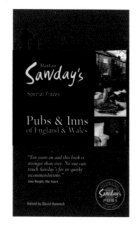

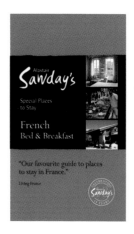

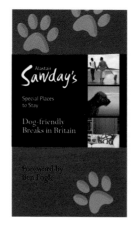

Alastair
Sawday's

Special Places to Stay

Eighteenth edition
Copyright © 2013
Alastair Sawday Publishing Co. Ltd
Published in September 2013
ISBN-13: 978-1-906136-63-5

Alastair Sawday Publishing Co. Ltd,
The Old Farmyard, Yanley Lane,
Long Ashton, Bristol BS41 9LR, UK
Tel: +44 (0)1275 395430
Email: info@sawdays.co.uk
Web: www.sawdays.co.uk

The Globe Pequot Press,
P. O. Box 480, Guilford,
Connecticut 06437, USA
Tel: +1 203 458 4500
Email: info@globepequot.com
Web: www.globepequot.com

Series Editor Alastair Sawday
Editors Nicola Crosse & Wendy Ogden
Editorial Assistance Helen Burke,
Sarah Claridge, Lianka Varga
Senior Editor Jo Boissevain
Picture Editor Alec Studerus
Production Coordinators Alex Skinner
& Sarah Frost Mellor
Writing David Ashby, Jo Boissevain,
Sarah Bolton, Nicola Crosse, Esther
Hubert, Annie Shillito, Wendy Ogden
Inspections David Ashby, Mandy Barnes,
Sue Birtwistle, Neil Brown, Anne Coates,
Angie Collings, Trish Dugmore, Naomi
Gorvin, Rebecca Harris, Esther Hubert,
Su Illingworth, Jackie King, Auriol
Marson, Margot Rawson, Aideen Reid,
Tristram Templer, Nicky Tennent, Jill
Tibbetts, Jacqui Vallis, Mandy Wragg
Special thanks to Angie Reid. Thanks also to
others who did an inspection or two.
Sales & Marketing & PR
01275 395433

Production: Pagebypage Co Ltd
Maps: Maidenhead Cartographic Services
Printing: Grafica Cems, Navarra, Spain
UK distribution: The Travel Alliance, Bath
Diane@popoutmaps.com

Cover photo credits.
Front 1. The Birches Mill, Shropshire, entry 414 2. Coromandel House, Sussex, entry 518 3. The Old
Manor House, Warwickshire, entry 527
Back: 1. Hanover House, Gloucestershire, entry 216 2. Wriggly Tin Shepherd's Huts, Hampshire, entry
242 3. Lower House, Herefordshire, entry 248

Alastair Sawday's

Special Places to Stay

British
Bed & Breakfast

4   Contents

5

houses more luxurious than many hotels. We encourage you to brave the simplicity of rooms in a university (with breakfast thrown in), and to enjoy engagingly quirky, and inexpensive, London 'DIY' B&Bs.

The commercial pressure is on us to play safe, but we are sticking to our guns and insist on including unusual, even eccentric, places that enrich your experience of Britain. As we continue, for example, to encourage the appreciation of local and organic food, so we also encourage the development of local enterprise, ideas and character.

So it is a joy to me to see an increase in applications from B&Bs who do things their own way. We have a bee sanctuary, a farm 'school' with a newt trail, a choice between bedrooms in the house or the VW camper van, virtually self-catering B&B in your own den in the garden, city places where you can have breakfast in the café below. All are breaking the rules of B&B: fewer notices, fewer restrictions, more fun. Another piece of good news is that B&B owners are serving weekend breakfasts later.

Eighteen years – that is how long this British Bed and Breakfast book has been going! Eighteen editions, each richer than the last. The website dances to the same tune – with sparkle, energy and conviction.

We continue to be very different from other 'collections'. We are, first and foremost, eclectic; we embrace variety, so we will never become just a collection of posh, comfortable houses that pamper you. We do much more: our *Special Places* delight, surprise and inspire those who use them. We range gaily from a lino-floored croft cottage with no central heating and a dash to the loo, to swish town and country

Just to show how different we are, this 18th edition includes some of our Canopy & Stars collection. They take our traditional emphasis on 'character' to a new level: huts, tents, boats, lorries, treehouses – all sorts of places can be made interesting and comfortable. Long live eclecticism!

Alastair Sawday

Photo: Tom Germain

It's simple. There are no rules, no boxes to tick. We choose places that we like and are fiercely subjective in our choices. We also recognise that one person's idea of special is not necessarily someone else's so there is a huge variety of places, and prices, in the book. Those who are familiar with our *Special Places* series know that we look for comfort, originality, authenticity, and reject the insincere, the anonymous and the banal. The way guests are treated comes as high on our list as the setting, the architecture, the atmosphere and the food.

Inspections

We visit every place in the guide to get a feel for how both house and owner tick. We don't take a clipboard and we don't have a list of what is acceptable and what is not. Instead, we chat for an hour or so with the owner and look round. It's all very informal, but it gives us an excellent idea of who would enjoy staying there. If the visit happens to be the last of the day, we may stay the night. Once in the book properties are re-inspected every four years or so, to keep things fresh and accurate.

Feedback

In between inspections we rely on feedback from our army of readers, as well as from staff members who are encouraged to visit properties across the series. This feedback is invaluable to us and we always follow up on comments. So do tell us whether your stay has been

a joy or not, if the atmosphere was great or stuffy, the owners cheery or bored. The accuracy of the book depends on what you, and our inspectors, tell us. A lot of the new entries in each edition are recommended by our readers, so keep telling us about new places you've discovered too. Please visit our site, www.sawdays.co.uk/recommend to tell us about your discoveries.

However, please do not tell us if the bedside light was broken, or the shower head was scummy. Tell the owner, immediately, and get them to do something about it. Most owners are more than happy to correct problems and will bend over backwards to help. Far better than bottling it up and then writing to us a week later!

Subscriptions

Owners pay to appear in this guide. Their fee goes towards the high costs of

Photo: Kaywana Hall, Devon, entry 115

inspecting, producing an all-colour book and developing our website. We only include places that we like and find special for one reason or another, so it is not possible for anyone to buy their way onto these pages. Nor is it possible for the owner to write their own description. We will say if the bedrooms are small, or if a main road is near. We do our best to avoid misleading people.

Disclaimer

We make no claims to pure objectivity in choosing these places. They are here simply because we like them. Our opinions and tastes are ours alone and this book is a statement of them; we hope you will share them. We have done our utmost to get our facts right but apologise unreservedly for any mistakes that may have crept in.

You should know that we don't check such things as fire regulations, swimming pool security or any other laws with which owners of properties receiving paying guests should comply. This is the responsibility of the owners.

Photo: Horsleygate Hall, Derbyshire, entry 99

Finding the right place for you

All these places are special in one way or another. All have been visited and then written about honestly so that you can take what you like and leave the rest. Those of you who swear by Sawday's books trust our write-ups precisely because we don't have a blanket standard; we include places simply because we like them. But we all have different priorities, so do read the descriptions carefully and pick out the places where you will be comfortable. If something is particularly important to you then do check when you book: a simple question or two can avoid misunderstandings.

Maps

Each property is flagged with its entry number on the maps at the front. These maps are a great starting point for planning your trip, but please don't use them as anything other than a general guide – use a decent road map for real navigation. Most places will send you detailed instructions once you have booked your stay.

Symbols

Below each entry you will see some symbols, which are explained at the very back of the book. They are based on the information given to us by the owners. However, things do change: bikes may be under repair or a new pool may have been put in. Please use the symbols as a guide rather than an absolute statement of fact and double-check anything that is important to you – owners occasionally

Photo: Keigwin Farmhouse, Cornwall, entry 49

bend their own rules, so it's worth asking if you may take your child or dog even if they don't have the symbol.

Children – The 🧍 symbol shows places which are happy to accept children of all ages. This does not mean that they will necessarily have cots, high chairs, etc. If an owner welcomes children but only those above a certain age, we have put these details at the end of their write-up. These houses do not have the child symbol, but even these folk may accept your younger child if you are the only guests. Many who say no to children do so not because they don't like them but because they may have a steep stair, an unfenced pond or they find balancing the needs of mixed age groups too challenging.

Pets – Our 🐕 symbol shows places which are happy to accept pets. It means they can sleep in the bedroom with you, but not on the bed. Be realistic about your pet – if it is nervous or excitable or doesn't like the company of other dogs, people, chickens, children, then say so. Do let the owners know when booking that you intend to bring your pet – particularly if it is not the usual dog!

Owners' pets – The 🐈 symbol is given when the owners have their own pet on the premises. It may not be a cat! But it is there to warn you that you may be greeted by a dog, serenaded by a parrot, or indeed sat upon by a cat.

Quick reference indices

At the back of the book you'll find a number of quick-reference indices that will help you choose the place that is just right for you.

In this edition you'll find listings of properties where:
• at least one bedroom or bathroom is accessible for wheelchair users
• a double costs £70 or less
• you can stay all day
• owners have a single room, or they let a double bedroom to guests travelling alone for half the double occupancy price, or less
• guests' pets can sleep in the bedroom (but not on the bed)

Photo: Aurora, Highland, entry 640

Types of places

Some houses have rooms in annexes or stables, barns or garden 'wings', some of which feel part of the house, some of which don't. If you have a strong preference for being in the throng or for being apart, check those details. Consider your surroundings when you are packing: large, ancient country houses may be cooler than you are used to; city places and working farms may be noisy at times; and that peacock or cockerel we mention may disturb you. Light sleepers should pack ear plugs, and take a dressing gown if there's a separate bathroom (though these are sometimes provided).

Some owners give you a front door key so you may come and go as you please; others like to have the house empty between, say, 10am and 4pm. If you would prefer not to wander far during the day then look for the places that have the 'Stay all day' quick reference at the back of the book.

Sawday's Canopy & Stars CANOPY&STARS

These are some of our more outdoor places. They could be anything from palatial treehouses to rustic wagons and everything in-between. The same standards of inspection and selection apply, but you might find things delightfully different to what you're used to. You could be clambering up a ladder to bed, throwing another log on the wood-burner or wheeling your luggage in a barrow, so take a look and keep your mind open to the outdoors. These entries

are highlighted with a green Canopy & Stars logo.

Rooms

Bedrooms – We tell you if a room is a double, twin/double (i.e. with zip and link beds), suite (with a sitting area), family or single. Most owners are flexible and can juggle beds or bedrooms; talk to them about what you need before you book. Staying in a B&B will not be like staying in a hotel; it is rare to be given your own room key and your bed will not necessarily be made during your stay, or your room cleaned. Make sure you are clear about the room that you have booked, its views, bathroom and beds, etc.

Bathrooms – Most bedrooms in this book have an en suite bath or shower room; we only mention bathroom details when they do not. So, you may get a 'separate' bathroom (yours alone but not en suite) or a shared bathroom. Under certain entries

Photo: Upper Larkstoke, Warwickshire, entry 528

we mention that two rooms share a bathroom and are 'let to same party only'. Please do not assume this means you must be a group of friends to apply; it simply means that if you book one of these rooms you will not be sharing a bathroom with strangers. If these things are important to you, please check when booking. Bath/shower means a bath with shower over; bath and shower means there is a separate shower unit.

Sitting rooms – Most B&B owners offer guests the family sitting room to share, or they provide a sitting room specially for guests, but do not assume that every bedroom or sitting room has a TV.

Meals

Unless we say otherwise, a full cooked breakfast is included. Some owners – particularly in London – will give you a good continental breakfast instead. Often you will feast on local sausage and bacon, eggs from resident hens, homemade breads and jams. In some you may have organic yogurts and beautifully presented fruit compotes. Some owners are fairly unbending about breakfast times, others are happy to just wait until you want it, or even bring it to you in bed.

Apart from breakfast, no meals should be expected unless you have arranged them in advance. Although we don't say so on each entry – the repetition a few hundred times would be tedious – all owners who provide packed lunch, lunch or dinner need ADVANCE NOTICE. And they want to get things right for you so, when booking, please discuss your diet and meal times. Meal prices are quoted per person, and dinner is often a social occasion shared with your hosts and other guests.

Do eat in if you can – this book is teeming with good cooks. And how much more relaxing after a day out to have to move no further than the dining room for an excellent dinner, and to eat and drink knowing there's only a flight of stairs between you and your bed. Very few of our houses are licensed, but most are happy for you to bring your own drink.

If you do decide to head out for supper, you can find recommendations of our favourite pubs on our *Special Places to Eat and Drink* microsite, see: www.sawdays.co.uk/pubs. If a B&B has a pub nearby, you can see this on their page on our website, too.

Prices and minimum stays

Each entry gives a price PER ROOM for two people. We also include prices for single rooms, and let you know if there will be any extra to pay, should you choose to loll in a double bed on your own.

The price range for each B&B covers a one-night stay in the cheapest room in low season to the most expensive in high season. Some owners charge more at certain times (during regattas or festivals, for example) and some charge less for stays of more than one night. Some owners ask for a two-night minimum stay and we mention this where possible. Most of our houses could fill many times over on peak weekends and during the summer; book early, especially if you have specific needs.

Booking and cancellation
You may not receive a reply to your booking enquiry immediately; B&Bs are not hotels and the owners may be away. When you speak to the owner double-check the price you will pay for B&B and for any meals.

Requests for deposits vary; some are non-refundable, especially in our London homes, and some owners may charge you for the whole of the booked stay in advance. Some cancellation policies are more stringent than others. It is also worth noting that some owners will take the money directly from your credit/debit card without contacting you to discuss it. Ask them to explain their cancellation policy clearly before booking to avoid a nasty surprise.

Payment
All our owners take cash and UK cheques with a cheque card. Some take credit cards; if they do we have given them the appropriate symbol. Check that your particular credit card is acceptable.

Tipping
Owners do not expect tips. If you have been treated with extraordinary kindness, write to them, or leave a small

gift. Please tell us, too – we love to hear, and we do note all feedback.

Arrivals and departures
Say roughly what time you will arrive (normally after 4pm), as most hosts like to welcome you personally. Be on time if you have booked dinner; if, despite best efforts, you are delayed, phone to give warning.

Closed
When given in months this means the whole of the month stated.

Photo: Bosvathick, Cornwall, entry 62

Priory Bay Yurts, Isle of Wight, entry 264

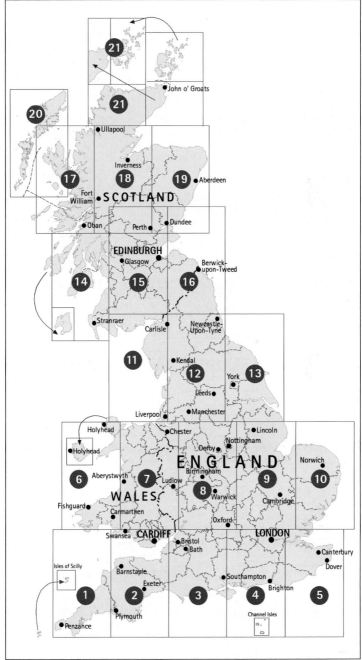

©Maidenhead Cartographic, 2013

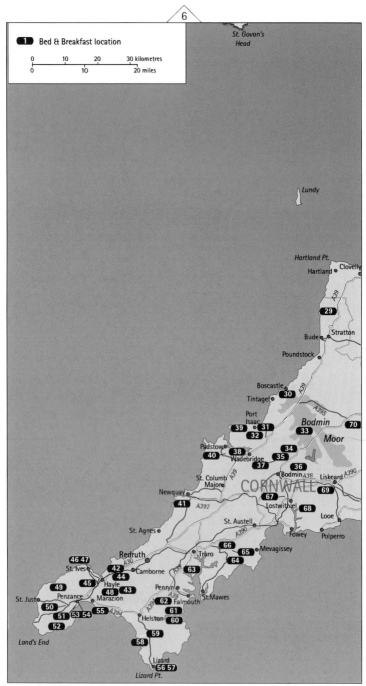

Bed & Breakfast location

0   10   20   30 kilometres
0   10   20 miles

Map 2 17

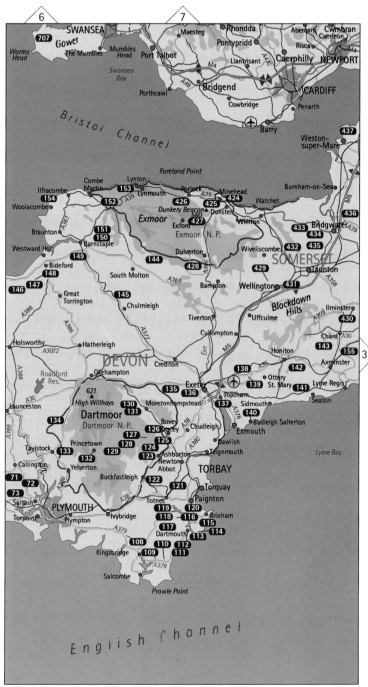

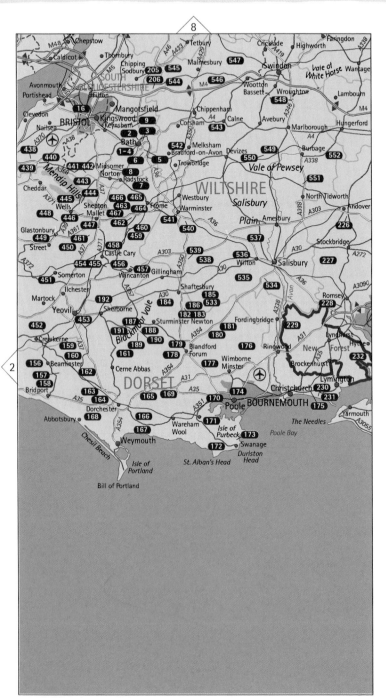

©Maidenhead Cartographic, 2013

Map 4   19

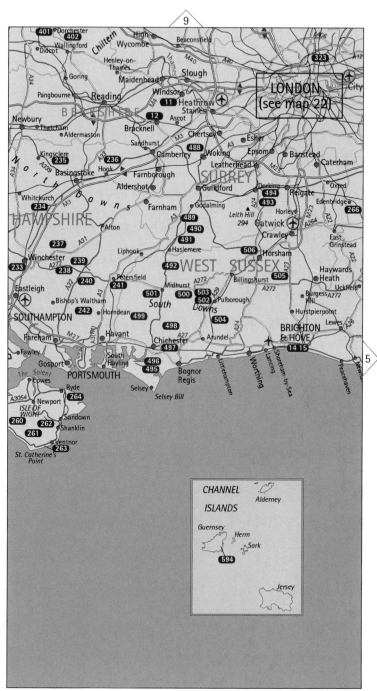

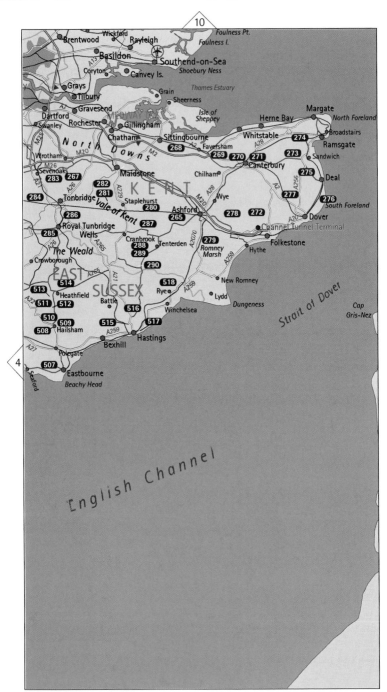

Map 6

21

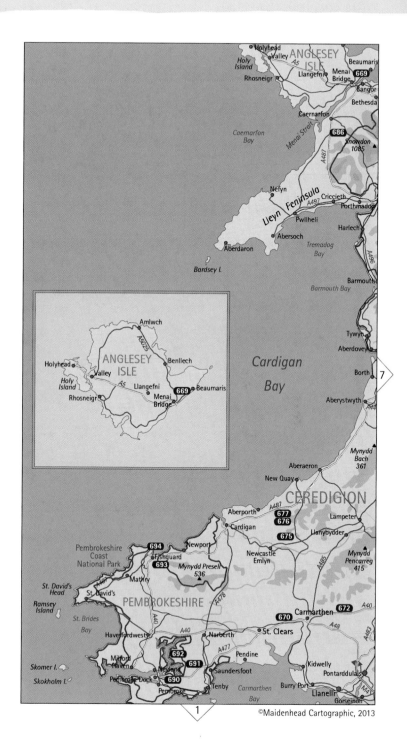

©Maidenhead Cartographic, 2013

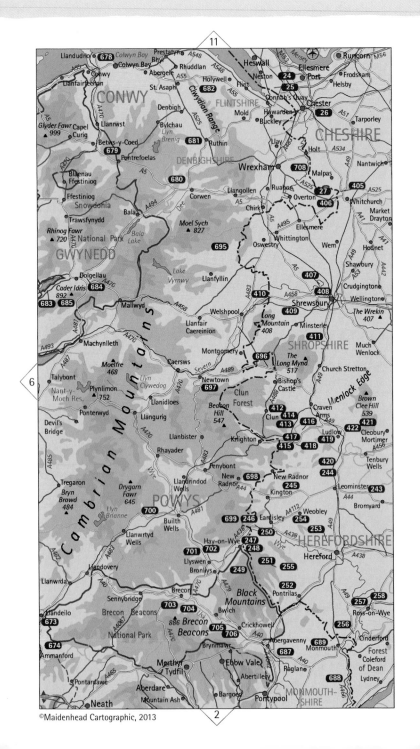

Map 8

23

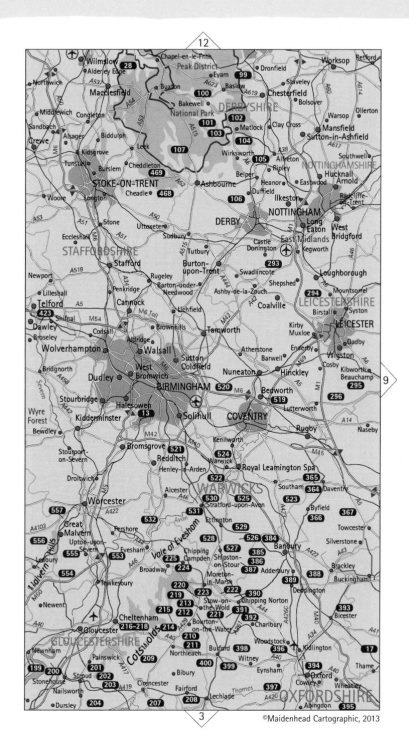

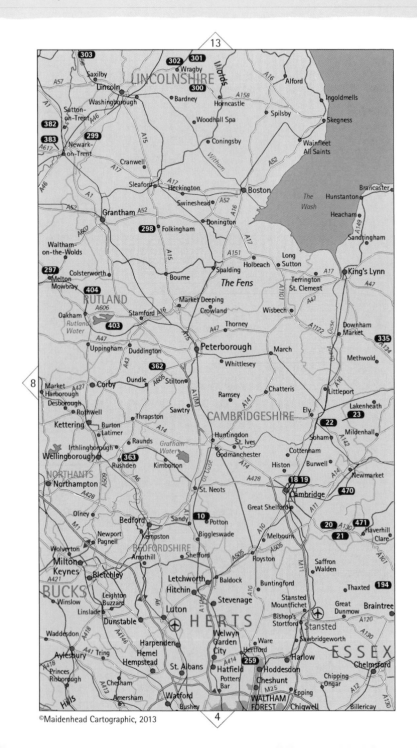

Map 10

25

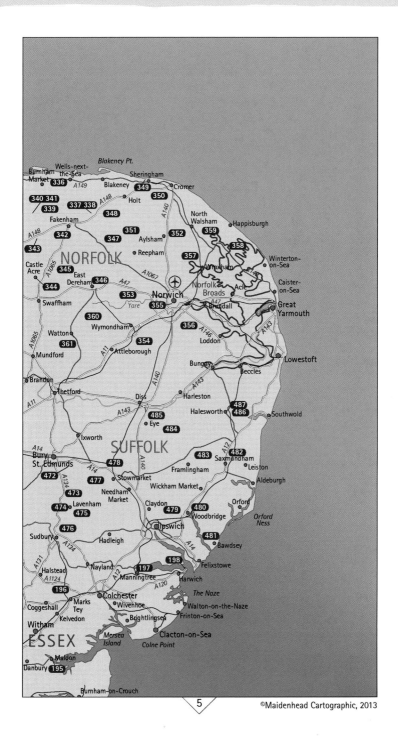

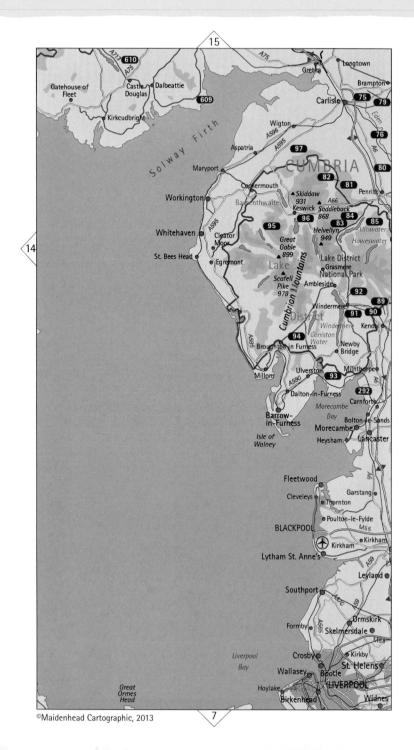

15

610
A713
A75
A75

Gatehouse of
Fleet

Castle
Douglas
Dalbeattie

609

Kirkcudbright

Gretna
Longtown

Brampton

Carlisle
75
79

Eden
A6
76

Wigton
A596

Solway Firth

Aspatria

A595

97

CUMBRIA

80

Maryport

82

81

Penrith

Cockermouth

Workington

Bassenthwaite

Skiddaw
931

Keswick

Saddleback
868

A66

84

85

Ullswater

Howeswater

Whitehaven

A595

Cleator
Moor

95

96

83

Helvellyn
949

St. Bees Head

Egremont

Great
Gable
899

Lake

Lake District
National Park

Grasmere

Scafell
Pike
978

Cumbrian Mountains

Ambleside

92

89

District

Windermere

91

90

Windermere

Kendal

Coniston
Water

Newby
Bridge

A595

94

Broughton-in-Furness

14

Millom

Ulverston

A590

93

Milnthorpe

A6

Dalton-in-Furness

Carnforth

292

Morecambe
Bay

Barrow-
in-Furness

Bolton-le-Sands

Morecambe

Isle of
Walney

Heysham

Lancaster

A6

Fleetwood

Cleveleys

Garstang

Thornton

Poulton-le-Fylde

M55

BLACKPOOL

Kirkham

Kirkham

Lytham St. Anne's

A59

Leyland

Southport

A576

59

Formby

A565

Ørmskirk

Skelmersdale

M58

Liverpool
Bay

Crosby

Kirkby

St. Helens

Wallasey

Bootle

Great
Ormes
Head

Hoylake

LIVERPOOL

Birkenhead

Widnes

Map 12

27

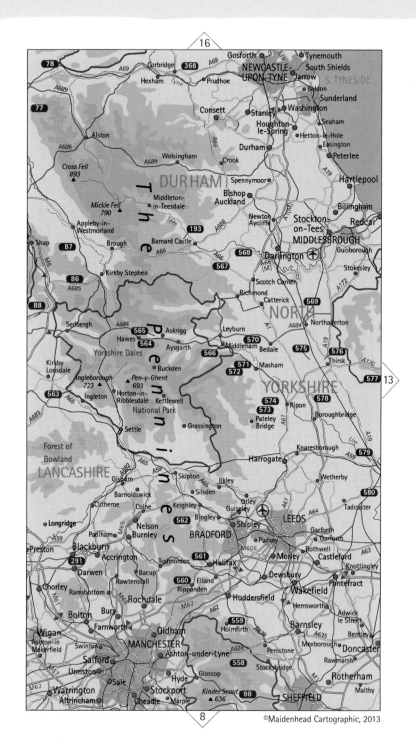

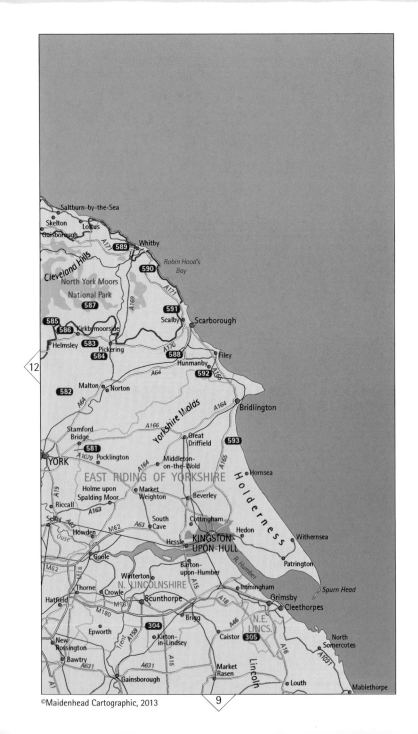

Map 14   29

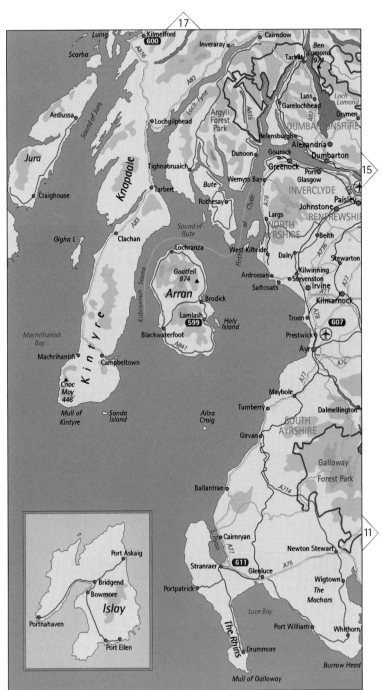

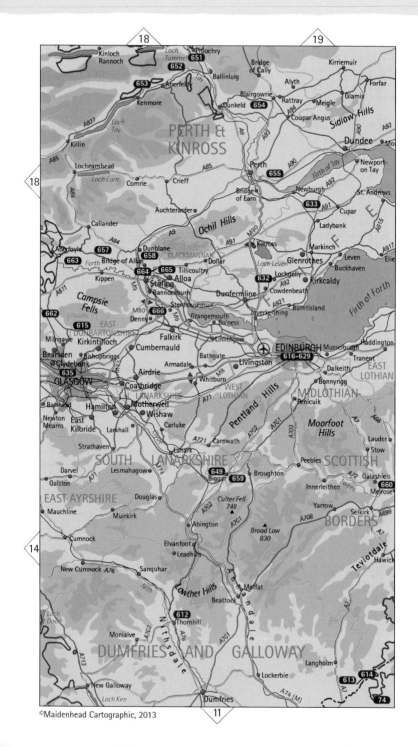

Map 16

31

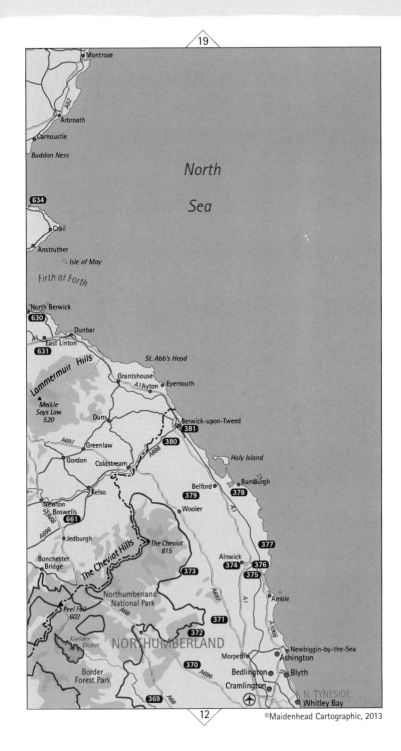

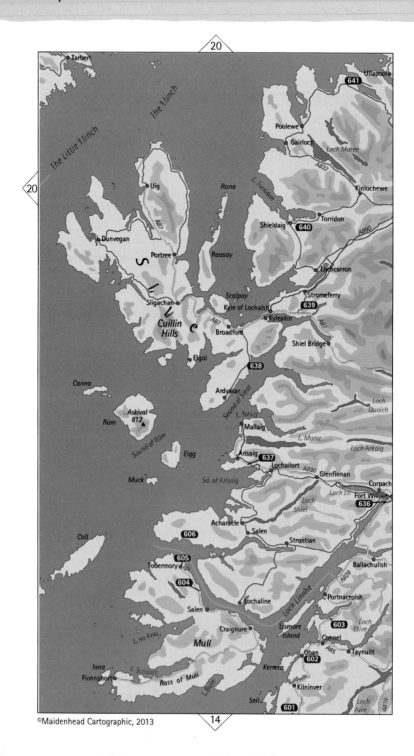

©Maidenhead Cartographic, 2013

Map 18 33

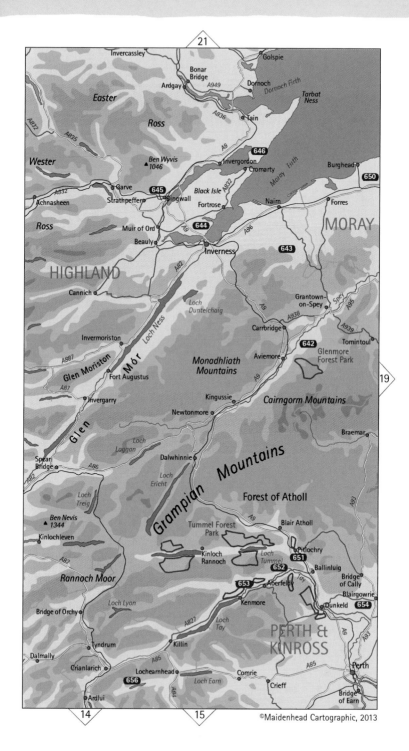

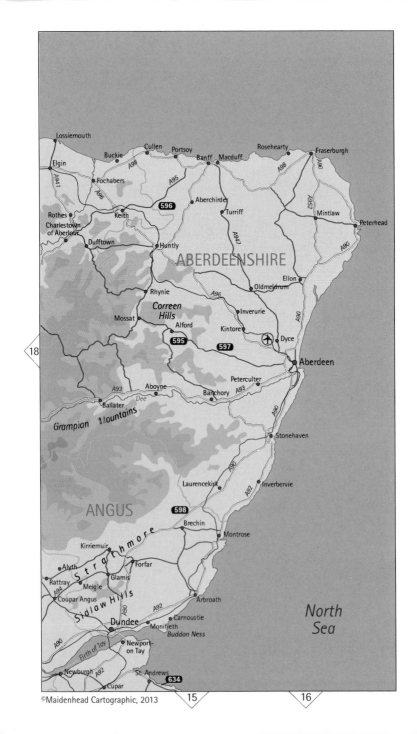

Map 20

35

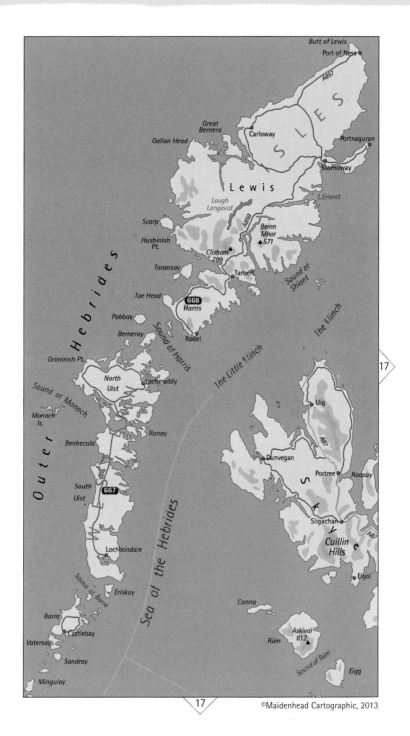

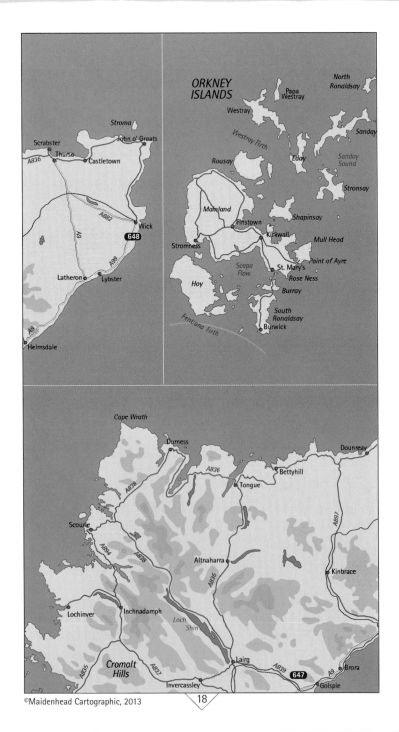

ORKNEY
ISLANDS

North
Ronaldsay

Papa
Westray

Westray

Westray Firth

Sanday

Stroma

John o' Groats

Scrabster

Thurso

Castletown

A836

Rousay

Eday

Sanday
Sound

Stronsay

Mainland

Finstown

Shapinsay

A882

Wick

648

Kirkwall

Mull Head

A9

Stromness

Point of Ayre

A99

Latheron

Lybster

Scapa
Flow

St. Mary's

Rose Ness

Hoy

Burray

A9

Burwick

South
Ronaldsay

Pentland Firth

Helmsdale

Cape Wrath

Durness

Dounreay

A836

Bettyhill

A836

Tongue

A897

Scourie

A894

A838

Altnaharra

A836

Kinbrace

Lochinver

Inchnadamph

Loch
Shin

A835

Cromalt
Hills

A837

Lairg

A839

647

A9

Brora

Invercassley

Golspie

Map 22   37

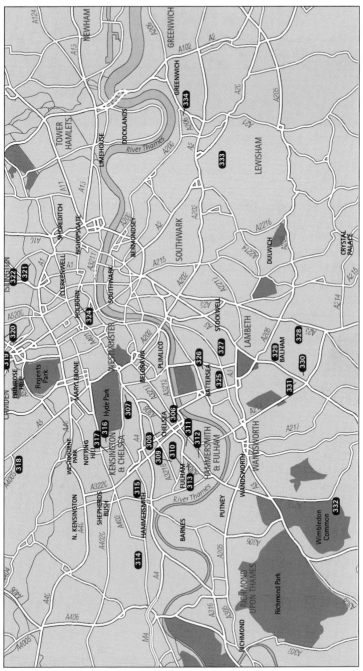

©Maidenhead Cartographic, 2013

Enjoy the special places in the West at your own pace.

Whether it's your first visit to the West of England or you're a frequent visitor, you'll find there's so much to see and do in this special part of the country. Whether you prefer sunning yourself on the miles of beautiful coastline, enjoying a slow glass of cider in our rural idyll, or soaking up the culture and heritage of Bristol or Bath there is something for everyone. And to help you decide how to make best use of your time during your stay, you may need some assistance in planning how to get around, and you can't beat a bit of insider local knowledge.

One of the most comprehensive sources for all things travel related in the West of England can be found at .travelwest.info.

It has been developed through the four local authorities covering the area (Bath & North East Somerset, Bristol, North Somerset and South Gloucestershire).

It contains up to the minute information for however you choose to travel, so you can use it to help plan your journey ahead by car, public transport, or under your own steam by bike or on foot.

There are some really useful downloadable resources such as maps and timetables, which you can use during your visit.

It is also a great help to have on your mobile phone browser when you are out and about, as it provides real time travel information so you can find out about any delays or disruptions on your route.

We suggest you'll get the best out of the West by taking life in the slow lane… you'll be surprised at what you find!

find your way with

travelwest+
www.travelwest.info

bike it   walk it   bus it

England

Discover the west at your own pace

Bath & N.E. Somerset

Pitt House

You couldn't be closer to the centre, nor on a calmer street. This Grade I-listed, seven-storey house, once home to William Pitt the Younger, is now inhabited by a warm, creative couple with a wry sense of humour. Inside: Georgian splendour matched by 21st-century eccentricity. Find sanded floorboards, walls of pure white, dazzling marble busts, a cow hide rug, a tumble of classical and oriental styles... collectors of antiques will keel over in a state of bliss. Bedrooms (up four flights of stairs) are only marginally less exotic, and share a fabulous bathroom and sitting room. Breakfast is the finest of continental. Outstanding.

Rooms	2 doubles sharing bath/shower.
Price	£90–£110. Singles £80.
Meals	Continental breakfast.
	Pubs/restaurants 2-minute walk.
Closed	Rarely.

	David & Sarah Bridgwater
	Pitt House,
	15 Johnstone Street,
	Bath,
	Bath & N.E. Somerset BA2 4DH
Tel	+44 (0)1225 471580
Mobile	+44 (0)7710 124376
Email	david.j.bridgwater@btinternet.com

Entry 1   Map 3

Bath & N.E. Somerset

77 Great Pulteney Street

Elegant stone steps lead down past exotic ferns to a spacious garden flat in this broad street of grand Grade I-listed houses. Inside all is pale wood, modern art, bergère chairs and palms. Downstairs is a large, smart bedroom and bathroom with loads of books and its own door to a delightful small sunny garden. On fine mornings you breakfast here, or choose the gorgeous upstairs dining room: fine local bacon and sausages and fruit from the allotment. Ian is a keen cook so dinner will also be special, but there are lots of good places to eat – and shop – nearby. Henry may play the Northumbrian pipes for you if you ask nicely...

Rooms	1 double.
Price	£85–£110. Singles from £60.
Meals	Dinner £25. Packed lunch from £5.
Closed	Rarely.

Ian Critchley & Henry Ford
77 Great Pulteney Street,
Bath,
Bath & N.E. Somerset BA2 4DL

Tel   +44 (0)1225 466659
Email   critchford@77pulteneyst.co.uk
Web   www.77pulteneyst.co.uk

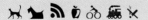

Entry 2   Map 3

Bath & N.E. Somerset

Sir Walter Elliot's House

Utterly wonderful hosts at this Grade I-listed house. On one of Bath's finest Regency terraces, it has been so beautifully restored that the BBC filmed it for *Persuasion*; Jane Austen Society members often stay. Up several stairs are bedrooms flooded with light, two with views over Sydney Gardens, one with a bathroom in marquina marble, cherrywood and ebony. Have breakfast in the convivial family kitchen, or in the plant-filled conservatory. For the adventurous, Mechthild will serve an Austrian alternative – cold meats and cheeses, fresh rye breads and homemade cakes. *Herrlich!*

Minimum stay two nights at weekends.

Rooms	3 twins/doubles.
Price	£95–£155. Singles £90–£115.
Meals	Pub/restaurant 300 yds.
Closed	Rarely.

Mechthild & Julian Self von Hippel
Sir Walter Elliot's House,
95 Sydney Place,
Bath,
Bath & N.E. Somerset BA2 6NE

Tel   +44 (0)1225 469435
Mobile +44 (0)7737 793772
Email   visitus@SirWalterElliotsHouse.co.uk
Web   www.sirwalterelliotshouse.co.uk

Entry 3   Map 3

Bath & N.E. Somerset

The Georgian Stables

Minutes from Bath centre... enjoy independence in converted stables, or choose Sydney Room in the main house. Bedrooms are stylish and snug, all is white and airy with splashes of colour and shelves of books. The stables have the original stone, a smart wet room and cobbled terrace; both rooms have their own sitting room. Breakfast is served by Hilary's friendly housekeeper: homemade muesli, fruits, free-range eggs, pains au chocolat. A canal runs past the end of lovely gardens with unbeatable views. Opposite: acres of National Trust land and the Skyline Circular Walk; take a picnic, watch the hot-air balloons rise over the city.

Minimum two nights at weekends.

Rooms	1 double & sitting room.
	Stables: 1 double & sitting room.
Price	£90–£150. Singles £90–£150.
Meals	Pubs/restaurants 8-minute walk.
Closed	Occasionally.

Hilary Cooper
The Georgian Stables,
41 Sydney Buildings,
Bath,
Bath & N.E. Somerset BA2 6DB

Tel   +44 (0)1225 465956
Mobile   +44 (0)7798 810286
Email   thegeorgianstables@gmail.com

Entry 4   Map 3

Bath & N.E. Somerset

55a North Road

Hidden down a narrow drive just a 25-minute walk from all that the centre of Bath has to offer and a short stroll to the very fine Prior Park, is a 1980s house full of surprises. Delightful owners Natalie and Guy offer you two elegant self-contained studios each with its own entrance, kitchen and wonderfully soothing mix of ultra-chic and traditional. Be spoiled by new oak floors, wool carpets, limestone tiles, old Irish bedheads and bed linen as soft as a cloud. And the most amazing breakfasts brought to your room – lavish, inventive and delicious.

Minimum two nights at weekends.

Rooms	2 studios: 1 double, 1 twin, each
	with small kitchen & own entrance.
Price	£120–£160. Singles from £100.
	(Room only: from £90; singles from £75.)
Meals	Pubs/restaurants within 1 mile.
Closed	Rarely.

Natalie & Guy Woods
55a North Road,
Combe Down, Bath,
Bath & N.E. Somerset BA2 5DF

Tel   +44 (0)1225 835593
Mobile   +44 (0)7977 904931
Email   info@55anorthroad.co.uk
Web   www.55anorthroad.co.uk

Entry 5   Map 3

De Montalt Wood

Deep valley views, acres of gardens and woodland to roam, pretty places to sit and muse... all just a couple of miles from Bath. Charles and Ann's Victorian house is a smart family home with a comfortable country feel. Airy bedrooms have big beds with fine linen, a sofa, TV, and garden vistas; bathrooms are luxurious with rain showers and scented things. You breakfast in the elegant dining room: a full English, smoked salmon and scrambled eggs, fruits on the sideboard, lashings of coffee. There are lovely walks with good pubs on the way, bluebells fill the woods in spring and Bath brims with history, spa and good restaurants.

Hollytree Cottage

Meandering lanes lead to this 16th-century cottage, with roses round the door, a grandfather clock in the hall and an air of genteel tranquillity. The cottage charm has been updated with Regency mahogany and sumptuous sofas. The bedrooms have views over undulating countryside; pretty bathrooms have oils and lotions. On sunny days breakfast is in the lovely garden room looking onto a colourful ornamental patio, sloping lawns, a pond, flowering shrubs and trees. A place to come for absolute peace, birdsong and walks; the joys of elegant Bath are 20 minutes away and Julia knows the area well; let her help plan your trips.

Rooms	2: 1 double; 1 double with separate bath.
Price	£110-£120.
Meals	Pubs/restaurants 5-minute drive.
Closed	Christmas & New Year.

Rooms	3: 1 double, 1 twin, 1 four-poster.
Price	£75-£90. Singles £45-£60.
Meals	Pub/restaurant 0.5 miles.
Closed	Rarely.

	Charles & Ann Kent
	De Montalt Wood,
	Summer Lane,
	Combe Down, Bath,
	Bath & N.E. Somerset BA2 7EU
Tel	+44 (0)1225 838001
Email	bookings@demontaltwood.co.uk
Web	www.demontaltwood.co.uk

	Julia Naismith
	Hollytree Cottage,
	Laverton, Bath,
	Bath & N.E. Somerset BA2 7QZ
Tel	+44 (0)1373 830786
Mobile	+44 (0)7564 196703
Email	jnaismith@toucansurf.com
Web	www.hollytreecottagebath.co.uk

Pitfour House

Georgian gentility in a village near Bath. This is where the rector would live in an Austen novel: it's handsome, respectable, and the feel extends inside, where convivial hosts Frances (a keen cook) and Martin (keen gardener) welcome you into their elegant home. The creamy guest sitting room gleams with period furniture, the dining room is panelled and parqueted, fresh flowers abound. The two bedrooms – one with en suite shower, one with a private bath – are compact but detailed with antiques. Take tea in the neat walled garden, admire the vegetable patch, then taste the spoils in one of Frances's fine suppers.

Easy access to park & ride into Bath.

The Power House

On top of Bath's highest hill lies Rikki's Bauhaus-inspired home, its glass walls making the most of a magical spot and a sensational view; on a clear day you can see the Welsh hills. In the vast open-plan living space downstairs – homely, inviting, inspiring – are treasures from a lifetime of travels: ancient Tuareg camel sacks, kitsch Art Deco pots, gorgeous Persian chests. Bedrooms are big, airy and light, with doors onto a huge balcony – and those views. Rikki is an incredible chef and uses the freshest and finest ingredients from Bath's farmers' market, ten minutes away. Breakfasts are superb.

Rooms	2: 1 twin/double;
	1 twin/double with separate bath.
Price	£88–£98.
Meals	Dinner £27–£32.
	Restaurant 1.5 miles.
Closed	Rarely.

Rooms	3: 1 double, 1 single.
	Studio: 1 double. 2 further small
	doubles available, sharing
	bathrooms.
Price	£100–£120. Singles £70.
Meals	Dinner £25.
	Pubs/restaurants 3-minute drive.
Closed	Rarely.

	Frances Hardman
	Pitfour House,
	High Street, Timsbury,
	Bath,
	Bath & N.E. Somerset BA2 0HT
Tel	+44 (0)1761 479554
Email	pitfourhouse@btinternet.com
Web	www.pitfourhouse.co.uk

	Rikki Howard
	The Power House,
	Brockham End,
	Lansdown,
	Bath,
	Bath & N.E. Somerset BA1 9BY
Tel	+44 (0)1225 446308
Email	rikkijacout@aol.com

Entry 8   Map 3

Entry 9   Map 3

Bedfordshire

Warren Farm Lodge

Horses run to greet you at the field gate. Their owners, the delightful Deirdre and husband Robert, have transformed the old stables and cowsheds of this red-brick dairy farm into a beautiful home. The stunning 'long room' is the hub of the house: reclaimed beams over the Aga, a wood-burner for chilly evenings, worn leather sofas on terracotta tiles. The rest of the house is a joy to explore: the sun room, the lounge with its grand piano, the library on the mezzanine. Masses of space, light, and comfy corners at every turn; big bedrooms have views of the lovely gardens. Bring the kids, stay the weekend.

Minimum stay two nights June-August weekends.

Rooms	3: 1 double, 1 suite, 1 family suite, each with separate bath.
Price	£70-£115. Family suite £135-£150. Singles £70-£100.
Meals	Lunch £8-£9. Dinner £20. Pubs/restaurants within 3 miles.
Closed	Rarely.

Deirdre Evans
Warren Farm Lodge,
Carthagena Road, Sutton,
Sandy,
Bedfordshire SG19 2NQ

Tel	+44 (0)1767 262927
Email	deirdre.evans@warrenfarmlodge.com
Web	www.warrenfarmlodge.com

Entry 10   Map 9

Berkshire

Gilbey's

Step up the stairs to your elegant top-floor studio; it's above a buzzy restaurant and in the heart of pretty Eton. Charming staff greet and look after you, and all is gleaming with rich autumn colours, cream carpets, immaculate linen, smart bathrooms and a rooftop view of Windsor Castle. Relax or work — there is a huge comfy sofa and flat-screen TV as well as useful desks. A generous continental breakfast is delivered to you: fresh bread and croissants, yogurts and fruit. There are interesting shops and galleries galore, you're a stroll from the college or river trips on the Thames, and Waterloo is 50 minutes by train.

Rooms	1 double.
Price	£175-£200.
Meals	Continental breakfast. Supper £18.50. Pubs/restaurants 300 yds.
Closed	Christmas.

Caroline Gilbey
Gilbey's,
82-83 High Street, Eton,
Windsor,
Berkshire SL4 6AF

Tel	+44 (0)1753 854921
Email	caroline@gilbeygroup.com
Web	www.gilbeygroup.com/eton

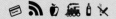

Entry 11   Map 4

Berkshire

Whitehouse Farm Cottage

In the quiet village of Binfield, an idyllic find: a 17th-century farmhouse with a gorgeous garden, and two charmingly converted buildings. Garden Cottage has a beamed drawing room downstairs and an immaculate gallery bedroom. The Forge – deliciously cosy – keeps the blacksmith's fireplace and overlooks an atmospheric courtyard garden with pebble mosaics. The single is in the house with its own cosy sitting room. Fabulous locally sourced breakfasts with freshly baked bread are served in the house by delightful Keir and Louise, film prop makers by profession. Hugely popular with guests and just about perfect!

NGS garden.

Rooms	1 single & sitting room. Garden Cottage: 1 double & sitting room. The Forge: 1 double & summerhouse.
Price	£85–£110. Singles £75–£90.
Meals	Pubs/restaurants within 1 mile.
Closed	Occasionally.

Keir & Louise Lusby
Whitehouse Farm Cottage,
Murrell Hill Lane, Binfield,
Bracknell,
Berkshire RG42 4BY
Tel   +44 (0)1344 423688
Mobile   +44 (0)7711 948889
Email   garden.cottages@ntlworld.com

Entry 12   Map 4

Birmingham

Woodbrooke Quaker Study Centre

A pleasure to find ten tranquil acres (woodlands, lawns, lake and walled garden) so close to the centre of Birmingham – run by such special people. This impressive Georgian mansion was donated by George Cadbury to the Quakers in 1903, as a place for study and contemplation. And so it remains. There are corridors aplenty and public rooms big and small: a library, a silent room, a lovely new garden lounge, and a dining hall where organic buffet meals feature fruit and veg from the grounds. Bedrooms, spread over several buildings, are carpeted, comfortable, light and airy, and most have en suite showers. Welcoming, nurturing, historic.

Rooms	59: 7 doubles, 7 twins, 45 singles (most rooms are en suite).
Price	£65. Singles from £42.50.
Meals	Lunch £10. Dinner £10. Pubs/restaurants 15-minute walk.
Closed	Christmas & Boxing Day.

Becky Thomas
Woodbrooke Quaker Study Centre,
1046 Bristol Road, Selly Oak,
Birmingham,
Birmingham B29 6LJ
Tel   +44 (0)121 472 5171
Email   enquiries@woodbrooke.org.uk
Web   www.woodbrooke.org.uk

Entry 13   Map 8

Brighton & Hove

The Art House Hove

Peaceful, close to the sea and in the heart of popular Hove, this Victorian villa is a friendly town treat. Bedrooms on the top floor are furnished in an eclectic style, mixing antique finds with quirky light-fittings; art books, flowers and splashes of colour complete the picture. Dexter and Liz give you a breakfast feast: muesli, fruit salad, patisseries fresh from the bakery that morning, eggs, smoked salmon, hash browns. Liz runs mosaic courses in the garden studio and her wonderful work decorates the house. Dozens of cafés and bistros are on the doorstep; Brighton is a 15-minute amble along the promenade.

Minimum two nights at weekends.

Rooms	3: 2 doubles, 1 single, all sharing bathroom & 2 extra wcs.
Price	£85–£95. Singles £65–£75.
Meals	Pubs/restaurants 0.5 miles.
Closed	Rarely.

Dexter Tiranti
The Art House Hove,
27 Wilbury Road,
Hove,
Brighton & Hove BN3 3PB

Tel	+44 (0)1273 775350
Email	enquiries@thearthousehove.co.uk
Web	www.thearthousehove.co.uk

Entry 14   Map 4

Brighton & Hove

4–5 Palmeira Square

Drift along Brighton seafront to emerge into the Regency splendour of Hove's Palmeira Square. Susie welcomes you into her spacious ground-floor flat where rooms are flooded with light, ceilings are high and furnishings have pizzazz – kilims on bamboo floors, funky chandeliers, elegant antiques. Bedrooms overlook a shrubbed courtyard at the back: one lovely and large with plum-coloured walls and a new wet room, the other peppermint cool. Susie has lived in Portugal, Brazil, Bordeaux, works from home and delivers a delicious breakfast to your door, or at a pretty seat in the window bay – turn your head to catch the sea.

Minimum stay two nights.

Rooms	2: 1 double; 1 twin/double with separate wc.
Price	£95–£130.
Meals	Continental breakfast. Pub/restaurant 500 yds.
Closed	Rarely.

Susie de Castilho
4–5 Palmeira Square, Flat 1,
Hove,
Brighton & Hove BN3 2JA

Tel	+44 (0)1273 719087
Mobile	+44 (0)7917 562771
Email	stay@2staybrighton.co.uk
Web	www.2staybrighton.co.uk

Entry 15   Map 4

Discover the west at your own pace

Bristol

9 Princes Buildings

A super city base with comfortable beds, charming owners and, without a doubt, the best views in Clifton. You're a hop from the elegant Suspension Bridge, restaurants, shops and pubs of the village and a ferry to whisk you to town or the station; yet all is quiet and the garden is large and leafy. You walk in to a big square hall; the drawing room has a peaceful feel and a veranda for the views. Bedrooms are sunny and traditional: one downstairs overlooks the garden, the top floor double is furnished more simply. Simon and Joanna give you a good, leisurely breakfast too: local sausages and bacon, homemade jams and marmalade.

Rooms	4: 2 doubles, 1 twin/double; 1 twin/double with separate bath.
Price	£85–£87. Singles from £60.
Meals	Pub/restaurant 100 yds.
Closed	Rarely.

Simon & Joanna Fuller
9 Princes Buildings,
Clifton,
Bristol,
Bristol BS8 4LB

Tel	+44 (0)117 973 4615
Email	info@9pb.co.uk
Web	www.9princesbuildings.co.uk

Entry 16   Map 3

Buckinghamshire

Long Crendon Manor

Masses of history and oodles of character at this timbered listed house with high chimneys, dating from 1187... no wonder film companies are keen to get through the arched entrance and into the courtyard! The vast dining room is a dramatic setting for breakfast: sausages from Sue's pigs, home-baked bread, plum and mulberry jam from the gardens. Windows on both sides bring light into the fire-warmed drawing room with leather sofas, gleaming furniture, family bits and bobs, pictures galore. Sleep soundly in comfortable, country-house style bedrooms (one with gorgeous yellow panelling). Peaceful.

Cambridgeshire

5 Chapel Street

Exemplary! Where: in a lovely, comfortable, refurbed Georgian house 20 minutes' walk from Cambridge centre. How: with warmth, pleasure, intelligence and local knowledge. Bedrooms have good quality mattresses, bedding and towels. Characterful pieces – an antique brass bed, a freestanding bath, oriental rugs – flowers, calm colours, garden views. The breakfasts: delicious, largely organic and local – fresh fruit salad, kedgeree with smoked Norfolk haddock, home baking (three types of bread; gluten free, no problem). If you'd like to swing a cat book the biggest room; borrow vintage bikes and thoroughly enjoy your break.

Rooms	3: 1 double, 1 four-poster; 1 double with extra twin in dressing room & shared bathroom.
Price	£100-£200. Singles £80-£100.
Meals	Supper £30. Pubs/restaurants 3-minute walk.
Closed	Occasionally.

Rooms	3: 2 doubles, 1 twin.
Price	£95-£120. Singles £85-£95.
Meals	Pubs/restaurants 5-minute walk.
Closed	Rarely.

	Sue Soar
	Long Crendon Manor,
	Frogmore Lane,
	Long Crendon, Aylesbury,
	Buckinghamshire HP18 9DZ
Tel	+44 (0)1844 201647
Email	sue.soar@longcrendonmanor.co.uk
Web	www.longcrendonmanor.co.uk

	Christine Ulyyan
	5 Chapel Street,
	Cambridge,
	Cambridgeshire CB4 1DY
Tel	+44 (0)1223 514856
Email	christine.ulyyan@gmail.com
Web	www.5chapelstreet.co.uk

Entry 17   Map 8

Entry 18   Map 9

Cambridgeshire

Cambridge University

Buses, bicycles and punting on the Cam: huge fun when you're in the heart of it all. Enter the Great Gate Tower of Christ's College to be wooed by tranquil, beautiful quadrangle gardens, breakfasts beneath portraits of hallowed masters, and a serene chapel. At smaller Sidney Sussex – 1598-old with additions – you can play tennis in gorgeous gardens, picnic on perfect lawns and start the day with rare-breed sausages. Churchill has a great gym, Downing has Quentin Blake paintings on the walls, St Catharine's has a candlelit chapel. Bedrooms (some shared showers) and lounges are functional. Well-informed porters are your first port of call.

Rooms spread across 13 colleges. For on-site parking, choose colleges out of town.

Rooms	1073: 60 doubles, 804 singles, 206 twins, 3 apartments for 2-3.
Price	£75-£128. Singles £41-£79. Apartments £85-£150.
Meals	Breakfast included. Some colleges offer dinner from £7. See website for details.
Closed	Mid-Jan to mid-March; May/June; Oct/Nov; Christmas. A few rooms available throughout year.

	University Rooms
	Cambridge University,
	Cambridge,
	Cambridgeshire
Web	www.cambridgerooms.co.uk

Entry 19 Map 9

Cambridgeshire

Springfield House

The former school house hugs the bend of a river, its French windows opening to delightful rambling gardens with scented roses... and a yew garden, and a mulberry tree that provides fruit for breakfast. It's an elegant home reminiscent of another age, with fascinating history on the walls and big comfortable bedrooms for guests; one is reached by narrow stairs and has outside steps to the garden. The conservatory, draped with a huge mimosa, is an exceptional spot for summer breakfasts, and the breakfasts are rather delicious. Good value and peaceful, yet close to Cambridge, of which kind Judith is a fund of knowledge.

Rooms	3: 2 doubles; 1 twin/double with separate bath.
Price	£70-£85. Singles £45-£60.
Meals	Pubs 150 yds.
Closed	Rarely.

	Judith Rossiter
	Springfield House,
	14-16 Horn Lane, Linton,
	Cambridgeshire CB21 4HT
Tel	+44 (0)1223 891383
Email	springfieldhouselinton@gmail.com
Web	www.springfieldhouselinton.com

Entry 20 Map 9

Cambridgeshire

Westoe Farm

Immerse yourself in miles of waving wheat and woodland. The house is a flint-knapped oasis of deep comfort with traditionally comfortable bedrooms, a large attractive hall and your own huge sitting room. Generous Tim and Henrietta are a capable pair and you are well looked after; they produce their own organic bacon, sausages, jams and honey, eggs are home-laid, breakfasts are award-winning and their home is self-sustaining in solar electricity. There's a fine, rose-filled garden, woods and fields – stroll around to your heart's content; visit Cambridge, Beth Chatto Gardens, antique shops... and Stansted is 25 minutes.

Rooms	2: 1 twin, 1 double.
Price	£110. Singles £75.
Meals	Pub 1 mile.
Closed	Christmas & New Year.

Henrietta Breitmeyer
Westoe Farm,
Bartlow,
Cambridgeshire CB21 4PR
Tel	+44 (0)1223 892731
Mobile	+44 (0)7776 258666
Email	enquire@bartlow.u-net.com
Web	www.westoefarm.co.uk

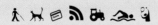

Entry 21   Map 9

Cambridgeshire

The Old Hall

You'll feel spoilt in this stunning house, transformed phoenix-like by the charming Morbeys, who look after guests in style. Arrive to tea and homemade cake in the beamed sitting room with paintings, photographs, fresh flowers, soft places to unwind and a dreamy view of the cathedral. Sleep well in smart, large bedrooms (cleverly planted trees disguise any road noise) and wake to Ely sausages, hot waffles with maple syrup, or smoked salmon and scrambled eggs on ciabatta toast. Cambridge is a short train ride away but there is history galore here, a formal garden and 15 acres of parkland with lakeside walks. Excellent value.

Rooms	5: 3 doubles, 1 twin/double, 1 four-poster.
Price	£120-£170. Singles from £100.
Meals	Pub/restaurant 1 mile.
Closed	Christmas & New Year.

Anthony & Alison Morbey
The Old Hall,
Stuntney,
Ely,
Cambridgeshire CB7 5TR
Tel	+44 (0)1353 663275
Email	stay@theoldhallely.co.uk
Web	www.theoldhallely.co.uk

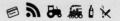

Entry 22   Map 9

Cambridgeshire

The Old Vicarage

Tug the bell pull and step inside a 19th-century parsonage with a labyrinth of rooms. Homemade flapjack and chocolates await, peaceful bedrooms are countrified and classy with stylish bathrooms – one a lovely en suite. Original artwork peppers every wall and is mostly for sale online. Take breakfast overlooking a big mature garden and brace yourself for a wonderful full English. Cats, dogs and chickens roam freely and if you're lucky you'll spot a proud peacock or muntjac deer within the trees. Explore Cambridge, walk Wicken Fen with its Konik ponies and birdlife, then stroll to one of the locals.

Ask about creative courses.

Rooms	2: 1 twin/double; 1 double with separate bath.
Price	£90–£100. Singles from £55–£60..
Meals	Pubs in village.
Closed	Christmas & New Year.

Gill Pedersen
The Old Vicarage,
7 Church Street,
Isleham,
Ely,
Cambridgeshire CB7 5RX

Tel	+44 (0)1638 780095
Email	gill@pedersen.co.uk
Web	www.oldvicarageisleham.co.uk

Entry 23   Map 9

Cheshire

Goss Moor

Crunch up the gravelled drive to the big white house, a beautifully run family home. Bedrooms are light, bright and decorated in creams and blues; bathrooms are spotless and warm. Be cosseted by fluffy bathrobes, biscuits, decanters of sherry – all is comfortable and inviting. After a day's exploring the Wirral and Liverpool, historic Chester and the wilds of north Wales – a short drive all – return to a kind welcome from Sarah. Expect a generous and delicious breakfast by the sunny bay window; in the summer, you are free to enjoy the garden and pool (not always heated!).

Rooms	2: 1 twin/double; 1 double with separate bath.
Price	£80–£85. Singles £50–£55.
Meals	Occasional dinner with wine, £25. Pub/restaurant 2 miles.
Closed	Rarely.

Chris & Sarah White
Goss Moor,
Mill Lane, Willaston,
Neston,
Cheshire CH64 1RG

Tel	+44 (0)151 327 4000
Mobile	+44 (0)7771 510068
Email	sarahcmwhite@aol.com
Web	www.gossmoor.co.uk

Entry 24   Map 7

Cheshire

Cheshire

Trustwood

Small and pretty and wrapped in beautiful country, Trustwood stands in peaceful gardens with National Trust woods at the end of the lane. Outside, sweetpeas flourish to the front, while lawns run down behind to a copse where bluebells thrive in spring. Inside, warm, fresh, contemporary interiors are just the ticket: super bedrooms, fabulous bathrooms, and a wood-burner and sofas in the sitting room. Free-range hens provide eggs for delicious breakfasts, Lin accounts for the lovely scones. As for the Wirral, much more beautiful than you probably imagine; coastal walks, botanic gardens and the spectacular Dee estuary all wait.

Cotton Farm

Only a four-mile hop from Roman Chester and its 900-year-old cathedral is this sprawling, red-brick farmhouse. Elegant chickens peck in hedges, ponies graze, lambs frisk and cats doze. The farm, run by conservationists Nigel and Clare, is under the Countryside Stewardship Scheme – there are wildflower meadows, summer swallows and 250 acres to roam. Farmhouse bedrooms are large, stylish and cosy with lovely fabrics, robes, a decanter of sherry and huge bath towels, but best of all is the relaxed family atmosphere. Breakfasts, with homemade bread, are delicious and beautifully presented.

Over tens welcome.

Rooms	2 doubles.
Price	£70. Singles £45.
Meals	Restaurants 2 miles.
Closed	Occasionally.

Rooms	3: 2 doubles, 1 twin.
Price	£57–£85. Singles £52.
Meals	Pub 1.5 miles.
Closed	Rarely.

Lin & Peter Friend
Trustwood,
Vicarage Lane, Burton,
Neston,
Cheshire CH64 5TJ

Tel	+44 (0)151 336 7118
Mobile	+44 (0)7550 012462
Email	lin@trustwood.freeserve.co.uk
Web	www.trustwood.freeserve.co.uk

Clare & Nigel Hill
Cotton Farm,
Cotton Edmunds,
Chester,
Cheshire CH3 7PG

Tel	+44 (0)1244 336616
Mobile	+44 (0)7840 682042
Email	information@cottonfarm.co.uk
Web	www.cottonfarm.co.uk

Entry 25   Map 7

Entry 26   Map 7

Cheshire

Mulsford Cottage

Delicious! Not just the food (Kate's a pro chef) but the sweet whitewashed cottage with its sunny conservatory and vintage interiors, and the green Cheshire countryside that bubble-wraps the place in rural peace. Chat – and laugh – the evening away over Kate's superb dinners, lounge by the sitting room fire, then sleep deeply in comfy bedrooms: cane beds, a bright red chair, a vintage desk. The double has a roll top bath, the twin a tiny shower-with-a-view. Step out to birdsong and the 34-mile Sandstone Trail to Shropshire. Wales starts just past the hammock, at the bottom of the large and lovely garden.

Rooms	2: 1 twin, 1 double, each with separate bath/shower.
Price	£80–£85. Singles £55.
Meals	Dinner from £18. Pub 1.5 miles.
Closed	Rarely.

Kate Dewhurst
Mulsford Cottage,
Mulsford, Sarn,
Malpas,
Cheshire SY14 7LP
Tel   +44 (0)1948 770414
Email   katedewhurst@hotmail.com
Web   www.mulsfordcottage.co.uk

Entry 27   Map 7

Cheshire

Harrop Fold Farm

Artists, foodies and walkers adore this antique-filled farmhouse with soul-lifting views. On the edge of the Peak District, the oldest building on the farm dates from 1694 (Bonnie Prince Charlie visited here). The B&B part has a warm peaceful breakfast room, a stone-flagged sitting room, a spectacular studio. Fresh flowers, antique beds, fine fabrics, hot water bottles with chic covers, bathrooms with fluffy robes: you get the best. Gregarious Sue and daughter Leah hold art and cookery courses so the food too is outstanding. Bedrooms have stupendous views – and flat-screen TVs and DVDs just in case they pall.

Minimum two nights at weekends.

Rooms	2 doubles.
Price	£95. Singles from £60.
Meals	Cookery demo & dinner £60. Pub 1.9 miles.
Closed	Rarely.

Sue Stevenson
Harrop Fold Farm,
Rainow,
Macclesfield,
Cheshire SK10 5UU
Tel   +44 (0)1625 560085
Email   stay@harropfoldfarm.co.uk
Web   www.harropfoldfarm.co.uk

Entry 28   Map 8

Cornwall

The Old Vicarage

The first sight of quirky chimneys – the spires of former owner Reverend Hawker's parish churches – sets the scene for a huge house packed with interest and steeped in Victoriana. Jill and Richard, both delightful, know the local history – and the cliff-top walks, which are glorious. Rooms are casually grand, dotted with *objets* – brass gramophone, magic lantern, eccentric Hawker memorabilia. Browse books in the study, play the grand piano, sip brandy over billiards. Bedrooms with wide floorboards are country-house pretty, bathrooms smart, lawns well tended and views are to the sea. Supper at a good pub is a stroll.

Rooms	3: 1 double, 1 twin, 1 single.
Price	£80-£90. Singles £40-£45.
Meals	Pub/tea rooms 5-10 minute walk.
Closed	December/January.

Jill & Richard Wellby
The Old Vicarage,
Morwenstow,
Cornwall EX23 9SR

Tel	+44 (0)1288 331369
Email	jillwellby@hotmail.com
Web	www.rshawker.co.uk

Entry 29   Map 1

Cornwall

The Old Parsonage

A spellbinding coastline, secret coves, spectacular walks. All this and a supremely comfortable Georgian rectory with pretty gardens. Morag and Margaret are relaxed and welcoming hosts. Superb pitch pine floors and original woodwork add warmth and a fresh glow, the big engaging bedrooms (one on the ground floor) have a quirky, upbeat mix of furniture and furnishings, and the bathrooms are pampering. Breakfasts are wonderful: savoury mushrooms, Cornish oak-roasted mackerel, French toast with bacon... In front of the house the land slopes away to the Atlantic, just a five-minute walk across a SSSI. A peaceful retreat.

Minimum stay two nights. Children over 12 welcome.

Rooms	5 twins/doubles.
Price	£92-£112. Singles from £75.
Meals	Packed lunch £5.95.
	Pub/restaurant 600 yds.
Closed	November-February.

Morag Reeve & Margaret Pickering
The Old Parsonage,
Forrabury, Boscastle,
Cornwall PL35 0DJ

Tel	+44 (0)1840 250339
Mobile	+44 (0)7890 531677
Email	morag@old-parsonage.com
Web	www.old-parsonage.com

Entry 30   Map 1

Cornwall

Tremoren

Views stretch sleepily over the Cornish countryside. You might feel inclined to do nothing more than wander the lovely garden or snooze by the pool, but the surfing beaches, the Camel Trail and the Eden Project are so close. The stone and slate former farmhouse has been smartly updated and your airy ground-floor bedroom comes with soft colours, pretty china, crisp linen, a comfortable bathroom, and its own sitting room, snug with sofas, books, maps and TV. For summer, there's a flower-filled terrace, perfect for a pre-dinner drink. Lanie, bubbly and engaging, runs her own catering company – dinner will be delicious!

Rooms	1 double & sitting room.
Price	£100-£110.
Meals	Dinner, 4 courses, £26.
	Pubs 0.5 miles.
Closed	Rarely.

Philip & Lanie Calvert
Tremoren,
St Kew,
Bodmin,
Cornwall PL30 3HA
Tel   +44 (0)1208 841790
Email   la.calvert@btopenworld.com

Entry 31   Map 1

Cornwall

The Corn Mill

This restored mill in a quiet Cornish valley is a relaxed and friendly home. Step inside and find a country cottage medley of flowers and family furniture, antique rugs and interesting market finds. Artist Suzie has her studio in a folly in the pretty garden; ducks and geese wander in the orchard. Cosy bedrooms have flowery fabrics, antique eiderdowns, warm blankets and good cotton; bathrooms are simple and fresh with fluffy towels. Breakfast well in the farmhouse kitchen on locally sourced food and bread fresh from the Rayburn. Exceptional coastal walking, music festivals, great beaches and Port Isaac are all nearby.

Rooms	2: 1 double, 1 family room.
Price	£80. Family room £80-£100.
Meals	Pub/restaurant 2 miles.
Closed	Christmas & New Year.

Susan Bishop
The Corn Mill,
Port Isaac Road, Trelill,
Bodmin,
Cornwall PL30 3HZ
Tel   +44 (0)1208 851079
Email   jemandsuzie@icloud.com

Entry 32   Map 1

Cornwall

The Barn at The Old Stables

The closer you inch down the lane to The Barn, the greener the fields become, the louder the spring-time bleating lambs. But that's all the noise here: this converted hay barn is a hubbub–free hideaway. Find a lavish double bedroom with fine touches: vast bathroom, sublime sink in' mattress and contemporary furniture made by Judith's son. Judith lives opposite and is most at home by her Aga, whipping up a delicious breakfast with local bacon or preparing extraordinary three–course suppers: after a day's walking or cycling the Camel Trail and Cornish coast, you can eat in the candlelit dining room, the valley unfolding beyond.

Minimum two nights at weekends.

Rooms	Barn: 1 double.
Price	£75-£100.
Meals	Dinner, 3 courses, £27.50. Pub/restaurant 5 miles.
Closed	Christmas & New Year.

Judith Argent
The Barn at The Old Stables,
Helland, Bodmin,
Cornwall PL30 4QE
Tel   +44 (0)1208 75543
Mobile +44 (0)7786 558641
Email juargent@hotmail.com
Web   www.thebarnincornwall.co.uk

Entry 33   Map 1

Cornwall

Higher Lank Farm

Families rejoice: you can only come if you have a child under five! Celtic crosses in the garden and original panelling hint at the house's 500-year history; bedrooms, newly decorated, have pocket sprung mattresses and large TVs. Nursery teas begin at 5pm, grown-up suppers are later and energetic Lucy will cheerfully babysit while the rest of you slink off to the pub. Farm-themed playgrounds are covered in safety matting and grass, there are piglets and chicks, eggs to collect, pony and trap rides, a sand barn for little ones and cream teas in the garden. Oh, and real nappies are provided!

Rooms	3 family rooms.
Price	£100. Singles by arrangement.
Meals	Supper £23. Nursery tea £7. Pub 1.5 miles.
Closed	November-Easter.

Lucy Finnemore
Higher Lank Farm,
St Breward,
Bodmin,
Cornwall PL30 4NB
Tel   +44 (0)1208 850716
Email lucyfin@higherlankfarm.co.uk
Web   www.higherlankfarm.co.uk

Entry 34   Map 1

Cornwall

Lavethan

A glorious house in the most glorious of settings: views sail down to the valley. It rambles on many levels and is part 15th century: walls are stone, floors are flagged, stairs are oak. The sunny bedroom in the house is best, with its panelled walls and smart bathroom; bedrooms across the courtyard are very private with their own entrances and have pretty quilted bedspreads. Catherine, a warm hostess, has decorated in country style; the guest sitting room is hugely welcoming with books, flowers and piano. All this and acres of ancient woods, Celtic crosses and a heated pool in the old walled garden.

Children over ten welcome.

Rooms	3: 1 double, 2 twins/doubles.
Price	£90. Singles £50.
Meals	Pub 0.25 miles.
Closed	Rarely.

	Christopher & Catherine Hartley
	Lavethan,
	Blisland,
	Bodmin,
	Cornwall PL30 4QG
Tel	+44 (0)1208 850487
Email	chrishartley@btconnect.com
Web	www.lavethan.com

Entry 35   Map 1

Cornwall

Cabilla Manor

There's a treasure round every corner and an opera house in one of the barns. Instant seduction as you enter the old manor house out on the moor, brimful of interest and colour. Rich exotic rugs and cushions, artefacts from around the world, Louella's sumptuous hand-stencilled quilts, huge beds, coir carpets, garden flowers. There's a dining room crammed floor to ceiling with books, many of them Robin's (a writer and explorer) and a lofty conservatory for friendly meals overlooking a semi-wild garden – with tennis and elegant lawns. The views are heavenly, the generous hosts wonderful and the final mile thrillingly wild.

Rooms	4: 1 double; 1 double with separate bath & shower; 1 double, 1 twin, sharing bath & shower (let to same party only).
Price	£90. Singles £45.
Meals	Dinner, 3 courses with wine, £35. Pub 4 miles. Restaurant 8-10 miles.
Closed	Christmas.

	Robin & Louella Hanbury-Tenison
	Cabilla Manor,
	Mount, Bodmin,
	Cornwall PL30 4DW
Tel	+44 (0)1208 821224
Mobile	+44 (0)7770 664218
Email	louella@cabilla.co.uk
Web	www.cabilla.co.uk

Entry 36   Map 1

Cornwall

Menkee

From this handsome Georgian farmhouse there are long views towards the sea; you're 20 minutes away from the coastal path and wild surf but you may not want to budge. Gage and Liz are deliciously unstuffy and look after you well: newspapers and a weather forecast appear with a scrumptious breakfast, your gorgeously comfortable bed is turned down in the evening and walkers can be dropped off and collected. The elegant house is filled with beautiful things, gleaming furniture, fresh flowers, roaring fires and pretty fabrics – all you have to do is slacken your pace and wind down.

Minimum two nights in high season.

Rooms	2: 1 double, 1 twin.
Price	£80-£90. Singles from £40.
Meals	Pub/restaurant 3 miles.
Closed	Rarely.

Gage & Liz Williams
Menkee,
St Mabyn, Wadebridge,
Cornwall PL30 3DD

Tel	+44 (0)1208 841378
Mobile	+44 (0)7999 549935
Email	gagewillms@aol.com
Web	www.cornwall-online.co.uk/menkee

Entry 37 Map 1

Cornwall

Roskear

Drive down the fields to this 17th-century working farmhouse, a blissfully peaceful escape. A snug sitting room with a log fire, a warm and smiling hostess, happy dogs, comfy bedrooms and simple bathrooms, a cheerful Aga, fabulous estuary views – country life at its most old-fashioned and charming. Delicious breakfasts are served on blue china, doors open to the sunny garden and there are acres of woodland and grassland all around. Good restaurants include Rick Stein's in Padstow, the ferry takes you to Rock, surfing is a short drive and the Camel cycle trail is nearby (hire bikes locally). Uncomplicated, good value B&B.

Rooms	2: 1 double with separate bath; 1 twin/double sharing bath (let to same party only).
Price	£70. Singles £35.
Meals	Pubs/restaurants 0.5-6 miles.
Closed	Never.

Rosina Messer-Bennetts
Roskear,
St Breock, Wadebridge,
Cornwall PL27 7HU

Tel	+44 (0)1208 812805
Mobile	+44 (0)7748 432013
Email	rosina@roskear.com
Web	www.roskear.com

Entry 38 Map 1

Cornwall

Porteath Barn

A converted 'upside-down' barn in an exquisite valley setting, elegantly uncluttered inside. Downstairs bedrooms – not vast – have fresh flowers, quilted bedspreads and beautiful bathrooms, and French windows that open onto a large and lovely garden. From here a path leads down to Epphaven Cove and the beach – fabulous. Continue further for wonderful walks on the coastal path if you're feeling hearty, return to a sitting room with seagrass flooring and a wood-burner. Jo and Michael are gracious and delightful and their breakfasts (kedgeree, kippers, pancakes, homemade jams) are superb.

Over 12s by arrangement.

Rooms	3: 2 twins/doubles, each with separate bath or shower; 1 double sharing bath (let to same party only).
Price	£80–£100. Singles by arrangement.
Meals	Pub 1.5 miles.
Closed	Rarely.

Jo & Michael Bloor
Porteath Barn,
St Minver,
Wadebridge,
Cornwall PL27 6RA
Tel   +44 (0)1208 863605
Email   m.bloor17@btinternet.com

Entry 39   Map 1

Cornwall

Molesworth Manor

It's a splendid old place, big enough to swallow hoards of people, peppered with art and interesting antiques. There are palms and a play area in the garden, two charming drawing rooms with an honesty bar and open fires for cosy nights, a carved staircase leading to bedrooms that vary in style and size – His Lordship's at the front, the Maid's in the eaves – and bathrooms that are lovely and pampering. The whiff of homemade muffins and a delicious breakfast lures you downstairs in the morning, Padstow and its food delights will keep you happy when you venture out. A superb bolthole run by Geoff and Jessica, youthful and fun.

Rooms	9: 7 doubles, 1 twin/double; 1 twin with separate shower.
Price	£85–£125. Singles by arrangement.
Meals	Pubs/restaurants 2 miles.
Closed	November-January. Open off-season by arrangement for larger parties.

Geoff French & Jessica Clarke
Molesworth Manor,
Little Petherick,
Padstow,
Cornwall PL27 7QT
Tel   +44 (0)1841 540292
Email   molesworthmanor@aol.com
Web   www.molesworthmanor.co.uk

Entry 40   Map 1

Cornwall

Myrtle Cottage

A proper cottage – beautifully kept, low-ceilinged and light – in a traditional Cornish village with a good foodie pub. Rooms, with distant sea views, are invitingly cosy: uneven white walls, prettily quilted beds, pale-carpeted or varnished creaking boards, flowers fresh from the garden. Sue does great breakfasts: homemade bread, muffins and preserves, local eggs and bacon, in the dining room, the sun room, or out on the patio. There are games and toys for tots and maps for walkers to borrow. You're a 15-minute stroll from the South West Coast Path so near many outstanding beaches; Porth Joke's a favourite. Lovely.

Rooms	2: 1 double; 1 twin with separate bath.
Price	£70. Singles £55.
Meals	Dinner £21. Pubs/restaurants 0.5 miles.
Closed	Rarely.

Sue Stevens
Myrtle Cottage,
Trevail, Cubert, Newquay,
Cornwall TR8 5HP

Tel	+44 (0)1637 830460
Mobile	+44 (0)7763 101076
Email	enquiries@myrtletrevail.co.uk
Web	www.myrtletrevail.co.uk

Entry 41   Map 1

Cornwall

Calize Country House

Beneath wheeling gulls and close to blond beaches, the big square 1870 guest house has amazing views of skies and sea. Virginia Woolf's lighthouse is in the bay, seals cavort at the colony nearby; a fresh uncomplicated décor brings the tang of the sea to every room. Artworks recall a world of surf; deckchair stripes clothe the dining table and dress the window; walls are pale or patterned; traditional sofas call for quiet times with a book. Homemade cake on arrival, binoculars in the rooms, perhaps a sea view. Jilly and Nigel look after you beautifully – and there's a great pub you can walk to.

Rooms	4: 2 doubles, 1 twin, 1 single.
Price	£80–£90. Singles £60.
Meals	Packed lunch £5. Pub 350 yds.
Closed	Rarely.

Nigel Whitaker
Calize Country House,
Gwithian,
Hayle,
Cornwall TR27 5BW

Tel	+44 (0)1736 753268
Email	jilly@calize.co.uk
Web	www.calize.co.uk

Entry 42   Map 1

Cornwall

Drym Farm

Rural, but not too deeply: the Tate at St Ives is a 15-minute drive. The 1705 farmhouse, beautifully revived, is surrounded by ancient barns, a dairy and a forge, fascinating to Cornish historians. Jan arrived in 2002, with an enthusiasm for authenticity and simple, stylish good taste. French limestone floors in the hall, eclectic art on the walls, a roll top bath, a *bateau lit*, an antique brass bed. Paintwork is fresh cream and taupe. There are old fruit trees and young camellias, a TV-free sitting room with two plump sofas and organic treats at breakfast. Charming and utterly peaceful.

Rooms	2 doubles.
Price	£80–£100. Singles from £70.
Meals	Pubs/restaurants within 1-4 miles.
Closed	Rarely.

	Jan Bright
	Drym Farm,
	Drym, Praze-an-Beeble,
	Camborne,
	Cornwall TR14 0NU
Tel	+44 (0)1209 831039
Email	drymfarm@hotmail.co.uk
Web	www.drymfarm.co.uk

Entry 43   Map 1

Cornwall

House at Gwinear

An island of calm, this grand old rambling house sits in bird-filled acres but is only a short drive from St Ives. The Halls are devoted to the encouragement of the arts and crafts which is reflected in their lifestyle. Find shabby chic with loads of character and no stuffiness – fresh flowers on the breakfast table, a piano in the corner, rugs on polished floors, masses of books. In a separate wing is your cosy bedroom and sitting room, with a fine view of the church from the bath. The large lawned gardens are there for bare-footed solace, and you can have breakfast in the Italianate courtyard on sunny days.

Rooms	1 twin/double with separate bath & sitting room.
Price	£80–£90.
Meals	Supper, 2 courses with wine, £25. Pub 1.5 miles.
Closed	Rarely.

	Charles & Diana Hall
	House at Gwinear,
	Gwinear,
	St Ives,
	Cornwall TR27 5JZ
Tel	+44 (0)1736 850444
Email	charleshall@btinternet.com

Entry 44   Map 1

Cornwall

Penquite

A doll's house of a B&B in a constellation of Cornwall's best attractions, set in a quiet village overlooking the Hayle estuary and bird reserve. A doctor's house from 1908, it oozes Arts and Crafts with chunky stone walls, sloping roof, winding stairs and polished oak enhanced by Stephanie's ceramics. All yours: a snug, bay-windowed sitting room; a private suite of cute bedrooms in the eaves; a mature garden of lofty pines, palms and summer house; a generous continental spread on the terrace or light-filled dining room. Stroll to pubs and deli, or past a golf course to the coastal path and St Ives Bay views.

Rooms	2: 1 family room for 3, 1 single with extra z-bed (let to same party only).
Price	Family room £85–£110. Singles £85–£110.
Meals	Continental breakfast. Restaurant 2-minute walk.
Closed	Rarely.

	Stephanie Pace
	Penquite,
	Vicarage Lane, Lelant,
	St Ives,
	Cornwall TR26 3EA
Tel	+44 (0)1736 755002
Email	stephaniepace@hotmail.com
Web	www.penquite-seasidesuite-cornwall.com

Cornwall

Organic Panda B&B & Gallery

A five-minute walk from St Ives, with a panoramic view of the bay, a cosy, comfortable B&B in perfect harmony with arty St Ives. The people are friendly, the house has a communal feel, and breakfasts are shared at the big rustic table. Spacious bedrooms have a laid-back style with organic linen, bamboo towels, chunky beds, white walls, and small but perfectly formed shower rooms. Andrea is an artist and theatre designer, Peter a photographer and organic chef, the food is delicious and the bread home-baked. The most beautiful coastal road in all England leads to St Just.

Whole house available to rent Christmas, New Year, Easter & school holidays.

Rooms	3: 2 doubles, 1 twin.
Price	£80–£150.
Meals	Packed lunch £10. Restaurants nearby.
Closed	Rarely.

	Peter Williams & Andrea Carr
	Organic Panda B&B & Gallery,
	1 Pednolver Terrace, St Ives,
	Cornwall TR26 2EL
Tel	+44 (0)1736 793890
Mobile	+44 (0)7787 854380
Email	info@organicpanda.co.uk
Web	www.organicpanda.co.uk

Cornwall

11 Sea View Terrace

In a smart row of Edwardian villas, with stunning harbour and sea views, is a delectable retreat. Sleek, softy coloured interiors are light and gentle on the eye – an Italian circular glass table here, a painted seascape there. Bedrooms are perfect with crisp linen and vistas of whirling gulls from private terraces; bathrooms are state of the art. Rejoice in softly boiled eggs with anchovy and chive-butter soldiers for breakfast – or continental in bed if you prefer. Grahame looks after you impeccably and design aficionados will be happy.

Over 12s welcome.

Rooms	3 suites.
Price	£100-£135. Singles from £75.
Meals	Dinner, with wine, from £25 (groups only). Packed lunch from £15. Pubs/restaurants 5-minute walk.
Closed	Rarely.

Grahame Wheelband
11 Sea View Terrace,
St Ives,
Cornwall TR26 2DH

Tel   +44 (0)1736 798440
Mobile   +44 (0)7973 953616
Email   info@11stives.co.uk
Web   www.11stives.co.uk

Entry 47   Map 1

Cornwall

Ennys

Prepare to be spoiled. A fire smoulders in the sumptuous sitting room, tea is laid out in the Aga-warm kitchen, bedrooms are luxurious (a king-size bed, an elegant modern four-poster, a powerful shower) and breakfasts are served at separate tables. The stylishness continues into the suites and everywhere there are fascinating artefacts from Gill's travels, designer fabrics and original art. The road ends at Ennys, so it is utterly peaceful; walk down to the river and along the old towpath to St Ives Bay. Or stay put: play tennis (on grass!) and swim in the heated pool sunk deep into the tropical gardens.

Children over 12 welcome.

Rooms	5: 3 doubles, 2 suites (twins/doubles) each with kitchenette.
Price	£95-£150. Suite £145-£195. Singles from £75.
Meals	Pub 3 miles.
Closed	25 October-1 April.

Gill Charlton
Ennys,
St Hilary,
Penzance,
Cornwall TR20 9BZ

Tel   +44 (0)1736 740262
Email   ennys@ennys.co.uk
Web   www.ennys.co.uk

Entry 48   Map 1

Cornwall

Keigwin Farmhouse

Off the glorious coast road to St Ives, in two walled acres overlooking the sea, is a very old farmhouse lived in by Gilly. Walk to the beach at Portheras Cove, dine well at Gurnard's Head, return to little whitewash-and-pine bedrooms with views that make you want to get out your paints, and a big shared bathroom with a massive old bath, fresh with organic cotton towels. A treat: Gilly's scones on arrival, eggs from her hens, stacks of books above the stairs and an arty feel – wide floorboards, creamy colours, family pieces, sculptures, ceramics, glass. A relaxed, delightful – and musical instrument-friendly – B&B.

Rooms	3: 2 doubles, 1 single, sharing 2 bathrooms (let to same party only).
Price	£70. Singles £35.
Meals	Pubs/restaurants 3 miles.
Closed	Rarely.

Gilly Wyatt-Smith
Keigwin Farmhouse,
Keigwin, Morvah,
Penzance,
Cornwall TR19 7TS
Tel +44 (0)1736 786425
Email sleep@keigwinfarmhouse.co.uk
Web www.keigwinfarmhouse.co.uk

Entry 49   Map 1

Cornwall

Trereife House

Sweep past ponies to a country house of high culture. Find period antiques, comfortable sofas and open fires, beautifully bound books, roll top baths, lavish rooms in powder-blues or greens, and sprawling grounds where summer fairs are held. A serene and special setting for a wedding or celebration, or a break from the daily grind – the delights of Penzance and the coast are an amble away. At breakfast, choose between the full English or kedgeree, or croissants and fig compote, served at the antique dining table. The family have lived on the estate for generations; an authentic, rich and marvellous place.

Minimum two nights.

Rooms	5: 4 doubles; 1 double sharing bath (let to same party only).
Price	£80-£140.
Meals	Pubs/restaurants 2 miles.
Closed	Rarely.

Peter Le Grice
Trereife House,
Penzance,
Cornwall TR20 8TJ
Tel +44 (0)1736 362750
Email trereifepark@btconnect.com
Web www.trereifepark.co.uk

Entry 50   Map 1

Cornwall

Marine Lodge

Come for independence in this 1970s hillside house at the top of little Newlyn – art and fishing hub. Your suite (bedroom and sitting room), decorated in natural tones with attractive lamps and splashes of colour from Richard's art, opens to a terrace and subtropical garden below, and a spectacular view of Mount's Bay. Your hosts are charming, and leave your laissez-faire continental breakfast for you. Wake when you want to homemade muesli and jams, dried fruit marinated in Earl Grey, toast, coffee… relish the privacy of it all. Watch the sun rise over St Michael's Mount, the dolphins in the bay and the fishing boats returning home.

Rooms	1 suite.
Price	£95. Singles £70.
Meals	Continental breakfast. Pubs/restaurants in village.
Closed	Rarely.

John Charlick
Marine Lodge,
Old Paul Hill, Newlyn,
Penzance,
Cornwall TR18 5BX
Tel   +44 (0)1736 362462
Email johncharlick@hotmail.co.uk
Web   www.marinelodgenewlyn.co.uk

Entry 51   Map 1

Cornwall

Cove Cottage

Down a long lane to a rose-clad cottage in the most balmy part of Cornwall… peace in a private cove. Your own door leads up steps to a gorgeous suite with luxurious linen on an antique four-poster, art, sofas… and a flowery balcony with spectacular views of the sea and subtropical gardens. Settle in happily to the sound of the waves. Sue is friendly and serves a great breakfast in the garden room: home-laid eggs, homemade jams and their own honey. The Penwith peninsula hums with gardens, galleries and stunning sandy beaches; Minack Theatre and Lamorna are close. Return for a salad supper of lobster or crab. Paradise!

Rooms	1 suite.
Price	£115–£120.
Meals	Cold platter £12.50. Dinner, in low season, £30. Pub/restaurant 3 miles.
Closed	Rarely.

Sue White
Cove Cottage,
St Loy, St Buryan,
Penzance,
Cornwall TR19 6DH
Tel   +44 (0)1736 810010
Email thewhites@covecottagestloy.co.uk
Web   www.covecottagestloy.co.uk

Entry 52   Map 1

Cornwall

Sophia's

Lovely Lynn welcomes you in her chef's whites – with a cappuccino and a truffle if you're lucky! Inspired by her father and his organic garden, she's opened this small sweet restaurant with rooms; word is spreading for the deliciousness of her food, especially the ocean-fresh fish. Upstairs are two light airy bedrooms, with white floorboards and window seats facing the sea; cross the road and you're on the prom. Mattresses are deep, bathrooms luxurious and breakfasts a delight: homemade breads and marmalade from organic oranges. Walk to Mousehole or St Michael's Mount, get high on sea breezes, unwind.

Rooms	2 doubles.
Price	£90-£100.
Meals	Dinner £12.90-£17.50. Restaurant downstairs.
Closed	End October-March.

Lynn Ryder
Sophia's,
Promenade, Penzance,
Cornwall TR18 4HH

Tel	+44 (0)1736 333363
Mobile	+44 (0)7811 025417
Email	info@sophiaspenzance.co.uk
Web	www.sophiaspenzance.co.uk

Entry 53   Map 1

Cornwall

Venton Vean

You can tell this place opened recently – everything is tip-top. Immensely helpful owners Philippa and David moved from London with their family and have transformed a dilapidated Victorian house into a supremely cool and elegant B&B. Moody colours, mid-century design classics and interesting reclamation finds make for a stunning and eclectic interior. Food is a passion – expect freshly ground coffee in your room and some of the most tantalising breakfasts around: Mexican, Spanish, even a good old full English will have you dashing down in the morning. Arty Penzance is a joy as is the craggy-coved beauty all around.

Rooms	3 doubles.
Price	£80-£105. Singles from £60.
Meals	Dinner, 3 courses, from £20. Packed lunch from £5. Cream tea £4.
Closed	Rarely.

Philippa McKnight
Venton Vean,
Trewithen Road,
Penzance,
Cornwall TR18 4LS

Tel	+44 (0)1736 351294
Email	info@ventonvean.co.uk
Web	www.ventonvean.co.uk

Entry 54   Map 1

Cornwall

Ednovean Farm

There's a terrace for each fabulous bedroom (one truly private) with views to the wild blue yonder and St Michael's Mount Bay, an enchanting outlook that changes with the passage of the day. Come for peace, space and the best of eclectic fabrics and colours, pretty lamps, Christine's sculptures, fluffy bathrobes and handmade soaps. The beamed open-plan sitting/dining area is an absorbing mix of exotic, rustic and elegant; have full breakfast here (last orders nine o'clock) or continental in your room. A footpath through the field leads to the village; walk to glorious Prussia Cove and Cudden Point, or head west to Marazion.

Rooms	3: 2 doubles, 1 four-poster.
Price	£95–£115.
Meals	Pub 5-minute walk.
Closed	Christmas & rarely.

Christine & Charles Taylor
Ednovean Farm,
Perranuthnoe,
Penzance,
Cornwall TR20 9LZ
Tel   +44 (0)1736 711883
Email info@ednoveanfarm.co.uk
Web   www.ednoveanfarm.co.uk

Entry 55 Map 1

Cornwall

Bay House

Perched on the edge of the map, high on rugged, seapink-tufted cliffs, Bay House is as close to the sea as you can get. Rooms are spacious (one with a bay window), the dining room defers to stunning sunsets and the attention to detail is immaculate. Expect fine original artwork and antiques, Ralph Lauren dressing gowns, designer linen, Molton Brown lotions, iPod docks and DVD players. Scramble down to secluded beaches, stroll to the famous Lizard Lighthouse or relax to the sound of the surf in the beautiful garden under rustling palms and hovering kestrels. Breakfast is outstanding – with John's homemade bread and jams.

Rooms	2 twins/doubles.
Price	£120–£160.
Meals	Pubs/restaurants 5-minute walk.
Closed	Christmas.

Carla Caslin
Bay House,
Housel Bay, The Lizard,
Cornwall TR12 7PG
Tel   +44 (0)1326 290235
Mobile +44 (0)7740 168805
Email   carla.caslin@btinternet.com
Web   www.mostsoutherlypoint.co.uk

Entry 56 Map 1

Cornwall

Landewednack House

The pug dogs will greet you enthusiastically and Susan will give you tea and biscuits in the drawing room of this immaculate house with a boutique hotel feel. Antony the chef keeps the wheels oiled and the food coming – treat yourself to green crab soup or succulent lobster; the wine cellar holds over 2,000 bottles so there's plenty of choice. Upstairs to bedrooms that are not huge and not all with sea views, but everything you could possibly need is there, from robes to brandy. The pool area is stunning, the garden is filled with interest and it's a three-minute walk to the sea.

Minimum two nights July & August.

Rooms	5: 4 doubles, 1 twin.
Price	£110. Singles £85.
Meals	Dinner, 3 courses, £38.
Closed	Rarely.

Susan Thorbek
Landewednack House,
Church Cove, The Lizard,
Helston,
Cornwall TR12 7PQ
Tel +44 (0)1326 290877
Email luxurybandb@landewednackhouse.com
Web www.landewednackhouse.com

Entry 57   Map 1

Cornwall

Halftides

Hugely enjoyable and special, surrounded by three acres with dazzling views down the coast and out to sea. Fresh funky bedrooms, not huge but filled with light, have gorgeous fabrics, crisp bedding, dreamy views; bathrooms (one a small pod-shower in the room) are sleek in glass and chrome. Susie is great fun, an artist and chef and gives you a delicious organic breakfast in the pretty, airy dining room. Take the coastal path north or south, visit the working harbour in the village, head for a swim down the private path to the beach below. A perfect place to relax and unwind.

Minimum two nights. Over threes welcome.

Rooms	3: 1 double; 1 double, 1 single, each with separate bath.
Price	£95-£120. Singles £35-£55.
Meals	Dinner, 2-3 courses with wine, £30-£35. Pub within walking distance.
Closed	February.

Charles & Susie Holdsworth Hunt
Halftides,
Laflouder Lane, Mullion, Helston,
Cornwall TR12 7HU
Tel +44 (0)1326 241935
Mobile +44 (0)7970 821261
Email halftides@btinternet.com
Web www.halftides.co.uk

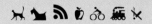

Entry 58   Map 1

Cornwall

Halzephron House

The coastal path runs through the grounds and the view is to die for – you can see St Michael's Mount on a clear day. Be greeted by homemade biscotti and organic coffee roasted in Cornwall: lovely Lucy and Roger are foodies as well as designers. Bedrooms are contemporary, quirky and full of charm: one in the house, with a velvet sofa and a French bed, the other, the Cabin, an enchanting nest for two – drift off under goosedown to the lapping waves below. Elsewhere: space, art and bowls of wild flowers. You can walk to three amazing beaches, a 13th-century church, a golf course and a gastropub. Heaven.

Dogs welcome in Cabin.

Rooms	2: 1 suite. Cabin: 1 suite.
Price	£80-£130.
Meals	Pub 0.25 miles.
Closed	Rarely.

	Lucy & Roger Thorp
	Halzephron House,
	Gunwalloe,
	Helston,
	Cornwall TR12 7QD
Mobile	+44 (0)7899 925816
Email	info@halzephronhouse.co.uk
Web	www.halzephronhouse.co.uk

Entry 59   Map 1

Cornwall

The Hen House

Greenies will be delighted: Sandy and Gary, truly welcoming, are passionately committed to sustainability and happy to advise on the best places to eat, visit and walk; there are OS maps on loan too. Enlightened souls will adore the spacious colourful rooms, the bright fabrics, the wildflower meadow with inviting sun loungers, the pond, the chance to try tai chi, the fairy-lit courtyard at night, the scrumptious locally sourced breakfasts, the birdsong. There's even a sanctuary room for reiki and reflexology set deep into the earth in this generous, peaceful retreat.

Minimum two nights. Over 12s welcome.

Rooms	3 doubles in 3 barns.
Price	£80-£90. Singles £70.
Meals	Pub/restaurant 1 mile.
Closed	Rarely.

	Sandy & Gary Pulfrey
	The Hen House,
	Tregarne, Manaccan,
	Helston, Cornwall TR12 6EW
Tel	+44 (0)1326 280236
Mobile	+44 (0)7809 229958
Email	henhouseuk@aol.com
Web	www.thehenhouse-cornwall.co.uk

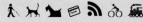

Entry 60   Map 1

Cornwall

Trerose Manor

Follow winding lanes through glorious countryside to find the prettiest, listed manor house, a warm family atmosphere and welcoming tea in the beamed kitchen. Large, light bedrooms, one with floor-to-ceiling windows, sit peacefully in your own wing and have views over the stunning garden. All are dressed in pretty colours, have comfy seats for gazing and smartly tiled bathrooms. A sumptuous breakfast can be taken outside in summer, there are wonderful walks over fields to river or beach and stacks of interesting places to visit. Lovely.

French, German & Italian spoken.

Rooms	3: 2 doubles, 1 twin/double.
Price	£115–£125. Singles £75.
Meals	Pubs/restaurants within walking distance.
Closed	Rarely.

Tessa Phipps
Trerose Manor,
Mawnan Smith,
Falmouth,
Cornwall TR11 5HX
Tel   +44 (0)1326 250784
Email   info@trerosemanor.co.uk
Web   www.trerosemanor.co.uk

Entry 61   Map 1

Cornwall

Bosvathick

A huge old Cornish house that's been in Kate's family since 1760 – along with Indian rugs, heavy furniture, ornate plasterwork, pianos, portraits, pets... even a harp. Historians will be in their element: pass three Celtic crosses dating from the 8th century before the long drive finds the imposing house (all granite gate posts and lions) and a rambling garden with grotto, lake, pasture and woodland. Bedrooms are simple and traditional, full of books and antiques; bathrooms are spick and span, one small and functional, one large. Come to experience a 'time warp' and charming Kate's good breakfasts. Close to Falmouth University, too.

Stair lift for guests' use.

Rooms	4: 1 twin/double, 1 twin, 2 singles; 2 bathrooms. Each party has sole use of a bathroom.
Price	£90. Singles £45–£70.
Meals	Supper, from £25. Packed lunch £5–£10. Pubs 2 miles.
Closed	Rarely.

Kate & Stephen Tyrrell
Bosvathick,
Constantine,
Falmouth,
Cornwall TR11 5RD
Tel   +44 (0)1326 340103
Email   kate@bosvathickhouse.co.uk
Web   www.bosvathickhouse.co.uk

Entry 62   Map 1

Cornwall

Trevilla House

Come for the position: the sea and Fal estuary wrap around you, and the King Harry ferry gives you an easy reach into the glorious Roseland peninsula. Inside find comfortable airy bedrooms with homemade quilts on the beds – the twin with a sofa and old-fashioned charm, the double with stunning sea views. Jinty rustles up delicious locally sourced breakfasts and homemade jams, and you eat in the sunny conservatory that looks south over the sea. Trelissick Gardens and the Copeland China Collection are just next door; the Maritime Museum, Eden, Tate, cycling, watersports and coastal walks are all close by.

Rooms	3: 1 double, 1 twin; 1 single sharing bath (let to same party only).
Price	£85-£95. Singles £50-£55.
Meals	Pubs/restaurants 1-2 miles.
Closed	Christmas & New Year.

Jinty & Peter Copeland
Trevilla House,
Feock, Truro,
Cornwall TR3 6QG
Tel   +44 (0)1872 862369
Mobile   +44 (0)7791 977621
Email   jinty@trevilla.com
Web   www.trevilla.com

Entry 63   Map 1

Cornwall

Hay Barton

Giant windows overlook many acres of farmland, and Jill and Blair look after you so well! Breakfasts are special with the best local produce, homemade granola, yogurt and more. Arrive for tea and lovely home-baked cake, laid out in a comfortable guest sitting room with a log fire and plenty of books and maps. Bedrooms are fresh and pretty with garden flowers, soft white linen on big beds and floral green walls. Gloriously large panelled bathrooms have long roll top baths and are painted in earthy colours. You can knock a few balls around the tennis court, and you're near to good gardens and heaps of places to eat.

Minimum stay two nights in summer.

Rooms	3 twins/doubles.
Price	£80-£90. Singles £60.
Meals	Pubs 1-2 miles.
Closed	Rarely.

Jill & Blair Jobson
Hay Barton,
Tregony, Truro,
Cornwall TR2 5TF
Tel   +44 (0)1872 530288
Mobile   +44 (0)7813 643028
Email   jill.jobson@btinternet.com
Web   www.haybarton.com

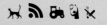

Entry 64   Map 1

Cornwall

Ashby Villa

Lesley is friendly and outgoing and invites you for a cream tea in the kitchen of her Edwardian home. The village is lively but the Dog House, for guests, is peacefully tucked behind, overlooking gardens and fields. Comfy bedrooms have a roll top tub or power shower, cosy rugs on tiled floors, local art, French country furniture and a shared terrace; one wood-lined studio has a wood-burner and its own patio. Zip over to the conservatory for a tasty breakfast and John's homemade bread. The Roseland Peninsula has secret coves and Truro is close. Return with fish for your own barbecue, then relax in the candlelit conservatory. Bliss.

Self-catering available. Dog-friendly.

Rooms	Dog House: 1 double, 1 family room for 3; 2 studios each with extra sofabed & kitchenette.
Price	£75. Family room £85. Singles on request.
Meals	Light meals available. Pub in village. Barbecue available. Picnic hamper on request.
Closed	Rarely.

Lesley Black
Ashby Villa,
Fore Street, Tregony,
Truro,
Cornwall TR2 5RW
Tel   +44 (0)1872 530189
Email blacklesley5@aol.com
Web   www.cornwallvillagebedandbreakfast.co.uk

Entry 65   Map 1

Cornwall

Creed House

A beautiful Georgian rectory surrounded by a truly lovely Cornish garden. Light pours into every elegant corner and your gracious hosts give you fresh, traditional bedrooms in a peaceful wing where sheets are crisp, colours are gentle, flowers are from the garden and you have your own cosy sitting room. Local breads and jams, fruit salads and a full English await you at breakfast – enjoyed in the handsome dining room warmed by a log fire. Perfect for exploring Cornwall's wonderful gardens and coast – excellent restaurants are nearby.

NGS garden.

Rooms	2: 1 double, 1 twin.
Price	£90–£100.
Meals	Pub/restaurant 1 mile.
Closed	Christmas & New Year.

Jonathon & Annabel Croggon
Creed House,
Creed, Grampound,
Truro,
Cornwall TR2 4SL
Tel   +44 (0)1872 530372
Email jrcroggon@btinternet.com
Web   www.creedhouse.co.uk

Entry 66   Map 1

Rambling Rose

Rambling Rose is tucked among the flowers from which it takes its name, in a little corner of Cornwall you can call your own. The caravan itself is Cornish to the core. Built in Penzance in the 1930s, she was restored by local craftsmen and decorated beautifully, with scrollwork and floral patterns, by Nick your friendly host. Panoramic views spread from her steps to the Fowey river valley and distant Bodmin Moor. Inside: a pull-out double, cosy and snug (check measurements first if you're tall!), books, radio and modern gas hob. There's charcoal for the barbecue and a welcome hamper of local goodies.

Minimum two nights. Book through Sawday's Canopy & Stars online or by phone.

Collon Barton

Come for the lofty position on a grassy hillside, the heartlifting views over unspoilt countryside and the pretty creekside village of Lerryn. This 18th-century house is a working sheep farm and an artistic household (sculptures galore, and family portraits). Anne and Iain give you eggs from their happy chickens in the old dairy, now a large, light breakfast room. Traditional airy bedrooms come in pink or blue and there's an elegant drawing room. On sunny days, Anne welcomes you with tea in the summer house. Wonderful riverside and coastal walks and good gardens abound; the Eden Project is 20 minutes away.

Children & pets by arrangement.

Rooms	Gypsy caravan for 2 with shower & wc 50 yards away.
Price	£75–£85.
Meals	BYO breakfast (welcome hamper provided). Pubs 1 mile.
Closed	Christmas & New Year.

Rooms	2: 1 twin/double, 1 twin/double with dressing room & extra beds.
Price	£80. Singles £50.
Meals	Pub 10-minute walk.
Closed	Rarely.

Sawday's Canopy & Stars
Rambling Rose,
Delancey House, Lostwithiel,
Cornwall PL22 0HU
Tel   +44 (0)1275 395447
Email   enquiries@canopyandstars.co.uk
Web   www.canopyandstars.co.uk/ramblingrose

Anne & Iain Mackie
Collon Barton,
Lerryn,
Lostwithiel,
Cornwall PL22 0NX
Tel   +44 (0)1208 872908
Mobile   +44 (0)7721 090186
Email   annemackie@btconnect.com

Entry 67   Map 1

Entry 68   Map 1

Cornwall

Trussel Barn

Views shoot off in all directions and landscaped gardens drop to the valley below, where the little branch line runs alongside the river linking Liskeard and Looe... fabulous. Ex-yacht skipper Richard and talented cook Kathy are full of plans for their new enterprise, and give you four comfortable, carpeted rooms (two are huge) with firm mattresses and new furniture. Bathrooms shine and breakfast is worth waking up for – full English, homemade everything and delicious preserves. After a day discovering Eden Project or coast, look forward to drinks on the great terrace – or a sink-into sofa and a roaring fire.

Rooms	4: 1 suite; 1 double, 1 twin, 1 single sharing bath (let to same party only).
Price	From £90. Singles from £50.
Meals	Dinner £20. Pubs/restaurants within 3 miles.
Closed	Rarely.

Richard Shields & Kathy Williams
Trussel Barn,
St Keyne, Liskeard,
Cornwall PL14 4QL

Tel	+44 (0)1579 340450
Mobile	+44 (0)7785 350552
Email	trusselbarn@btinternet.com
Web	www.trusselbarn.com

Entry 69 Map 1

Cornwall

Hornacott

The garden, in its lovely valley setting, has seats in little corners poised to catch the evening sun – perfect for a pre-dinner drink. The peaceful house is named after the hill and you have a private entrance to your airy suite: a room with a large bed plus a lofty sitting room with a balcony and windows that look down onto the wooded valley. With CD player, music, chocolates and magazines you are truly self-contained. Jos, a kitchen designer, and Mary-Anne love having guests and living the slow life – busily! – and give you top-notch local produce and free-range eggs for breakfast.

Rooms	2: 1 suite; 1 twin with separate shower.
Price	£70. Suite £95. Singles £50.
Meals	Dinner, 3 courses, £20. BYO. Pubs/restaurants 4.5 miles.
Closed	Christmas.

Jos & Mary-Anne Otway-Ruthven
Hornacott,
South Petherwin,
Launceston,
Cornwall PL15 7LH

Tel	+44 (0)1566 782461
Email	otwayruthven@btinternet.com
Web	www.hornacott.co.uk

Entry 70 Map 1

Cornwall

Cadson Manor

This lovely old manor, with spectacular views across the Lynher valley, has been in the Crago family for generations. Chatty and friendly Brenda looks after you well; expect flowers, log fires, homemade cakes and delicious breakfasts with eggs from the hens. Everything shines, from the slate hall floor and antique furniture to the pretty china and talkative parrot. Fish in the lake, picnic in the grounds or walk Cadson Bury among Highland cattle. Bedrooms and bathrooms have hotel comfort, rich drapes and thoughtful extras. Historic houses, gardens, the Eden Project, golf and the coast are all close, and the walks are sublime.

Rooms	4: 2 doubles; 1 double, 1 twin sharing bath (let to same party only).
Price	£96. Singles £65.
Meals	Pub/restaurant 3 miles.
Closed	Occasionally.

Brenda Crago
Cadson Manor,
Callington,
Cornwall PL17 7HW
Tel   +44 (0)1579 383969
Email   brenda.crago@btconnect.com
Web   www.cadsonmanor.co.uk

Entry 71   Map 2

Cornwall

Pentillie Castle

So many temptations: woodland gardens that tumble down to the Tamar, a walled Victorian kitchen garden still being restored, a magnificent Victorian bathing hut... and Pentillie beef cattle, uniquely theirs, grazing either side of the great drive up to the handsome house. Bedrooms are smart, spacious and deeply comfortable, bathrooms pamper. Ted and Sarah, with daughter Sammie, have mastered that delicate balancing act between luxury and stuffiness, bringing out one and banishing the other. It's the sort of place where you gasp at the perfection of it all and then throw your shoes off before diving into the sofa.

Rooms	9: 8 twins/doubles, 1 four-poster suite.
Price	£130–£195. Suite £185–£210.
Meals	Dinner, 3 courses, £30. Pubs/restaurants 15-minute drive.
Closed	Rarely.

Sammie Coryton
Pentillie Castle,
St Mellion, Saltash,
Cornwall PL12 6QD
Tel   +44 (0)1579 350044
Email   contact@pentillie.co.uk
Web   www.pentillie.co.uk

Entry 72   Map 2

Cornwall

Lantallack Farm

You will be inspired here, in generous Nicky's heart-warming old Georgian farmhouse. Find a straw-yellow sitting room with a log fire, books to read and a grand piano; views are breathtaking across countryside, streams and wooded valley. Bedrooms have deliciously comfy beds; Polly's Bower, a romantic hideaway in the old cider barn, is a charming open-plan space with whitewash and old beams, wood-burner and freestanding tub. Breakfast in the walled garden on fine days: apple juice from the orchard and bacon and sausages from down the road. There are 40 acres to explore, a leat-side trail and a heated outdoor pool; marvellous.

Minimum two nights.

Rooms	2: 1 double. Polly's Bower: 1 double with sitting area & kitchen.
Price	£100–£120. Polly's Bower £125–£135.
Meals	Supper on request in Polly's Bower, £25. Pubs/restaurants 1 mile.
Closed	Rarely.

Nicky Walker
Lantallack Farm,
Landrake, Saltash,
Cornwall PL12 5AE

Tel	+44 (0)1752 851281
Email	enquiries@lantallack.co.uk
Web	www.lantallackgetaways.co.uk

Entry 73 Map 2

Cumbria

Mallsgate Hall

Moss-walled lanes wend through wonderful scenery to this intriguing 17th-century fortified manor house and busy working farm. The aim is for self-sufficiency and Christopher and Ilona (he an environmental law barrister) pour energy into the place. Estate produce stars in meals by Ilona's cousin Alice, a Ballymaloe-trained cook. You eat in the Library or Great Hall, sleep in the big vault-ceilinged bedroom (children in a small bunk-bedded room), and bathe in the equally beamed and comfortably old-fashioned bathroom. The gardens – overlooked by the pretty Georgian façade – are a joy. Bring jumpers, wellies and wander!

Bunk room available for 2 children (sharing bathroom with double).

Rooms	1 double.
Price	£120. Singles £80.
Meals	Supper, 2 courses, £25. Pubs 3 miles.
Closed	November–February.

Ilona Boyle
Mallsgate Hall,
Roweltown, Carlisle,
Cumbria CA6 6LX

Tel	+44 (0)1697 748292
Email	ilonaboyle@gmail.com
Web	www.mallsgate.co.uk

Entry 74 Map 15

Warwick Hall

The position here is magnificent, a slice of English heaven. The house stands resplendently in 260 acres on the banks of the river Eden, one of the best salmon beats in the country; a two-mile stroll hugs the water. Inside, everything is gorgeous: vast windows that flood the place with light; a wonderful drawing room with sofas in front of the fire; a dining room with views of hill and river. Delightful country-house bedrooms have high ceilings, beautiful fabrics, super bathrooms; one has its own fire. Bonnie Prince Charlie once stayed, though not in the comfort you can expect. Delicious food and a great atmosphere, too.

Ask about exclusive use for house parties.

Drybeck Farm

Steve and Paula do what they love at Drybeck Farm, on the banks of the Eden river. You can breakfast while watching the kingfishers, and a hamper is included on the first morning (their own eggs, jam, bread, sausage, bacon). There are wood-burners for cosiness; showers and compost loos are a step away; and both yurts and wagon have their own spot in the 'cookhouse with a view'. Stock up on farm produce for the barbecue, try charcoal burning or green wood-working with Steve, help feed rare breeds. You're off the tourist trail but Carlisle is nearby should you miss civilisation. Most guests choose to stay put…

Minimum three nights. Book through Sawday's Canopy & Stars online or by phone.

Rooms	9: 7 twins/doubles; 2 suites with kitchenettes.
Price	£120. Suites £180. Self-catering house party rates available.
Meals	Dinner, 3 courses, £30. Restaurant 1 mile.
Closed	Rarely.

Rooms	2 yurts for 4, 1 wagon for 2, sharing 2 showers & dry compost wcs, close by.
Price	Wagon £58-£64. Yurts £98-£108.
Meals	BYO breakfast (hamper for first morning). Pubs within 2 miles.
Closed	December-March.

	Val Marriner
	Warwick Hall,
	Warwick-on-Eden, Carlisle,
	Cumbria CA4 8PG
Tel	+44 (0)1228 561546
Mobile	+44 (0)7818 448756
Email	info@warwickhall.org
Web	www.warwickhall.org

	Sawday's Canopy & Stars
	Drybeck Farm,
	Armathwaite, Carlisle,
	Cumbria CA4 9ST
Tel	+44 (0)1275 395447
Email	enquiries@canopyandstars.co.uk
Web	www.canopyandstars.co.uk/ drybeckfarm

Cumbria

Sirelands

Sirelands, once a gardener's cottage, stands among rhododendrons and spreading trees on a sunny slope, a stream trickling by: a stunning spot. The Carrs have lived here for years and the house has a relaxed and homely feel. Enjoy home-grown produce at dinner on a polished table, then retire to the sitting room, delightful with log basket, honesty bar, flowers and books. Sash windows overlook the wooded garden, visited by roe deer and a wide variety of birds. Bedrooms and bathrooms are pleasant, peaceful and spotless; one loo has an amazing view! Friendly Angela loves cooking and treats you to tea and homemade cake.

Rooms	2: 1 twin; 1 double with separate bath/shower.
Price	£100. Singles £50-£60.
Meals	Dinner, 2-3 courses, £22-£27.50. Pubs within 5 miles.
Closed	Christmas & New Year.

David & Angela Carr
Sirelands,
Heads Nook,
Brampton, Carlisle,
Cumbria CA8 9BT
Tel   +44 (0)1228 670389
Mobile   +44 (0)7748 101513
Email   carr_sirelands@btconnect.com

Entry 77   Map 12

Cumbria

Willowford Farm

Lauren and Liam are enthusiastic about their organic farm and their guests. Two single-storey stone byres have been converted environmentally with thermafleece wool in the roof and a wood-burning boiler for heated slate floors. In one byre: the bedrooms, fresh, stylish, with slate floors and lofty beams, perhaps windows looking onto the farmyard, or skylights for the stars. In the other: a cosy sitting room with views of sheep and hills, and tables for meals of home-reared lamb and beef, and tasty veggy dishes; or head off to the pub! Hadrian's Wall, forts, museums and walks are all here – and Millie the sheepdog welcomes yours.

Rooms	Barn: 1 double, 4 twins/doubles (2 let to same party only).
Price	£75-£80. Singles from £50.
Meals	Dinner, 3 courses, £18. Packed lunch £6. Pubs/restaurants 1 mile.
Closed	Sunday & Monday. Mid-November-February.

Liam McNulty & Lauren Harrison
Willowford Farm,
Gilsland,
Brampton,
Cumbria CA8 7AA
Tel   +44 (0)1697 747962
Email stay@willowford.co.uk
Web   www.willowford.co.uk

Entry 78   Map 12

Cumbria

Cumbria

Chapelburn House

Yomp in the most dramatic scenery close to the best bits of Hadrian's Wall, then head for Chapelburn House. Matt and Katie are young, charming, unflappable, food is reared happily then cooked with more flavour than fuss. Honey is from their bees, bread is home-baked. You have a sitting room with an open fire, lots of books and squishy sofas, *and* a south-facing garden room for summer dreaming. Bedrooms are deeply comfortable and bathrooms (one definitely not for fatties!) brand spanking new. Children are more than welcome to join in. This would delight exhausted refugees from London, too.

Lazonby Hall

The pinky sandstone façade rises, château-like, from bright flowers, box hedges, crunchy gravel: enchanting. Views, from sash windows and garden folly, yawn over the Eden valley to the Pennines. Step past pillars to panelled, antique-filled rooms of heavy curtains, marble fires, mahogany and oils. Formal, yet not daunting – the Quines and their daschunds bring life, flexibility, and delicious Cumbrian breakfasts. Wake to birdsong and garden views. This sweet area of winding lanes and dry stone walls is near the north Lakes, Penrith, Carlisle, Scotland, ripe for exploration by foot, bike, canoe or train.

Rooms	2 doubles.
Price	£70-£90.
Meals	Dinner, 3 courses, £25. Packed lunch £5-£7.50. Restaurant 5 miles.
Closed	Christmas & New Year.

Rooms	4: 2 doubles; 1 double, 1 twin sharing bath.
Price	£80-£125. Singles £75-£100.
Meals	Supper, 3 courses, £25-£50. Pub/restaurant 2 miles.
Closed	Rarely.

Matthew & Katie McClure
Chapelburn House,
Low Row, Brampton,
Cumbria CA8 2LY
Tel +44 (0)1697 746595
Email stay@chapelburn.com
Web www.chapelburn.com

Mr & Mrs Quine
Lazonby Hall,
Lazonby, Penrith,
Cumbria CA10 1BA
Tel +44 (0)1768 870800
Email info@lazonbyhall.co.uk
Web www.lazonbyhall.co.uk

Entry 79 Map 11

Entry 80 Map 11

Johnby Hall

You are ensconced in the quieter part of the Lakes and have independence in this Elizabethan manor house – once a fortified Pele tower, now a family home. Two suites (one in the studio, next to the main house) are fresh and light: each has its own sitting room with lots of books and pictures, squashy sofas, pretty fabrics and whitewashed walls. Beds have patchwork quilts, windows have stone mullions and there is absolute quiet. Henry gives you sturdy breakfasts, and good home-grown suppers by a roaring fire in the great hall; he and Anna can join you or leave you in peace. Walks from the door are sublime.

Scales Plantation

Beautiful Cumbrian mini camps in woodland clearings. Choose from one of three shepherd's huts, a big safari tent or a double bell tent. Each is tucked away in its own corner of woodland with the backdrop of the North Lake fells to gaze out on. Feather down duvets and sheepskin rugs soften rustic spaces and keep you warm and cosy along with oven wood-burners and gas-fired baths. Try your hand at campfire cookery on the fire pit and tripod. Tabitha and Rob are wonderful hosts, and, besides giving you the basics including farm eggs, can take your order for farm shop provisions and have them waiting when you get there.

Minimum three nights. Book through Sawday's Canopy & Stars online or by phone.

Rooms	2: 1 twin/double & sitting room. Studio: 1 family room & sitting room.	Rooms	3 shepherd's huts for 4. Bell tent for 4. Safari tent for 8 with shower on porch & compost loo 10 yards away.
Price	£110-£125. Singles £80-£90.		
Meals	Supper, 2 courses, £20. Pub 1 mile.	Price	Shepherd's huts £70-£130. Bell tent camp £80-£130. Safari tent £150-£184.
Closed	Rarely.		
		Meals	BYO breakfast (welcome pack provided). Pub 3 miles.
		Closed	Never.

	Henry & Anna Howard		Sawday's Canopy & Stars
	Johnby Hall,		Scales Plantation,
	Johnby, Penrith,		Berrier, Penrith,
	Cumbria CA11 0UU		Cumbria CA11 0XE
Tel	+44 (0)17684 83257	Tel	+44 (0)1275 395447
Email	bookings@johnbyhall.co.uk	Email	enquiries@canopyandstars.co.uk
Web	www.johnbyhall.co.uk	Web	www.canopyandstars.co.uk/ scalesplantation

Entry 81   Map 11

Entry 82   Map 11

Cumbria

Lowthwaite

Leave your worries behind as you head up the lanes to the farmhouse tucked into the fell. Jim, ex-hiking guide, and Danish Tine moved back from Tanzania with their daughters in 2007 and give you four peaceful bedrooms in the view-filled barn wing. Handsomely chunky twin beds are of recycled dhow wood, crisp light bathrooms sport organic soaps and you wake to the smell of homemade bread; breakfasts are fine Scandinavian and English inspired spreads. In a garden full of bird feeders and pheasants a stream trickles through one of the guest terraces, and there are endless fells to explore. A treat for peace-seekers and families.

Rooms	4: 2 twins/doubles, 2 family rooms.
Price	£60-£90. Singles £40-£70.
Meals	Packed lunch £6. Dinner £18-£27. Pubs 2.5 miles.
Closed	Christmas.

	Tine & Jim Boving Foster
	Lowthwaite,
	Matterdale,
	Penrith,
	Cumbria CA11 0LE
Tel	+44 (0)1768 482343
Email	info@lowthwaiteullswater.com
Web	www.lowthwaiteullswater.com

Entry 83   Map 11

Cumbria

Greenah

Tucked into the hillside off a narrow lane, this 1750s smallholding is surrounded by fells, so is perfect for walkers. Absolute privacy for four friends or family with your own entrance to a beamed and stone-flagged sitting room with wood-burning stove, creamy walls and cheery floral curtains. Warm bedrooms have original paintings, good beds, hot water bottles, bathrobes and a sparkling bathroom with a loo with a remarkable view. Malcolm is a climber; Marjorie is totally committed to organic food so you get a fabulous breakfast, and good advice about the local area. Fell walking is not compulsory!

Over eights welcome.

Rooms	2: 1 double; 1 twin sharing shower with double (let to same party only).
Price	£90-£95. Singles £60-£65.
Meals	Pubs/restaurants 3 miles.
Closed	November/January.

	Marjorie & Malcolm Emery
	Greenah,
	Matterdale, Penrith,
	Cumbria CA11 0SA
Tel	+44 (0)1768 483387
Mobile	+44 (0)7767 213667
Email	info@greenah.co.uk
Web	www.greenah.co.uk

Entry 84   Map 11

Cumbria

Whitbysteads

Swing into the yard of a gentleman's farmhouse at the end of a drive lined with gorse, stone walls and sheep. It's a working farm, so lots going on with four-wheel drives, dogs, busy hens and relaxed bustle. Victoria does styles and periods well: warm rugs, flowery sofas with plain linen armchairs, modern family paintings. The main bedroom is sumptuous and stylish, the smaller rooms simpler; bathrooms are wonderfully vintage, eclectic and big. Great hosts who make you feel instantly at home here; enjoy the breathtaking views over the fells – easy for the M6 too. Dress up in the evening for dinner at Sharrow Bay.

Rooms	3: 1 double; 1 double, 1 twin sharing bath (let to same party only).
Price	£90–£110. Singles £45.
Meals	Dinner from £20. Children's tea £5. Pub 0.5 miles.
Closed	Rarely.

Victoria Lowther
Whitbysteads,
Askham, Penrith,
Cumbria CA10 2PG

Tel	+44 (0)1931 712284
Mobile	+44 (0)7976 276961
Email	victoria@whitbysteads.org
Web	www.whitbysteads.org

Entry 85   Map 11

Cumbria

Kelleth Old Hall

Glorious unimpeded views of fields, cows and the Howgill Fells from this fun and characterful B&B. Charlotte – chutney enthusiast, writer of three novels – has moved into an ancient manor (the fourth owner in 400 years); now it glows with paintings, antiques and books. Short steep stairs lead from 17th-century flagstones to a big canopied brass bed and yellow silk curtains at mullion windows. All is warm, charming, inviting, and that includes the roll top bath beneath a vaulted ceiling. Fuel up on a Cumbrian breakfast, return to a delicious supper of exotic flavours. Near the A685 but peaceful at night.

Rooms	1 double (with extra single bed).
Price	£80–£90. Singles £60–£65.
Meals	Dinner, 2–3 courses, £18–£22. Pub/restaurant 5 miles.
Closed	Occasionally.

Charlotte Fairbairn
Kelleth Old Hall,
Kelleth, Penrith,
Cumbria CA10 3UG

Tel	+44 (0)1539 623344
Mobile	+44 (0)7754 163941
Email	charlottefairbairn@hotmail.co.uk
Web	www.kelletholdhall.co.uk

Entry 86   Map 12

Cumbria

Drybeck Hall

Looking south to fields, woodland and beck this Grade II* listed, 1679 farmhouse has blue painted mullion windows and exposed beams. Expect a deeply traditional home with good furniture, an open fire and pictures of Anthony's predecessors looking down on you benignly; the family has been in the area for 800 years. Comfortable bedrooms have pretty floral fabrics and oak doors; bathrooms are simple but sparkling. Lulie is relaxed and charming and a good cook: enjoy a full English with free-range eggs in the sunny dining room, and home-grown vegetables and often game for dinner. A genuine slice of history.

Rooms	2: 1 double, 1 twin.
Price	£90. Singles £45.
Meals	Dinner, 3 courses, £25. Pub/restaurant 4 miles.
Closed	Rarely.

Lulie & Anthony Hothfield
Drybeck Hall,
Appleby-in-Westmorland,
Cumbria CA16 6TF
Tel   +44 (0)1768 351487
Email   lulieant@aol.com
Web   www.drybeckhall.co.uk

Entry 87   Map 12

Cumbria

Lapwings Barn

In the back of most-beautiful-beyond, down narrow lanes, this converted barn is a gorgeous retreat for two – or four. Delightful generous Gillian and Rick give you privacy and an upstairs sitting room with log stove, sofa and a balcony with views. Bedrooms downstairs (separate entrances) are pleasingly rustic with beams and modern stone-tiled bathrooms. Breakfast is delivered: sausages and bacon from their Saddlebacks, eggs from their hens, superb homemade bread and marmalade. Stroll along lowland tracks, watch curlews and lapwings, puff to the top of Whinfell. Ambleside and Beatrix Potter's house are near. One of the best.

Rooms	Barn: 2 twins/doubles & sitting room.
Price	£60-£90. Singles from £35.
Meals	Packed lunch £5. Pub/restaurant 3.5 miles.
Closed	Rarely.

Rick & Gillian Rodriguez
Lapwings Barn,
Whinfell, Kendal,
Cumbria LA8 9EQ
Tel   +44 (0)1539 824373
Mobile   +44 (0)7901 732379
Email   stay@lapwingsbarn.co.uk
Web   www.lapwingsbarn.co.uk

Entry 88   Map 12

Cumbria

Summerhow House

In four acres of fine landscaping and fun topiary is a large and inviting home of flamboyant wallpapers and shades of aqua, lemon and rose. Stylish but laid-back, grand but unintimidating, both house and hosts are a treat. Bedrooms have gilt frames and marble fireplaces, Molton Brown goodies and garden views, there are two sitting rooms to retreat to and breakfasts to delight you – fruits from the orchard, eggs from Sizergh Castle (John's family home). Two miles from Kendal: hop on the train to the Lakes. Walkers, sailors, skiers, food-lovers, dog-lovers will be charmed… aspiring actors too (talk to Janey!).

Rooms	2: 1 double, 1 twin.
Price	£80-£120. Singles £50-£69.
Meals	Pub/restaurant 1.5 miles.
Closed	Occasionally.

	Janey & John Hornyold-Strickland
	Summerhow House,
	Shap Road,
	Kendal,
	Cumbria LA9 6NY
Tel	+44 (0)1539 720763
Email	stay@summerhowbedandbreakfast.co.uk
Web	www.summerhowbedandbreakfast.co.uk

Entry 89   Map 11

Cumbria

Gillthwaite Rigg

All is calm and ordered in this airy and tranquil Arts and Crafts house. Come for nature and to be surrounded by lake and fell countryside – you may spot a badger or deer in the garden! Find panelled window seats, gleaming oak floors, leaded windows, wooden latched doors and motifs moulded into white plaster. Bedrooms with original fireplaces and large comfy beds have an uncluttered simplicity and views. Banks of books, wood-burners, proper Cumbrian breakfasts and kind, affable hosts add cheer. Rhoda and Tony are passionate about conservation and wildlife in their 14 acres of garden and woodland.

Babies & children over six welcome.

Rooms	2: 1 double, 1 twin/double.
Price	£70-£85. Singles £55.
Meals	Pubs/restaurants 1 mile.
Closed	Christmas & New Year.

	Rhoda M & Tony Graham
	Gillthwaite Rigg,
	Heathwaite Manor, Lickbarrow Rd,
	Windermere, Cumbria LA23 2NQ
Tel	+44 (0)1539 446212
Mobile	+44 (0)7765 415934
Email	tonyandrhodagraham@hotmail.com
Web	www.gillthwaiterigg.co.uk

Entry 90   Map 11

Cumbria

Gilpin Mill

Come to be seriously spoiled. Down leafy lanes is a pretty white house by a mill pond, framed by pastures and trees. Steve took a year off to build new Gilpin Mill, and Jo looks after hens, labs and guests – beautifully. In the country farmhouse sitting room oak beams span the ceiling and a slate faux-lintel sits above the log fire. Bedrooms are equally inviting: beds are topped with duck down, luscious bathrooms are warm underfoot. Alongside is a lovely old barn where timber was made into bobbins; in the mill pond is a trout ladder and dam, soon to provide power for the grid. And just six cars pass a day!

Children over ten welcome.

Rooms	3 twins/doubles.
Price	£86-£106. Singles £58-£68.
Meals	Pub 2.5 miles.
Closed	Christmas.

Jo & Steve Ainsworth
Gilpin Mill,
Crook, Windermere,
Cumbria LA8 8LN
Tel   +44 (0)1539 568405
Email   info@gilpinmill.co.uk
Web   www.gilpinmill.co.uk

Entry 91   Map 11

Cumbria

Fellside Studios

Off the beaten tourist track, a piece of paradise in the Troutbeck valley: seclusion, stylishness and breathtaking views. Prepare your own candlelit dinners, rise when the mood takes you, come and go as you please. The flower beds spill with heathers, hens cluck, and there's a decked terrace for continental breakfast in the sun – freshly prepared by your gently hospitable hosts who live in the attached house. In your studio apartment you get oak floors, slate shower rooms, immaculate kitchenettes with designer touches, DVD players, comfy chairs, luxurious towels. Wonderful.

Minimum stay two nights.

Rooms	2 studios for 2: each with 1 double or 1 twin/double & kitchenette.
Price	£70-£90. Singles from £45.
Meals	Continental breakfast. Pub/restaurant 0.5 miles.
Closed	Rarely.

Monica & Brian Liddell
Fellside Studios,
Troutbeck, Windermere,
Cumbria LA23 1PE
Tel   +44 (0)1539 434000
Email   brian@fellsidestudios.co.uk
Web   www.fellsidestudios.co.uk

Entry 92   Map 11

Cumbria

Broughton House

Down lanes edged with dry stone walls and hedges, with distant views of the Lakeland mountains… what peace! You feel instantly at home too, in a house full of books and colour. Bedrooms come with a jar of Cate's homemade brownies, a bowl of fruit and a deep mattress: a brass bed in one, privacy in the wing, snug simplicity in Ben's Cabin. Wake to fresh juice, pancakes, homemade bread, local bacon and sausages, smoked salmon and scrambled eggs. Muffin the dog, Minty the cat, a host of hens and a large garden all add to the charm. Perfect for cycling, a hop from lake Windermere and eating out in pretty Cartmel is a treat.

Rooms	3: 1 double; 1 double with separate bath. Cabin: 1 twin, kitchen & sitting room in a yurt (May-Sept).
Price	£80. Cabin £60. Singles £50.
Meals	Pub 1 mile.
Closed	Rarely.

Cate Davies
Broughton House,
Field Broughton, Grange-over-Sands,
Cumbria LA11 6HN

Tel	+44 (0)1539 536439
Email	info@broughtonhousecartmel.co.uk
Web	www.broughtonhousecartmel.co.uk

Entry 93   Map 11

Cumbria

Cockenskell Farm

The house and hill farm garden with its wild rhododendrons and damson orchard sits at the southern end of Lake Coniston and the views are glorious. Inside find beamed rooms, art and antique pine; bedrooms have pretty patchwork covers and lovely wallpapers. Relax with a book in the conservatory, stroll through the magical, bird-filled garden or tackle a bit of the Cumbrian Way which meanders through the fields to the back. On sunny days Sara will give you breakfast in the conservatory. History seeps from every pore, the place glows with loving care and to stay here is a treat.

Children over 12 welcome.

Rooms	2: 1 twin; 1 twin with separate bath.
Price	£90. Singles from £45.
Meals	Packed lunch £7.50. Pubs 2-4 miles.
Closed	November-February.

Sara Keegan
Cockenskell Farm,
Blawith, Ulverston,
Cumbria LA12 8EL

Tel	+44 (0)1229 885217
Mobile	+44 (0)7909 885086
Email	keegan@cockenskell.co.uk
Web	www.cockenskell.co.uk

Entry 94   Map 11

Cumbria

New House Farm

The large comfy beds, the extravagant baths, the linen, the fabrics, the pillows – comfort par excellence! The renovation is impressive, too; the plasterwork stops here and there to reveal old beam, slate or stone. A trio of the bedrooms are named after the mountain each faces; Swinside brings the 1650s house its own spring water. The breakfast room has a wood-burner, hunting prints and polished tables for Hazel's breakfasts to fuel your adventures, the sitting room sports fireplaces and brocade sofas, and walkers will fall gratefully into the hot spring spa. Luxurious, and huge fun.

Children over six welcome.

Rooms	5: 2 doubles, 1 twin/double. Stables: 2 four-posters.
Price	£110–£170. Singles £60–£85.
Meals	Lunch from £6 (April–November). Dinner, 3–5 courses, £32–£38. Packed lunch £8. Afternoon tea £5. Pubs 2.5 miles.
Closed	Rarely.

Hazel Thompson
New House Farm,
Lorton,
Cockermouth,
Cumbria CA13 9UU
Mobile   +44 (0)7841 159818
Email   hazel@newhouse-farm.co.uk
Web   www.newhouse-farm.com

Entry 95   Map 11

Cumbria

Howe Keld

Dismiss all thoughts of the chintzy Keswick guest house: David and Val have swept through with carpets made of Herdwick sheep wool, bedroom furniture made by a local craftsman, gorgeous fabrics, striking wallpaper and smart bathrooms with green slate. It's luxurious but not flashy, and there's a cosy sitting room in primary colours crammed with local info; theatre, shops and restaurants are all strolling distance (choose rooms at the front if you need total quiet). Fill up at breakfast on home-baked bread, freshly made smoothies or a jolly good fry-up.

Minimum stay two nights at weekends, three on bank holidays.

Rooms	14: 13 doubles, 1 single.
Price	£90–£130. Singles £55–£60.
Meals	Pub/restaurant 300 yds.
Closed	Part of December including Christmas. Most of January excluding New Year.

David Fisher
Howe Keld,
5/7 The Heads,
Keswick,
Cumbria CA12 5ES
Tel   +44 (0)1768 772417
Email   david@howekeld.co.uk
Web   www.howekeld.co.uk

Entry 96   Map 11

Cumbria

Boltongate Old Rectory

The setting of this lovely old rectory could hardly be more pastoral; many of its rooms face south and have superb fells views. Furniture is a beautiful mix of antique and contemporary – handmade Harris mattresses, big chunky sofas – in a house whose roots go back to 1360. The treats continue at table: Gill is passionate about sourcing organic and local ingredients for her kitchen, David knows his wines and you eat by candlelight in a 16th-century room. They're relaxed and charming and, when the place is full, create a fabulous house-party feel. Outside: red squirrels and well-fed rabbits, a croquet lawn and stunning Skiddaw

Rooms	3: 1 double, 1 twin/double; 1 double with separate bath.
Price	£120–£130. Singles from £95.
Meals	Dinner, 3 courses, £33. Pub 10-minute drive.
Closed	Sunday & Monday. December/January.

Gill & David Taylor
Boltongate Old Rectory,
Boltongate, Ireby,
Wigton, Cumbria CA7 1DA

Tel	+44 (0)1697 371647
Mobile	+44 (0)7763 242969
Email	boltongate@talk21.com
Web	www.boltongateoldrectory.com

Entry 97   Map 11

Derbyshire

Underleigh House

A Derbyshire longhouse in Brontë country built by a man called George Eyre. The position is unbeatable – field, river, hill, sky – but the stars of the show are Philip and Vivienne, dab hands at spoiling guests rotten. There's a big sitting room with maps for walkers, a dining room hall for hearty breakfasts, and tables and chairs scattered about the garden. Back inside, bedrooms vary in size, but all have super beds, goose down duvets and good views; a couple have doors onto the garden, the suites have proper sitting rooms. Fantastic walks start from the front door, Castleton Caves are on the doorstep, Chatsworth is close.

Minimum two nights at weekends. Children over 12 welcome.

Rooms	5: 3 doubles, 2 suites.
Price	£90–£95. Suite £105–£110. Singles from £70.
Meals	Packed lunches £6. Pubs/restaurants 0.5 miles.
Closed	Christmas & January.

Philip & Vivienne Taylor
Underleigh House,
Lose Hill Lane, Hope,
Hope Valley,
Derbyshire S33 6AF

Tel	+44 (0)1433 621372
Email	Info@underleighhouse.co.uk
Web	www.underleighhouse.co.uk

Entry 98   Map 12

Derbyshire

Horsleygate Hall

Hens and guinea fowl animate the charming old stable yard, and the gardens are vibrant and fascinating, with stone terraces and streams, hidden patios, modern sculptures and seats in every corner... the Fords, attentive and kind, encourage you to explore. Inside the 1783 house, Margaret has created yet more charm. There is a warm, timeless, harmonious feel, with worn kilims on pine boards, striped and floral wallpapers, deep sofas and pools of light. Breakfast is served round a big table in the old schoolroom — homemade jams and oatcakes, garden fruit, eggs from the hens. Special.

Children over five welcome.

Rooms	3: 1 double; 1 family room, 1 twin sharing bath.
Price	£70–£85. Singles £45–£55.
Meals	Pubs/restaurant 1 mile.
Closed	23 December–4 January.

Robert & Margaret Ford
Horsleygate Hall,
Horsleygate Lane,
Holmesfield,
Derbyshire S18 7WD
Tel   +44 (0)1142 890333

Entry 99   Map 8

Derbyshire

River Cottage

Well-travelled Gilly and John have restored their large house — built in the 1740s — and given it a fresh modern twist. Interiors are light and airy, with mirrors, antiques and immaculate fabrics giving each room a charm of its own. Attention to detail includes Gilly's legendary breakfasts — and five types of tea! Outside: a lovely tiered garden with the river Wye running through; easy to ignore the busy A6 when settled here with a glass of wine. Ashford-in-the-Water is one of the prettiest villages in the Peaks, fishing can be arranged and you are ten minutes from Chatsworth — there's a bus stop right outside the door.

Minimum two nights at weekends Easter-Oct.

Rooms	4: 3 doubles; 1 double with separate bath.
Price	£85–£125. Singles from £75.
Meals	Pubs 800 yds.
Closed	Mid-December to mid-February.

Gilly & John Deacon
River Cottage,
Buxton Rd, Ashford-in-the-Water,
Bakewell, Derbyshire DE45 1QP
Tel   +44 (0)1629 813327
Email   info@rivercottageashford.co.uk
Web   www.rivercottageashford.co.uk

Entry 100   Map 8

Derbyshire

Dale End House

One of those places where you get your own annexe – in this case, the former milking parlour of the listed farmhouse. It certainly has scrubbed up nicely. The ground-floor bedroom has a finely dressed antique bed and magnificent chandelier while the well-equipped kitchen is a boon if you don't fancy venturing out for supper. Friendly, helpful Sarah takes orders for breakfasts – eggs from her hens, local sausages and bacon – and delivers to your door. No open fire but cosy underfloor heating warms you after a blustery yomp in any direction. Bring your four-legged friends – canine or equine – to this happy house.

Self-catering option.

Rooms	Lodge: 1 double with kitchen & dining/sitting room.
Price	£85.
Meals	Pubs/restaurants 2.5 miles.
Closed	Rarely.

Sarah & Paul Summers
Dale End House,
Gratton, Bakewell,
Derbyshire DE45 1LN

Tel	+44 (0)1629 650380
Email	thelodge@daleendhouse.co.uk
Web	www.daleendhouse.co.uk

Entry 101   Map 8

Derbyshire

Tinkersley Cottage

Sarah has painstakingly reassembled two run-down cottages at the very top of a hill, with the giddiest views over the Peak District's loveliest parts. You can tell she's a stylist: find pretty stripes and florals, painted wood panelling, chandeliers and shabby chic. Your small, comfortable garden suite, restful with antique linen and painted French bed, is delightfully private with its own sitting area, a terrace for the views and entrance up steps from the garden. Sarah is bright and bubbly and loves having guests; breakfast is sourced locally; Chatsworth farm shop and Bakewell farmers' market are nearby.

Rooms	Garden Room: 1 suite.
Price	£85.
Meals	Pubs/restaurants within 1 mile.
Closed	Rarely.

Sarah Copley
Tinkersley Cottage,
Tinkersley, Rowsley,
Matlock,
Derbyshire DE4 2NJ

Tel	+44 (0)7802 494814
Email	sarahcopley16@hotmail.co.uk
Web	www.tinkersleycottage.co.uk

Entry 102   Map 8

Derbyshire

Old Shoulder of Mutton

The lively village of Winster is mega-pretty; the Old Shoulder of Mutton, once a pub, sits in its middle. Steven and Julie are welcoming and their home is as cosy as can be. Find a warm contemporary and traditional mix, framed clay pipes (found during renovations), a charming drawing room, luxurious bedrooms and snazzy en suite bathrooms. Breakfast is by the wood-burner: feast on eggs Benedict, homemade jam, local bacon and the famous Derbyshire oatcakes. There's a lovely and unexpected garden at the back; Bakewell, with its legendary Monday market and Chatsworth House, is a short drive, and the walking is dreamy.

Over 12s welcome. Minimum two nights.

Rooms	3: 2 doubles, 1 twin/double.
Price	£95.
Meals	Pubs in village.
Closed	Rarely.

Steven White
Old Shoulder of Mutton,
West Bank, Winster,
Matlock,
Derbyshire DE4 2DQ
Tel   +44 (0)1629 650005
Email   steven@theoldshoulderofmutton.co.uk
Web   www.oldshoulderofmutton.co.uk

🐕 🔊 🚂 ✕

Entry 103   Map 8

Derbyshire

Manor Farm

Between two small dales, close to great houses (Chatsworth, Hardwick Hall, Haddon Hall), lies this cluster of ancient farms and church; welcome to the 16th century! Simon and Gilly, warm, delightful and fascinated by the history, have restored the east wing to create big, beamy rooms in the old hayloft and a pretty garden room on the ground floor; a cosy and quaint bedroom overlooks the church. Wake to a scrumptious breakfast in the cavernous Elizabethan kitchen. There's a 'book exchange' in the old milking parlour and a lovely garden with sweeping views across the valley and distant hills.

Children over six welcome.

Rooms	4: 1 double, 2 twins/doubles, 1 family room for 2-4.
Price	£80-£90. Family room £80-£140. Singles £55-£70.
Meals	Pubs within 10-minute drive.
Closed	Rarely.

Simon & Gilly Groom
Manor Farm,
Dethick, Matlock,
Derbyshire DE4 5GG
Tel   +44 (0)1629 534302
Mobile +44 (0)7944 660814
Email   gilly.groom@w3z.co.uk
Web   www.manorfarmdethick.co.uk

♿ 📖 🔊 🚜 🚂 ✕

Entry 104   Map 8

Derbyshire

Mount Tabor House

On a steep hillside between the Peaks and the Dales, a chapel in a pretty village with a peaceful aura and great views. Enter a hall where light streams through stained-glass windows – this is a relaxed, easy place to stay with a distinctive and original interior, a log-burner to keep you toasty and a sweet dog called Molly. Fay is charming and generous and breakfast, in a dining room with open stone walls, is delicious: mainly from the village shops and as organic as possible; you can eat on the balcony in summer. Walk to the pub for dinner, come home to a fabulous wet room and a big inviting bed.

Usually minimum two nights at weekends.

Rooms	1 twin/double.
Price	£85. Singles £60.
Meals	Occasional dinner £25. Pub 100 yds.
Closed	Rarely.

Fay Whitehead
Mount Tabor House,
Bowns Hill, Crich,
Matlock,
Derbyshire DE4 5DG

Tel	+44 (0)1773 857008
Mobile	+44 (0)7813 007478
Email	mountabor@msn.com

Entry 105   Map 8

Derbyshire

Park View Farm

An extravagant refuge after a long journey, run by hospitable hosts. Daringly decadent, every inch of this Victorian farmhouse brims with flowers, sparkling trinkets, polished brass, plump cushions and swathes of chintz. Bedrooms with beautiful views dance in swirls of colour, frills, gleaming wood, lustrous glass, buttons and bows; fresh eggs, fresh fruits, homemade breads and their own rare-breed sausages accompany the grand performance. Have afternoon tea on the vine-covered terrace, roam the 370 organic acres. Kedleston Hall Park provides a stunning backdrop.

Rooms	3: 2 four-posters; 1 four-poster with separate bath.
Price	£90. Singles £45.
Meals	Pub/restaurant 1 mile.
Closed	Christmas.

Linda Adams
Park View Farm,
Weston Underwood, Ashbourne,
Derbyshire DE6 4PA

Tel	+44 (0)1335 360352
Mobile	+44 (0)7771 573057
Email	enquiries@parkviewfarm.co.uk
Web	www.parkviewfarm.co.uk

Entry 106   Map 8

Derbyshire

Alstonefield Manor

Country manor house definitely, but delightfully understated and cleverly designed to look natural. This family home, sitting in walled gardens, is high in the hills above Dovedale. Local girl Jo spoils you with homemade scones and tea when you arrive, served on the lawns or by the fire in the elegant drawing room. Beautiful bedrooms have antiques, flowers, lovely fabrics, painted floors and garden views; wood panelled bathrooms have showers or a roll top tub. Wake to birdsong – and a candlelit breakfast with local bacon and Staffordshire oatcakes. After a great walk, stroll across the village green for supper at The George. A joy.

Minimum two nights. Children over 12 welcome.

Rooms	3: 1 double; 2 doubles each with separate bathroom. Extra suite available
Price	£130-£150. Singles from £95.
Meals	Pub 100 yds.
Closed	Christmas & occasionally.

Robert & Jo Wood
Alstonefield Manor,
Alstonefield,
Ashbourne,
Derbyshire DE6 2FX
Tel   +44 (0)1335 310393
Email   stay@alstonefieldmanor.com
Web   www.alstonefieldmanor.com

Entry 107   Map 8

Devon

Annapurna

Rural bliss: the garden of this pretty, cream-painted longhouse surrounded by fields of cows looks down the folded valley to the steeple of Modbury Church. Carol and Peter spoil you with blueberry pancakes, organic home-baked bread and eggs from their happy hens for breakfast. Charming bedrooms (one is smaller) with a fresh country feel have garden flowers, sparkling bathrooms and wonderfully comfortable beds. The views over the church and valley stretch for miles, fabulous walking starts from the door and you are close to the watery delights of Salcombe and Dartmouth. Guests love this place: "Carol and Peter are perfect hosts!"

Rooms	2: 1 twin/double; 1 single (double bed) with separate bath.
Price	£70-£80. Singles £35-£40.
Meals	Pubs/restaurants 1 mile.
Closed	Rarely.

Carol Farrand & Peter Foster
Annapurna,
Mary Cross, Modbury,
Devon PL21 0SA
Tel   +44 (0)1548 831299
Mobile   +44 (0)7977 200324
Email   carolfarrand@tiscali.co.uk
Web   www.annapurna-devon.co.uk

Entry 108   Map 2

Devon

Keynedon Mill

Welcome to an ancient stone mill, and beautiful rooms in the old miller's house. There's a big friendly kitchen with old stone floors and a cheerful red Aga, a beamed dining room with a long polished table, a guest sitting room with a wood-burner, and a pretty garden with a stream running through – picnic, read, enjoy a glass of wine in peaceful corners. Elegant bedrooms have superb beds, antique linen curtains, fresh flowers, morning tea trays and garden views. A delicious breakfast of home-baked bread and local produce will set you up for the day: walk the coastal path, discover secluded coves.

Minimum two nights at weekends. Children over eight welcome.

Rooms	4: 1 double, 1 family room for 3; 2 twins/doubles, each with separate bath/shower.
Price	£85–£100. Singles £50–£65.
Meals	Dinner, 2 or 3 courses from £15. Picnics and lunches by arrangement. Pub 0.5 miles.
Closed	Rarely.

Stuart & Jennifer Jebb
Keynedon Mill,
Sherford, Kingsbridge,
Devon TQ7 2AS
Tel   +44 (0)1548 531485
Mobile   +44 (0)7775 501409
Email   bookings@keynedonmill.co.uk
Web   www.keynedonmill.co.uk

Entry 109   Map 2

Devon

Stokenham House

Lovely Stokenham House gazes at the sea and the bird-rich Slapton Ley. Iona and Paul – an energetic, thoughtful and artistic couple – have created a super South Hams base: huge chill-out cushions on the lawn, summerhouse in the pretty banked garden, BBQ by the pool. It's grand yet laid-back, with a fine drawing room, big conservatory and a family-friendly feel. Learn to cook or grow veg, invite friends for dinner, host your own party: Iona is a superb cook. The funky large annexe suite is very private; generous bedrooms in the house are decked in vintage fabrics and papers, and have single rooms off.

Dogs welcome in downstairs room. Cots & highchairs available.

Rooms	4: 1 suite, 1 family room for 4; 1 twin/double, 1 single sharing separate bath.
Price	£140. Family room £140–£210. Singles £45.
Meals	Dinner from £30. Pubs/restaurants 2-minute walk.
Closed	Rarely.

Iona & Paul Jepson
Stokenham House,
Stokenham, Kingsbridge,
Devon TQ7 2ST
Tel   +44 (0)1548 581257
Mobile   +44 (0)7720 443132
Email   ionajepson@googlemail.com
Web   www.stokenhamhouse.co.uk

Entry 110   Map 2

Devon

Strete Barton House

Contemporary, friendly, exotic and exquisite: French sleigh beds and Asian art, white basins and black chandeliers, and a garden with sofas for the views. So much to love – and best of all, the coastal path outside the door. Your caring hosts live the dream, running immaculate B&B by the sea, in an old manor house at the top of the village. Breakfasts are exuberantly local (village eggs, sausages from Dartmouth, honey from the bay), there's a wood-burner in the sitting room, warm toasty floors and Kevin and Stuart know exactly which beach, walk or pub is the one for you. Heavenly.

Minimum two nights in summer.

Rooms	6: 3 doubles, 1 twin/double; 1 twin/double with separate shower. Cottage: 1 suite & sitting room.
Price	£105–£140. Suite £150–£160.
Meals	Pub/restaurant within 50 yds.
Closed	Rarely.

Stuart Litster & Kevin Hooper
Strete Barton House,
Totnes Road, Strete,
Dartmouth,
Devon TQ6 0RU
Tel   +44 (0)1803 770364
Email   info@stretebarton.co.uk
Web   www.stretebarton.co.uk

Entry 111   Map 2

Devon

Campbells

Above the hurly-burly of Dartmouth is a reassuringly traditional B&B. Captain Campbell is charming, looks after you beautifully and is dedicated to your getting the most out of your stay. The entrance at the rear doesn't prepare you for the lovely estuary scene that spreads out on the southerly, terraced side. Inside: thick carpets, good family furniture, silverware in glass-fronted cabinets and two bedrooms with watery views. Breakfast is bolstering – full English, with good Devon ingredients. You are just across the way from the Naval College, and five minutes' walk from shops, boats, restaurants and cafés.

Rooms	2 doubles.
Price	£80–£100.
Meals	Pubs/restaurants 0.5 miles.
Closed	October–March.

Colin Campbell
Campbells,
5 Mount Boone,
Dartmouth,
Devon TQ6 9PB
Tel   +44 (0)1803 833438

Entry 112   Map 2

Devon

Nonsuch House

The photo says it all! You are in your own crow's nest, perched above the flotillas of yachts zipping in and out of the estuary mouth: stunning. Kit and Penny are great fun and look after you well; ex-hotelier Kit smokes his own fish fresh from the quay and produces brilliant dinners. Further pleasures lie across the water... and a five-minute walk brings you to the ferry that transports you, and your car, to the other side. Breakfasts in the conservatory are a delight, bedrooms are big and comfortable, and fresh bathrooms sparkle.

Minimum two nights at weekends. Over tens welcome.

Rooms	4: 1 doubles, 3 twins/doubles.
Price	£115–£170. Singles £90–£145.
Meals	Dinner, 3 courses, £37.50. (Not Tues/Wed/Sat.) Pub/restaurant 5-minute walk & short boat trip.
Closed	Rarely.

Kit & Penny Noble
Nonsuch House,
Church Hill, Kingswear,
Dartmouth,
Devon TQ6 0BX

Tel	+44 (0)1803 752829
Email	enquiries@nonsuch-house.co.uk
Web	www.nonsuch-house.co.uk

Entry 113   Map 2

Devon

Brightwater House

Hearts will soar: you're right up in the crow's nest here and feeling smugly private, with breathtaking views over the yacht-spotted river to Dartmouth and the Naval College. Painter Susie's 1930s house is splashed with sunlight from three sides in the tiled conservatory with Lloyd Loom chairs, fresh flowers, shelves of books; you breakfast heartily here while boat-watching. The bedroom has its own entrance from the garden terrace (down steep steps), and is small and pretty with white painted furniture, pale silk curtains and Susie's paintings; the bathroom is modern, new and fresh with cream stone tiles. Beguiling.

Rooms	1 twin.
Price	£105–£125. Singles £95–£115.
Meals	Pubs/restaurants 5-minute walk.
Closed	Rarely.

Susie Bennett
Brightwater House,
Higher Contour Road, Kingswear,
Dartmouth,
Devon TQ6 0DE

Tel	+44 (0)1803 752898
Email	sben2121@yahoo.co.uk
Web	www.brightwaterhouse.co.uk

Entry 114   Map 2

Devon

Kaywana Hall

With glossy modern lines and sparkling glass in its own wooded valley, this is a 'Grand Designs' project in the making. All is smart and contemporary from the great oil paintings and slate and wooden floors to the ultra-crisp bed linen and immaculate bathrooms. The bedrooms are separate from the main house and up steps; one has views over the pool, and all have private terraces. The feel is spacious and uncluttered but warm and cosy, too. Friendly Tony gives you delicious locally sourced choices at breakfast, you can hop on the ferry for Dartmouth and close by are regattas, gardens to visit, beaches and steam train and river trips.

No children.

Rooms	3: 2 doubles, 1 twin/double.
Price	£140-£165. Singles £120-£155.
Meals	Pub/restaurant 0.5 miles.
Closed	Rarely.

Anthony Pithers & Gordon Craig
Kaywana Hall,
Higher Contour Road,
Kingswear,
Dartmouth,
Devon TQ6 0AY

Tel	+44 (0)1803 752200
Email	res@kaywanahall.co.uk
Web	www.kaywanahall.co.uk

Entry 115   Map 2

Devon

Kerswell Farmhouse

Close to Totnes yet out in the wilds, this house and barn sit on a ridge with glorious views to Dartmoor. Twelve years ago the Devon longhouse was in poor repair: you'd never know now! All has been transformed by oak – seasoned and new – while the front sports a gorgeous conservatory. Graham sells British art (on fabulous display), Nichola is an interior designer, together they run truly welcoming B&B. Bedrooms are super-comfortable with electronic slatted blinds, bathrooms are state of the art, and the suite comes with its own slice of garden. Books and DVDs are on tap, food and wines are a serious treat.

Over 12s welcome.

Rooms	5: 2 doubles; 1 single with separate bath. Barn: 1 twin/double, 1 suite.
Price	£100-£110. Suite £130. Singles £60-£98.
Meals	Supper £20. Dinner £30. Restaurants 2 miles.
Closed	1 December-3 January.

Graham & Nichola Hawkins
Kerswell Farmhouse,
Kerswell, Cornworthy,
Totnes,
Devon TQ9 7HH

Tel	+44 (0)1803 732013
Mobile	+44 (0)7503 335507
Email	gjnhawkins@rocketmail.com
Web	www.kerswellfarmhouse.co.uk

Entry 116   Map 2

Devon

Pippin the Gypsy Caravan

Pippin was hand-painted by specialist wagon restorer Nick Dow, whose clients include Ronnie Wood. Nestled in Jane and Will's Devon apple orchard, your miniature home on wheels is adorable but snug – tall guests beware! The bowtop is traditionally furnished and fabrics are Cath Kidson-pretty, so step back in time as you cook dinner slowly on a tripod over the fire, and bathe in a wood-fired shower in a rustic wet room. Jane's cedar wood hot tub is in the far corner – the perfect spot for a sociable soak with some local cider beneath the starry sky. Jane's welcome is warm, the setting is idyllic, Boho Totnes is close.

Minimum three nights. Book through Sawday's Canopy & Stars online or by phone.

Rooms	Gypsy caravan for 2 with wet room & wc 50 yards away.
Price	£85.
Meals	BYO breakfast. Welcome hamper provided. Pubs within 3 miles.
Closed	October-March.

Sawday's Canopy & Stars
Pippin the Gypsy Caravan,
Cleave Farm,
Butterwells,
Totnes,
Devon TQ9 7JS

Tel	+44 (0)1275 395447
Email	enquiries@canopyandstars.co.uk
Web	www.canopyandstars.co.uk/pippin

🐾 📖 🚜 ✗

Entry 117   Map 2

Devon

Riverside House

The loveliest 18th-century house with the tidal river estuary bobbing past with boats and birds; dip your toes in the water while sitting in the garden. Felicity, an artist, and Roger, a passionate sailor, give you pretty bedrooms with paintings, poetry, little balconies, wide French windows and binoculars; spot swans at high tide, herons (perhaps a kingfisher) when the river goes down. Stroll to the pub for quayside barbecues and jazz in summer; catch the ferry from Dittisham to Agatha Christie's house; discover delightful Dartmouth. Kayaks and inflatables are welcome by arrangement.

Minimum two nights at weekends.

Rooms	2: 1 double; 1 double with separate shower.
Price	£80-£95. Singles from £65.
Meals	Pubs 100 yds.
Closed	Rarely.

Felicity & Roger Jobson
Riverside House,
Tuckenhay,
Totnes,
Devon TQ9 7EQ

Tel	+44 (0)1803 732837
Mobile	+44 (0)7710 510007
Email	felicity.riverside@hotmail.co.uk
Web	www.riverside-house.co.uk

🧒 📶 ✗

Entry 118   Map 2

Devon

Avenue Cottage

The tree-lined approach is steep and spectacular; the cottage sits in 11 wondrous acres of rhododendron, magnolia and wild flowers with a lily-strewn pond, grassy paths and lovely views over the river. Find a quiet spot in which to read or simply sit and absorb the tranquillity. Richard is a gifted gardener, and the archetypal gardener's modesty and calm have penetrated the house itself – it is uncluttered, comfortable and warmed by a log fire. The old-fashioned twin room has a big, faded bathroom with a faux-marble basin and a balcony with sweeping valley views; the pretty village and pub are a short walk away.

Rooms	2: 1 twin/double; 1 double sharing shower with owner.
Price	£60–£80. Singles £40–£50.
Meals	Pub 0.25 miles.
Closed	Rarely.

Richard Pitts
Avenue Cottage,
Ashprington, Totnes,
Devon TQ9 7UT

Tel	+44 (0)1803 732769
Mobile	+44 (0)7719 147475
Email	richard.pitts@btinternet.com
Web	www.avenuecottage.com

Entry 119   Map 2

Devon

Stoke Gabriel Lodgings

Deep in dreamy Devon countryside – but up, up high, free, above the river Dart – a deliciously simple, shiny new house where balconies gulp in long light views and large rooms are shot with rich raspberry, deep turquoise and purple hues. David and Helen's enthusiasm is infectious, both for their home (white walls, oak floors, silk and swish fittings) and village (millpond, jetty, pubs, café and ancient yew). So let them spoil you: cream tea on arrival, smoked salmon for breakfast, an open fire in the family sitting room, a crossword in the conservatory. With these hosts, with this view – you won't want to go home.

Rooms	3: 2 doubles, 1 twin/double.
Price	£90–£100. Singles £60–£65
Meals	Pubs/restaurants within walking distance.
Closed	Rarely.

Helen & David Littlefair
Stoke Gabriel Lodgings,
Badger's Retreat, 2 Orchard Close,
Stoke Gabriel, Totnes,
Devon TQ9 6SX

Tel	+44 (0)1803 782003
Mobile	+44 (0)7785 710225
Email	info@stokegabriellodgings.com

Entry 120   Map 2

Devon

Manor Farm

Sarah is a happy gardener, keeping bees and hens too so you can have honey and eggs for breakfast, served in a super red dining room. Michael produces vegetables that will find their way into your (excellent) dinner, and raspberries for your muesli. The farmhouse, facing a communal courtyard, twists and turns around unexpected corners thanks to ancient origins, and its good traditional bedrooms in bright farmhouse colours are reached via two separate stairs – nicely private. Sarah and Michael's labradors are charming and the village is pure Devon: surrounded by apple orchards and with two good pubs for eating out.

Rooms	2: 1 double; 1 twin with separate bath/shower.
Price	£70-£75. Singles £55-£65.
Meals	Dinner £20-£25. Packed lunch £7.50. Pubs 500 yds.
Closed	Rarely.

Sarah Clapp
Manor Farm,
Broadhempston,
Totnes,
Devon TQ9 6BD
Tel   +44 (0)1803 813260
Email mandsclapp@btinternet.com

Entry 121   Map 2

Devon

Kilbury Manor

You can stroll down to the Dart from the garden and onto their little island, when the river's not in spate! Back at the Manor – a listed longhouse from the 1700s – are four super-comfortable bedrooms, the most private in the stone barn. Your genuinely welcoming hosts (with dogs Dillon and Buster) moved to Devon to renovate a big handsome house and open it to guests. Julia does everything beautifully so there's organic smoked salmon and delicious French toast for breakfast, baskets of toiletries by the bath, the best linen on the best beds and a drying room for wet gear – handy if you've come to walk the Moor. Spot-on B&B.

Rooms	4: 1 double; 1 double with separate bath. Barn: 2 doubles.
Price	£80-£90. Singles from £65.
Meals	Pubs/restaurants 1.5-4 miles.
Closed	Rarely.

Julia & Martin Blundell
Kilbury Manor,
Colston Road,
Buckfastleigh,
Devon TQ11 0LN
Tel   +44 (0)1364 644079
Email info@kilburymanor.co.uk
Web   www.kilburymanor.co.uk

Entry 122   Map 2

Devon

Agaric Rooms at Tudor House

A merchant's townhouse now happily given over to rooms for the Agaric Restaurant. Sophie and Nick are young, fun and very clever: in these mostly large, individually styled rooms, fabrics are plush, colours rich and bathrooms have roll tops, robes and smart towels; the ground floor double has a striking wet room. A breakfast room is cool with leather and palms; full English or anything else you want is served here. Don't come without booking into the restaurant for fabulous modern British cooking – then stagger two steps down the street to your well-earned bed. Ashburton bustles with good food shops, antiques and books.

Devon

Penpark

Clough Williams-Ellis of Portmeirion fame did more than design an elegant house; he made sure it communed with nature. High on a hill overlooking the valley, light pours in to this lovely house from every window, and the views stretch across rolling farmland to Dartmoor and Hay Tor. The big double has a comfy sofa and its own balcony; the spacious private suite has arched French windows to gardens and pretty woodland beyond, and an extra room for young children. All is traditional and comforting: antiques, heirlooms, African carvings, silk and fresh flowers, richly coloured rugs. Your charming, generous hosts look after you well.

Rooms	4: 2 doubles, 1 family room, 1 single.
Price	£120. Family room £140–£170. Singles £58–£70.
Meals	Owners' restaurant next door. Packed lunch from £10 for 2.
Closed	Rarely.

Rooms	3: 1 family suite, 2 twins/doubles, all with separate bath/shower.
Price	£76–£84. Singles by arrangement.
Meals	Pubs/restaurants 3 miles.
Closed	Rarely.

	Sophie & Nick Coiley
	Agaric Rooms at Tudor House,
	36 North Street, Ashburton,
	Devon TQ13 7QD
Tel	+44 (0)1364 654478
Email	eat@agaricrestaurant.co.uk
Web	www.agaricrestaurant.co.uk

	Madeleine & Michael Gregson
	Penpark,
	Bickington, Ashburton,
	Devon TQ12 6LH
Tel	+44 (0)1626 821314
Email	maddy@penpark.co.uk
Web	www.penpark.co.uk

Entry 123   Map 2

Entry 124   Map 2

Devon

Hooks Cottage

At the end of a long bumpy track, the hideaway mine captain's house may have few original features but the woodland setting is gorgeous. Mary and Dick have a finely judged sense of humour; labradors Archie and Cobble will charm you. It is simple, rural, close to the Moors, with woodland birds and a gentle river to unwind stressed souls. Carpeted bedrooms have a faded floral charm and pretty stream views; bathrooms are plain. Enjoy local sausages and Mary's marmalade for breakfast, a lovely garden and amazing bluebells in spring; walks from the house are sublime. Great value, and dogs are welcome too!

Rooms	2: 1 double en suite (wc across landing); 1 twin with separate bath.
Price	£60–£65. Singles from £40.
Meals	Pub/restaurant 2 miles.
Closed	Rarely.

Mary & Dick Lloyd-Williams
Hooks Cottage,
Bickington, Ashburton,
Devon TQ12 6JS
Tel   +44 (0)1626 821312
Email   hookscottage@yahoo.com
Web   www.hookscottage.co.uk

Entry 125   Map 2

Devon

Highfield House

Come for complete peace in the Dartmoor National Park and be bowled over by the glorious garden. Helen is charming and her smart contemporary house gleams; light floods in through huge windows and the south-facing terrace runs the length of the house. Large bedrooms with armchairs are sumptuous, one has its own roof terrace with views of the moor; bathrooms are sparkling and modern. The birds sing, the pale oak floors are heated from underneath and the locally sourced breakfast is generous. Wonderful walks start at the end of the garden and the pretty village has a friendly pub serving good food.

Minimum stay two nights. Children over 12 welcome.

Rooms	3: 1 double, 2 twins/doubles.
Price	£80–£90. Singles £75–£85.
Meals	Pub 300 yds. Restaurants within 5 miles.
Closed	December/January.

Helen Waterworth
Highfield House,
Mapstone Hill, Lustleigh,
Newton Abbot, Devon TQ13 9SE
Tel   +44 (0)1647 277577
Email   helen@highfieldhousedevon.co.uk
Web   www.highfieldhousedevon.co.uk

Entry 126   Map 2

Devon

Bagtor House

A ten-minute walk and you're on top of the moor; the views are glorious. Enfolded by five acres of garden and pasture, the listed 15th-century house with the Georgian façade is the last remaining manor in the parish. Find ancient beauty in granite flagstones, oak-panelled walls, great fireplaces glowing with logs, country dressers brimming with china. Your hosts are charming; Sue looks after hens, geese, labradors, grows everything and makes her own muesli. The large family suite has a polished wood four-poster, colourful rugs and an adjoining twin room. Warm, homely, civilised, and now with hydro-electric power!

Minimum two nights.

Rooms	1 family suite with separate bath/shower (adjoining twin room).
Price	£80–£120. Singles by arrangement.
Meals	Restaurants/pubs 1.5 miles.
Closed	Christmas.

Sue & Nigel Cookson
Bagtor House,
Ilsington, Newton Abbot,
Devon TQ13 9RT
Tel   +44 (0)1364 661538
Email   sawreysue@hotmail.com
Web   www.bagtormanor.co.uk

Entry 127   Map 2

Devon

Corndonford Farm

An ancient Devon longhouse and an engagingly chaotic haven run by warm and friendly Ann and Will, along with their Dartmoor ponies. Steep, stone circular stairs lead to bedrooms: bright colours, a four-poster with lacy curtains, gorgeous views over the cottage garden and a bathroom with a beam to duck. A place for those who want to get into the spirit of it all – maybe help catch an escaped foal, chatter to the farm workers around the table; not for fussy types or Mr and Mrs Tickety Boo! Delicious Aga breakfasts and good for walkers too – the Two Moors Way is on the doorstep.

Under tens by arrangement.

Rooms	2: 1 four-poster; 1 twin with separate bath.
Price	£80. Singles £40.
Meals	Pub 2 miles.
Closed	Rarely.

Ann & Will Williams
Corndonford Farm,
Poundsgate,
Newton Abbot,
Devon TQ13 7PP
Tel   +44 (0)1364 631595
Email   corndonford@btinternet.com

Entry 128   Map 2

Devon

Heron Cottage

Folded into a valley in an idyllic corner of Dartmoor is a freshly renovated riverside B&B – one of two adjoining 18th-century cottages. Down by the water – complete privacy in your own Swedish style cabin – a light, airy, roomy space with cosy triple-glazing and sparkling shower room. Your hosts – outgoing, musical, hospitable and well-travelled – bring you delicious breakfasts (local eggs and sausages, homemade bread and jams) at flexible times; in summer it's served beside the tumbling river with buzzards soaring above. The Two Moors Way runs right by the door and this magical haven is loved by all who stay.

Rooms	Garden house: 1 double.
Price	£85. Singles £55.
Meals	Pub 2 miles.
Closed	Rarely.

Sue Bottomley
Heron Cottage,
Jordan, Widecombe-in-the-Moor,
Newton Abbot,
Devon TQ13 7PN

Tel   +44 (0)1364 631596
Email   sue@patrickgarvey.demon.co.uk
Web   www.heroncottagedartmoor.co.uk

Entry 129   Map 2

Devon

Cyprian's Cot

A charming 16th-century terraced cottage filled with beams and burnished wood. The old stone fireplace is huge, the grandfather clock ticks, the views are stunning and Shelagh is warm and welcoming. Guests have their own sitting room with a crackling fire; up the narrow stairs and into cosy bedrooms – a small double and a tiny twin. Tasty breakfasts, served in the dining room, include free-range eggs, sausages and bacon from the local farm and garden fruits. Discover the lovely town with its pubs, fine restaurant and interesting shops. With the Dartmoor Way and the Two Moors Way on the doorstep, the walking is wonderful too.

Rooms	2: 1 twin; 1 double with separate bath.
Price	£60–£65. Singles from £30.
Meals	Pubs/restaurants 4-minute walk.
Closed	Rarely.

Shelagh Weeden
Cyprian's Cot,
47 New Street, Chagford,
Newton Abbot,
Devon TQ13 8BB

Tel   +44 (0)1647 432256
Email   shelaghweeden@btinternet.com
Web   www.cyprianscot.co.uk

Entry 130   Map 2

Devon

Easdon Cottage

Replenish your soul in this light and beautifully proportioned cottage; if the charming big double in the house is taken, you may stay in the nearby barn. Both have tranquillity and delightful moorland views. Inside are wood-burners in the dining and drawing rooms, and an enchanting mix of good pictures, oriental rugs, books, plants and some handsome Victorian finds. You are in a classic Devon valley, Dartmoor lies beyond, and the sweet cottage garden is filled with birds. Liza and Hugh's organic veggie and vegan breakfasts are imaginative and delicious.

Children by arrangement. Reduction for three nights or more. Self-catering available in barn.

Rooms	1 twin/double.
Price	£70–£80. Singles £70.
Meals	Occasional supper £12–£25. Pub/restaurant 3 miles.
Closed	Rarely.

Liza & Hugh Dagnall
Easdon Cottage,
Long Lane,
Manaton,
Devon TQ13 9XB
Tel +44 (0)1647 221389
Email easdondown@btopenworld.com
Web www.easdoncottage.co.uk.

Entry 131 Map 2

Devon

Tor Royal Farm

A Georgian farmhouse with a regal history, and sweeping views over the rolling moor; a peace-seeker's dream. Behind the listed façade find an enclosed courtyard and bell tower, a big light-filled sitting room, plush beds (one downstairs, the rest up), soft carpets and soothing colours. Farmer's wife Justine serves a full English breakfast (almost all their own produce, from apple juice to bacon) at antique drop-leaf tables, loves meeting guests and will happily tell you of the history. Spot foxes, badgers, plovers in the garden, gallop off on a horse, stroll to the village pubs — and return to a lovely warm wood-burner.

Rooms	5: 2 doubles, 2 twins/doubles, 1 single.
Price	£80. Singles from £50.
Meals	Dinner from £30. Packed lunch available. Pubs/restaurants 1 mile.
Closed	Rarely.

Justine Colton
Tor Royal Farm,
Tor Royal Road, Princetown,
Yelverton, Devon PL20 6SL
Tel +44 (0)1822 890189
Mobile +44 (0)7892 910666
Email stay@torroyal.co.uk
Web www.torroyal.co.uk

Entry 132 Map 2

Devon

Mount Tavy Cottage

Between Dartmoor and Tavistock, this 250-year-old former gardener's bothy has been made into a warm and welcoming home by Jo and Graham. Pretty bedrooms in the house have stripped floorboards, a four-poster or half-tester bed and freestanding baths. Two simpler bedrooms, each with a big shower, are across the courtyard in the garden studios; here you can be completely independent, or trot over to the house for a delicious breakfast. Lots to enjoy outside too: a cider orchard with beehives, a walled garden, rare-breed pigs in the wood and a lake with a thatched dining spot.

Arrivals after 5pm, unless previously arranged.

Rooms	4: 1 double, 1 four-poster, both with separate bath. 2 studios: 1 twin/double & kitchenette each.
Price	£70–£80. Singles from £35.
Meals	Dinner, 3 courses, £25. Pub 2 miles.
Closed	Rarely.

G H Moule
Mount Tavy Cottage,
Tavistock,
Devon PL19 9JL
Tel   +44 (0)1822 614253
Mobile   +44 (0)7776 181576
Email   mounttavy@btinternet.com
Web   www.mounttavy.co.uk

Entry 133   Map 2

Devon

Burnville House

Granite gateposts, Georgian house, rhododendrons, beechwoods and rolling fields of sheep: that's the setting. But there's more. Beautifully proportioned rooms reveal subtle colours, elegant antiques, squishy sofas and bucolic views, stylish bathrooms are sprinkled with candles, there are sumptuous dinners and pancakes at breakfast. Your hosts left busy jobs in London to settle here, and their place breathes life – space, smiles, energy. Swim, play tennis, walk to Dartmoor from the door, take a trip to Eden or the sea. Or... just gaze at the moors and the church on the Tor and listen to the silence, and the sheep.

Rooms	3 doubles.
Price	£85–£95. Singles £60.
Meals	Dinner from £19. Pub 2 miles.
Closed	Rarely.

Victoria Cunningham
Burnville House,
Brentor, Tavistock,
Devon PL19 0NE
Tel   +44 (0)1822 820443
Mobile   +44 (0)7881 583471
Email   burnvillef@aol.com
Web   www.burnville.co.uk

Entry 134   Map 2

Devon

Devon

Brook Farmhouse

Tuck yourself up in the peace and quiet of Paul and Penny's whitewashed, thatched cottage, surrounded by glorious countryside. Inside find your own charming sitting room with a huge inglenook, good antiques, fresh flowers, and comfy sofa and chairs; breakfast here on homemade apple juice, eggs from the owners' hens and delicious local bacon and sausages. Up the ancient spiral stone stairs is your warm, beamed bedroom with smooth linen, chintzy curtains, lots of cushions. You are near Dartmoor and can reach the Devon beaches and the north Cornish coast; perfect for hearty walkers, birdwatchers, surfers and picnic-lovers.

Old Orchard Shepherd's Hut

A homely shepherd's hut on an organic community farm, not far from Exeter. The epitome of simple elegance, with hand-stitched white curtains and roses round the door, it is constructed from everything local... even the wrought-iron curtain rods were forged on site. There's a standard double bed and a wood-burner to keep you cosy, a small fire pit outside the door (and cups, and kettle), and a bench for two. Breakfast — bacon and eggs, homemade granola — arrives when you want it, and the electric shower is in the bathroom hut, a few paces away. Farm events include guided walks, talks, and chances to get your hands dirty!

Minimum two nights. Book through Sawday's Canopy & Stars online or by phone.

Rooms	1 double with separate bath.
Price	£80-£90. Singles £50.
Meals	Pub 2 miles.
Closed	Rarely.

Rooms	Shepherd's hut for 2 with separate shower & compost loo.
Price	£65.
Meals	Pubs within walking distance.
Closed	November-March.

Paul & Penny Steadman
Brook Farmhouse,
Tedburn St Mary,
Exeter,
Devon EX6 6DS
Tel   +44 (0)1647 270042
Email penny.steadman@btconnect.com
Web   www.brook-farmhouse.co.uk

Sawday's Canopy & Stars
Old Orchard Shepherd's Hut,
West Town Farm, Ide,
Exeter, Devon EX2 9TG
Tel   +44 (0)1275 395447
Email enquiries@canopyandstars.co.uk
Web   www.canopyandstars.co.uk/
oldorchard

Entry 135   Map 2

Entry 136   Map 2

Devon

Beach House

Lapping at the riverside garden is the Exe estuary, wide and serene. Birds and boats, the soft hills beyond, a gorgeous Georgian house on the river and interesting hosts who have been here for years. The garden is pretty with quirky rooster-shaped topiary and old apple trees; you may have a locally sourced breakfast in the conservatory or dining room, and there are raspberries and blackberries from the garden when in season. Relax on comfortable chairs in bedrooms with lovely estuary views; charmingly old-fashioned bathrooms are sparkling. Cycle into Exeter for culture and cathedral; an RSPB reserve is five minutes away.

Rooms	2: 1 twin, 1 double.
Price	£90. Singles £60.
Meals	Pubs/restaurants 8-minute walk.
Closed	December-March.

Trevor & Jane Coleman
Beach House,
45 The Strand,
Topsham,
Exeter,
Devon EX3 0BB
Tel   +44 (0)1392 876456
Email   janecoleman45@hotmail.com

Entry 137   Map 2

Devon

Larkbeare Grange

Expectations rise as you follow the tree-lined drive to the immaculate Georgian house... to be warmly greeted with homemade cakes. The upkeep is perfect, the feel is chic and the whole place exudes well-being. Sparkling sash windows fill big rooms with light, floors shine and the grandfather clock ticks away the hours. Expect the best: good lighting, goose down duvets, luxurious fabrics and fittings, a fabulous suite for a small family, flexible (and delicious) breakfasts and lovely views from the bedrooms at the front. Charlie, Savoy-trained, and Julia are charming and fun; and there are bikes to borrow. Exceptional B&B!

Rooms	4: 2 doubles, 1 twin/double, 1 suite.
Price	£105-£135. Suite £165-£190. Singles £85-£115.
Meals	Pub 1.5 miles.
Closed	Rarely.

Charlie & Julia Hutchings
Larkbeare Grange,
Larkbeare, Talaton,
Exeter,
Devon EX5 2RY
Tel   +44 (0)1404 822069
Email   stay@larkbeare.net
Web   www.larkbeare.net

Entry 138   Map 2

Devon

Lower Allercombe Farm

Horses in the paddock and no-frills bedrooms at this down-to-earth, very friendly B&B. Don't expect twinsets and pearls; Susie, ex-eventer, may greet you in two-tone jodhpurs instead. She and Lizzie (her terrier) live at one end of the listed longhouse, guests at the other. There's a sitting room with horsey pictures and wood-burner, and bedrooms upstairs that reflect the fair price. You'll feast on home eggs and tomatoes in the morning, and rashers from award-winning pigs. Very handy for Exeter, the south coast and Dartmoor; the airport is ten minutes away, the A30 is one mile.

Stabling available.

Rooms	3: 1 double, 1 twin; 1 double with separate bath.
Price	£60–£80. Singles £50.
Meals	Pub/restaurant 2 miles.
Closed	Rarely.

	Susie Holroyd
	Lower Allercombe Farm,
	Rockbeare, Exeter,
	Devon EX5 2HD
Tel	+44 (0)1404 822519
Mobile	+44 (0)7800 636961
Email	holroyd.s@gmail.com
Web	www.lowerallercombefarm.co.uk

Entry 139   Map 2

Devon

Rosehill Rooms and Cookery

A stunning original veranda runs along this fine listed Victorian house, and busy Budleigh is a five-minute walk. Sharon and Willi, natural, warm and friendly, run a cookery school here with exciting courses that you can book. Upbeat bedrooms have seaside names, garden views and sofas; bathrooms with slate style floors gleam. Nip downstairs for a delicious breakfast of porridge with honey and cream, muffins, croissants, a full English, and a choice of seven mueslis! The rose-filled cottage garden has sunny seats. Exeter and Sidmouth are close, the coastal path and the beach are a mere saunter.

Minimum two nights.

Rooms	4 doubles.
Price	£100–£125.
Meals	Pubs/restaurant 5-minute walk.
Closed	Rarely.

	Willi & Sharon Rehbock
	Rosehill Rooms and Cookery,
	30 West Hill,
	Budleigh Salterton,
	Devon EX9 6BU
Tel	+44 (0)1395 444031
Email	info@rosehillroomsandcookery.co.uk
Web	www.rosehillroomsandcookery.co.uk

Entry 140   Map 2

Devon

Glebe House

Set on a hillside with fabulous views over the Coly valley, this late-Georgian vicarage is now a heart-warming B&B. The views will entice you, the hosts will delight you and the house is filled with interesting things. Chuck and Emma spent many years at sea – he a Master Mariner, she a chef – and have filled these big light rooms with cushions, kilims and treasured family pieces. There's a sitting room for guests, a lovely conservatory with a vintage vine, peaceful bedrooms with blissful views and bathrooms that sparkle. All this, two sweet pygmy goats, wildlife beyond the ha-ha and the fabulous coast a hike away.

Minimum stay two nights July & August weekends & bank holidays.

Rooms	3: 1 double, 1 family room, 1 twin/double.
Price	£80. Family room £80–£110. Singles £50.
Meals	Dinner, 3 courses £25. Pubs/restaurants 2.5 miles.
Closed	Christmas & New Year.

Emma & Chuck Guest
Glebe House,
Southleigh, Colyton,
Devon EX24 6SD
Tel   +44 (0)1404 871276
Mobile   +44 (0)7867 568569
Email   emma_guest@talktalk.net
Web   www.guestsatglebe.com

Entry 141   Map 2

Devon

West Colwell Farm

Devon lanes, pheasants, bluebell walks *and* sparkling B&B. The Hayes clearly love what they do; ex-TV producers, they have converted this 18th-century farmhouse and barns into a cosy, warm and stylish place to stay. Be charmed by original beams and pine doors, heritage colours and clean lines. Bedrooms feel self-contained, two have terraces overlooking the wooded valley and the most cosy is tucked under the roof. Linen is luxurious, showers are huge and breakfasts (Frank's pancakes, lovely bacon, eggs from next door) are totally flexible. A pretty garden in front, beaches nearby, peace all around. Bliss.

Rooms	3 doubles.
Price	£85–£95. Singles £70.
Meals	Restaurants 3 miles.
Closed	December/January.

Frank & Carol Hayes
West Colwell Farm,
Offwell,
Honiton,
Devon EX14 9SL
Tel   +44 (0)1404 831130
Email   stay@westcolwell.co.uk
Web   www.westcolwell.co.uk

Entry 142   Map 2

Devon

Applebarn Cottage

A tree-lined drive leads to a long white wall, and a gate opening to an explosion of colour – the garden. Come for a deliciously restful place and the nicest, most easy-going hosts; the wisteria-covered 17th-century cottage is full of books, paintings and fresh flowers. Bedrooms – one in an extension that blends in beautifully – are large, traditional, wonderfully comfortable, and the views down the valley are sublime. Patricia trained as a chef and dinners at Applebarn are delicious and great fun. Breakfast, served in a lovely oak-floored dining room, includes a neighbour's homemade honey.

Minimum two nights.

Rooms	2 suites.
Price	£78-£83. Dinner, B&B option (dinner & aperitif) £41.50-£67 p.p.
Meals	Dinner, 3 courses & aperitif, £28.
Closed	November to mid-March.

Patricia & Robert Spencer
Applebarn Cottage,
Bewley Down, Axminster,
Devon EX13 7JX
Tel +44 (0)1460 220873
Email paspenceruk@yahoo.co.uk
Web www.applebarn.wordpress.com

Entry 143   Map 2

Devon

Sannacott

On the southern fringes of Exmoor you're in peaceful rolling hills, hidden valleys and a Designated Dark Sky area. The Trickeys breed horses from their Georgian style farmhouse; find roaring log fires, antiques, pretty fabrics, fresh flowers and a relaxed feel. Bedrooms are traditional and comfortable (one in an annexe), some with views over the garden and countryside. Generous breakfasts include homemade bread and jams and organic or local goodies. There's a pretty bird-filled garden to wander, walkers can enjoy the North Devon coastal path, birdwatchers and riders will be happy and there are well-known gardens to visit.

Rooms	3: 1 double, 1 twin/double sharing bath/shower (let to same party only). Annexe: 1 twin & kitchenette.
Price	£80. Singles £45.
Meals	Occasional dinner, 3 courses, £25. Pub 2.5 miles.
Closed	Rarely.

Clare Trickey
Sannacott,
North Molton,
Devon EX36 3JS
Tel +44 (0)1598 740203
Email mct@sannacott.co.uk
Web www.sannacott-exmoor.co.uk

Entry 144   Map 2

Devon

Hillbrow House

This lovely 'house on the hill' has a deep veranda and glorious views over the Taw valley, Exmoor (and, on a clear day, to distant Dartmoor). The light, uncluttered rooms are neat as a pin with coordinated colours, thick fabrics, antiques and your own upstairs studio sitting room; bedrooms have feather pillows, proper blankets and luxurious bathrooms. Golfers and walkers will be in paradise, Highbullen Golf Club is a short walk, surfers can reach Croyde easily and many gentler beaches lie in the other direction. RHS Rosemoor is also within striking distance; stoke up on Clarissa's delicious homemade granola for breakfast.

Rooms	2: 1 double;
	1 double with separate bath.
Price	£90–£100. Singles £50.
Meals	Dinner, 3 courses, £30.
	Pubs/restaurants within walking distance.
Closed	Christmas.

Clarissa Roe
Hillbrow House,
Chittlehamholt, Umberleigh,
Devon EX37 9NS
Tel   +44 (0)1769 540214
Mobile +44 (0)7774 784601
Email   clarissaroe@btinternet.com
Web   www.hillbrowhouse.com

Entry 145   Map 2

Devon

Leworthy Barton

Biscuits, scones, sweet vases of hedgerow flowers. Breakfasts are left for you to cook and come courtesy of Rupert's Tamworth pigs and happy hens; bread and jams are homemade, wellies and waxed jackets are on tap. Rupert is a busy farmer and designer who chooses to give guests what he would most like himself. So... you have the whole of the stables, tranquil, beautifully restored and with field and sky views. Downstairs is open-plan, with kitchen and log-burner; up are sloping ceilings, wooden floors, big bed, soft towels. It's cosy yet spacious, stylish yet homely, and the Atlantic coast is the shortest drive.

Rooms	Barn: 1 double, sitting room
	& kitchen.
Price	£80–£100. Singles £60.
Meals	Pub 3 miles.
Closed	Rarely.

Rupert Ashmore
Leworthy Barton,
Woolsery,
Bideford,
Devon EX39 5PY
Tel   +44 (0)1237 431140

Entry 146   Map 2

Devon

Beara Farmhouse

The moment you arrive at the whitewashed farmhouse you feel the affection your hosts have for their home and gardens. Richard is a lover of wood and a fine craftsman – every room echoes his talent; he also created the pond that's home to mallards and geese. Ann has laid brick paths, stencilled, stitched and painted, all with an eye for colour; bedrooms and guest sitting room are delectable and snug. Open farmland all around, sheep, pigs and hens in the yard, the Tarka Trail on your doorstep and hosts happy to give you 6.30am breakfast should you plan a day on Lundy Island. Guests love this place.

Minimum two nights at weekends, bank holidays and June-Sept.

Rooms	2: 1 double, 1 twin.
Price	£75. Singles by arrangement.
Meals	Pub 1.5 miles.
Closed	20 December–5 January.

Ann & Richard Dorsett
Beara Farmhouse,
Buckland Brewer,
Bideford,
Devon EX39 5EH
Tel   +44 (0)1237 451666
Web   www.bearafarmhouse.co.uk

Entry 147   Map 2

Devon

South Yeo

In Devon – down windy lanes with tall grassy banks and the smell of the sea – is a lovely Georgian country house with two walled gardens and barns at the back. You'll fall for this place the moment you arrive, and its owners: Jo runs an interiors business, Mike keeps the cattle and sheep that graze all around. You have an inviting bedroom overlooking the valley, a small pretty sitting room (adjoining) with TV, an elegant drawing room with a real fire... find a cream French bed, a pretty quilted cover, a claw-foot bath. Delicious breakfasts with home eggs and homemade jams are brought to a snug room that catches the morning sun.

Rooms	1 double & sitting room.
Price	£85–£105. Singles £75.
Meals	Pub 1.5 miles.
Closed	Rarely.

Joanne Wade
South Yeo,
Yeo Vale, Bideford,
Devon EX39 5ES
Tel   +44 (0)1237 451218
Mobile +44 (0)7766 201191
Email   stay@southyeo.com
Web   www.southyeo.com

Entry 148   Map 2

Devon

Hollamoor Farm

If it's a civilised retreat you're after then head to where the Taw and Torridge meet... to Tarka country, and this rambling 300-year-old farm. Roses ramble, swallows swoop and there are 500 acres to explore. One bedroom is in a barn next to the house and combines stone rusticity and country house grandeur with aplomb; the soft furnishings are exquisite. The bedroom in the house is equally plush and both have fun bathrooms. There's a huge fireplace in the dining room and a well-loved sitting room where you can meet the Wreys (past and present). A real family home where the door is always open – elegant informality at its very best.

Rooms	2: 1 twin/double with separate bath. Barn: 1 twin/double.
Price	£90. Singles £48.
Meals	Occasional dinner £25. Pubs/restaurants 3 miles.
Closed	Rarely.

Sir George & Lady Caroline Wrey
Hollamoor Farm,
Tawstock,
Barnstaple,
Devon EX31 3NY
Tel +44 (0)1271 373466
Mobile +44 (0)7766 700904
Email carolinewrey@gmail.com

Entry 149   Map 2

Devon

Holly Cottage

Our inspectors eat a lot of breakfasts, so when one gets awarded top marks, you know it's seriously good! Generous amounts of local bacon, sausages and eggs, buttery mushrooms and blueberry muffins put a spring in your step. Stephanie, friendly and easy-going, has created a simple, light, raftered annexe suite. Peace and privacy are yours: from your pine bed, drink in the views through the floor-to-ceiling window towards Bideford Bay and Hartland Point. All around, north Devon hills rise and fall; picnic by the River Barle, explore the 11th-century church next door. This is great value, and babysitting is available.

Babes in arms welcome. Small, well-behaved dogs welcome – in house only (not in bedrooms).

Rooms	1 double.
Price	£75. Singles £40.
Meals	Pubs/restaurants 2.5 miles.
Closed	Rarely.

Stephanie Lion
Holly Cottage,
Stoke Rivers, Barnstaple,
Devon EX32 7LD
Tel +44 (0)1598 710550
Mobile +44 (0)7785 798809
Email stephanie.lion@yahoo.co.uk
Web www.hollycottagebbdevon.co.uk

Entry 150   Map 2

Devon

Rosehill Barn

Up and down the rolling hills of Devon, along the long grassy track, to the oldest house in the hamlet and Rob and Rosie full of warmth and smiles. Your very private barn is surrounded by cottage garden loveliness, in a garden you may share. The old stone barn, fabulously stocked with books, is warm and cheerful: pale blue armchairs on a wooden floor, white walls, fresh flowers, a decanter of sherry, lashings of hot water and a gorgeously comfortable bed. Breakfasts, served in the lofty 16th-century Open Hall, are a feast of homemade deliciousness straight from the Aga. Walks from the door abound.

Rooms	Barn: 1 double & sitting room.
Price	£85. Singles from £60.
Meals	Pub 4 miles.
Closed	Rarely.

Robert Ingram
Rosehill Barn,
Hill, Loxhore,
Barnstaple,
Devon EX31 4SU

Tel	+44 (0)1271 850415
Email	rob@hill-loxhore.co.uk
Web	www.rosehillbarn.co.uk

Devon

Beachborough Country House

Welcome to this gracious 18th-century rectory with stone-flagged floors, lofty windows, wooden shutters and glorious rugs. Viviane is vivacious and spoils you with dinners and breakfasts from the Aga; dine in the elegant dining room before a twinkling fire. Hens cluck, horses whinny but otherwise the peace is deep. Ease any walker's pains away in a steaming roll top tub; lap up country views from big airy bedrooms. There's a games room for kids in the outbuildings and a stream winds through the garden, a delicious three acres of vegetables and roses. Huge fun.

Rooms	3: 1 twin/double (extra single available), 2 doubles.
Price	£80. Singles from £50. Dogs £5.
Meals	Dinner, 2-3 courses, from £19. Catering for house parties. Pub 3 miles.
Closed	Rarely.

Viviane Clout
Beachborough Country House,
Kentisbury, Barnstaple,
Devon EX31 4NH

Tel	+44 (0)1271 882487
Mobile	+44 (0)7732 947755
Email	viviane@beachborough.freeserve.co.uk
Web	www.beachboroughcountryhouse.co.uk

Devon

North Walk House

Sea views, brass bedsteads and big rooms at this calm retreat, perfectly positioned on a cliff-top path – super for walkers and foodies. Ian and Sarah welcome you with homemade cake in a cosy guest lounge, and give you light bedrooms with sparkling bathrooms and seductive beds. Enjoy the coastal and Exmoor walks, or genteel Lynton and Lynmouth; return to log fire and armchairs. Take your tea on a sea-view terrace, or be tempted by Sarah's four-course supper, seasonal and mostly organic. Everything here is thoughtful, from the welcome to the décor and the refreshments: arrive, unpack, unwind…

Rooms	5: 4 doubles, 1 twin.
Price	£80-£150. Singles £50-£100.
Meals	Dinner, 4 courses, from £27. Pub/restaurant 0.25 miles.
Closed	Rarely.

Ian & Sarah Downing
North Walk House,
North Walk,
Lynton,
Devon EX35 6HJ
Tel +44 (0)1598 753372
Email walk@northwalkhouse.co.uk
Web www.northwalkhouse.co.uk

Entry 153   Map 2

Devon

Victoria House

Beachcombers, surfers and walkers will be in their element here. You stay in the beach-hut annexe with a big romantic deck facing the sea; complete with funky daybed and a magnificent view. The owners live next door in the Edwardian seaside villa: Heather is lively and fun, she and David are ex-RAF and go out of their way to give you the best tour de force breakfasts – fruits, yogurts, waffles, eggs Benedict or the full Monty. Sip a sundowner on the deck or stir yourself to go further; you are on the coastal road to Woolacombe (of surfing and kite surfing fame) and the beach is a ten-minute walk. A top spot for couples.

Check-in between 4pm & 9pm, unless arranged. Special diets catered for.

Rooms	Annexe: 1 double.
Price	£100-£115. Singles £70-£80.
Meals	Pubs/restaurants 200 yds.
Closed	Rarely.

Heather & David Burke
Victoria House,
Chapel Hill, Mortehoe,
Woolacombe,
Devon EX34 7DZ
Tel +44 (0)1271 871302
Email heatherburke59@fsmail.net
Web www.victoriahousebandb.co.uk

Entry 154   Map 2

Crafty Camping

Seven sweet spaces dotted throughout an enchanting patch of woodland: a forest village around a big pond. Most have their own piping hot 'tree showers'; the three bell tents share two. Pick up homemade pizza dough from the honesty shop, fire up the wood oven, sample local ciders while you wait. Everything is joined by wooden walkways lit with LEDs that glow, then dim as you pass: you'll not lose your way! Follow paths to the sauna yurt, or the big central kitchen where Dorset Cereals and Clipper teas are free (just bring milk). River Cottage Canteen at Axminster is nearby; Regency Lyme Regis is close.

Minimum two nights. Book through Sawday's Canopy & Stars online or by phone.

Crosskeys House

In previous lives a pub, a cobbler's shop and a smithy, this listed stone house, right on the village crossroads, is well settled into its B&B role. Robin and Liz offer you a fabulous breakfast, in the conservatory or dining room, and will happily advise on the glories of west Dorset (walks, pubs, stately homes): nothing is too much trouble. Their sitting room is softly traditional – plump sofas, family portraits and antiques, flowers, glossy magazines – while lovely cosy bedrooms have king-size beds and interesting books. The house is near the road but there's a pretty flower-filled garden and water fresh from the well.

Rooms	2 yurts for 2, 1 tipi for 2, 1 hut for 2, each with separate shower & wc; 3 bell tents for 2, sharing 2 showers & wcs.
Price	Bell tents £70-£90. Yurts, tipi & shepherd's hut £100-£125.
Meals	BYO breakfast (cereal, tea & coffee provided).
Closed	Mid-November to March.

Rooms	3: 1 double, 2 twins/doubles.
Price	£85-£90. Singles from £70.
Meals	Pub 200 yds.
Closed	Rarely.

Sawday's Canopy & Stars
Crafty Camping,
Woodland Workshop,
Yonder Hill, Holditch,
Dorset TA20 4NL
Tel   +44 (0)1275 395447
Email enquiries@canopyandstars.co.uk
Web   www.canopyandstars.co.uk/
         craftycamping

Robin & Liz Adeney
Crosskeys House,
High Street, Broadwindsor,
Beaminster,
Dorset DT8 3QP
Tel   +44 (0)1308 868063
Email robin.adeney@care4free.net
Web   www.crosskeyshouse.com

Entry 155   Map 2

Entry 156   Map 3

Dorset

Pear Tree Farm

Just four miles from bustling Bridport, this traditional pretty Dorset farmhouse is reached down secret narrow lanes and surrounded by deep valleys. A keen traveller and garden designer, Emma has created a vibrant home brimming with interesting art, good antique furniture, rugs, comfy old armchairs and books galore; there is an extraordinary collection of glass walking sticks. The garden is a delight and blissful views from flowery bedrooms will charm you. Wake to a breakfast of local bacon and home-laid eggs in the sunny kitchen. Close to River Cottage, Bridport Literary Festival and the coast; a walker's paradise.

Rooms	2: 1 twin/double; 1 twin sharing bath (2nd room let to same party only).
Price	£75-£80. Singles £50.
Meals	Pubs/restaurants within 4 miles.
Closed	Christmas & Easter.

Emma Poë
Pear Tree Farm,
Loscombe,
Bridport,
Dorset DT6 3TL
Tel +44 (0)1308 488223
Email poe@gotadsl.co.uk
Web www.peartreefarmbedandbreakfast.co.uk

Entry 157 Map 3

Dorset

No 27

In a peaceful side street in Bridport is a historic artisan's house with masses of charm. Find walls painted in chalky hues, flagstones toasty underfoot, painted floorboards topped with kilims, and books, paintings, antiques and flowers. Juliet invites you to use the house like a home, and breakfasts are generous, delicious and served around a large table in the kitchen extension; admire the garden from a wall of glass. Explore the pubs, seafood restaurants and market stalls of Bridport, the beaches of Lyme Regis and the wonderful Jurassic coast; come home to fresh, airy bedrooms, both with views to garden and hills.

Ask about parking.

Rooms	2: 1 double; 1 double with separate bath.
Price	£75-£120.
Meals	Supper from £15. Pubs/restaurants in town.
Closed	Rarely.

Juliet Lewis
No 27,
27 Barrack Street,
Bridport,
Dorset DT6 3LX
Tel +44 (0)1308 426378
Email julietalewis@gmail.com
Web www.no27bridport.co.uk

Entry 158 Map 3

Dorset

Wooden Cabbage House

Leafy lanes and a private drive lead you to Martyn and Susie's beautifully restored hamstone house, hidden in rolling West Dorset. Leave the hubbub behind, savour the stunning valley views, relax in this spacious stylish home amongst flowers, fine antiques and paintings. Cosy bedrooms have country-house charm. A delicious breakfast is served in the gorgeous garden room – home-grown fruits, local eggs and sausages – and French windows open to a productive potager and terraced gardens. Local walks are good and the Jurassic coast is half-an-hour away; return to comfy sofas by the log fire. Fabulous hosts – nothing is too much trouble.

Garage parking.

Rooms	3: 2 doubles, 1 twin.
Price	£100–£110. Singles from £80.
Meals	Dinner, 3 courses with wine, £40. Supper, 2 courses with wine, £30. Pubs/restaurants 3 miles.
Closed	Rarely.

	Martyn & Susie Lee
	Wooden Cabbage House,
	East Chelborough,
	Dorchester,
	Dorset DT2 0QA
Tel	+44 (0)1935 83362
Mobile	+44 (0)7805 378583
Email	relax@woodencabbage.co.uk
Web	www.woodencabbage.co.uk

Entry 159   Map 3

Dorset

Old Forge

Snug in a stream-tickled hamlet, deep in Hardy country, this B&B is as pretty as a painting – and just as peaceful. That is, until owner Judy starts to giggle: she is full of smiles and laughter. This is a happy place, a real country home, a no-rules B&B. The one guest double, sharing the former forge with a self-catering pad for two, is neat, warm and cosy with yellow hues, thick carpets and trinkets from travels. The 17th-century farmhouse opposite is where you breakfast: Prue Leith-trained Judy serves a neighbour's eggs, a friend's sausages, in an eclectically furnished room with bucolic views to garden, meadows and hills.

Rooms	Old Forge: 1 double.
Price	£80–£90. Extra person £15.
Meals	Restaurant 1.5 miles.
Closed	Rarely.

	Judy Thompson
	Old Forge,
	Lower Wraxall Farmhouse,
	Lower Wraxall,
	Dorchester,
	Dorset DT2 0HL
Tel	+44 (0)1935 83218
Email	judyjthompson@hotmail.co.uk
Web	www.lowerwraxall.co.uk

Entry 160   Map 3

Dorset

Holyleas House

In a lovely village, a fabulous house, comfortable, peaceful and easy – and Tia and her two friendly dogs give the warmest welcome. You breakfast by a log fire in an elegant dining room in winter, on free-range eggs, bacon and sausages from the farmers' market, homemade jams and marmalade. Sleep in light, softly coloured bedrooms with lovely views across well-tended gardens; bathrooms are spotless. Walkers and explorers will be happy to roam the Dorset Downs, then return to a roaring fire and a cosy book in the drawing room.

Minimum two nights in high season & at weekends. Babysitting possible.

Rooms	3: 1 double, 1 family room; 1 single with separate bath.
Price	£80-£90. Singles £40.
Meals	Pub a short walk.
Closed	Christmas & New Year.

Tia Bunkall
Holyleas House,
Buckland Newton,
Dorchester,
Dorset DT2 7DP

Tel	+44 (0)1300 345214
Mobile	+44 (0)7968 341887
Email	tiabunkall@holyleas.fsnet.co.uk
Web	www.holyleashouse.co.uk

Entry 161   Map 3

Dorset

Fullers Earth

Such an English feel: the village with pub, post office and stores, the rose-filled walled garden with fruit trees beyond, the tranquil church view. This listed house – its late-Georgian frontage added in 1820 – is a treat: flowers and white linen, a lovely sitting room where you settle with tea and cake by the fire, roomy bedrooms with comfortable beds, books and views. At breakfast enjoy perfect compotes and jams from the garden, homemade muesli and local produce. Friendly Ian and Wendy will plan great walks with you in this AONB, the Jurassic coast is 20 minutes away and you can walk to the pub through the garden.

Rooms	3: 1 double; 1 double, 1 single sharing bath/shower (let to same party only).
Price	£80-£90. Singles from £40.
Meals	Pub in village.
Closed	Christmas.

Wendy Gregory
Fullers Earth,
Cattistock,
Dorchester,
Dorset DT2 0JL

Tel	+44 (0)1300 320190
Mobile	+44 (0)7792 654543
Email	stay@fullersearth.co.uk
Web	www.fullersearth.co.uk

Entry 162   Map 3

Dorset

Manor Farm

You are high up on the chalk hills that fall to the Jurassic Coast. Tessa's family have lived in the flint and stone house since 1860 and it is crammed with history: solid antiques, books galore, pictures, maps and photographs. From all the windows views soar to sheep-dotted hills. You can settle by the wood-burner in the snug, and your Aga-cooked breakfast or supper is served in the handsome dining room, or the garden in summer; cooking is one of Tessa's passions. Bedrooms are without frills but clean and comfortable; the bathroom is large and sparkling. Outdoor heaven is yours; find a pet pig called Pork!

Rooms	2: 1 double, 1 twin sharing bath (let to same party only).
Price	£70–£100.
Meals	Dinner, 2-3 courses, from £15. Pub/restaurant 4 miles.
Closed	Rarely.

Tessa Russell
Manor Farm,
Compton Valence, Dorchester,
Dorset DT2 9ES
Tel   +44 (0)1308 482227
Mobile +44 (0)7818 037184 (signal unreliable)
Email   tessa.nrussell@btinternet.com
Web   www.manor-farm.uk.com

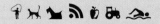

Entry 163   Map 3

Dorset

Whitfield Farm Cottage

Jackie and David are warm, delightful hosts, and their pretty thatched 18th-century cottage is full of charm. A delicious breakfast is served in the large beamed kitchen, or in the walled courtyard on sunny days, and the garden brims with roses, lavender and sweet peas. Your bedroom (with its own shower) is immaculate in blue and white and opens onto the garden; the sitting room is cosy and comfy with inglenook fireplace and window seats. Dorchester is close, you're eight miles from the stunning Jurassic coast, and you can enjoy a day's fishing on the river Frome (tickets are sometimes available).

Minimum two nights at weekends.

Rooms	1 twin/double. Extra room available.
Price	£80–£85. Singles £50.
Meals	Pubs/restaurants 1.25 miles.
Closed	Christmas & Easter.

Jackie & David Charles
Whitfield Farm Cottage,
Poundbury Road,
Dorchester,
Dorset DT2 9SL
Tel   +44 (0)1305 260233
Email dcharles@gotadsl.co.uk
Web   www.whitfieldfarmcottage.co.uk

Entry 164   Map 3

Dorset

The White Cottage

Strolling distance from lovely old Athelhampton House and its gardens is this thatched cottage where Lindsay and Mark are slowly becoming self-sufficient. You will be well fed: home-grown vegetables, bacon from the pigs, eggs from Clarissa the chicken. It's a lively young-family household with gorgeous bedrooms: super linen, plump pillows; generous bathrooms have thick towels and eco-friendly lotions. The suite has its own entrance and a big comfortable sitting room. Help feed the animals and enjoy the river Piddle running through the garden – fish for brown trout but please put them back!

Rooms	3: 1 double, 1 suite for 2-4 (with sofabed); 1 twin/double with separate bath.
Price	£75-£85. Suite £100-£120. Singles from £55.
Meals	Pubs 1 mile.
Closed	Rarely.

Lindsay & Mark Piper
The White Cottage,
Athelhampton,
Dorchester,
Dorset DT2 7LG
Tel   +44 (0)1305 848622
Mobile   +44 (0)7788 166322
Email   bookings@white-cottage-bandb.co.uk
Web   www.white-cottage-bandb.co.uk

Entry 165   Map 3

Dorset

Yoah Cottage

Rosemary and Furse are ceramic sculptors; she makes delicate, sometimes humorous, pieces, he creates bold animals and birds; their thatched, cob-walled, rambling house is a jaw-dropping gallery of modern art, ceramics, fabrics. The cottage garden's colours complete the vibrant picture. Originally two cottages, you sleep on one side in a country-pretty double and a twin under the eaves, sharing (with friends or family) a bathroom and a sitting room with log fire. Breakfast (full English, homemade jams and marmalade) is next to the couple's studio. Such enthusiastic, artistic owners – and you're deep in Hardy country.

Minimum two nights.

Rooms	2: 1 double, 1 twin sharing bath (let to same party only).
Price	£65-£85. Singles £40-£50.
Meals	Pub next door.
Closed	Christmas & Easter.

Furse & Rosemary Swann
Yoah Cottage,
West Knighton,
Dorchester,
Dorset DT2 8PE
Tel   +44 (0)1305 852087
Email   roseswann@tiscali.co.uk
Web   www.yoahcottage.co.uk

Entry 166   Map 3

Dorset

Marren

On the Dorset coastal path overlooking Weymouth Bay – a blissful spot for Jurassic Coast adventures. The owners have transformed this 1920s house, set in six acres of terraced and wooded garden, and their style reflects their penchant for natural materials and country life. Bedrooms are elegant and comfortable; one has a door onto the garden; from the other you can marvel at the sun setting over the sea. Enjoy superb Slow Food spreads of farm produce and homemade bread, then head off to the secluded beach below and a turquoise sea swim. Leave the low-slung Morgan at home: the track is steep!

Minimum two nights at weekends. Children over 12 welcome.

Rooms	2 doubles.
Price	£95-£135.
Meals	Pub 1 mile.
Closed	Rarely.

Peter Cartwright
Marren,
Holworth,
Dorchester,
Dorset DT2 8NJ
Tel   +44 (0)1305 851503
Mobile   +44 (0)7957 886399
Email   marren@lineone.net
Web   www.marren.info

Entry 167   Map 3

Dorset

Waddon House

Don't be daunted when this magnificent manor house swings into view: it's grand, gracious, filled with flowers... and Suzie is lovely. The house breathes 500 years of history – there's a fine artefact or period feature at every turn, from white hounds in the courtyard entrance to silver tureens in the handsome dining room. Bedrooms are in the east wing, one a vision of yellow silk and antiques, the other a raftered Art Deco dream with stained-glass windows and furniture from the Queen Mary Liner. Formal gardens envelop the house – a maze of balustrades, finials, statues and steps, with stunning views to the Jurassic coast. Unique!

Rooms	2: 1 twin/double with sofabed; 1 four-poster with separate bath.
Price	£110-£150. Singles £90-£100.
Meals	Dinner, 4 courses, £28. Pub/restaurant 2 miles.
Closed	Rarely.

Suzie Chaffyn-Grove
Waddon House,
Waddon, Portesham,
Weymouth,
Dorset DT3 4ER
Tel   +44 (0)1305 871241
Mobile   +44 (0)7966 436420
Email   suzie@waddonhouse.co.uk
Web   www.waddonhouse.co.uk

Entry 168   Map 3

Dorset

Honeycombe Cottage

As dreamy as its name, the 16th-century cottage in the village, with deep walls, open fireplaces and flagged floors houses one dog and gentle, generous Heather. Now her children have flown the nest, she gives you a garden that blooms as wonderfully as the house and, up under the eaves, soft curtains, soothing colours, aromatic oils and delicious beds. Have breakfast (homemade honey, bacon from up the road) in the homely kitchen, or outside on fine days, where lawns and borders drift effortlessly into orchard, fields and hills. An all-year-round delight.

Children over five welcome.

Dorset

Bering House

Fabulous in every way. Renate's attention to detail reveals a love of running B&B: the fluffy dressing gowns and bathroom treats, the biscuits, fruit and sherry... she and John are welcoming and delightful. Expect pretty sofas, golden bath taps, a gleaming breakfast table, and a big sumptuous suite with views across sparkling Poole harbour to Brownsea Island and Purbeck Hills. Breakfasts are served on blue and white Spode china: exotic fruits with Parma ham, smoked salmon with poached eggs and muffins, kedgeree, smoked haddock gratin, warm figs with Greek yogurt and honey: the choice is superb. An immaculate harbourside retreat.

Rooms	2: 1 twin/double; 1 double with separate shower.
Price	£80.
Meals	Pubs/restaurants 0.33 miles.
Closed	Rarely.

Rooms	2: 1 twin/double, 1 suite with kitchenette.
Price	£80. Suite £95. Singles £70–£85.
Meals	Pub 400 yds. Restaurant 500 yds.
Closed	Rarely.

	Heather Loxton
	Honeycombe Cottage,
	Shitterton,
	Bere Regis,
	Dorset BH20 7HU
Tel	+44 (0)1929 471660
Mobile	+44 (0)7717 783839
Email	info@honeycombecottage.com
Web	www.honeycombecottage.com

	Renate & John Wadham
	Bering House,
	53 Branksea Avenue,
	Hamworthy,
	Poole,
	Dorset BH15 4DP
Tel	+44 (0)1202 673419
Email	johnandrenate1@tiscali.co.uk

Entry 169   Map 3

Entry 170   Map 3

Dorset

Gold Court House

Anthea and Michael have created a mood of restrained luxury and uncluttered, often beautiful, good taste in their Georgian townhouse. Restful bedrooms have antiques, beams, linen armchairs, radios and TVs. There's an eye-catching collection of aquamarine glass, interesting art, and a large drawing room and pretty walled garden in which to relax after a day out. Views are soft and lush yet you are in the small square of this attractive town with cafés and galleries a short walk. Your hosts are delightful – "they do everything to perfection," says a guest; both house and garden are a refuge.

Over tens welcome.

Rooms	3: 1 double; 2 twin/doubles each with separate bathroom.
Price	£85. Singles £60.
Meals	Restaurants 50 yds.
Closed	Rarely.

	Anthea & Michael Hipwell
	Gold Court House,
	St John's Hill, Wareham,
	Dorset BH20 4LZ
Tel	+44 (0)1929 553320
Email	info@goldcourthouse.co.uk
Web	www.goldcourthouse.co.uk

Entry 171 Map 3

Dorset

Lower Lynch House

On the glorious Isle of Purbeck, between the old stone village of Corfe Castle and Kingston atop a hill, this wisteria-strewn house sits at the end of a long woodland track. Aga-cooked breakfast is served at tables overlooking courtyard and garden; cosy, traditional bedrooms with pale colours and florals are as peaceful as can be. No sitting room, but a small sofa in the double. You are a five-minute drive from the coastal path: a great spot for walkers and peace-seekers. Bron and Nick are warm and friendly, their home a relaxing retreat with a mature garden to wander and wild deer roaming.

Minimum two nights.

Rooms	2: 1 twin; 1 double with separate bath.
Price	£80.
Meals	Pub 0.75 miles.
Closed	Christmas & New Year.

	Bron & Nick Burt
	Lower Lynch House,
	Kingston Hill,
	Corfe Castle,
	Dorset BH20 5LG
Tel	+44 (0)1929 480089
Email	bronburt@btinternet.com

Entry 172 Map 3

Dorset

The Old Post Office

The stunning coastal path comes past the front door of this restored bungalow on a private cliff-top estate. Clamber down to a hidden beach and a short walk will take you to Swanage. The house glows with warm colour and a friendly, informal feel. Comfortable sunny bedrooms have painted furniture and French windows onto an inviting veranda, set with rocking chairs and candles. Toasty bathrooms sparkle. Artist Rowena and rare-book dealer David look after you very well; Rowena loves to cook and chat and breakfast is local and delicious, with mushrooms, herby potatoes and eggs from Arabella the hen. To stay is a treat!

Rooms	2: 1 twin;
	1 double with separate bath.
Price	£85. Singles £55.
Meals	Pub/restaurant 0.3 miles.
Closed	Rarely.

Rowena Bishop
The Old Post Office,
4 Ballard Estate, Swanage,
Dorset BH19 1QZ

Tel	+44 (0)1929 422041
Mobile	+44 (0)7976 356013
Email	rowena@outwardbound.plus.com
Web	www.oldpostofficeswanage.co.uk

🐈 📶 🚂 ✕

Entry 173   Map 3

Dorset

The Park 24

All is lush, leafy and quiet, yet a mere stroll from the centre. The garden teems with lavender and agapanthus in summer, and tea on the terrace is glorious. Chris and Fiona's Edwardian home has a relaxing open house feel; the elegant sitting room gleams with beautiful antiques and flowers, and a log fire in winter keeps you toasty. Cosy chic ground-floor bedrooms have ultra sleek shower rooms. Chat away at the refectory table while Fiona cooks breakfast, tuck into porridge with cinnamon and cream. Work it off on the beach, then back for a summerhouse nap – and a possible sighting of a sweet spaniel nosing through the undergrowth!

Minimum stay two nights at busy times.

Rooms	2 doubles.
Price	£88-£135. Singles from £70.
Meals	Pub/restaurant 1 mile.
Closed	Rarely.

Chris & Fiona Dixon-Box
The Park 24,
24 Meyrick Park Crescent,
Talbot Woods, Bournemouth,
Dorset BH3 7AQ

Tel	+44 (0)1202 296473
Mobile	+44 (0)7740 425623
Email	info@thepark24.co.uk
Web	www.thepark24.co.uk

♿ 🐈 📧 📶 🚂 ✕

Entry 174   Map 3

Dorset

Sondela

All is leafy and sedate, with tall pines and rhododendrons hiding large houses: a short drive sweeps you to the front of this colonial style bungalow smothered in roses. Glynda and Selwyn, warm and intelligent, have filled their lovely light home with interesting antiques, textiles and artefacts from their years in South Africa; guests have their own sitting room in soft blues with a stone fireplace and fresh flowers. Bedrooms are quiet (the double is bigger and more contemporary) with pure white cotton sheets and splashes of colour from bedspreads or cushions; on sunny days you breakfast in the glorious garden.

Rooms	2: 1 double, 1 twin.
Price	£70-£90. Singles £60.
Meals	Restaurant 5-minute walk.
Closed	Rarely.

Glynda & Selwyn Morrison
Sondela,
20 Chewton Farm Road,
Highcliffe, Christchurch,
Dorset BH23 5QN

Tel	+44 (0)1425 270978
Mobile	+44 (0)7734 991034
Email	morglyn@hotmail.com
Web	www.chewtonbedandbreakfast.com

Entry 175   Map 3

Dorset

Thornhill

This pretty thatched house has peaceful views from every window… of fields, woods and superb gardens. Sara and John are charming hosts and love having people to stay; they have lots of local knowledge too. Downstairs are pastel walls, polished antiques, beautiful cedar floors and interesting art. All is neat, tidy, spacious and spotless, and Sara pays great attention to detail: fruit, chocolates and a choice of teas in comforting bedrooms with an old-fashioned feel. You can spot deer on the lawn, stride out straight from the door, visit the Minster, drive to beaches. Come on a Thursday if you like to play bridge!

Rooms	3: 1 double, 1 twin, 1 single, all sharing 2 baths. Possible use of separate bath.
Price	£64. Singles from £32.
Meals	Pub/restaurant 400 yds.
Closed	Rarely.

John & Sara Turnbull
Thornhill,
Holt,
Wimborne,
Dorset BH21 7DJ

Tel	+44 (0)1202 889434
Email	scturnbull@lineone.net

Entry 176   Map 3

Dorset

Crawford House

Below, the river Stour winds through the valley and under the medieval, nine-arched bridge. Above, an Iron Age hill fort; between is Crawford House. It's an elegant Georgian house in an acre of walled garden, soft and pretty inside with an easy, relaxed atmosphere. Carpeted bedrooms are homely and warm, with long curtains; one room has four-poster twin beds with chintz drapes. The sun streams through the floor-to-ceiling windows of the downstairs rooms, and charming 18th- and 19th-century oil paintings hang in the dining room. Andrea is fun, and a great host, with lots of local knowledge.

Broadband available.

Rooms	3: 1 twin/double; 1 twin with separate bath; 1 twin with separate shower.
Price	£70-£75. Singles £40.
Meals	Pub in village.
Closed	Mid-October to mid-April.

Andrea Lea
Crawford House,
Spetisbury,
Blandford Forum,
Dorset DT11 9DP

Tel   +44 (0)1258 857338
Email   andrea@lea8.wanadoo.co.uk

Entry 177   Map 3

Dorset

Stickland Farmhouse

Charming Dorset... welcome to a soft, delightful thatched cottage in an enviably rural setting. Sandy and Paul have poured love into this listed farmhouse and garden, the latter bursting with lupins, poppies, foxgloves, clematis, delphiniums. Sandy gives you delicious breakfasts with homemade muesli, eggs from the hens and soda bread from the Aga. Pretty, cottagey bedrooms have crisp white dressing gowns and lots of books and pictures – one room opens onto your own seating area in the garden. The village has a good pub, and Cranbourne Chase, rich in barrows and hill forts, is close by.

Minimum two nights at weekends in summer. Over tens welcome.

Rooms	3: 2 doubles, 1 twin.
Price	£70-£75. Singles £60.
Meals	Pub 3-minute walk.
Closed	Rarely.

Sandy & Paul Crofton-Atkins
Stickland Farmhouse,
Winterborne Stickland,
Blandford Forum,
Dorset DT11 0NT

Tel   +44 (0)1258 880119
Mobile   +44 (0)7932 897774
Email   sandysticklandfarm@tiscali.co.uk
Web   www.sticklandfarmhouse.co.uk

Entry 178   Map 3

Dorset

Hill House

A classically smart, immaculately comfortable, 1920s townhouse on the edge of Blandford Forum. Warm, hospitable Jan and Geoff ensure you'll want for nothing. Choose pretty much anything for breakfast – smoked salmon and scrambled egg, French toast, bacon and maple syrup – in a sunny dining room overlooking the garden with its fishpond and croquet lawn. Beds are big and beautifully dressed, bathrooms pristine and spoiling, and there's an open fire in the guest living room. You're ten minutes' walk from the centre of 'one of the best preserved Georgian towns in England'. Geoff can advise on great fishing and golf.

Minimum two nights at weekends.

Rooms	3: 1 double, 2 twins/doubles each with extra bed.
Price	£75–£100. Singles from £75.
Meals	Pubs/restaurants 5-minute walk.
Closed	Rarely.

Jan & Geoff McGratty
Hill House,
49 Salisbury Road,
Blandford Forum,
Dorset DT11 7HT

Tel	+44 (0)1258 480074
Email	mcgratty@btinternet.com
Web	www.hillhousedorset.co.uk

Entry 179   Map 3

Dorset

Launceston Farm

Farmhouse chic in the most glorious of surroundings. The bedrooms, all named after the fields, are an exquisite blend of contemporary and traditional; two have roll tops in the room itself. Take tea by the open fire or find a secluded spot in the ornamental, walled gardens. Breakfast and candlelit dinner are farm-sourced and deliciously rustic. Sarah, who was born in this listed house, provides a truly relaxing stay; son Jimi's organic farm tours are a must and there are footpaths through the surrounding AONB from the door. You will leave this country retreat feeling completely rejuvenated.

Over 12s welcome.

Rooms	6: 4 doubles, 2 twins/doubles.
Price	£90–£115. Singles from £55.
Meals	Dinner, 2 courses, £22.50 (Mon & Fri only). Pub 1 mile.
Closed	Rarely.

Sarah Worrall
Launceston Farm,
Tarrant Launceston,
Blandford Forum,
Dorset DT11 8BY

Tel	+44 (0)1258 830528
Email	info@launcestonfarm.co.uk
Web	www.launcestonfarm.co.uk

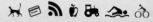

Entry 180   Map 3

Dorset

Sarunds Cottage

Steep lanes tumble down to wooded Farnham and the famous Museum Inn. A little further, up a gravelled driveway, are Josephine's interior design studio and elegant Georgian house. Through a gate, privately in its own lane, is a cottage housing your suite – spacious, luxurious, on the first floor and bliss for independent souls. Light-filled and beamy, with a rococo-esque bed and toile de Jouy curtains, it's a vision of cream, grey and soft ochre; the chandelier'd bathroom is stunning too. Breakfast in a basket is a cook-your-own affair. Deer bound in the forests of Cranborne Chase, Salisbury is 20 minutes away.

Rooms	1 suite with sitting room & kitchenette.
Price	£120. Singles £80-£100.
Meals	Pub/restaurant 200 yds.
Closed	Rarely.

Josephine Browning
Sarunds Cottage,
Farnham,
Blandford Forum,
Dorset DT11 8DE
Tel   +44 (0)1725 552555
Email   jb@countryhouse-interiordesign.co.uk
Web   www.sarundscottage.co.uk

🚶 ▤ 🔊 ✕

Entry 181   Map 3

Dorset

The Old Forge, Fanners Yard

Step back in time in this beautifully restored forge: retro signs, museum pieces, ponies in the paddock and a simpler, slower way of life... Tim and Lucy's smallholding gives you a taste of harmonious living with the seasons, and they recycle everything. This includes Tim's classic cars, a cosy gypsy caravan and a vintage shepherd's hut. The attic bedrooms are snug – Lucy's quilts, country antiques, sparkling bathrooms, flowers – and their breakfasts are renowned: eggs from their hens, organic bacon and sausages, home-grown jams, apple juice straight from the orchard. A happy place, a tonic to stay.

Self-catering in the Smithy. Over eights welcome.
Minimum two nights in caravan & shepherd's hut.

Rooms	4: 1 double, 1 family. Gypsy caravan (Rosie) & shepherd's hut (Sam): 1 double (each with shower/wc close by).
Price	£75-£95. Family room £80-£125. Singles £60-£75. Gypsy caravan & shepherd's hut £95.
Meals	Pub/restaurant within 1 mile.
Closed	Rarely.

Tim & Lucy Kerridge
The Old Forge,
Fanners Yard,
Compton Abbas, Shaftesbury,
Dorset SP7 0NQ
Tel   +44 (0)1747 811881
Email   theoldforge@ymail.com
Web   www.theoldforgedorset.co.uk

🐈 ▤ 🔊 ✕

Entry 182   Map 3

Dorset

Dorset

Rosie & Sam

The immaculately restored gypsy caravan and the shepherd's hut at The Old Forge overlook orchard, paddock (home of Scrumpy Jack the donkey) and a view of beautiful Fontmell Down. Rosie's colours are true Romany – deep burgundy and cream – while Sam's vintage charm is unmistakable, with curtains patchworked from 1970s Laura Ashley dresses. Each has a double bed – Rosie's is authentically snug – and its own outside space; sit and watch the sun set over the fields. Your shower room is next to the retro petrol pump and you join the B&B guests for lovely Lucy's breakfasts: a delicious (award-winning) start to the day.

Minimum two nights. Book through Sawday's Canopy & Stars online or by phone.

Lawn Cottage

In a quiet village in the Blackmore Vale, the path to this spacious cottage is lined with tulips and vegetables. Easy-going June is a collector of pretty things; fine sketches and watercolours, antiques and china blend charmingly with soft colours and zingy kilims. There's a delightful, sunny, en suite bedroom downstairs, with a private entrance and touches of toile de Jouy, and a double room upstairs. Breakfast is served in the big kitchen or out in the cottage garden; the tiny sitting room is a perfect snug. Visit Sherborne for its abbey, castle and smart shops; walk from the gate to Duncliffe Woods. Perfect Dorset B&B!

Rooms	Gypsy caravan for 2, shepherd's hut for 2, each with separate shower & wc.	
Price	£95.	
Meals	Breakfast in house included. Pub/restaurant within 1 mile.	
Closed	Never.	

Rooms	2: 1 twin/double; 1 double with separate bathroom.
Price	£70. Singles £40.
Meals	Pub/restaurant 1 mile.
Closed	Rarely.

	Sawday's Canopy & Stars
	Rosie & Sam,
	The Old Forge, Fanners Yard,
	Compton Abbas,
	Dorset SP7 0NQ
Tel	+44 (0)1275 395447
Email	enquiries@canopyandstars.co.uk
Web	www.canopyandstars.co.uk/ theoldforge

	June Watkins
	Lawn Cottage,
	Stour Row,
	Shaftesbury,
	Dorset SP7 0QF
Tel	+44 (0)1747 838719
Mobile	+44 (0)7809 696218
Email	enquiries@lawncottagedorset.co.uk
Web	www.lawncottagedorset.co.uk

Entry 183   Map 3

Entry 184   Map 3

Dorset

Rose Cottage

You are buried deep in a quiet corner here, just perfect for long walks: return to a wood-burner and a pot of tea and home-made cake in a beamed sitting room full of sofas and books. Bedrooms are light and charming with chintzy curtains and fabulous views over the garden (flowers, vegetables, stream); loll in big beds with cushions and crisp white sheets. Breakfast is a fairly flexible, mostly organic treat with Rose Cottage honey, served in an elegant dining room with glowing furniture and dollops of morning sunshine. Amanda, warm and welcoming, looks after you very well indeed.

Babies & children over eight welcome.

Rooms	2: 1 twin/double; 1 twin/double with separate bath/shower.
Price	£85. Singles from £50. Child £15.
Meals	Snacks & packed lunch available. Pub/restaurant 1 mile.
Closed	Christmas.

Giles & Amanda Vardey
Rose Cottage,
Watery Lane,
Donhead St Mary,
Shaftesbury,
Dorset SP7 9DF

Tel   +44 (0)1747 828449
Email   amanda@rosecottage.uk.com
Web   www.rosecottage.uk.com

Entry 185   Map 3

Dorset

Glebe Farm

You're in Dorset's highest village – views from the house sprawl for miles. Ian farms 1,000 acres, Tessa looks after horses, ponies and chickens. Their home, newly built, comes with green oak, soaring ceilings and walls of glass that frame spectacular views ("Emmerdale meets Grand Designs" to quote a happy guest). Aga-cooked breakfasts include local bacon and home-laid eggs, while bedrooms, one up, one down, have warm colours, big beds, beautiful views, super bathrooms. The Wessex Ridgeway starts in the village, so follow it over to magnificent Hambledon Hill, an Iron Age hill fort. Dine on the terrace in summer.

Over 14s welcome.

Rooms	2 twins/doubles.
Price	£100–£120. Singles from £60.
Meals	Dinner, 2 courses, £25 (by prior arrangement). Pubs 2 miles.
Closed	Christmas & New Year.

Tessa & Ian Millard
Glebe Farm,
High Street, Ashmore,
Salisbury,
Dorset SP5 5AE

Tel   +44 (0)1747 811974
Mobile   +44 (0)7799 858961
Email   stay@glebefarmbandb.co.uk
Web   www.glebefarmbandb.co.uk

Entry 186   Map 3

Dorset

Golden Hill Cottage

Deep in the countryside lies Stourton Caundle and this charming thatched cottage. You have the peace and privacy of your own sitting room, traditionally furnished with antiques, paintings and open fire; up a private stair is your carpeted twin room with a small shower. Anna, courteous and kind, brings you splendid platefuls of local bacon and sausage, homemade jams and Dorset honey for breakfast; nothing is too much trouble for these hosts. There are glorious walks from the village, a good pub that serves food and real ales, and Sherborne, Montacute and Stourhead for landscape, culture and history.

Babes in arms welcome.

Rooms	1 twin & sitting room.
Price	£80–£90. Singles £50.
Meals	Pubs/restaurants within 3 miles.
Closed	Rarely.

Anna & Andrew Oliver
Golden Hill Cottage,
Stourton Caundle,
Sturminster Newton,
Dorset DT10 2JW

Tel	+44 (0)1963 362109
Email	anna@goldenhillcottage.co.uk
Web	www.goldenhillcottage.co.uk

Entry 187   Map 3

Dorset

Gorse Farm House

Start your day with a generous and locally sourced breakfast in the sunny conservatory; maps and books about walking and cycling will help you forge out into the dreamy Dorset countryside. Wendy throws open her lovely house, so wander the garden, grab a book, laze in the conservatory or settle into the snug. Upstairs are light-filled, peaceful bedrooms (one with triple aspect windows for the views), a bowl of sweets, dainty china and more books; the en suite bathroom has a roll top bath. Lee's sculptures peek out from clever planting in the garden: find a pretty spot and enjoy the bird-filled peace.

Children over 12 welcome.

Rooms	2: 1 twin/double; 1 twin/double with separate bath.
Price	£75. Singles £45–£55.
Meals	Pub/restaurant 2 miles.
Closed	Christmas.

Wendy Dickenson
Gorse Farm House,
Fifehead St Quintin,
Sturminster Newton,
Dorset DT10 2AW

Tel	+44 (0)1258 475343
Mobile	+44 (0)7725 238344
Email	contactus@gorsefarmhousebb.co.uk
Web	www.gorsefarmhousebb.co.uk

Entry 188   Map 3

Dorset

Old Causeway Bakery

Opposite the village playing field, footsteps from the pub, is this warm, cosy, beamy B&B. Your relaxed hosts, fond of country pursuits, know all the best walks (as do Henry and Bertie, the adorable dogs) and have guidebooks galore; beautiful Bulbarrow Hill is close. You start the day with a delicious cooked breakfast, and end it by the wood-burner, amid soft lamps and deep colours: the guest lounge is most inviting. In the self-contained wing, up the stairs, is a super-private room with a theatrical air. But all the rooms ooze comfort, with their plush bedheads, soft carpets, polished antiques and super bathrooms.

Dogs welcome.

Rooms	3: 2 twins/doubles. Bakery Wing: 1 twin/double.
Price	£80–£120. Singles £75–£85.
Meals	Pub 30 yds.
Closed	Rarely.

Sandra Williams & Simon Boggon
Old Causeway Bakery,
Hazelbury Bryan,
Sturminster Newton,
Dorset DT10 2BH
Tel   +44 (0)1258 817228
Mobile   +44 (0)7825 815796
Email   sandrasimonbw@btinternet.com
Web   www.oldcausewaybakery.co.uk

Entry 189   Map 3

Dorset

Munden House

This is a super B&B – a couple of farm cottages and assorted outbuildings beautifully stitched together. It's run with great warmth by Colin and Annie, who buy and sell colourful rugs and have travelled the world to do it. Outside, long views shoot off over open country; inside, airy interiors, pretty bedrooms and lots of colour. The garden studios are bigger and more private; one has a galleried bedroom above a lovely sitting room. Annie cooks fantastic food – local meat, fish from Brixham – but her vegetarian dishes will seduce die-hard carnivores. You eat at smartly dressed tables; breakfast is on the terrace in good weather.

Rooms	7: 2 doubles, 1 twin/double, 1 four-poster, 3 garden studios.
Price	£80–£130. Singles from £70.
Meals	Dinner, 3 courses, £27. Pub 0.5 miles.
Closed	Christmas.

Annie & Colin Fletcher
Munden House,
Mundens Lane,
Alweston,
Sherborne,
Dorset DT9 5HU
Tel   +44 (0)1963 23150
Email   stay@mundenhouse.co.uk
Web   www.mundenhouse.co.uk

Entry 190   Map 3

Dorset

Glebe House

Clematis and wisteria cover much of the mellow brickwork of this spacious and uncluttered 1950s house, down a quiet lane in a tiny hamlet in the heart of stunning Blackmore Vale. From the hall look right through to the mature pretty garden; it's open house and David and Barbara love having guests to stay. Enjoy tea and scones in the garden room, neat-as-a-pin bedrooms and bathrooms, and wide views from every window. Tuck into all sorts of tasty choices at breakfast, by the fire in the dining room. Magnificent castle and abbey are close, and walks from the door are outstanding – you could stay a week and never do the same one twice!

Rooms	2: 1 double, 1 twin/double.
Price	£70–£80. Singles £50.
Meals	Pub/restaurant within 1 mile.
Closed	Rarely.

	David & Barbara Fifield
	Glebe House,
	Folke, Sherborne,
	Dorset DT9 5HP
Tel	+44 (0)1963 210337
Mobile	+44 (0)7980 864033
Email	glebe.house@hotmail.com
Web	www.glebehouse-dorset.co.uk

Entry 191   Map 3

Dorset

Windrush Farm

Fun to eat in the light farmhouse kitchen with its Aga, polished oak table, and rag-rolled dresser full of colourful plates. Upstairs, too, is delightful – creaky floors, sloping ceilings and a maze of corridors brightened by new Zoffany wallpapers. Pretty bedrooms are in soft colours; everywhere there are paintings, prints and photos. On colder evenings, your charming hosts will light a fire for you in the guest sitting room – lived-in and snug with artwork and piles of books – while for summer there's a scented rambler-strewn garden and a terrace with the loveliest views. Bustling Sherborne is a ten-minute drive.

Rooms	2: 1 double with separate bath; 1 twin sharing bath (2nd room let to same party only).
Price	£80. Singles from £55.
Meals	Dinner £25. Pub/restaurant 1 mile.
Closed	Christmas.

	Richard & Jenny Gold
	Windrush Farm,
	Stowell,
	Sherborne,
	Dorset DT9 4PD
Tel	+44 (0)1963 370799
Email	jennygold@hotmail.co.uk
Web	www.windrushfarmbedandbreakfast.com

Entry 192   Map 3

Durham

Cooper House Farm

Lucy's clever and original use of vibrant colours, combined with antique and vintage pieces, produces astonishing results! And there are lots of wonderful pictures of cows. Hearty breakfasts are served at one large table in the kitchen with orange Aga, juke box and jolly sofas. Stoke up on homemade bread and jams, eggs from their hens – walk it off furiously in the glorious Dales or amble along the river; perhaps visit Barnard Castle. Return to hugely comfortable colourful bedrooms with pastoral views, warm shining bathrooms, a guests' sitting room with a roaring fire and three gentle dogs.

Over sevens welcome.

Rooms	2: 1 twin/double; 1 twin/double with separate bath.
Price	£95. Singles £55.
Meals	Pubs/restaurants 1-3 miles.
Closed	Rarely.

Lucy Blackmore
Cooper House Farm,
Cotherstone,
Barnard Castle,
Durham DL12 9QR
Tel   +44 (0)1833 650187
Email   contact@cooperhouse.org.uk
Web   www.cooperhouse.org.uk

Entry 193   Map 12

Essex

Brook Farm

Large low Georgian windows fill the house with light, unpretentious family pieces warm the bedrooms, and the stunning carved crossbeam in the interconnecting family rooms is late-medieval. Anne, a country lover, has farmed here for over 30 years; outbuildings dot the yard, sheep and horses roam the acres. In Anne's sitting room logs fill the copper and hunting prints line the walls – no TV, but magazines and books aplenty – and you breakfast (deliciously) at a long table with fine antique benches. The handsome pink farmhouse oozes history and a faded country charm, there are some good pubs nearby and Stansted is 30 minutes.

Rooms	3: 1 twin; 1 double, 1 family room, each with separate bath.
Price	£70-£80. Family room £70-£175. Singles £40-£45.
Meals	Packed lunch £3-£5. Pubs within 2 miles.
Closed	Rarely.

Anne Butler
Brook Farm,
Wethersfield, Braintree,
Essex CM7 4BX
Tel   +44 (0)1371 850284
Mobile +44 (0)7770 881966
Email   abutlerbrookfarm@aol.com
Web   www.brookfarmwethersfield.co.uk

Entry 194   Map 9

32 The Hythe

The Thames barge in all her glory: the Gibbs' garden runs almost into the river Blackwater where these majestic old craft are moored and the mudflats are a bird-watcher's dream. Summer breakfast on the deck – local smoked kippers and free-range eggs – watching the barges sail up the river is a rare treat. Beneath wide limpid skies this sensitively extended fisherman's cottage looks out to 12th-century St Mary's at the back where Kim and Gerry ring the Sunday bells. It's immaculate and comfortable inside, an inspired mix of modern and antique lit by myriad candles, among other romantic touches.

Over 14s welcome.

Rooms	2: 1 double;
	1 double with separate bath.
Price	£90. Singles £70.
Meals	Pub 100 yds.
Closed	Christmas & Boxing Day.

Kim & Gerry Gibbs
32 The Hythe,
Maldon,
Essex CM9 5HN
Tel   +44 (0)1621 859435
Mobile   +44 (0)7753 135108
Email   gibbsie@live.co.uk
Web   www.thehythemaldon.co.uk

Entry 195   Map 10

Caterpillar Cottage

Traditional brick and clapboard, dormer windows, tall chimney – this looks like the real thing. But the 'converted farm building' in the grounds of Patricia's former grand old house is fairly young. Filled with fine furniture, family photographs and *objets* from far-flung travels, it invites relaxation. The double-height, vaulted sitting room brims with sofas and books, logs crackle on chilly nights and bedrooms are simple and comfortable with decent-sized bathrooms. Patricia, a lively grandmother, adores children while her big garden promises home-grown fruit and tranquillity.

Rooms	2: 1 triple; 1 double with separate
	bath/shower. Camp bed available.
Price	£65–£70. Triple £75–£85.
	Singles from £35.
Meals	Packed lunch available.
	Pubs 50 yds.
Closed	Rarely.

Patricia Mitchell
Caterpillar Cottage,
Fordstreet, Aldham,
Colchester,
Essex CO6 3PH
Tel   +44 (0)1206 240456
Mobile   +44 (0)7776 202713
Email   bandbcaterpillar@tiscali.co.uk
Web   www.caterpillarcottage.co.uk

Entry 196   Map 10

Essex

Emsworth House

Unexpectedly tranquil is this 1937 vicarage, with wide views over the Stour and some wonderful light for painting. Penny, an artist, is a flexible and generous host and you can laze or picnic in her two-acre garden. This is Constable country – great for walking; you are near to Frinton beach and golf, sailing and riding. Return to comfy sofas and chairs, open fires and good books, and redecorated bedrooms with a country feel and the odd African throw or splash of colour. There's heaps of lovely art and a garden full of birds. Penny has camp beds and high chairs and a can-do attitude. Great fun.

Rooms	3: 1 double, 1 twin; 1 double with separate bath.
Price	£55-£80. Singles from £55.
Meals	Pub/restaurant 0.5 miles.
Closed	Rarely.

Penny Linton
Emsworth House,
Ship Hill, Station Road,
Bradfield, Manningtree,
Essex CO11 2UP

Tel	+44 (0)1255 870860
Mobile	+44 (0)7767 477771
Email	emsworthhouse@hotmail.com
Web	www.emsworthhouse.co.uk

🎡 🐈 📶 🚂 ✕

Entry 197   Map 10

Essex

Esplanade House

Through Harwich Old Town and along the waterfront, this handsome house overlooks the harbour entrance, ships, fishing boats and sandy beach. Books and artwork fill every corner, the elegant drawing room is inviting – comfortable sofas, board games, jigsaws – and Liz and Martin are delightful. Bedrooms over four floors have fantastic views, fine linen, robes, hot water bottles and smart, warm bathrooms; children can hop up the stairs to the attic room. Wake for homemade blueberry muffins and jams, local bacon and sausages; venture forth for nautical sites. Lights dance on the water at night and Constable country is on the doorstep.

Parking for four cars.

Rooms	3: 1 double with sofabed & separate bath/shower; 1 double, 1 twin sharing bath (2nd room let to same party).
Price	£80-£120. Singles £80.
Meals	Dinner £30. Supper £20. Picnic available. Pubs/restaurants 5-minute walk.
Closed	Rarely.

Liz & Martin Evans
Esplanade House,
32 Kings Quay Street,
Harwich,
Essex CO12 3ES

Tel	+44 (0)1255 508235
Mobile	+44 (0)7887 724055
Email	enquiries@esplanadehouse.co.uk
Web	www.esplanadehouse.co.uk

🎡 🐈 📶 🐕 🚂 ✕

Entry 198   Map 10

Discover the west at your own pace

Gloucestershire

Grove Farm

Boards creak and you duck, in a farmhouse of the best kind: simple, small-roomed, stone-flagged, beamed, delightful. The walls are white, the polished furniture is good and there are pictures everywhere. In spite of great age (16th century), it's light, with lots of pretty windows. The 400 acres are farmed organically and Penny makes award-winning cheese and a grand breakfast — continental at busy times. Stupendous views across the Severn estuary to the Cotswolds, the Forest of Dean on the doorstep, and woodland walks carpeted with spring flowers. And there is simply no noise — unless the guinea fowl are in voice.

Rooms	2: 1 double; 1 twin/double with separate bath.
Price	£70. Singles £40.
Meals	Packed lunch £5. Pub 2 miles.
Closed	Rarely.

	Penny & David Hill
	Grove Farm,
	Bullo Pill, Newnham,
	Gloucestershire GL14 1DZ
Tel	+44 (0)1594 516304
Mobile	+44 (0)7990 877984
Email	davidandpennyhill@btopenworld.com
Web	www.grovefarm-uk.com

Entry 199   Map 8

Gloucestershire

Frampton Court

Deep authenticity in this magnificent Grade I-listed house. The manor of Frampton on Severn has been in the family since the 11th century and although Rollo and Janie look after the estate, it is artist Gillian who greets you on their behalf and looks after you. There are exquisite examples of decorative woodwork and, in the hall, a cheerful log fire; perch on the Mouseman fire seat. Bedrooms are traditional with antiques, panelling and long views. Beds have fine linen, one with embroidered Stuart hangings. Stroll around the ornamental canal, soak up the old-master views. An architectural masterpiece.

Arrivals after 5pm.

Rooms	3: 1 double, 1 twin/double, 1 four-poster.
Price	£135–£170.
Meals	Dinner £29–£40. Pub across the green. Restaurant 3 miles.
Closed	Rarely.

	Gillian Keightley
	Frampton Court,
	Frampton on Severn,
	Gloucestershire GL2 7EX
Tel	+44 (0)1452 740267
Email	framptoncourt@framptoncourtestate.co.uk
Web	www.framptoncourtestate.co.uk

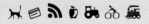

Entry 200   Map 8

Gloucestershire

St Annes

Step straight off the narrow pavement into a sunny hall and a warm and welcoming family home. Iris and Greg have made their pretty 17th-century house, in the heart of this lovely bustling village, as eco-friendly as possible. Comfy bedrooms are charming; the four-poster room has a tiny en suite shower room. Farmers' market breakfasts are a feast, bantams wander into the kitchen and Rollo the dog loves children. Painswick is known as 'the Queen of the Cotswolds': enjoy superb walks through orchid meadows and beech woods carpeted with bluebells; visit good pubs on the way. Great value.

Minimum two nights at weekends April-Sept.

Rooms	3: 1 double, 1 twin, 1 four-poster.
Price	£70–£75. Singles £50. Dogs £5.
Meals	Packed lunch £6. Pubs/restaurants in village.
Closed	Rarely.

	Iris McCormick
	St Annes,
	Gloucester Street, Painswick,
	Gloucestershire GL6 6QN
Tel	+44 (0)1452 812879
Email	iris@st-annes-painswick.co.uk
Web	www.st-annes-painswick.co.uk

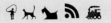

Entry 201   Map 8

Gloucestershire

Nation House

Three cottages were knocked together to create this wisteria-clad, listed village house, now a terrific B&B. Beams are exposed, walls are pale and hung with prints, floors are close-carpeted, the sitting room is formally cosy and quiet. Smart, comfortable bedrooms have patchwork quilts, low beams and padded seats at lattice windows; the bathroom is spotless and the small shower room gleaming. In summer, breakfast in the conservatory on still-warm homemade bread, local bacon and sausages, Brenda's preserves. The village is a Cotswold treasure, with two good eating places and with many walks from the door.

Rooms	3: 1 family room; 2 doubles sharing bath (let to same party only).
Price	£75-£85. Singles £60.
Meals	Dinner £10-£12. Pubs 50 yds.
Closed	Rarely.

	Brenda Hammond
	Nation House,
	George Street, Bisley,
	Gloucestershire GL6 7BB
Tel	+44 (0)1452 770197
Email	stay@nationhouse.co.uk
Web	www.nationhouse.co.uk

Entry 202   Map 8

Gloucestershire

Well Farm

Perhaps it's the gentle, unstuffy attitude of Kate and Edward. Or the great position of the house with its glorious views across the valley. Whichever, you'll feel comforted and invigorated by your stay. It's a real family home and you get both a fresh, pretty bedroom that feels very private and the use of a comfortable, book-filled sitting room opening to a flowery courtyard: Kate is an inspired gardener. Sleep soundly on the softest of pillows, wake to the deep peace of the countryside and the delicious prospect of eggs from their own hens, local sausages and good bacon. The area teems with great walks – lovely pubs too.

Rooms	1 twin/double & sitting room.
Price	£85-£90.
Meals	Dinner from £20. Pubs nearby.
Closed	Rarely.

	Kate & Edward Gordon Lennox
	Well Farm,
	Frampton Mansell, Stroud,
	Gloucestershire GL6 8JB
Tel	+44 (0)1285 760651
Email	kategl@btinternet.com
Web	www.well-farm.co.uk

Entry 203   Map 8

Gloucestershire

Lodge Farm

A plum Cotswolds position and Nicky's truly striking garden – five distinct areas divided by stone walling, full of interest and colour. Your flexible, busy hosts, who also help wedding groups, give you supper en famille next to the Aga or something smart and candlelit around the dining room table: perfect for a house party. Sometimes there's home-reared lamb for dinner, always fresh coffee at breakfast, homemade bread and yogurt, local sausages and their free-range eggs; the sitting room has flowers, family photographs and lots of magazines. Peace-and-quiet lovers will delight – yet you are a short walk from Tetbury.

Rooms	4: 2 twins/doubles, 1 family room; 1 twin/double with separate bath.
Price	£80-£90. Family room £95-£125. Singles from £60.
Meals	Dinner, 2-3 courses, £18.15-£30. Pub/bistro 2.5 miles.
Closed	Rarely.

	Robin & Nicky Salmon
	Lodge Farm,
	Chavenage, Tetbury,
	Gloucestershire GL8 8XW
Tel	+44 (0)1666 505339
Mobile	+44 (0)7836 221457
Email	nsalmon.lodgefarm@btinternet.com
Web	www.lodgefarm.co.uk

Entry 204   Map 8

Gloucestershire

The Moda House

A fine house and a big B&B, but one that retains a deeply homely feel; Duncan and Jo are hugely well-travelled and have filled it with pictures and artefacts from all over the world. Bedrooms differ (three are in a neat annexe) but all are cosy and well decorated with lovely colours, good fabrics, pocket sprung mattresses and bright bathrooms with thick towels. Breakfast – locally sourced, cooked on the Aga and brought to round tables – sets you up for fabulous walks: you are a mile from the Cotswold Way. Return to a basement sitting room with comfy armchairs and lots of books, and a bustling town full of restaurants and shops.

Minimum two nights over busy weekends & minimum three nights during Badminton.

Rooms	11: 8 doubles, 3 singles.
Price	£82-£95. Singles from £62.
Meals	Pubs/restaurants within 100 yards.
Closed	Rarely.

	Duncan & Jo MacArthur
	The Moda House,
	1 High Street,
	Chipping Sodbury,
	Gloucestershire BS37 6BA
Tel	+44 (0)1454 312135
Email	enquiries@modahouse.co.uk
Web	www.modahouse.co.uk

Entry 205   Map 3

Gloucestershire

Little Smithy

Minutes from the M4, the farming village is fairly quiet and your little cottage with mullioned windows completely private. Your front door opens into a hallway which runs the length of the building: at one end, the creamy twin with bright red bedspreads and sparkling bathroom next door, at the other, your L-shaped sitting room with an electric wood-burner. Upstairs is the comfy double and another smart bathroom; all is as neat as a pin. Joanna gives you breakfast in the main house, or on warm days in the garden: eggs from next door's hens, homemade bread and marmalade. Right on the Cotswold Way so perfect for walkers.

Rooms	2: 1 double, 1 twin/double.
Price	£75. Singles £60.
Meals	Pub/restaurant 1 mile.
Closed	Christmas & Easter.

Joanna Bowman
Little Smithy,
Smithy House, Tormarton,
Badminton,
Gloucestershire GL9 1HU
Tel   +44 (0)1454 218412
Email joannabowman@uk2.net
Web   www.littlesmithy.com

Entry 206   Map 3

Gloucestershire

The Old Rectory

English to the core – and to the bottom of its lovely garden, with a woodland walk and plenty of quiet places to sit. You sweep into the circular driveway to a yellow labrador welcome. This beautiful 17th-century high gabled house is comfortably lived-in with an understated décor, antiques, creaky floorboards and a real sense of history. The bedrooms, one with a garden view, have good beds, a chaise longue or an easy chair; bathrooms are vintage and functional but large. Caroline is calm and competent and serves breakfasts with organic eggs and local bacon at the long table in the rich red dining room. A welcoming place.

Rooms	2: 1 double, 1 twin/double; extra bed available.
Price	£85–£100. Singles from £52.
Meals	Pub 200 yds.
Closed	December/January.

Roger & Caroline Carne
The Old Rectory,
Meysey Hampton,
Cirencester,
Gloucestershire GL7 5JX
Tel   +44 (0)1285 851200
Email carolinecarne@cotswoldwireless.co.uk
Web   www.meyseyoldrectory.co.uk

Entry 207   Map 8

Great Farm

Three riverside spots here, all named after the wildlife. Otter is a Swallows & Amazons-style haven, Nightingale is romantic with a claw-foot tub, and Barn Owl's two bowtop wagons with chill-out pod are perfect for families; fairy lights glow on the decking. Each feels very private, with a flushing loo, a hot shower or a bath, a covered outdoor kitchen, a fire pit for toasting marshmallows. Leonie can bring you a breakfast hamper, and you can walk along the river bank to pretty Lechlade, with pubs, antique shops and row boats for hire. For adventurous chefs there are crayfish in the river – and traps provided!

Minimum two nights. Book through Sawday's Canopy & Stars online or by phone.

The Guest House

You get your own new timber-framed house with masses of light and space, a terrace, and spectacular valley and woodland views. The living room has wooden floors, lovely old oak furniture and French windows onto the rose-filled garden. Sue brims with enthusiasm and is a flexible host: breakfast can be over in her kitchen or continental in yours. Look forward to the eggs from the hens and delicious dinners with produce from the veg patch. The bedroom is a charming up-in-the-eaves room with oriental rugs, colourful linen and a big comfy bed; your fresh, simple wet room is downstairs. A peaceful, secluded place.

Rooms	Carriage for 2, shepherd's hut for 2, each with separate shower or bathroom alongside. Gypsy caravan set-up for 2-6 (2 doubles, 2 child beds).
Price	Camp for 2, £90-£95. Camp for 2-6, £115-£140.
Meals	Full breakfast hamper for 2, £32. Pubs 2 miles.
Closed	Never.

Rooms	Cottage: 1 double, sitting room & kitchenette.
Price	£130-£150.
Meals	Dinner, 2 courses, from £15; 3 courses, from £20. Pub 1 mile.
Closed	Rarely.

Sawday's Canopy & Stars
Great Farm,
Whelford, Fairford,
Gloucestershire GL7 4EA
Tel   +44 (0)1275 395447
Email   enquiries@canopyandstars.co.uk
Web   www.canopyandstars.co.uk/
          greatfarm

Sue Bathurst
The Guest House,
Manor Cottage, Bagendon,
Cirencester,
Gloucestershire GL7 7DU
Tel   +44 (0)1285 831417
Email   heritage.venues@virgin.net
Web   www.cotswoldguesthouse.co.uk

Gloucestershire

Clapton Manor

Karin and James's 16th-century manor is as all homes should be: loved and lived-in. And, with three-foot-thick walls, rich Persian rugs on flagstoned floors, sit-in fireplaces and stone-mullioned windows, it's gorgeous. The garden, enclosed by old stone walls, is full of birdsong and roses. One bedroom has a secret door leading to a fuchsia-pink bathroom; the other room, smaller, has a Tudor stone fireplace and wonderful garden views. Wellies, dogs, a comfy guest sitting room with lots of books... and breakfast by a vast fireplace: homemade bread, award-winning marmalade and eggs from the hens. A happy, charming family home.

Rooms	2: 1 double, 1 twin/double.
Price	£110-£130. Singles from £100.
Meals	Pub/restaurants within 15-minute drive.
Closed	Rarely.

Karin & James Bolton
Clapton Manor,
Clapton-on-the-Hill,
Gloucestershire GL54 2LG

Tel	+44 (0)1451 810202
Mobile	+44 (0)7967 144416
Email	bandb@claptonmanor.co.uk
Web	www.claptonmanor.co.uk

Entry 210   Map 8

Gloucestershire

Sherborne Forge

You are in a quiet Cotswolds corner, in your own restored cottage across the garden from the owner's 17th-century house, and overlooking Sherborne Brook. Walk in to a large living space with a high beamed ceiling, comfy sofas, bright rugs, antiques, flowers, books and a dining table and chairs. You have your own small kitchen for toast and tea; Karen brings over a delicious organic breakfast, served on a private terrace on sunny mornings. Your bedroom has pretty fabrics and fine linen; the bathroom has a big tub for long soaks. Fish for trout in the brook, head off for glorious walks and bike rides... this is a sanctuary.

Minimum two nights preferred.

Rooms	Cottage: 1 twin/double, sitting room & kitchenette.
Price	£100-£110. Singles £80.
Meals	Pub/restaurant 2.5 miles.
Closed	Rarely.

Karen Kelly
Sherborne Forge,
Number 1 Sherborne, Cheltenham,
Gloucestershire GL54 3DW

Tel	+44 (0)1451 844286
Mobile	+44 (0)7796 146130
Email	karen.j.kelly@btinternet.com
Web	www.sherborneforge.co.uk

Entry 211   Map 8

Gloucestershire

Rectory Farmhouse

Once a monastery, now a farmhouse with style. Passing a development of converted farm buildings to reach the Rectory's warm Cotswold stones makes the discovery doubly exciting. More glory within: Sybil, a talented designer, has created something immaculate, fresh and uplifting. A wood-burner glows in the sitting room, bed linen is white, walls cream; beds are superb, bathrooms sport cast-iron slipper baths and power showers and views are to the church. Your hosts are naturally friendly; Sybil used to own a restaurant and her breakfasts – by the Aga or in the conservatory under a rampant vine – are a further treat.

Children over 14 welcome.

Rooms	2 doubles.
Price	£98–£105. Singles £75–£85.
Meals	Pubs/restaurants 1 mile.
Closed	Christmas & New Year.

Sybil Gisby
Rectory Farmhouse,
Lower Swell, Stow-on-the-Wold,
Cheltenham,
Gloucestershire GL54 1LH

Tel	+44 (0)1451 832351
Email	rectoryfarmhouse@yahoo.com
Web	www.rectoryfarmhouse.yolasite.com

Entry 212   Map 8

Gloucestershire

The Mews

Down the cobbled mews, a beautifully presented mews house – luxury and parking in the heart of Stow. Hostess Jan has her own self-contained space so is on hand to help, and gives you breakfast in a big, light, multi-purpose living room – metallic grey kitchen units at one end, a triptych mirror at the other, and a large sofa. Up the black, grey and cream stair carpet is a super-private bedroom on the first floor: a circular mirror floating above an immaculate bed, a wall of wardrobes, a mews' view, and a fabulous state-of-the-art bathroom. Old Stow, stuffed with galleries and antique shops, is a charming, civilised Cotswolds base.

Off-street parking. Minimum two nights at weekends

Rooms	1 double.
Price	£100–£120.
Meals	Pub/restaurant within walking distance.
Closed	Rarely.

Jan Winters
The Mews,
1 Fox Lane, Digbeth Street,
Stow-on-the-Wold, Cheltenham,
Gloucestershire GL54 1BN

Mobile	+44 (0)7767 206923
Email	jan@themews-stowonthewold.com
Web	www.themews-stowonthewold.com

Entry 213   Map 8

Gloucestershire

Fieldways

High in the Wolds, close to a sleepy village green, are a secluded house and garden where life ticks over beautifully inside and out. Rosewood mahogany, heaps of flowers, a pretty gazebo and a staircase lined with art – all this is the creation of Scottish-Canadian Alan, generous to a fault, a perfectionist in all he does. Marble bathrooms have heated floors while classic country bedrooms are full of deep-carpeted comfort. An immaculate, traditional drawing room and conservatory are yours to share. Wake to the prospect of a fine cooked breakfast, homemade jams, teas from all over the world. Marvellous.

Rooms	3: 1 double, 2 twins.
Price	£85–£110. Singles £65–£75. Dogs £5.
Meals	Lunch £15–£20. Dinner from £40. Pub 50 yds.
Closed	Rarely.

Alan Graham
Fieldways,
12 Chapel Lane,
Cold Aston, Cheltenham,
Gloucestershire GL54 3BJ
Tel   +44 (0)1451 810659
Mobile   +44 (0)7790 024532
Email   cascadegroup@aol.com
Web   www.fieldways.com

Entry 214   Map 8

Gloucestershire

Aylworth Manor

Set in a peaceful Cotswolds valley and surrounded by attractive gardens, John and Joanna's gorgeous manor is immaculate. Sit beside the wood-burner in the comfy snug or play the piano in a grand drawing room, rich with art and family photos: your hosts have that happy knack of making you feel instantly at home. Large sunny bedrooms come with garden and valley views, perfect linen on seriously cushy beds, antiques and lavish bathrooms. Wake refreshed for breakfast in the dining room: homemade bread, eggs from the ducks and hens, coffee in a silver pot. The Windrush Way passes the gate at the end of the drive. What a treat!

Children over 12 welcome.

Rooms	2: 1 double; 1 twin/double with separate bath.
Price	£90–£110. Singles £60.
Meals	Pub 2.5 miles.
Closed	Rarely.

John & Joanna Ireland
Aylworth Manor,
Naunton,
Cheltenham,
Gloucestershire GL54 3AH
Tel   +44 (0)1451 850850
Mobile   +44 (0)7768 810357
Email   enquiries@aylworthmanor.co.uk
Web   www.aylworthmanor.co.uk

Entry 215   Map 8

Gloucestershire

Hanover House

The former home of Elgar's wife, in a Victorian terrace in Cheltenham's heart, is warm, elegant, inviting and surprisingly peaceful. There are big trees all around and the river Chelt laps at the foot of the garden. Inside, find a graceful period décor enlivened by exuberant splashes of colour; the delectable drawing room, with pale walls and a trio of arched windows, is the perfect foil for great art, books and rugs. Bedrooms are beautiful in vibrant red and amber; bathrooms are simply stylish. Breakfast is superb and served in the dining room window. Best of all are Veronica and James: musical, well-travelled, irresistible.

Rooms	3: 1 double, 1 twin; 1 double with separate bath.
Price	£100. Singles £70.
Meals	Pubs/restaurants 200 yds.
Closed	Rarely.

Veronica & James Ritchie
Hanover House,
65 St George's Road,
Cheltenham,
Gloucestershire GL50 3DU
Tel   +44 (0)1242 541297
Email   info@hanoverhouse.org
Web   www.hanoverhouse.org

Entry 216   Map 8

Gloucestershire

Detmore House

Down a private drive, surrounded by seven acres, this smart shiny house has been the home of poets, artists and writers. Gill carries on the creativity with her cooking, interior design, jewellery, gardening and chickens; she and Hugh are easy natural hosts. Supremely comfortable bedrooms have a smart hotel feel, bathrooms are immaculate and you and your dinner party guests will be spoiled with organic produce from the garden. There are wide lawns and mature trees and you can lap up the views across Charlton Hills from lots of lovely sitting spots. Cheltenham and the Cotswold Way are on the doorstep.

Rooms	4: 2 twins/doubles, 1 family room for 3, 1 twin.
Price	£85–£95. Family room £120–£150. Singles from £65.
Meals	Dinner from £28.50 (for groups of 6+). Packed lunch £6. Pub 1 mile.
Closed	Christmas & New Year.

Gill Kilminster
Detmore House,
London Road, Charlton Kings,
Cheltenham,
Gloucestershire GL52 6UT
Tel   +44 (0)1242 582868
Email   gillkilminster@btconnect.com
Web   www.detmorehouse.com

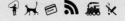

Entry 217   Map 8

Gloucestershire

The Courtyard Studio

This smart first-floor studio, attractive in reclaimed red brick, is reached via its own wrought-iron staircase; you are beautifully private. The friendly owners live next door, and will cook you a delicious breakfast in the house, or leave you a continental one in your own fridge. Find a clever, compact, contemporary space with a light and uncluttered living area, a mini window seat opposite two very comfortable boutiquey beds, fine linen, wicker armchair, and a patio area for balmy days. A 20-minute walk brings you to the centre of Cheltenham and you're a two-minute canter from the races.

Minimum two nights.

Rooms	Studio: 1 twin.
Price	£80.
Meals	Restaurants/pubs within 1 mile.
Closed	Rarely.

John & Annette Gill
The Courtyard Studio,
1 The Cleevelands Courtyard,
Cleevelands Drive, Cheltenham,
Gloucestershire GL50 4QF

Tel	+44 (0)1242 573125
Mobile	+44 (0)7901 978917
Email	courtyardstudio@aol.com

Gloucestershire

Windy Ridge House

Everyone loves Windy Ridge. It's comfortable, it's cosy, it's run by cheerful staff and it's well positioned for touring the Cotswolds. Nick's father was in construction and built this in traditional style using the finest timbers and stone; it's seen much refurbishment since then too. There's a green marble bathroom with mirrored walls, a proper four-man lift, a pine-panelled drawing room and polished things at every turn. Take a book to a velveteen sofa and help yourself from the honesty bar; visit the arboretum, the prize-winning gardens and the summer heated pool.

Rooms	4: 2 doubles; 1 double, 1 twin/double each with separate bath.
Price	£100-£110. Singles from £80.
Meals	Pub 100 yds.
Closed	Rarely.

Nick & Jennifer Williams
Windy Ridge House,
Longborough,
Moreton-in-Marsh,
Gloucestershire GL56 0QY

Tel	+44 (0)1451 830465
Email	nick@windy-ridge.co.uk
Web	www.windy-ridge.co.uk

Gloucestershire

Donnington Manor

Through the pillared entrance find a slice of English life – old-fashioned grandeur in the Cotswolds. Kat and Henry, affable and interesting, keep their own chickens, bake their own bread, and breakfasts and dinners are delicious. Bedrooms (floral drapes, sinks in the room) have high ceilings and wonderful views, bathrooms (baths not showers) are a leisurely size and the drawing room and snug are to share: cosy log fires and paintings of ancestors. In summer, the natural gardens come into their own and the views from the terrace reach for miles. Walkers rejoice: the Heart of England Way runs right by.

Rooms	2: 1 double, 1 twin each with separate bath.
Price	£100–£120. Singles £75.
Meals	Dinner, 3 courses, £25. Pub/restaurant 2 miles.
Closed	Rarely.

Katherine & Henry Dennis
Donnington Manor,
Donnington,
Moreton-in-Marsh,
Gloucestershire GL56 0YB
Tel   +44 (0)1451 830255
Mobile   +44 (0)7913 461551
Email   katdnns@gmail.com

Entry 220   Map 8

Gloucestershire

Trinity House

Meet Zelie: generous, charming, and passionate about the Cotswolds. Off a lane in dreamy Upper Oddington is a smart modern house with a crisp gravel drive and newly planted borders. Inside, a country elegance prevails. Antique furniture shines with care and polish, walls are covered with 20th-century art and splendid sofas front the fire. Bedrooms and bathrooms ooze comfort and joy: one with a private balcony, the other with its own terrace, all with village views. But don't snuggle under the goose down for too long: breakfast verges on the sinful and is locally sourced and delicious. Prepare to be thoroughly spoiled!

Rooms	2 twins/doubles.
Price	£100–£130. Singles from £60.
Meals	Pubs within walking distance.
Closed	Rarely.

Zelie Mason
Trinity House,
Upper Oddington,
Moreton-in-Marsh,
Gloucestershire GL56 0XH
Tel   +44 (0)1451 831284
Mobile   +44 (0)7809 429365
Email   info@trinityhousebandb.co.uk
Web   www.trinityhousebandb.co.uk

Entry 221   Map 8

Gloucestershire

The Old School

So comfortable and filled with understated style is this 1854 Cotswold stone house. Wendy and John are generous, beds are huge, linen is laundered, towels and robes are fluffy. Your own mini fridge is carefully hidden and pretty lamps cast a warm glow. Best of all is the upstairs sitting room: a chic, open-plan space with church style windows letting light flood in and super sofas, good art, lovely fabrics. A wood-burner keeps you toasty, Wendy is a grand cook and all is flexible. A gorgeous, relaxing place to stay – on the A44 but peaceful at night – that positively hums with hospitality. Guests say "even better than home!"

Rooms	4: 3 doubles, 1 twin/double.
Price	£120-£150. Singles from £96.
Meals	Dinner, 4 courses, £32.
	Supper, 2 courses, £18.
	Supper tray £12. Pub 0.5 miles.
Closed	Rarely.

Wendy Veale & John Scott-Lee
The Old School,
Little Compton, Moreton-in-Marsh,
Gloucestershire GL56 0SL
Tel   +44 (0)1608 674588
Mobile   +44 (0)7831 098271
Email   wendy@theoldschoolbedandbreakfast.com
Web   www.theoldschoolbedandbreakfast.com

Entry 222   Map 8

Gloucestershire

Wren House

Barely two miles from Stow-on-the-Wold, this peaceful house sits charmingly on the edge of a tiny hamlet. It was built before the English Civil War and Kiloran spent two years stylishly renovating it; the results are a joy. Downstairs, light-filled, elegant rooms with glowing rugs on pale Cotswold stone; upstairs, delicious bedrooms, spotless bathrooms and a doorway to duck. Breakfast in the vaulted kitchen is locally sourced and organic, where possible, and the well-planted garden, in which you are encouraged to sit, has far-reaching views. Explore rolling valleys and glorious gardens; Kiloran can advise.

Minimum two nights.

Rooms	3: 1 twin/double; 1 twin/double
	with separate bath & shower;
	1 twin with separate bath.
Price	£110. Singles from £85.
Meals	Pubs/restaurants 1 mile.
Closed	Rarely.

Kiloran McGrigor
Wren House,
Donnington, Stow-on-the-Wold,
Gloucestershire GL56 0XZ
Tel   +44 (0)1451 831787
Mobile   +44 (0)7802 676673
Email   enquiries@wrenhouse.net
Web   www.wrenhouse.net

Entry 223   Map 8

Gloucestershire

The Court

Just off the high street this huge honey-hued Jacobean house has been in the family since it was built in 1624 by Sir Baptist Hicks. Dogs sound the alarm when you knock… step inside to find a relaxed faded splendour. Delicate ornaments sit on exquisite antiques, family portraits and spectacular oils line the walls; up winding stairs, bedrooms (all with TVs) have comfy beds, books, a mix of beautiful and functional furniture and breathtaking views of rooftops or gardens. Jane's friendly housekeeper cooks your Aga breakfast – eggs and jams are from the garden. The walking is superb, Hidcote and Kiftsgate are close. Great value.

Rooms	3: 1 family room; 1 family room, 1 double, each with separate bath.
Price	£70-£80. Family rooms £60-£100. Singles from £50.
Meals	Pub/restaurant 30 yds.
Closed	Christmas, Easter, Whitsun bank holiday & half term.

Jane Glennie
The Court,
Calf Lane,
Chipping Campden,
Gloucestershire GL55 6JQ

Tel   +44 (0)1386 840201
Email   j14glennie@aol.com
Web   www.thecourtchippingcampden.co.uk

Entry 224   Map 8

Gloucestershire

Seymour House

A gorgeous golden house, right on the high street of one of the Cotswolds' prettiest towns. It was a hotel until your hosts returned it to a family home, with two children and a dog it is most welcoming and appealing. There's a generous walled garden that slopes upwards at the back, and a long sash-window'd drawing room at the front, elegant and inviting: magazines and open fire at one end, breakfast tables at the other. Sarah loves to cook so expect the best. Bedrooms have madly comfortable beds, rich cream towels, delicious linen, a country-house feel. Nearby there are markets and gardens galore.

Over tens welcome.

Rooms	5: 3 doubles, 2 twins/doubles.
Price	£120-£130. Singles £80.
Meals	Pubs/restaurants within walking distance.
Closed	Rarely.

Sarah Taylor
Seymour House,
High Street,
Chipping Campden,
Gloucestershire GL55 6AG

Tel   +44 (0)1386 840064
Email   sarah@seymourhousebandb.co.uk
Web   www.seymourhousebandb.co.uk

Entry 225   Map 8

Hampshire

Meadow Lodge

A summerhouse treat, tucked away beside the handsome Lodge, overlooking a pool and pretty landscaped gardens. French windows open to a terrace of tumbling wisteria, shrubs and pots. The huge bedroom is elegant and light, the bathroom luxurious; beds are well-dressed, there are books to read, rattan sofa and chairs, wide-screen TV, CDs and a lovely mix of family pieces, antiques and Liza's art. A traditional English with home-laid eggs is brought over; help yourself to cereals, patisserie, toast, coffee… and your fridge is stocked with nibbles and drinks. Amble over the trout-filled river Anton and meadows for a pub supper.

Hampshire

Yew Tree House

Philip and Janet's house is artistic and tranquil. The views, the house and the villagers are said to have inspired Dickens, who escaped London for the peace of the valley. The exquisite red brick was there 200 years before him; the rare dovecote in the next door churchyard, to which you may have the key, 300 years before that. Thoughtful hosts, interesting to talk to, have created a home of understated elegance: a yellow-ochre bedroom with top quality bed linen, cashmere/silk curtains designed by their son, enchanting garden views, flowers in every room, a welcoming log fire. Breakfast with good coffee is delicious too.

Rooms	Summerhouse: 1 double. Single room and extra beds available.
Price	£100–£200. (£140 for 3; £180 for 4; £200 for 5). Singles £85.
Meals	Dinner, 2 courses, £20. Pubs 5-minute walk.
Closed	Rarely.

Rooms	2: 1 twin; 1 double with separate bath.
Price	£85. Singles by arrangement.
Meals	Pub in village.
Closed	Rarely.

	Elizabeth Butterworth Meadow Lodge, Green Meadow Lane, Goodworth Clatford, Andover, Hampshire SP11 7HH
Tel	+44 (0)1264 352965
Mobile	+44 (0)7930 532822
Email	liza.butterworth@googlemail.com
Web	www.greenmeadowlodge.co.uk

	Philip & Janet Mutton Yew Tree House, Broughton, Stockbridge, Hampshire SO20 8AA
Tel	+44 (0)1794 301227
Email	pandjmutton@onetel.com

Entry 226   Map 3

Entry 227   Map 3

Hampshire

Lee Manor

Cross the river Test, amble down a quiet country lane, arrive at Deb and Phil's family home. Their pretty manor is elegant yet friendly and the sitting room is inviting: books, games, sofas and open fire. Lovely bedrooms have feather toppers on good beds, beautiful fabrics, a decanter of port and homemade biscuits. Expect huge breakfasts: Phil's home-roasted coffee, black pudding, waffles, kippers, eggs from the hens... delicious! There are historic houses to visit (admire the roses at Montisfont Abbey), trout fishing can be arranged and the Southampton Boat Show and New Forest are a hop.

Rooms	3: 2 doubles, 1 twin/double. Extra single available.
Price	£85–£140. Singles from £45.
Meals	Dinner, 3 courses, £25 (min 4 guests). Pubs/restaurants 2.5 miles.
Closed	Rarely.

	Deb Newman
	Lee Manor,
	Lee Lane, Lee,
	Romsey,
	Hampshire SO51 9LH
Tel	+44 (0)2380 730123
Email	leemanorbandb@gmail.com
Web	www.leemanor.co.uk

Entry 228   Map 3

Hampshire

Sandy Corner

Stride straight onto open moorland from this smallholding on the edge of the New Forest – a good place for anyone who enjoys walking, cycling, riding, wildlife and the great outdoors. And there's plenty of room for wet clothes and muddy boots. You may hear the call of a nightjar in June, Dartford warblers nest nearby, hens cluck around the yard. Sue also keeps a horse, two cats, a few sheep. You have a little guest sitting room, fresh sunny bedrooms, your own spot in the garden and a marvellous, away-from-it-all feel. You can walk to one pub; others are nearby.

Rooms	2 doubles.
Price	£78. Singles from £50.
Meals	Packed lunch £8. Pub within walking distance.
Closed	Rarely.

	Sue Browne
	Sandy Corner,
	Ogdens North,
	Fordingbridge,
	Hampshire SP6 2QD
Tel	+44 (0)1425 657295

Entry 229   Map 3

Hampshire

Vinegar Hill Pottery

A sylvan setting, stylish pottery, a young and talented family. The cobalt blues and rich browns of David's ceramics fill the old stables of a Victorian manor house. Take pottery courses (one hour to a long weekend) or just enjoy the creative Mexican-inspired décor. A narrow staircase spirals up to a modern loft: crisp whites, cathedral ceiling with sunny windows, brilliant shower. The ground-floor garden suite has a patio (with a gorgeous Showman's wagon!), sitting room, painted bed and optional children's beds. Lucy brings breakfast to your room. Stroll to the beach: stretch out and you almost touch the Isle of Wight.

Min. two nights at weekends April-Oct; 3 on bank holidays.

Rooms	3: 1 double, 1 suite for 2-4. Showman's wagon for 2 (with separate wet room) available in summer.
Price	£80. Suite £85. Wagon £80. Singles from £60.
Meals	Pub/restaurant 0.25 miles.
Closed	Rarely.

Lucy Rogers
Vinegar Hill Pottery,
Vinegar Hill,
Milford on Sea,
Hampshire SO41 0RZ

Tel	+44 (0)1590 642979
Email	info@vinegarhillpottery.co.uk
Web	www.vinegarhillpottery.co.uk

Entry 230   Map 3

Hampshire

Bay Trees

The Isle of Wight and the Needles loom large as you approach Milford on Sea: the beach is shingle, the views are amazing. Mark and Sarah have become dab hands at B&B and welcome you in to a sun-filled conservatory with Ercol elm and beech tables and chairs; the home-bakes and award-winning breakfasts are delicious. Comfortable bedrooms, with good linen, are spotless and warm; bathrooms ooze white towels. One room opens to the lush garden: magnolias, weeping willow and pond; and chickens that lay your breakfast eggs! With Mark's background in hospitality and Sarah's passion for cooking the service here is second to none.

Usually minimum two nights at weekends.

Rooms	3: 1 double, 1 family room, 1 four-poster.
Price	£90-£110. Singles £80.
Meals	Restaurants 100 yds.
Closed	Rarely.

Mark & Sarah Clayson
Bay Trees,
8 High Street,
Milford on Sea, Lymington,
Hampshire SO41 0QD

Tel	+44 (0)1590 642186
Email	mark.clayson@btinternet.com
Web	www.baytreebedandbreakfast.co.uk

Entry 231   Map 3

Hampshire

Home Close

The setting is gorgeous, surrounded by the New Forest – walks start from the gate. The house, once a farm belonging to the Beaulieu estate, is now home to friendly Sally and Bob. You sleep in a sunshine-yellow bedroom overlooking the lovely garden, there are Lloyd Loom chairs for reading or TV, bottled water, proper milk, homemade shortbread. A generous breakfast, sometimes with home-baked bread, is taken in the pretty blue dining room at a solid oak table, from where you can watch the comings and goings of interesting birds beneath the arbour. Perfect for exploring the New Forest or a day trip to the Isle of Wight.

Rooms	1 double.
Price	£80–£90.
Meals	Packed lunch £7. Pubs/restaurants within 7 miles.
Closed	Christmas, New Year & occasionally.

Sally Brearley
Home Close,
Hill Top,
Beaulieu,
Hampshire SO42 7YR
Tel   +44 (0)1590 612287
Email   homeclose@talktalk.net
Web   www.homeclosebedandbreakfast.co.uk

Entry 232   Map 3

Hampshire

Brymer House

Complete privacy in a B&B is rare. Here you have it, just a 12-minute walk from town, cathedral and water meadows. Relax in your own half of a Victorian townhouse immaculately furnished and decorated, and with a garden to match – all roses and lilac in the spring. Breakfasts are sumptuous, there's a log fire in the guests' sitting room and fresh flowers abound. An 'honesty box' means you may help yourselves to drinks. Bedrooms are small and elegant, with antique mirrors, furniture and bedspreads; bathrooms are warm and spotless. Guy and Fizzy have charmed Special Places guests for many years.

Children over seven welcome.

Rooms	2: 1 double, 1 twin.
Price	£75–£85. Singles £55–£65.
Meals	Pubs/restaurants nearby.
Closed	Rarely.

Guy & Fizzy Warren
Brymer House,
29-30 St Faith's Road,
St Cross, Winchester,
Hampshire SO23 9QD
Tel   +44 (0)1962 867428
Email   brymerhouse@aol.com
Web   www.brymerhouse.co.uk

Entry 233   Map 4

Hampshire

Weston Farm

Country life at its loveliest: a beautifully restored Georgian house and farm; fresh-laid eggs; a donkey and pony in the paddock, and generous, helpful hosts who will fetch you off the London train. Horse and hound wallpaper gallops over the hall, the sitting room has wood panelling, sash windows and a giant marble fireplace; comfortable bedrooms have writing desks, pretty curtains and white linen. A footpath traces the 800-acre arable farm so roam free over water meadows. Stroll to the typical Hampshire village of Micheldever (thatched cottages, handsome church) for dinner – or it's eight miles to historic Winchester.

Hampshire

Browninghill Farm

Complete independence here: your own prettily converted threshing barn down an oak-lined lane. Hattie lives in the farm next door and looks after you well; breakfasts and dinners are rustled up for you in your little kitchen – eggs from the hens, homemade bread and jams and local produce. The attractive dining/sitting space has a soaring ceiling, beams, a duck egg blue dresser holding cheerful crockery and a picture window with views across the fields. Bedrooms (one up, one down) are cosy with comfy feather pillows and white linen; bathrooms are small yet perfect with robes and big towels. Snug and romantic.

Minimum two nights.

Rooms	2: 1 twin/double, 1 four-poster.
Price	£80. Singles £50.
Meals	Pub 1.5 miles.
Closed	Christmas.

Rooms	Barn: 1 double, 1 single.
Price	£110. Singles £50-£75.
Meals	Supper, 2 courses, £25.
	Pubs/restaurants 0.5 miles.
Closed	Rarely.

	Laura Stevens
	Weston Farm,
	Weston Down Lane,
	Weston Colley, Winchester,
	Hampshire SO21 3AG
Tel	+44 (0)1962 774791
Mobile	+44 (0)7999 816417
Email	westonfarmbandb@googlemail.com
Web	www.westonfarmaccommodation.co.uk

	Hattie Pigot
	Browninghill Farm,
	Browninghill Green,
	Baughurst, Tadley,
	Hampshire RG26 5JZ
Tel	+44 (0)1189 815537
Mobile	+44 (0)7789 431220
Email	hattie@browninghillfarm.com
Web	www.browninghillfarm.com

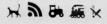

Entry 234   Map 4

Entry 235   Map 4

Hampshire

Little Cottage

Just 45 minutes from Heathrow but the peace is deep, the views are long and the wildlife thrives — watch fox and deer, listen out for the rare nightjar. Chris and Therese grow summer salads and soft fruits and give you superb home cooking; eat in a big conservatory filled with greenery. Guests have a lovely sitting room with an eclectic mix of modern and antique furniture, and a pretty terrace overlooks the garden; bedrooms, likewise, are on the ground-floor, fresh and light, the double with distant views. Perfect for walkers and those who seek solace from urban life but don't want to stray too far.

Minimum two nights at weekends. Over 12s welcome.

Rooms	3: 1 double, 1 twin/double, 1 single.
Price	£80–£95. Singles £55.
Meals	Dinner from £20. Pub 1.5 miles.
Closed	Christmas, New Year & occasionally.

Chris & Therese Abbott
Little Cottage,
Hazeley Heath,
Hartley Wintney, Hook,
Hampshire RG27 8LY

Tel	+44 (0)1252 845050
Mobile	+44 (0)7721 462214
Email	info@little-cottage.co.uk
Web	www.little-cottage.co.uk

Entry 236   Map 4

Hampshire

Mulberry House

Deep in Jane Austen country, among apple trees and rose bushes, is Mulberry House — the red-brick stable block of Old Alresford House. Peter and Sue are charming and relaxed, and so is their home, filled with interesting pictures, fresh flowers and family photos. Private, quietly elegant guest rooms share a sitting room and kitchenette; the one in the eaves overlooks a pretty courtyard where a fountain plays. In fine weather you breakfast beneath the wisteria and vine-hung pergola on home-laid eggs and homemade jams. Comfortably English with a rich and lovely garden framed by ancient beech trees.

Rooms	2: 1 double, 1 twin/double.
Price	£90. Singles £65.
Meals	Pubs/restaurants within 15-minute walk.
Closed	Rarely.

Sue & Peter Paice
Mulberry House,
Colden Lane, Old Alresford,
Alresford,
Hampshire SO24 9DY

Tel	+44 (0)1962 735518
Mobile	+44 (0)7801 931905
Email	suepaice@btinternet.com
Web	www.mulberryhousebnb.com

Entry 237   Map 4

Hampshire

Marne Cottage

This Victorian cottage has bay trees at the porch, cottage garden borders and a brimming Peter Rabbit vegetable patch. Julia's warm welcome includes tea and cakes – served in the cosy drawing room or out in the colourful garden. Find eclectic art, pretty furniture, country chintz; Alfie the dog adds to the friendly feel. Beautifully decorated bedrooms have white cotton, colourful throws and waffle robes. A locally sourced full English breakfast, lighter continental choices or 'Mrs Morgan's Omelettata' set you up for coastal jaunts, gardens, Jane Austen's house... if you're off to the opera you can order a hamper.

Rooms	3: 1 double; 1 double with separate bath; 1 single (sharing either bathroom).
Price	£100. Singles £55-£75.
Meals	Pub 300 yds.
Closed	Rarely.

Julia Morgan
Marne Cottage,
Kilmeston Road, Kilmeston,
Alresford,
Hampshire SO24 0NJ
Tel   +44 (0)1962 771418
Email   info@marnecottagebandb.co.uk
Web   www.marnecottagebandb.co.uk

Entry 238   Map 4

Hampshire

The Threshing Barn

You are on the edge of the rolling Meon valley in South Downs National Park, the approach through hedge-lined lanes is bucolic and the beautifully restored barn sits on a conservation award-winning farm run by John. You have quiet independence in the glorious bothy – a beamed and light space with a big walk-in shower. Find flowers, a comfortable bed and feather and down pillows. Guests are greeted with tea, breakfast is a local or home-grown extravaganza (check out Emma's borage honey) and views are to one of the tallest village church spires in Hampshire.

Minimum two nights.

Rooms	Bothy: 1 twin/double.
Price	£100. Singles £85.
Meals	Packed lunch £7-£8. Pub 2 miles.
Closed	Rarely.

Emma Bird
The Threshing Barn,
Stocks Lane, Privett,
Hampshire GU34 3NZ
Tel   +44 (0)1730 828382
Mobile   +44 (0)7980 841154
Email   emmacbird@stocksfarmprivett.co.uk
Web   www.thethreshingbarn.co.uk

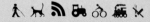

Entry 239   Map 4

Hampshire

Hampshire

Shafts Farm

The 1960s farmhouse has many weapons in its armoury: a tremendous South Downs thatched-village setting, owners who know every path and trail, comfortable, generous bedrooms and a stunning rose garden designed by David Austin Roses (parterres, obelisks, meandering paths). The two bedrooms are fresh in cream, florals and plaids, each with a shower room with heated floors to keep toes toasty. Homemade granola, garden fruit and the full English make a fine start to the day; the airy, cane-furnished conservatory is the place for afternoon tea and a read. Your hosts are both geographers and have an intriguing display of maps.

Mizzards Farm

The central hall is three storeys high, its vaulted roof open to the rafters. This is the oldest part of this lovely, wisteria-clad, mostly 16th-century farmhouse: kilims and fine antiques look splendid against old flagstones and wooden floors. There's a drawing room for musical evenings and an upstairs conservatory from which you can see the garden with its lake, outdoor chess and Harriet's sculptures. The four-poster is luxuriously kitsch with electric curtains, the other bedrooms are traditional and fresh. Take care on the long driveway – the weather has taken its toll!

Children over eight welcome. Min. two nights.

Rooms	2 twins.
Price	£80. Singles £50.
Meals	Dinner, 3 courses, £17. Pubs/restaurants 500 yds.
Closed	Rarely.

Rooms	3: 1 double, 1 twin, 1 four-poster.
Price	£82–£92. Singles by arrangement.
Meals	Pubs 0.5 miles.
Closed	Christmas & New Year.

	Rosemary Morrish
	Shafts Farm,
	West Meon,
	Petersfield,
	Hampshire GU32 1LU
Tel	+44 (0)1730 829266
Email	info@shaftsfarm.co.uk
Web	www.shaftsfarm.co.uk

	Harriet & Julian Francis
	Mizzards Farm,
	Rogate,
	Petersfield,
	Hampshire GU31 5HS
Tel	+44 (0)1730 821656
Email	francis@mizzards.co.uk

Hampshire

Herefordshire

Wriggly Tin Shepherd's Huts

Butser and Beacon are very fine huts that Alex has hand-wrought himself, indulging his passion for all things vintage and mechanical. He has kept the theme of restoration alive right throughout, with the kitchenware and furnishings scoured locally and contributing to the feel of another age (the 1940s maybe!). The huts are off-grid but the wood-burner (with oven) keeps you cosy whatever the weather and hurricane lamps cast an atmospheric glow. Storage space is under super comfy beds, leaving you space to relax in; showers and loo, shared between the two, are housed in an even more ingenious conversion.

Minimum two nights. Book through Sawday's Canopy & Stars online or by phone.

Grendon Manor

The best of traditional meets modern country living: this 16th-century manor house is a super mix of the very old and very new. A working sheep and cattle farm is wrapped around it and you can walk over fields and down to a pretty Norman church. Jane is easy company and looks after you well. Guests in their own wing will rejoice in bedrooms with old beams, crisply comfortable linen and new bathrooms, while the guest sitting room downstairs has marvellous dark oak panelling, rich colours and glowing lamps. A farmhouse-tasty breakfast sets you up for beautiful Herefordshire walks, and Ludlow is close.

Rooms	Shepherd's hut for 2, shepherd's hut for 3, sharing 2 showers & compost loos.	Rooms	3: 2 doubles, 1 twin.
Price	£75-£107.	Price	£100. Singles £50.
Meals	Breakfast basket for 2, £20. Supper, £8.50pp. Pubs within 2 miles.	Meals	Dinner £25 (groups only). Pub/restaurant 2 miles.
Closed	November-March.	Closed	Rarely.

	Sawday's Canopy & Stars		Jane Piggott
	Wriggly Tin Shepherd's Huts,		Grendon Manor,
	Brook Lane, Hambledon,		Bredenbury, Bromyard,
	Hampshire PO7 4TF		Herefordshire HR7 4TH
Tel	+44 (0)1275 395447	Tel	+44 (0)1885 482226
Email	enquiries@canopyandstars.co.uk	Mobile	+44 (0)7977 493083
Web	www.canopyandstars.co.uk/	Email	jane.piggott@btconnect.com
	wrigglytin	Web	www.grendonmanor.com

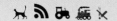

Herefordshire

Bunns Croft

The timbers of this medieval yeoman's house are quite possibly a thousand years old. Little of the structure has ever been altered: it's an absolute delight. Stone floors, rich colours, a piano, dogs, books, cosy chairs – all give a homely, warm feel. Cruck-beamed bedrooms are snugly small, the stairs are steep, and the twin's bathroom has its own sweet fireplace. The countryside is 'pure', too, with 1,500 acres of National Trust land a short drive away. Anita is charming, loves to look after her guests, grows her own fruit and vegetables and makes fabulous dinners. Just mind your head.

Rooms	4: 1 twin; 1 double, 2 singles, sharing bath (let to same party only).
Price	£80-£85. Singles from £40.
Meals	Dinner, 3 courses, £25. Pub 7 miles.
Closed	Rarely.

Anita Syers-Gibson
Bunns Croft,
Moreton Eye,
Leominster,
Herefordshire HR6 0DP
Tel   +44 (0)1568 615836

Entry 244   Map 7

Herefordshire

Staunton House

This handsome Georgian rectory with light, colourful and well-proportioned rooms brims with beautiful furnishings. The original oak staircase leads to peaceful bedrooms with comfortable beds; the blue room looks onto garden and pond. It's a house that matches its owners – quiet, traditional and country-loving. Wander through the lovely garden, drive to Hay or Ludlow, stride some ravishing countryside, play golf near Offa's Dyke; return to Rosie and Richard's lovely home to relax in their drawing room before enjoying a delicious dinner in the elegant dining room. You will be well tended here.

Rooms	2: 1 double, 1 twin/double.
Price	£85-£95. Singles from £55.
Meals	Dinner, 3 courses, £25. Pub/restaurant 2.5 miles.
Closed	Rarely.

Rosie & Richard Bowen
Staunton House,
Staunton-on-Arrow, Pembridge,
Leominster,
Herefordshire HR6 9HR
Tel   +44 (0)1544 388313
Mobile   +44 (0)7780 961994
Email   rosbown@aol.com
Web   www.stauntonhouse.co.uk

Entry 245   Map 7

Herefordshire

Hall's Mill House

Quiet lanes bring you to this most idyllic spot – a stone cottage in a light and open valley. The sitting room is snug with wood-burner and sofas but the kitchen is the hub of the place – delicious breakfasts and dinners are cooked on the Aga. Grace, chatty and easy-going, obviously enjoys living in her modernised mill house. Rooms are small, fresh, with exposed beams and slate sills; only the old mill interrupts the far-reaching, all-green views. Drift off to sleep to the sound of the Arrow burbling by – a blissful tonic for walkers and nature lovers. Great value, too.

Children over four welcome.

Rooms	3: 1 double; 1 double, 1 twin, sharing bath.
Price	£60-£65. Singles £27.50-£32.50.
Meals	Dinner from £15. Pub/restaurant 3 miles.
Closed	Christmas.

Grace Watson
Hall's Mill House,
Huntington,
Kington,
Herefordshire HR5 3QA
Tel   +44 (0)1497 831409
Email   hallsmillhouse@hotmail.co.uk

Entry 246   Map 7

Herefordshire

Tinto House

Bang in the centre of Hay-on-Wye, opposite the clock tower, amid a sea of bookshops, this beautiful Georgian townhouse brims with period features and original art. John and Karen have decorated their home with love: in the dining room, John's eye-catching paintings set off oak antiques, bookshelves, a fireplace; bedrooms bear mementos of France; one room holds art exhibitions. The garden, on the Wye's banks, is resplendent with roses and sculptures. Breakfast on local sausages and compotes from home-grown fruit before hitting the Black Mountains or Hay's independent shops. Perfect for lovers of outdoor and armchair pursuits.

Rooms	4: 2 doubles, 1 twin; 1 double with separate bath.
Price	£85-£95.Singles £60-£80.
Meals	Packed lunch £6.50. Pub/restaurant 100 yds.
Closed	Christmas & New Year.

Karen Clare
Tinto House,
13 Broad Street, Hay-on-Wye,
Herefordshire HR3 5DB
Tel   +44 (0)1497 821556
Mobile   +44 (0)7985 559355
Email   tintohouse13@gmail.com
Web   www.tinto-house.co.uk

Entry 247   Map 7

Herefordshire

Lower House

A luxuriant garden in a magical valley; strike out for the Black Mountains from the door. The house, itself a forest of old timber, is almost lost within the garden. It is old, but restored with affection. Stairs twist and creak, the unexpected awaits you. Irresistible bedrooms are panelled or timber-clad; bathrooms are fresh. There's a handsome room downstairs where you eat breakfast (plentiful, delicious), play the piano or read by the fire. Nicky and Pete are kind and generous and offer an exquisite self-catering retreat in the garden too. You're next to Offa's Dyke path and on the Welsh border. One of the best!

Minimum two nights. Children over ten welcome. Parking available.

Rooms	2: 1 double; 1 double with separate bath/shower.
Price	£95-£100. Singles £90.
Meals	Pubs/restaurants in Hay-on-Wye, 1 mile.
Closed	Rarely.

Nicky & Peter Daw
Lower House,
Cusop Dingle, Hay-on-Wye,
Herefordshire HR3 5RQ

Tel	+44 (0)1497 820773
Mobile	+44 (0)7779 480783
Email	nicky.daw@btinternet.com
Web	www.lowerhousegardenhay.co.uk

Entry 248   Map 7

Herefordshire

Ty-Mynydd

Six miles over open heathland from Hay-on-Wye, and up the mountainside to this remote, renovated, stone-flagged farmhouse. Sheep graze the hillside, the views are simply the best. Relax by the log-burner on leather sofas wrapped in a cosy Welsh blanket. Turn on the taps and taste water straight from your hosts' own mountain stream. Awake to delicious rare-breed sausages and eggs produced in the fields around you (this is a working organic farm). The lovely young family give you two sweetly restful rooms on the ground floor, one with 'that view', and a simple country bathroom complete with roll top bath. The sunsets are magical.

Minimum two nights at weekends.

Rooms	2 doubles sharing bath (let to same party only).
Price	£90. Singles £60.
Meals	Pubs 6-8 miles.
Closed	Christmas & New Year.

Niki Spenceley
Ty-Mynydd,
Llanigon, Hay-on-Wye,
Herefordshire HR3 5RJ

Tel	+44 (0)1497 821593
Mobile	+44 (0)7896 020459
Email	nikispenceley@gmail.com
Web	www.tymynydd.co.uk

Entry 249   Map 7

The Fresh Spring Yurt

The yurt is almost an extension of owner Daphne herself, as is everything at the New Inn Brilley, a former pub. It radiates charm, peace and happiness, from the hand-made double bunk to the converted Cow Shed kitchen/dining room. A short trek up the hill are two hot showers (please use sparingly!) and loos. Guinea fowl, hens – Araucana and feathery legged Pekins – roam the grounds along with the occasional flock of sheep. The yurt sleeps six at a pinch, with a raised double, two folding-chair beds and an extra double futon, and you can choose to join the B&B guests for breakfast. Perfect for a rest and a spiritual tune-up.

Minimum two nights. Book through Sawday's Canopy & Stars online or by phone.

Yew Tree House

Sue and John's gorgeous 19th-century home is surrounded by gardens bejewelled with roses and fruit trees – plus stunning views across the Golden Valley to Hay Bluff. Meet these delightful people over tea and homemade cake in a tastefully decorated guest sitting room with comfy sofas, an open fire and shelves groaning with books. Generous bedrooms in pretty pastels are supremely comfortable, bathrooms have plenty of fluffy towels. Wake to the smell of baking bread, hasten to the dining room for a delicious breakfast of local produce. Dore Abbey's down the road, and Hay-on-Wye a half-hour jaunt. The countryside is glorious.

Rooms	Yurt for 2-6 with shower & wc close by.		Rooms	3: 1 double, 1 twin, 1 suite.
Price	£70-£90.		Price	£80-£95.
Meals	Continental breakfast, £4. Dinner, 2 courses, £12.50. Pub 4 miles.		Meals	Dinner, 3 courses, £25. Pub/restaurant 3.5 miles.
Closed	Rarely.		Closed	Rarely.

	Sawday's Canopy & Stars		John & Susan Richardson
	The Fresh Spring Yurt,		Yew Tree House,
	Brilley, Whitney-on-Wye,		Batcho Hill,
	Hereford,		Vowchurch,
	Herefordshire HR3 6HE		Hereford,
			Herefordshire HR2 9PF
Tel	+44 (0)1275 395447	Tel	+44 (0)1981 251195
Email	enquiries@canopyandstars.co.uk	Email	enquiries@yewtreehouse-hereford.co.uk
Web	www.canopyandstars.co.uk/ freshspringyurt	Web	www.yewtreehouse-hereford.co.uk

Entry 250 Map 7

Entry 251 Map 7

Herefordshire

Rock Cottage

Birds, books and beautiful Black Mountain views highlighted by morning sun, turning to an inky black line at dusk; the cottage glows. There's an instant feeling of warmth and friendliness as you step into the snug hall; find rich autumnal colours, old rugs, a big wood-burner and comfy sitting rooms. Local art and photos line the walls, bedrooms have sumptuous beds, perfect linen and garden posies. You eat (very well) at the communal oak table, or out on the pretty terrace. Thoughtful Chris and Sue will take you to hear the dawn chorus and there are food and literary festivals, bookshops and walks galore.

Dogs by arrangement.

Rooms	2 doubles.
Price	£70–£90. Singles £60–£75.
Meals	Packed lunch £6. Dinner, 3 courses, £20. Pub/restaurant 4 miles.
Closed	Christmas & New Year.

Chris & Sue Robinson
Rock Cottage,
Newton St Margarets,
Hereford,
Herefordshire HR2 0QW
Tel   +44 (0)1981 510360
Email   robinsrockcottage@googlemail.com
Web   www.rockcottagebandb.co.uk

Entry 252   Map 7

Herefordshire

Burghill Grange

A big, happy, friendly family house. Harriet and John are marvellous hosts and their home – all waxed elm floors, beams and fine 18th-century ceilings – is a delight. Your cosy bright sitting room has a fire, bold fabrics and interesting books; enjoy home-laid eggs, fresh bread, delicious coffee and sausages from Ludlow, as you gaze over the peaceful garden and pond. A first-floor double is calm and uncluttered, the others beamed and large with great views to church tower and orchards; smart bathrooms have chunky roll tops, big towels, oodles of hot water and organic bubbles. Handy for Hay, golf, antiques and the Brecon Beacons.

Rooms	3: 1 double; 1 twin/double with separate shower; 1 twin with separate bath.
Price	£110. Singles from £60.
Meals	Occasional dinner £20. Pubs/restaurants 1–4 miles.
Closed	Rarely.

Harriet Gordon
Burghill Grange,
Burghill, Hereford,
Herefordshire HR4 7SE
Tel   +44 (0)1432 761016
Mobile   +44 (0)7525 215414
Email   enquiries@burghillgrange.com
Web   www.burghillgrange.com

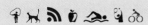

Entry 253   Map 7

Herefordshire

Garnstone House

Come for peace and quiet in the Welsh Marches, good food and lovely, humorous, down-to-earth hosts. The atmosphere is easy, and the furniture a lifetime's accumulation of eclectic pieces and pictures of horses, hounds and country scenes. After dinner and good conversation, climb the picture-lined stairs to a comfortable, pretty bedroom in soft colours – either a twin or a double – and a bathroom that is properly old-fashioned. Delicious breakfasts (homemade jams and eggs from the hens), tasty dinners and a stunning garden to explore – the variety and colour of the springtime flowers are astonishing and the clematis is a glory.

Herefordshire

Ladywell House

Wrapped by ancient oaks and a deep peacefulness, a wonderful place to relax in the Golden Valley. Charles and Sarah are generous hosts; their Edwardian dower house is welcoming and informal and glows with colour, family paintings and antiques. Luxurious bedrooms have handsome fabrics, garden views, flat-screen TVs and smart immaculate bathrooms. A superb, local or organic breakfast with homemade bread is served in the conservatory; enjoy afternoon tea and cakes, or drinks, in the garden's Breeze House on summer days, or by the open fire in winter. Walk from the door, explore the Black Mountains, browse in bustling Hay-on-Wye.

Rooms	2: 1 double, 1 twin, sharing bathroom (let to same party only).
Price	£90-£100. Singles from £50.
Meals	Dinner from £25. Pub/restaurant 1 mile.
Closed	Rarely.

Rooms	2: 1 four-poster; 1 twin with separate bath.
Price	£65-£90. Singles from £65.
Meals	Dinner on request, £25. Bistro 5-minute drive. Pub 10-minute drive.
Closed	Occasionally.

Dawn & Michael MacLeod
Garnstone House,
Weobley,
Herefordshire HR4 8QP
Tel   +44 (0)1544 318943
Email   macleod@garnstonehouse.co.uk
Web   www.garnstonehouse.co.uk

Charles & Sarah Drury
Ladywell House,
Turnastone, Vowchurch,
Herefordshire HR2 0RE
Tel   +44 (0)1981 550235
Mobile +44 (0)7970 510110
Email   sarah@ladywellhouse.com
Web   www.ladywellhouse.com

Entry 254   Map 7

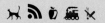

Entry 255   Map 7

Herefordshire

Granton House

Climbing roses, the hum of bees, frogs splashing in the pond... the walled garden of Liz and John's 17th-century village home is as bountiful as it is beautiful. Liz picks fruit for muesli and preserves which combine with John's home-baked bread, Gloucester Old Spot sausages and local honey for breakfast. Rooms are soothingly elegant with beams, fireplaces and stained-glass windows; the garden bedroom is a sun-filled joy with dazzling views of Coppet Hill. Venture forth to local glories like Symonds Yat, the Forest of Dean and the Brecon Beacons; return to relax in the garden or by an open fire in chilly months.

Minimum stay two nights at weekends & bank holidays.

Rooms	3: 2 doubles, 1 triple.
Price	£95-£110. Singles £70.
Meals	Pubs/restaurants within 1 mile.
Closed	Christmas & New Year.

Liz & John Bloxham
Granton House,
Goodrich,
Ross-on-Wye,
Herefordshire HR9 6JE

Tel	+44 (0)1600 890277
Email	granton@stayonwye.com
Web	www.stayonwye.com

Entry 256   Map 7

Herefordshire

Caradoc Court

Down the long drive, past the grand pillars and the Wellingtonia pines, to a lovely Jacobean manor, former seat of the Viscounts Scudamore. In 2009 the Handbys arrived, created four uncluttered, soft-carpeted bedrooms for guests and are mindfully making their mark on the place. Be wowed by impressive fireplaces and mullioned windows, massive oak roof trusses and polished sleigh beds, billiard room, ballroom and 12 wooded, landscaped acres, high on a bluff overlooking the Wye. The vistas are superb, the peace is restorative, the breakfasts are exemplary and there's a civilised pub at the end of the drive.

Rooms	4: 3 doubles, 1 twin.
Price	£90-£120. Singles £75-£90.
Meals	Pub 500 yds.
Closed	November-February.

Kathy Handby
Caradoc Court,
Sellack,
Ross-on-Wye,
Herefordshire HR9 6LS

Tel	+44 (0)1989 730257
Email	kathy@caradoccourt.co.uk
Web	www.caradoccourt.co.uk

Entry 257   Map 7

Herefordshire

The Coach House

Pots of flowers by the front door and Farne the friendly terrier greet you. Iola and Michael are warm, friendly, and give you a continental breakfast of homemade breads and preserves, eggs from Michael's hens, croissants from the local bakery. Their house is airy and pleasing with comfy sofas and an open fire in the sitting room, a huge dining room overlooking farmland and an inviting bedroom with painted beams, good linen and a bookcase full of novels. Sit in the garden and admire the glorious views to the south; head off for Ross-on-Wye, Ledbury, the music festival in Malvern, Cheltenham races and Wye valley walks.

Rooms	1 double.
Price	£80. Singles £50.
Meals	Continental breakfast.
	Pubs/restaurants 1 mile.
Closed	Rarely.

	Iola & Michael Fass
	The Coach House,
	Old Gore,
	Ross-on-Wye,
	Herefordshire HR9 7QT
Tel	+44 (0)1989 780339
Email	iolafass@btinternet.com
Web	www.thecoachhousebandb.com

Entry 258   Map 7

Hertfordshire

Number One

It's worth hopping out of bed for Annie's breakfast: luxury continental with raspberry brioche or the full delicious Monty. Her house is a sparkling Aladdin's cave of mirrors, bunches of white twigs with birds atop, candles, cherubs, painted wooden floors, big open fires and generous bunches of roses. Bedrooms are lavishly done; nifty bathrooms have Italian tiles – and more roses! Close to the centre, this good-looking Georgian terrace house featured in Pevsner's guide to Hertfordshire, and the market town is busy with theatre, shops and galleries. Return for a gourmet dinner in the magical courtyard garden – when the sun is shining!

Rooms	3: 2 twins/doubles; 1 double with
	separate bath/shower.
Price	£95-£130.
Meals	Dinner £25. BYO.
	Pubs/restaurants 5-minute walk.
Closed	Rarely.

	Annie Rowley
	Number One,
	1 Port Hill, Hertford,
	Hertfordshire SG14 1PJ
Tel	+44 (0)1992 587350
Mobile	+44 (0)7770 914070
Email	annie@numberoneporthill.co.uk
Web	www.numberoneporthill.co.uk

Entry 259   Map 9

Isle of Wight

Northcourt

A Jacobean manor in matchless grounds: 15 acres of terraced gardens, exotica and subtropical flowers. The house is magnificent too; huge but a lived-in home, its big comfortable bedrooms wait in two wings. The formal dining room has separate tables, where delicious homemade bread and jams, garden fruit, honey and local produce are served. There's a snooker table in the library, a chamber organ in the hall and a grand piano in the vast music room. Groups are welcome and John offers garden tours. The peaceful village is in lovely downland – and you can walk from the garden to the Needles.

Rooms	6 twins/doubles.
Price	£70-£105. Singles £47.50-£67.50
Meals	Pub 3-minute walk through the gardens.
Closed	Rarely.

John & Christine Harrison
Northcourt,
Shorwell,
Isle of Wight PO30 3JG

Tel	+44 (0)1983 740415
Mobile	+44 (0)7955 174699
Email	christine@northcourt.info
Web	www.northcourt.info

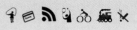

Entry 260   Map 4

Isle of Wight

Gotten Manor

Miles from the beaten track and bordered by old stone barns, the guest wing of this Saxon house is charmingly simple. Up steep stone steps (you must be nimble!) and through a low doorway find big bedrooms in laid-back rustic, funky French style: beams, limewashed stone, wooden floors, Persian rugs and a sweet window. Sleep on a rosewood bed and bathe by candlelight – in a roll top tub in your room. Friendly, informal Caroline serves breakfast in the old creamery: homemade yogurts, compotes and organic produce. There's a walled garden and a guest living room with cosy wood-burner.

Minimum two nights at weekends. Over 12s welcome.

Rooms	2 doubles.
Price	£85-£100. Singles by arrangement.
Meals	Pub 1.5 miles.
Closed	Rarely.

Caroline Gurney-Champion
Gotten Manor,
Gotten Lane, Chale,
Isle of Wight PO38 2HQ

Tel	+44 (0)1983 551368
Mobile	+44 (0)7746 453398
Email	as@gottenmanor.co.uk
Web	www.gottenmanor.co.uk

Entry 261   Map 4

Isle of Wight

Redway Farm

Immerse yourself in the rolling landscape of the sunny Arreton Valley... up a winding lane find a handsome, south-facing Georgian farmhouse and friendly Linda. Bedrooms are quiet, large, light and sumptuous with thick mattresses, gorgeous linen and lovely views over the gardens; warm bathrooms sparkle. Downstairs is delightful with antiques, roaring fires and fresh flowers. You breakfast on fresh croissants from the Aga – or the full works with eggs from the hens, in the sun-filled morning room or the dining room with wood-burner. Explore acres of garden with birdsong, cycle to sandy beaches. Bliss.

Rooms	2 doubles, each with separate bath.
Price	£89-£99. Singles £69-£79.
Meals	Pub 3 miles.
Closed	Rarely.

	Linda James
	Redway Farm,
	Budbridge Lane, Merstone,
	Newport,
	Isle of Wight PO30 3DJ
Tel	+44 (0)1983 865228
Mobile	+44 (0)7775 480830
Email	lindajames.redway@gmail.com
Web	www.bedbreakfast.redwayfarm.co.uk

Entry 262   Map 4

Isle of Wight

Lisle Combe

How many gardens sport tall palms, miniature donkeys and lawns that slope down to woods, fields and beach – with Botanic Gardens next door? The grounds are huge, the position is uplifting and upper rooms have views of the sea. Author Alfred Noyes lived here in the 1930s and the feel is timeless; today grandson Robert, wife Ruth and their young family, run gentle, charming, traditional B&B. After a day exploring Ventnor and all the coves and beaches, return to carpeted corridors, faded satin sofas, delightful gilt-framed oils and old-fashioned tranquillity. Bedrooms are homely, lofty, with floral cotton bedspreads.

Minimum two nights July & August.

Rooms	3: 1 double; 1 double, 1 triple, each with separate bath/shower.
Price	£75-£100. Child £25.
Meals	Pubs/restaurants 2 miles.
Closed	December-February.

	Robert & Ruth Noyes
	Lisle Combe,
	Undercliff Drive,
	St Lawrence,
	Ventnor,
	Isle of Wight PO38 1UW
Tel	+44 (0)1983 852582
Email	enquiries@lislecombe.co.uk
Web	www.lislecombe.co.uk

Entry 263   Map 4

Isle of Wight

Kent

Priory Bay Yurts

Listen to the sound of the surf from the decked terrace of these glorious yurts. They sit in the grounds of the Priory Bay Hotel and its two fabulous restaurants; you'll eat well here. Artfully but softly decorated with a lovely fresh feel, the yurts come with sofas and big double beds, elegant claw-foot tubs and flushing loos, and a view of woodland or sea. Out on the deck, through French doors, the private beach waits invitingly below. You have full use of the hotel pool and tennis courts, you can stroll the coastal paths and – for a special occasion – charter the hotel yacht and cruise the bay.

Minimum two nights at weekends. Book through Sawday's Canopy & Stars online or by phone.

Snoadhill Cottage

You'll feel at home the moment you arrive at Yvette and Philip's friendly cottage. Once a medieval 'hall house', it's awash with huge oak beams. Up steep stairs and past shelves of books find fresh, sunny bedrooms with lovely views. Enjoy a flagstone terrace for summery breakfasts or a fireside spot in the dining room; expect eggs from the hens, homemade jams, kippers perhaps or a full English. You're surrounded by glorious open countryside, walks and cycle rides start from the door and it's just 25 minutes from the Channel Tunnel. Dip in the swimming pond, chat to Rocky the labrador… and the gardens are blooming.

Rooms	3 yurts for 2.		Rooms	2: 1 double with separate shower, 1 twin with separate bath.
Price	£200-£250. Child £40.		Price	£80-£85. Singles £65.
Meals	Breakfast, at hotel, included. Lunch £22.50. Dinner, 3 courses, £35.		Meals	Pub 1 mile.
Closed	Never.		Closed	Rarely.

	Sawday's Canopy & Stars Priory Bay Yurts, Priory Bay Hotel, Priory Road, Seaview, Isle of Wight PO34 5BU	
Tel	+44 (0)1275 395447	
Email	enquiries@canopyandstars.co.uk	
Web	www.canopyandstars.co.uk/ priorybay	

	Yvette James Snoadhill Cottage, Snoadhill, Bethersden, Ashford, Kent TN26 3DY
Tel	+44 (0)1233 822377
Email	enquiries@snoadhillcottage.co.uk
Web	www.snoadhillcottage.co.uk

Entry 264   Map 4

Entry 265   Map 5

Gabriel & Bathsheba

Escape London and be here in an hour, and in the morning you will be breakfasting on the veranda overlooking a field of llamas! Tempt your woolly neighbours with breakfast of their own (there's a jar-full in the hut). The setting is stunning, you sleep in Gabriel (the bigger hut) and you bathe in Bathsheba, in a luxurious slipper bath... The water comes piping hot from the gas boiler, and the loo is plumbed in. A distressed dresser displays pretty bone china, the décor is pastoral, the wood-burner keeps you cosy. Lovely hosts Gary and Michelle can pop by with a basket of breakfast treats, or cook dinner on request.

Minimum two nights. Book through Sawday's Canopy & Stars online or by phone.

Rooms	Shepherd's hut for 2 with separate bath & wc.
Price	£90–£110.
Meals	Continental breakfast hamper for 2, £10. Dinner for 2, £25.
Closed	December–March.

Sawday's Canopy & Stars
Gabriel & Bathsheba,
Little Brookstreet, Hartfield Rd,
Edenbridge, Kent TN8 5NH
Tel   +44 (0)1275 395447
Email enquiries@canopyandstars.co.uk
Web   www.canopyandstars.co.uk/
       gabrielandbathsheba

Entry 266   Map 4

Ransoms

Originally designed to be attached to a steam roller during roadworks, Ransoms has been transformed into something just a little more comfortable. Now featuring a full-sized double bed and a stained-glass window from Rye Cinque Port, the wagon has rumbled up from its resting place in Oxford to settle at The Nut Plat. Fresh and lovely inside, with its traditional green and yellow livery intact and fitting beautifully into its rural setting, it sits 36 paces from a purpose-built kitchen hut and a gas-powered shower. The site is completely free from such disturbances as light pollution, traffic noise and... other guests!

Minimum two nights. Book through Sawday's Canopy & Stars online or by phone.

Rooms	Shepherd's hut for 2 with separate kitchen, gas shower & dry wc.
Price	£85–£100.
Meals	Breakfast hamper for 2, £20. Pub 300 yards
Closed	November–March.

Sawday's Canopy & Stars
Ransoms,
The Nut Plat, Stone Cottage,
Roughway,
Kent TN11 9SH
Tel   +44 (0)1275 395447
Email enquiries@canopyandstars.co.uk
Web   www.canopyandstars.co.uk/ransoms

Entry 267   Map 5

Kent

Dadmans

Once the dower house to Lynsted Park, Dadmans sits in parkland with nearby orchards and grazing cattle and sheep. Your breakfast eggs are laid by rare-breed hens and Amanda sources fantastic local produce for dinner, served in the dining room on gleaming mahogany or in the Aga-warmed kitchen. There's an elegant drawing room to enjoy, and lovely bedrooms have indulgent beds, flowers, views and good bathrooms. Pretty outside too with ancient trees, walled areas, a nuttery and box-edged herb garden, and plenty of castles and cathedrals to visit nearby. A special retreat where you feel part of the family.

Rooms	2: 1 twin; 1 double with separate bath.
Price	£85. Singles by arrangement.
Meals	Dinner, 4 courses, £35. Supper from £15. Pubs/restaurants nearby.
Closed	Rarely.

	Amanda Strevens
	Dadmans,
	Lynsted,
	Sittingbourne,
	Kent ME9 0JJ
Tel	+44 (0)1795 521293
Mobile	+44 (0)7931 153253
Email	amanda.strevens@btopenworld.com
Web	www.dadmans.co.uk

Entry 268   Map 5

Kent

The Linen Shed

A weatherboard house with a winding footpath to the front door and a pot-covered veranda out the back: sit here and nibble something delicious and homemade while you contemplate the pretty garden with its gypsy caravan. Vickie, wreathed in smiles, has created a 'vintage' interior: find wooden flooring, reclaimed architectural pieces, big old roll tops, a mahogany loo seat. Bedrooms (two up, one down) are painted in the softest colours, firm mattresses are covered in fine linen, cotton or linen dressing gowns wait patiently in the smart bathrooms. Food is seriously good here, and adventurous – try a seaside picnic hamper!

Rooms	3: 2 doubles each with separate bath/shower; 1 double with separate bath (occasionally sharing with family).
Price	£95-£110. Singles from £75.
Meals	Picnic hamper from £20. Pub/restaurant 300 yds.
Closed	Rarely.

	Vickie Hassan
	The Linen Shed,
	104 The Street,
	Boughton-under-Blean, Faversham,
	Kent ME13 9AP
Tel	+44 (0)1227 752271
Mobile	+44 (0)7714 646469
Email	bookings@thelinenshed.com
Web	www.thelinenshed.com

Entry 269   Map 5

7 Longport

A delightful, unexpected hideaway bang opposite the site of St Augustine's Abbey and a five-minute walk to the cathedral. You pass through Ursula and Christopher's elegant Georgian house to emerge in a pretty courtyard, with fig tree and rambling rose, to find your self-contained cottage. Downstairs is a cosy sitting room with pale walls, tiled floors and plenty of books, and a clever, compact wet room with mosaic tiles. Then up steep stairs to a swish bedroom with crisp cotton sheets on a handmade bed and views of magnolia and ancient wisteria. You breakfast in the main house or in the courtyard on sunny days. Perfect.

Rooms	Cottage: 1 double & sitting room.
Price	£90. Singles £60.
Meals	Restaurants 5-minute walk.
Closed	Rarely.

Ursula & Christopher Wacher
7 Longport,
Canterbury,
Kent CT1 1PE
Tel   +44 (0)1227 455367
Email   info@7longport.co.uk
Web   www.7longport.co.uk

Entry 270   Map 5

14 Westgate Grove

Slap bang in the city, overlooking the river Stour and within strolling distance of the cathedral... step inside to find a surprising, cool contemporary feel. Pippa is an interior designer, her husband an architect, and fresh bedrooms have good lighting, smart fabrics and pretty flowers. Bathrooms come with the fluffiest towels; the one for the cosy smaller double has a rain shower and Brazilian black slate. On warm days you breakfast in the walled garden with ancient vines, olives, lemons, mimosa; for cooler evenings there is an outdoor fireplace. Pippa is welcoming and friendly; a great place to stay for exploring Canterbury.

Rooms	2: 1 double;
	1 double with separate bath.
Price	£80–£100.
Meals	Pub/restaurant 50 yds.
Closed	Rarely.

Pippa Clague
14 Westgate Grove,
Canterbury,
Kent CT2 8AA
Tel   +44 (0)1227 769624
Mobile +44 (0)7815 107032
Email   pippaclague@me.com

Entry 271   Map 5

Kent

Park Gate

Peter and Mary are a generous team and their conversation is informed and easy. Behind the wisteria-clad façade are two sitting rooms with inglenook fireplaces, ancient beams and polished wood. Fresh comfortable bedrooms have TVs, gorgeous views over the garden to the fields beyond and gleaming bathrooms. Meals are delicious! More magic outside: croquet, tennis and thatched pavilions, wildlife and roses and a sprinkling of sheep to mow the paddock. The house dates back to 1460 and has a noble history: Sir Anthony Eden lived here and Churchill visited during the war. Great value, and convenient for Channel Tunnel and ferries.

Rooms	3: 2 twins/doubles; 1 single with separate shower.
Price	£85. Singles £45.
Meals	Occasional dinner, 3 courses, £30. Simple supper £17.50. Pubs/restaurants 1 mile.
Closed	Christmas, New Year & January.

Peter & Mary Morgan
Park Gate,
Elham,
Canterbury,
Kent CT4 6NE
Tel   +44 (0)1303 840304
Email   marylmorgan@hotmail.co.uk

Entry 272   Map 5

Kent

Great Weddington

The listed house of perfect proportions was built by a Sandwich brewer of ginger beer. The décor is classic country house, the bedrooms desirable and cosy, the bathrooms snug and spotless, and Katie fills the rooms with flowers; she also arranges the flowers for Canterbury Cathedral. The drawing room has vast sofas, shelves of books, tables of magazines, fine watercolours and much-loved antiques. Outside, stunning hedges and lawns and a terrace for tea in the summer. A grand house in a farmland setting; you're close to the north Kent coast and the area hums with history.

Minimum two nights at weekends April-Sept. Dogs by arrangement.

Rooms	2 twins/doubles.
Price	£90-£130.
Meals	Supper from £25. Dinner from £40. Both occasional and not on Sundays.
Closed	Christmas & New Year.

Katie & Neil Gunn
Great Weddington,
Ash, Canterbury,
Kent CT3 2AR
Tel   +44 (0)1304 813407
Email   greatweddington@hotmail.com
Web   www.greatweddington.co.uk

Entry 273   Map 5

Kent

Hoo Farmhouse

Jane and Nicolas are keen shrimpers – let them take you to Minnis Bay and cook your catch for supper! They are generous hosts and their striking Georgian farmhouse has a warm, relaxed atmosphere; Jane welcomes you with home-baked cake or scones. Big, sunny bedrooms have huge sash windows, books and incredibly comfortable beds. Wake refreshed for breakfast in the charming dining room, or out in the walled garden: homemade jams, fruit and local produce. Lots to explore in the area with Canterbury Cathedral, Whitstable, castles and sandy beaches all nearby. Return to a perfect drawing room with deep sofas, garden views and log fire.

Rooms	2 twins/doubles.
Price	£90. Singles £65.
Meals	Pub 1 mile.
Closed	Rarely.

Jane Irwin
Hoo Farmhouse,
Monkton Road, Minster,
Ramsgate,
Kent CT12 4JB
Tel   +44 (0)1843 821322
Email   stay@hoofarmhouse.com
Web   www.hoofarmhouse.com

Entry 274   Map 5

Kent

Orchard Barn

Alison knows how to spoil (big beds, bread from the mill, home-grown soft fruit, homemade jams), David knows the wildlife, and they both love doing B&B. The big beautiful barn has been sympathetically restored, its middle section left open to create a stunning covered courtyard: find soaring beams, a comfortable leather sofa, fresh flowers. You get two snug, carpeted bedrooms up in the eaves – pale beams, bright colours, and a sweet bath (or shower) room. A delightful village, the ancient port of Sandwich nearby and egrets, kingfishers, swallows and squirrels a walk away. Superb.

Minimum two nights. Children over seven welcome.

Rooms	2: 1 double, 1 twin/double.
Price	£80-£85. Singles from £50.
Meals	Pubs/restaurants within 1.5 miles.
Closed	Christmas & January.

David & Alison Ross
Orchard Barn,
Felderland Lane, Worth,
Kent CT14 0BT
Tel   +44 (0)1304 615045
Mobile   +44 (0)7950 599304
Email   orchardbarnworth@gmail.com
Web   www.orchardbarn-worth.co.uk

Entry 275   Map 5

Kent

Kent

Kingsdown Place

Wow. A huge white villa set in terraced gardens running down to the sea; on clear days you can see France! Tan has renovated house and garden with panache: modern art festoons the walls, statues lurk and all is light and contemporary. Upstairs are superb bedrooms: one four-poster with garden views, and, up a spiral staircase in the loft, a very private suite with a sitting room and terrace. All have Conran mattresses and white linen. Breakfast on scrambled eggs and smoked salmon or the full works, out on the terrace in good weather. Seaside chic and a mere hop from Deal, Dover, Walmer and Sandwich.

Farthingales

Deep in rural Kent (yet 15 minutes from Canterbury and Dover) is a village hall-house of great character with a Victorian draper's shop addition. Welcome to a warm, cosy and inviting B&B, with the private guest quarters, overlooking Nonington Church and fields beyond, in the 'shop' wing. Find comfy beds and fluffy towels upstairs (even headphones for the TV), and a spacious sitting room down, delightful with Knole sofa and wood-burner. Ex-radio presenter Peter brings a fine English breakfast to your table as you gaze on beautiful orchard, pond, treehouse and lawns; you can breakfast outside on balmy days.

Cots & highchairs available.

Rooms	3: 1 suite; 1 double, 1 four-poster, each with separate bath & sitting room.	Rooms	3: 1 double, 2 twins.
		Price	£75-£95. Singles £65.
Price	£95-£100. Suite £120-£130. Singles from £75.	Meals	Pubs 1 mile.
		Closed	Rarely.
Meals	Packed lunch £10. Dinner £25. Restaurant 500 yds. Pub 0.5 miles.		
Closed	Christmas & New Year.		

	Tan Harrington		**Peter Deeley**
	Kingsdown Place,		Farthingales,
	Upper Street,		Old Court Hill,
	Kingsdown,		Nonington, Dover,
	Kent CT14 8EU		Kent CT15 4LQ
Tel	+44 (0)1304 380510	Tel	+44 (0)1304 840174
Email	tan@tanharrington.com	Email	farthingalesbandb@yahoo.co.uk
		Web	www.farthingales.co.uk

Entry 276   Map 5

Entry 277   Map 5

Kent

Stowting Hill House

A classic manor house in an idyllic setting, close to Canterbury and the North Downs Way. This warm, civilised home mixes Tudor beams with Georgian proportions; there's a huge conservatory full of greenery, a guest sitting room with sofas and log fire, and breakfasts fresh from the Aga. Traditional bedrooms are carpeted and cosily furnished. Your charming, country-loving hosts welcome you with tea and flowers from the garden – a perfect summer spot with its lawns, tree-lined avenue and stone obelisk. You are ten minutes from the Chunnel but this is worth more than one night.

Children over ten welcome.

Rooms	2: 1 twin/double, 1 twin.
Price	£95–£100. Singles £70.
Meals	Dinner from £30. Pub 1 mile.
Closed	Christmas & New Year.

	Richard & Virginia Latham
	Stowting Hill House,
	Stowting,
	Ashford,
	Kent TN25 6BE
Tel	+44 (0)1303 862881
Email	lathamvj@gmail.com
Web	www.stowtinghillhouse.co.uk

Entry 278   Map 5

Kent

The Old Rectory

On a really good day (about once every five years) you can see France. But you'll be more than happy to settle for the superb views over Romney Marsh, the Channel in the distance. The big, friendly house, built in 1850, has impeccable, elegant bedrooms and good bathrooms; the large, many-windowed sitting room is full of books, pictures and flowers from the south-facing garden. Marion and David are both charming and can organise transport to Ashford International for you. It's remarkably peaceful – perfect for walking (right on the Saxon Shore path), cycling and bird-watching.

Children over ten welcome.

Rooms	2: 1 twin; 1 twin with separate bath/shower.
Price	£80. Singles £50.
Meals	Pubs within 4 miles.
Closed	Christmas & New Year.

	Marion & David Hanbury
	The Old Rectory,
	Ruckinge,
	Ashford,
	Kent TN26 2PE
Tel	+44 (0)1233 732328
Email	oldrectory@hotmail.com
Web	www.oldrectoryruckinge.co.uk

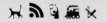

Entry 279   Map 5

Kent

Hereford Oast

Jack the Jack Russell will meet you, swiftly followed by Suzy – and tea and cake in the garden: sheer heaven in summer. The 1876 oast house, set back from a country road and gazing on lush fields, has become the loveliest B&B. Downstairs is the dining room, as unique as it is round. Upstairs is the guest room, sunny, fresh and bright, with a blue and white theme and a rural view. As for the village – white-clapboard cottages, pubs, fine church – it's the prettiest in Kent. Sausages from Pluckley and homemade soda bread set you up for cultured jaunts: Leeds Castle, Sissinghurst, Great Dixter… all marvellously close.

Rooms	1 twin/double.
Price	£75–£85. Singles £50–£55.
Meals	Pubs 1 mile.
Closed	Rarely.

Suzy Hill
Hereford Oast,
Smarden Bell Road, Smarden,
Ashford,
Kent TN27 8PA
Tel   +44 (0)1233 770541
Email   suzy@herefordoast.fsnet.co.uk
Web   www.herefordoast.co.uk

Entry 280   Map 5

Kent

Merzie Meadows

You get your own suite in this lovely ranch-style house with huge windows, pergolas groaning with climbers, and a Mediterranean-style swimming pool in the twittering garden. Pamela is just as light and bright: she keeps horses and hens and gives you locally sourced breakfasts. Your bedroom has a contemporary, uncluttered feel and is beautifully dressed in pale colours with pretty fabrics and a super bed, your own sitting room looks onto the garden and the bathroom is sleek with Italian marble and plump towels. All is peaceful; garden and nature lovers will adore it here.

Minimum two nights at weekends April-September.

Rooms	1 suite for 2-3.
Price	£98–£110. Singles £98.
Meals	Pub 2.5 miles.
Closed	Mid-December to February.

Pamela Mumford
Merzie Meadows,
Hunton Road, Marden,
Maidstone,
Kent TN12 9SL
Tel   +44 (0)1622 820500
Mobile +44 (0)7762 713077
Email   merziemeadows@me.com
Web   www.merziemeadows.co.uk

Entry 281   Map 5

Kent

Reason Hill

Brian and Antonia's 200-acre fruit farm is perched on the edge of the Weald of Kent, with stunning views over orchards and oast houses. The farmhouse has 17th-century origins (low ceilings, wonky floors, stone flags) and a conservatory for sunny breakfasts; colours are soft, antiques gleam, the mood is relaxed. A roomy twin has a bay window and armchairs, the pretty double looks over the garden. Come in spring for the blossom, summer for the fresh fruit and veg from the garden and anytime for a break. The Greensand Way runs along the bottom of the farm, you are close to Sissinghurst Castle and 45 minutes from the Channel Tunnel.

Rooms	4: 2 twins; 1 double, 1 single sharing shower (let to same party only).
Price	£80-£85. Singles £50.
Meals	Pubs within 1 mile.
Closed	Christmas & New Year.

Brian & Antonia Allfrey
Reason Hill,
Linton, Maidstone,
Kent ME17 4BT
Tel   +44 (0)1622 743679
Mobile   +44 (0)7775 745580
Email   antonia@allfrey.net
Web   www.reasonhill.co.uk

Entry 282   Map 5

Kent

Ightham

Lord it through electric oak gates to find B&B in your own modern barn. Gardening enthusiast Caroline's house is close but not hugely visible: you're wonderfully independent. Bedrooms on the ground floor are eclectic and appealing, with pine floors, dazzling white walls and slatted wooden blinds for a moody light; the bathroom is big and contemporary with a walk-in shower. Upstairs: an enormous family space for sitting, eating, playing, and glass doors on to a terrace for outdoor fun. Breakfast is delivered: eggs from the hens, pancakes, French toast. Great walks start from the door; return for supper – Caroline loves to cook.

Rooms	Barn: 1 double, 1 twin (let to same party only).
Price	£115.
Meals	Dinner, 3 courses, £25. Pub/restaurant 5-minute walk.
Closed	Rarely.

Caroline Standish
Ightham,
Hope Farm, Sandy Lane,
Ightham, Sevenoaks,
Kent TN15 9BA
Tel   +44 (0)1732 884359
Email   clstandish@gmail.com
Web   www.ighthambedandbreakfast.co.uk

Entry 283   Map 5

Kent

Charcott Farmhouse

The 1750 tile-hung brick farmhouse is very much a family home; if you don't come expecting an immaculate environment you will enjoy it here. There's a pretty sitting room in the old bakehouse with original beams and bread oven, and cats and a dog to keep you company. Bedrooms are unfussy, with oriental rugs, antiques, pretty country fabrics and simple bathrooms. Ginny is charming and loves books while Nicholas – a tad eccentric for some – is knowledgeable about the area and a brilliant chef. Breakfast is an unrushed, happy affair with heaps of homemade bread and marmalade and eggs from the free-range chickens. Come and go as you please.

Rooms	3: 2 twins; 1 twin with separate bath.
Price	£65-£85. Singles from £50.
Meals	Pub 5-minute walk.
Closed	Rarely.

Nicholas & Ginny Morris
Charcott Farmhouse,
Charcott, Leigh, Tonbridge,
Kent TN11 8LG

Tel	+44 (0)1892 870024
Mobile	+44 (0)7508 683985
Email	charcottfarmhouse@btinternet.com
Web	www.charcottfarmhouse.com

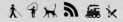

Entry 284   Map 5

Kent

40 York Road

A smart Regency townhouse, slap bang in the centre of Royal Tunbridge Wells and a five-minute walk from the beautiful Pantiles. Patricia will enjoy cooking for you; in another life she served up delights for hungry skiers coming off the French mountains. A delightful host, she leaves you to come and go as you please; guests have a comfy sitting room, bright spotless bedrooms that are quieter than you may think and thoughtful extras. In the summer you will breakfast deliciously in the pretty courtyard garden – try the lemon pancakes! Wander into town for great little shops and restaurants. Truly excellent.

Over 12s welcome.

Rooms	2 twins/doubles.
Price	£80. Singles from £50.
Meals	Supper £13. Dinner, 4 courses with wine, £25. Picnic available. Pub/restaurant nearby.
Closed	23 December-2 January.

Patricia Lobo
40 York Road,
Tunbridge Wells,
Kent TN1 1JY

Tel	+44 (0)1892 531342
Email	yorkrd@uwclub.net
Web	www.yorkroad.co.uk

Entry 285   Map 5

Kent

22 Lansdowne Road

Built in 1861, the house in leafy Tunbridge Wells "has never been as Victorian as it is now". So says Harold, whose devotion to Victoriana knows no bounds. Deep colours, rich velvets, marble tables, authentic wallpapers, tasselled lamps, portraits of Queen Victoria, tea and scones by the fire… be prepared to take a serious step back in time. Bedrooms are simple in comparison: ruched chintz in the double, damask in the twin – and a door to the conservatory. Bathrooms have large mirrors and brand new fittings, breakfast is a locally sourced spread. Those in search of heritage will marvel.

Off-street parking.

Rooms	3: 1 double, 1 twin/double; 1 studio with shower & kitchenette.
Price	£80–£120. Singles £80.
Meals	Dinner, 2 courses, £30. Pubs/restaurants within 5-minute walk.
Closed	January.

Harold Brown
22 Lansdowne Road,
Tunbridge Wells,
Kent TN1 2NJ
Tel +44 (0)1892 533633
Mobile +44 (0)7714 264489
Email info@thevictorianbandb.com
Web www.thevictorianbandb.com

Kent

Barclay Farmhouse

Lynn's breakfasts are fabulous: fresh fruit, warm croissants, home-baked breads and a daily changing twist on the traditional English. The weatherboarded guest barn may be in perfect trim but has a been-here-for-ever feel; you have country-cosy dining tables for breakfast, a patio for summer, a big peaceful garden. Gleaming bedrooms have handmade oak bedheads, chocolates, slippers, discreet fridges, radios, TVs; shower rooms are in perfect order. Couples, honeymooners, garden lovers – many would love it here (but no children: the garden pond is deep). Warm-hearted B&B, and glorious Sissinghurst nearby.

Minimum two nights at weekends in high season.

Rooms	Barn: 3 doubles.
Price	£90. Singles from £70.
Meals	Pubs/restaurants 1 mile.
Closed	Rarely.

Lynn Ruse
Barclay Farmhouse,
Woolpack Corner,
Biddenden,
Kent TN27 8BQ
Tel +44 (0)1580 292626
Email info@barclayfarmhouse.co.uk
Web www.barclayfarmhouse.co.uk

Kent

Ramsden Farm

A truly interesting and comfortable house, with south-facing views across the Wealds; charming Sally has renovated these former farm buildings with flair. Unhurried, very good breakfasts are eaten in the huge kitchen with a lemon-coloured Aga and floor to ceiling glass doors opening on to a wooden deck; spill outside on warm days. After a hearty walk you can doze in front of a tree-devouring inglenook; find lovely sunny bedrooms too, with more of that view from each, tip-top mattresses and the crispest white linen. Fantastic bathrooms have travertine marble and underfloor heating. Spoiling and completely peaceful.

Self-catering in cottage.

Rooms	3: 1 double, 1 twin; 1 double with separate bath.
Price	£85–£110.
Meals	Pub 1 mile.
Closed	Rarely.

Sally Harrington
Ramsden Farm,
Dingleden Lane,
Benenden,
Kent TN17 4JT
Tel +44 (0)1580 240203
Email sally@ramsdenfarmcottage.co.uk
Web www.ramsdenfarmcottage.co.uk

Entry 288   Map 5

Kent

Pullington Barn

Up a private drive and straight in to a vast, beamed expanse of bright light, warm colours, beautiful art and a cheery welcome from Gavin and Anne in their converted barn. There are endless books to choose: settle in the comfy drawing room with its grand piano. Or sit in the pretty south-facing garden on a fine day; on the other side, views from the orchard spread over oast houses and church spires. Big bedrooms (one on the ground floor) have good mattresses, coordinated bed linen and feather pillows. You breakfast well on local and homemade produce, served at the travertine table in the dining hall. Lovely walks from the door.

Children over nine welcome, other ages by arrangement.

Rooms	2: 1 double, 1 twin.
Price	£80–£95. Singles from £60.
Meals	Pub/restaurant 0.5 miles.
Closed	Christmas.

Gavin & Anne Wetton
Pullington Barn,
Benenden,
Kent TN17 4EH
Tel +44 (0)1580 240246
Mobile +44 (0)7849 759929
Email anne@wetton.info
Web www.wetton.info/bandb

Entry 289   Map 5

Kent

Lamberden Cottage

Down a farm track find two 1780 cottages knocked into one, with flagstone floors, a cheery wood-burner in the guest sitting room and welcoming Beverley and Branton. There's a traditional country-cottage feel with pale walls, thick oak beams, soft carpeting and very comfortable bedrooms (the twin has an adjoining bedroom); views from all are across the Weald of Kent. Wander the lovely gardens to find your own private spot, sip a sundowner on the terrace, eat a hearty breakfast in the family dining room; home-grown fresh fruits, home-made marmalades and yogurts. Near to Sissinghurst, Great Dixter and many historic places.

Rooms	2: 1 double; 1 twin with adjoining children's twin.
Price	£75–£100. Singles from £65.
Meals	Pub 1 mile.
Closed	Christmas & New Year.

Beverley & Branton Screeton
Lamberden Cottage,
Rye Road, Sandhurst,
Cranbrook,
Kent TN18 5PH

Tel	+44 (0)1580 850743
Mobile	+44 (0)7768 462070
Email	thewalledgarden@lamberdencottage.co.uk
Web	www.lamberdencottage.co.uk

Entry 290   Map 5

Lancashire

Sagar Fold House

In a spectacular setting, a 17th-century dairy and two perfect studios, one up, one down. Private entrances lead to big beamed spaces that marry immaculate efficiency with unusual beauty – very here and now. A gorgeous Indian doorframe serves as a bedhead upstairs, soft colours and contemporary touches lift the spirit, plentiful books and DVDs entertain you and a continental breakfast is supplied – homemade and organic whenever possible. Now gaze over the Italian knot garden, which ties in lines of a lovely landscape. Take walks in deeply peaceful countryside; top-notch places to eat are an easy drive.

Rooms	2 studios, each with kitchenette.
Price	Studio £85–£90.
Meals	Continental breakfast in fridge. Pubs/restaurants 1-2 miles.
Closed	Rarely.

Helen & John Cook
Sagar Fold House,
Higher Hodder, Clitheroe,
Lancashire BB7 3LW

Tel	+44 (0)1254 826844
Mobile	+44 (0)7850 750709
Email	helencook14@gmail.com
Web	www.sagarfoldhouse.co.uk

Entry 291   Map 12

Lancashire

Challan Hall

The wind in the trees, the boom of a bittern and birdsong. That's as noisy as it gets. On the edge of the village, delightful Charlotte's former farmhouse overlooks woods and Lake Haweswater; deer, squirrels and Leighton Moss Nature Reserve are your neighbours. The Cassons are well-travelled and the house, filled with a colourful mish-mash of mementos, is happily and comfortably traditional. Expect a sofa-strewn sitting room, a smart red and polished-wood dining room and two freshly floral bedrooms. Morecambe Bay and the Lakes are on the doorstep – come home to lovely views and stunning sunsets.

Rooms	2: 1 twin/double; 1 twin/double with separate bath.
Price	£75. Singles from £45.
Meals	Dinner, 2 courses, £25. Packed lunch available. Pubs 1 mile.
Closed	Rarely.

Charlotte Casson
Challan Hall,
Silverdale,
Lancashire LA5 0UH
Tel   +44 (0)1524 701054
Mobile   +44 (0)7790 360776
Email   cassons@btopenworld.com
Web   www.challanhall.co.uk

Entry 292   Map 11

Leicestershire

Breedon Hall

Through high brick walls find a listed Georgian manor house in an acre of garden, and friendly Charlotte and Charles. Make yourselves at home in the fire-warmed drawing room full of fine furniture and pictures; carpets and curtains are in the richest, warmest reds and golds. Charlotte is a smashing cook and gives you homemade granola, jams and marmalade with local eggs, bacon and sausages; you'd kick yourself if you didn't book dinner. Bedrooms are painted in soft colours, fabrics are thick, beds covered in goose down; bathrooms are immaculate. Borrow a bike and discover the glorious countryside right on the cusp of two counties.

Minimum two nights at weekends.

Rooms	2 doubles.
Price	£95–£110. Singles £85.
Meals	Dinner, 3 courses, £35. Pub/restaurant 1-minute walk.
Closed	Rarely.

Charlotte Meynell
Breedon Hall,
Main Street,
Breedon-on-the-Hill,
Derby,
Leicestershire DE73 8AN
Mobile   +44 (0)7973 105467
Email   charlottemeynell@btinternet.com

Entry 293   Map 8

Leicestershire

Curtain Cottage

A pretty village setting for this cottage on the main street, next door to Sarah's interior design shop. You have your own entrance by the side and through a large garden, which backs onto fields with horses and the National Forest beyond. A conservatory is your sitting room: wicker armchairs, wooden floors, a contemporary take on the country look. Bedrooms are light and fresh: linen from The White Company on sumptuous beds, slate-tiled bathrooms, stunning fabrics. Breakfast is full English with eggs from the hens or fresh fruit and croissants from the local shop – all is delivered to you. Perfect privacy.

Rooms	2: 1 double, 1 twin.
Price	£85. Singles £60.
Meals	Pubs/restaurants 150 yds.
Closed	Rarely.

	Sarah Barker
	Curtain Cottage,
	92-94 Main Street,
	Woodhouse Eaves,
	Leicestershire LE12 8RZ
Tel	+44 (0)1509 891361
Mobile	+44 (0)7906 830088
Email	sarah@curtaincottage.co.uk
Web	www.curtaincottage.co.uk

Entry 294   Map 8

Leicestershire

Kicklewell House

The last house in the village overlooks miles of fields and the garden includes paddocks and stables. Fiona, easy, hospitable, great fun, loves horses, dogs and fine art; her cream walls glow with artwork, much of which she frames and sells. The house is warm, inviting and a visual delight: big deep sofas, bright ethnic rugs, a trusty Aga, heaps of books. After a scrumptious local breakfast, stride off to the lovely Foxton Canal, or visit one of the big local houses and gardens like Cottesbrooke Hall and Holdenby. Bedrooms are as peaceful and as charming as can be; good dogs are welcomed with open arms.

Rooms	2: 1 twin, 1 double.
Price	£90. Singles £50.
Meals	Dinner, 3 courses, £25.
	Packed lunch £7.50. Pubs 2 miles.
Closed	Christmas & Easter.

	Fiona Shann
	Kicklewell House,
	Laughton,
	Lutterworth,
	Leicestershire LE17 6QF
Tel	+44 (0)1162 404173
Email	fonishann@hotmail.co.uk

Entry 295   Map 8

Leicestershire

The Grange

Behind the mellow brick exterior (Queen Anne in front, Georgian at the back) is a warm family home. Log fires brighten chilly days and you are greeted with kindness and generosity by Mary and Shaun and their sweet dog. Big, beautifully quiet bedrooms, one an atmospheric beamed room in the attic, are hung with strikingly unusual wallpapers and furnished with excellent beds and pretty antiques; bathrooms are simple yet impeccable. Wake to breakfast in the big, flagstoned hall: homemade bread, local bacon and award-winning sausages. The newly designed garden has a treehouse and is large enough to roam.

NGS garden.

Rooms	2: 1 twin, 1 double.
Price	£80. Singles £50.
Meals	Pubs/restaurants 0.5-1.5 miles.
Closed	Christmas & New Year.

Shaun & Mary Mackaness
The Grange,
Kimcote,
Leicestershire LE17 5RU
Tel   +44 (0)1455 203155
Mobile +44 (0)7808 242530
Email   shaunandmarymac@hotmail.com
Web   www.thegrangekimcote.co.uk

Entry 296   Map 8

Leicestershire

The Gorse House

Passing cars are less frequent than passing horses – this is a peaceful spot in a pretty village. Lyn and Richard's 17th-century cottage has a feeling of lightness and space; there's a fine collection of paintings and furniture, and oak doors lead from dining room to guest sitting room. Country style bedrooms have green views and are simply done. The garden layout was designed by Bunny Guinness, you can bring your horse (there's plenty of stabling) and it's a stroll to a good pub dinner. The house is filled with laughter, breakfasts with home-grown fruits are tasty and the Cowdells are terrific hosts who love having guests to stay.

Rooms	3: 1 double, 1 family room.
	Stable: 1 triple & kitchenette.
Price	£65. Family room £65-£120.
	Triple £65-£98. Singles £35.
Meals	Packed lunch £5.
	Pub 75 yds (closed on Sun eves).
Closed	Rarely.

Lyn & Richard Cowdell
The Gorse House,
33 Main Street, Grimston,
Melton Mowbray,
Leicestershire LE14 3BZ
Tel   +44 (0)1664 813537
Mobile +44 (0)7780 600792
Email   cowdell@gorsehouse.co.uk
Web   www.gorsehouse.co.uk

Entry 297   Map 9

Lincolnshire

The Barn

Simon and Jane – the nicest people – have farmed for 30 years and love having guests to stay. Breakfasts and suppers are entirely local or home-grown, and delicious; there are endless extras and nothing is too much trouble. In this light-filled barn conversion find old beams, new walls and good antiques; a brick-flanked fireplace glows and heated floors keep toes warm. Above the high-raftered main living/dining room is a comfy, good-sized double; in the adjoining stables, two further rooms, a crisp feel, sparkling showers, restful privacy. Views are to sheep-dotted fields and the village is on a 25-mile cycle trail.

Rooms	3: 1 twin/double. Stables: 1 double (extra single available); 1 single with separate bath/shower.
Price	£70–£75. Singles £50.
Meals	Supper, 2 courses, £17.50. Dinner, 3 courses, £25. BYO. Pubs in village & 2 miles.
Closed	Rarely.

Simon & Jane Wright
The Barn,
Spring Lane, Folkingham,
Sleaford,
Lincolnshire NG34 0SJ

Tel	+44 (0)1529 497199
Mobile	+44 (0)7876 363292
Email	sjwright@farming.co.uk
Web	www.thebarnspringlane.co.uk

Entry 298   Map 9

Lincolnshire

Brills Farm

An early Georgian farmhouse at the top of one of Lincolnshire's rare hills. Built of warm brick near a Roman settlement site, it shines with country elegance and charm, subtle colours and antique furniture. The flower-filled drawing and dining rooms overlook the valley, the beautiful airy bedrooms (one a super king-size) have goose down duvets and lovely linen. The Whites are a delightful, enthusiastic couple with a flourishing family (Sophie is a professional cook and event rider). They offer great dinners, and cookery courses, during the winter; bacon from their pigs all year round.

Children over 12 welcome.

Rooms	3: 2 doubles, 1 twin/double.
Price	£90–£100. Singles £55–£60.
Meals	Supper £20. Dinner £30. Packed lunch £10. Pubs 5-min drive.
Closed	Christmas & New Year.

Charles & Sophie White
Brills Farm,
Brills Hill, Norton Disney,
Lincoln,
Lincolnshire LN6 9JN

Tel	+44 (0)1636 892311
Mobile	+44 (0)7947 136228
Email	admin@brillsfarm-bedandbreakfast.co.uk
Web	www.brillsfarm-bedandbreakfast.co.uk

Entry 299   Map 9

Lincolnshire

Baumber Park

Lincoln red cows and Longwool sheep surround this attractive rosy-brick farmhouse – once a stud that bred a Derby winner. The old watering pond is now a haven for frogs, newts and toads; birds sing lustily. Maran hens conjure delicious eggs, and charming Clare, a botanist, is hugely knowledgeable about the area. Bedrooms are light and traditional with mahogany furniture; two have heart-stopping views. Guests have their own wisteria-covered entrance, sitting room with an open fire, dining room with local books and the lovely garden to roam. This is good walking, riding and cycling country; seals and rare birds on the coast.

Usually minimum two nights at weekends in high season.

Rooms	3: 2 doubles; 1 twin with separate bath.
Price	£60-£70. Singles from £45.
Meals	Pubs 1.5 miles.
Closed	Christmas & New Year.

Clare Harrison
Baumber Park,
Baumber,
Horncastle,
Lincolnshire LN9 5NE
Tel   +44 (0)1507 578235
Mobile   +44 (0)7977 722776
Email   mail@baumberpark.com
Web   www.baumberpark.com

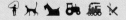

Entry 300   Map 9

Lincolnshire

The Grange

Wide open farmland and an award-winning farm on the edge of the Lincolnshire Wolds. This immaculately kept farm has been in the family for generations; Sarah and Jonathan are delightful and make you feel instantly at home. Find acres of farmland and a two mile farm trail to explore, a trout lake to picnic by and an open fire to warm you in an elegant drawing room with Georgian windows. Sarah gives you delicious homemade cake on arrival and huge Aga breakfasts with home-laid eggs and local produce. Comfortable bedrooms have TVs, tea trays and gleaming bathrooms. Fabulous views stretch to Lincoln Cathedral and the walks are superb.

Rooms	2 doubles.
Price	£70-£75. Singles £45.
Meals	Supper from £18. Dinner, 2 courses, from £25. BYO. (No meals during harvest.) Pub/restaurant 1 mile.
Closed	Christmas & New Year.

Sarah & Jonathan Stamp
The Grange,
Torrington Lane,
East Barkwith,
Lincolnshire LN8 5RY
Tel   +44 (0)1673 858670
Mobile   +44 (0)7951 079474
Email   sarahstamp@farmersweekly.net
Web   www.thegrange-lincolnshire.co.uk

Entry 301   Map 9

Lincolnshire

The Manor House

One guest's summing up reads: "Absolutely perfect – hostess, house, garden and marmalade." Delightful Ann – interested in horses, food, photography, people – makes you feel immediately at home. You have the run of downstairs: all family antiques, fresh flowers and space. Chintzy, carpeted bedrooms have dreamy views of the lovely sweeping gardens and duck-dabbled lake; dinners are delicious: game casserole, sticky toffee pudding with homemade ice cream… Perfect stillness at the base of the Wolds and a pretty one-mile walk along the route of the old railway that starts from the front door. Very special, and great value.

Rooms	2: 1 double, 1 twin.
Price	£70–£75. Singles £50.
Meals	Dinner from £20. BYO. Pub/restaurant 2 miles.
Closed	Christmas.

Ann Hobbins
The Manor House,
West Barkwith,
Lincolnshire LN8 5LF

Tel	+44 (0)1673 858253
Mobile	+44 (0)7751 891274

Entry 302   Map 9

Lincolnshire

Knaith Hall

This intriguing place, medieval church at its gate, dates from the 16th century. Lawns slope down to the river Trent; daffodils, lambs, a passing barge and waterfowl pattern the serenity. And the skyscapes are terrific; at night, a distant power station shines, enhancing that 'great rurality of taste' referred to in Pevsner. Indoors, diamond-paned windows, a domed dining room and fine furniture are softened by an easy décor and a log fire twinkles in the drawing room. Bedrooms are large with comfortable beds; wake to breakfast with award-winning sausages. An appealing family house, with friendly hosts and a relaxed atmosphere.

Rooms	2: 1 double with separate shower; 1 twin with separate bath.
Price	£70–£80. Singles from £40.
Meals	Dinner, 3 courses with wine, £20. Pub 4 miles.
Closed	Rarely.

John & Rosie Burke
Knaith Hall,
Knaith, Gainsborough,
Lincolnshire DN21 5PE

Tel	+44 (0)1427 613005
Mobile	+44 (0)7796 881328
Email	rosemary@knaith.com

Entry 303   Map 9

Lincolnshire

The Manor House

At the end of a neatly raked gravel drive, a new manor house with wide views and stunning sunsets over the peaceful Trent valley. The Days have farmed in the village since 1898 and look after you with rich warm comfort and friendly ease. Rooms have opulent curtains with chintzy roses, period furniture and rural art. Beautiful gardens are awash with summer roses, ducks on the pond, horses in the paddock, sunny patios – one in front of the annexe is for guests' exclusive use. You can fish for carp in the lake, shooting can be arranged and there are music and art festivals, antique fairs and walks in abundance.

Rooms	2: 1 double. Annexe: 1 twin/double with kitchenette.
Price	£70. Singles £45.
Meals	Pub/restaurant 3.5 miles.
Closed	Christmas & New Year.

Judy Day
The Manor House,
Manton, Kirton Lindsey,
Gainsborough,
Lincolnshire DN21 4JT

Tel	+44 (0)1652 649508
Mobile	+44 (0)7712 766347
Email	enquiries@manorhousebedandbreakfast.co.uk
Web	www.manorhousebedandbreakfast.co.uk

Entry 304   Map 13

Lincolnshire

The Old Farm House

Hidden in the Lincolnshire Wolds, an 18th-century, ivy-covered house – and Nicola's father still farms the fields beyond the ha-ha. The stone-flagged, terracotta-washed hall gives a hint of warm colours to come; creamy walls show off tawny fabrics, prints and antiques; the beamed sitting/breakfast room has a big, rosy brick inglenook fireplace and tranquil views. Such a welcoming, tucked-away place, hopping with pheasant but just an easy drive from shops, golf and racing in the nearby towns. Excellent value, good plentiful food, and perfect if you fancy privacy and space.

Children over eight welcome.

Rooms	3: 2 doubles, 1 triple.
Price	£80. Triple £90–£120. Singles £55.
Meals	Pub 2 miles.
Closed	Christmas, New Year & occasionally.

Nicola Clarke
The Old Farm House,
Low Road, Hatcliffe,
Grimsby,
Lincolnshire DN37 0SH

Tel	+44 (0)1472 824455
Mobile	+44 (0)7818 272523
Email	clarky.hatcliffe@btinternet.com
Web	www.oldfarmhousebandbgrimsby.com

Entry 305   Map 13

London

90 Old Church Street

In a quiet street facing the Chelsea Arts Club is an enticing, contemporary haven. Softly spoken Nina is passionate about the arts, knows Chelsea inside out and takes real pleasure in looking after her guests. Antique shop spoils stand alongside more modern delights, the attention to detail is amazing and there are plentiful bunches of flowers. A lush carpet takes you up to the second floor and your super-private, surprisingly peaceful and deliciously designed bedroom and bathroom. Breakfast – fruit platters, yogurt and croissants – is shared with Nina in the kitchen. We love No. 90 – and the little black poodles!

Tube: South Kensington.

Rooms	1 double.
Price	£115–£130. Singles from £100.
Meals	Continental breakfast £10. Restaurants nearby.
Closed	Occasionally.

Nina Holland
90 Old Church Street,
Chelsea,
London SW3 6EP
Tel   +44 (0)20 7352 4758
Mobile +44 (0)7831 689167
Email   ninastcharles@gmail.com
Web   www.chelseabedbreakfast.com

Entry 306 Map 22

London

37 Trevor Square

A three-minute walk from Hyde Park or Harrods – a fabulous find. The square is peaceful, private, exquisite, so find a pretty corner and enjoy. Margaret runs an interior design company – rather successfully, by the look of things – and serves a superb full English breakfast in the kitchen/diner; there's also a small conservatory you are welcome to use. Bedrooms (one downstairs has an enormous bed and a little patio) have goose down pillows, cashmere duvets, electric blankets and a mini fridge; slip on your robe, listen to some music or watch a DVD – it's all here. Blissful luxury in the middle of Knightsbridge.

Tube: Knightsbridge. Nearest car park £25 for 24 hrs (closed overnight).

Rooms	3: 1 twin/double; 1 double, 1 twin sharing shower (let to same party only).
Price	£185. Singles £120.
Meals	Restaurants 200 yds.
Closed	Occasionally.

Margaret & Holly Palmer
37 Trevor Square,
Knightsbridge,
London SW7 1DY
Tel   +44 (0)20 7823 8186
Email   margaret@37trevorsquare.co.uk
Web   www.37trevorsquare.co.uk

Entry 307 Map 22

London

6 Oakfield Street

This district dates from the mid-1660s and local historian Simon has maps to prove it; their road is the second smallest in London. Hospitable Margaret and Simon, language, art and Egypt lovers, live in a stylish 1860s house with a beautiful roof mural (hers), a marble-topped table in the dining room and a collection of Egyptian prints. There's an open-plan feel to the kitchen, and a roof terrace where you can sit in summer. Bedrooms are at the top of the house: the twin is little but, being at the back, is silent at night; the double has a big wooden bed and an antique armoire. Stroll to restaurants on Hollywood Road.

Tube: Earl's Court, 12-minute walk. South Kensington 20-minute walk or 5-minute bus ride on 14 or 414. Nearest car park £25 for 24 hrs.

Rooms	2: 1 double, 1 twin.
Price	£90-£135. Singles £90.
Meals	Restaurants nearby.
Closed	Occasionally.

Margaret & Simon de Maré
6 Oakfield Street,
Little Chelsea,
London SW10 9JB
Tel   +44 (0)20 7352 2970
Mobile   +44 (0)7990 844008
Email   margaretdemare@googlemail.com
Web   www.athomeinnchelsea.com

Entry 308   Map 22

London

15 Delaford Street

A pretty Victorian, terraced Fulham home, inside all charming and spacious. In a tiny, sun-trapping courtyard you can have continental breakfast in good weather – tropical fruits are a favourite and the coffee is very good; a second miniature garden bursts with life at the back. The bedroom, up a spiral staircase, looks down on it all. Expect perfectly ironed sheets on a comfy bed, a quilted throw, books in the alcove, a sunny bathroom and fluffy white towels. The tennis at Queen's is in June and on your doorstep. Tim and Margot – she's from Melbourne – are fun, charming and happy to pick you up from the nearest tube.

Tube: West Brompton. Parking free eves & weekends; otherwise pay & display. 74 bus to West End nearby.

Rooms	1 double.
Price	£95-£100. Singles £75.
Meals	Restaurants nearby.
Closed	Occasionally.

Margot & Tim Woods
15 Delaford Street,
Fulham,
London SW6 7LT
Tel   +44 (0)20 7385 9671
Email   woodsmargot@hotmail.co.uk

Entry 309   Map 22

35 Burnthwaite Road

Near Queen's Club and Wimbledon for tennis and Fulham Broadway's tube, a sweet terraced house on the sunny side of the street. A fresh aqua carpet ushers you up to a bright bedroom on the second floor, and a spotless white bathroom squeezed under the eaves. It's as peaceful as can be. No sitting room but a rather smart dining table for breakfast – croissants, cereals, fresh fruit salad. A traditional and civilised feel prevails, thanks to lovely family pieces, fine china, touches of chintz – and friendly Diana who helps you plan your day. Buses to Piccadilly and Westminster, a stroll to the Thames, all of London at your feet.

Tube: Fulham Broadway, 6-minute walk. Parking pay & display. Bus: 211, 414, 14.

Rooms	1 twin/double.
Price	£95-£120. Singles from £80.
Meals	Pubs/restaurants within walking distance.
Closed	Rarely.

Diana FitzGeorge-Balfour
35 Burnthwaite Road,
Fulham,
London SW6 5BQ
Tel	+44 (0)20 7385 8081
Mobile	+44 (0)7831 571449
Email	diana@dianabalfour.co.uk
Web	www.dianabalfour.co.uk

Entry 310   Map 22

21 Barclay Road

The grand piano is a magnet for conductors and music professors from around the world. Delightful Charlotte and Adrian host lively social music evenings; Charlotte, who does something unspeakably high-powered by day, happily advises the best outings. All is swish here: polished oak floors, a sunny roof terrace, beautifully done bedrooms with decanters of sherry and luxuriously dressed beds (one a splendid king), and smart sparkling bathrooms. Help yourself to good espresso and a light breakfast tray in your room before setting off to tour London. Bring your instrument... a great city find.

Use of grand piano by arrangement. Tube: Fulham Broadway, 2-minute walk. Parking free 8pm-9am & all Sunday. 9am-8pm pay & display.

Rooms	2 doubles.
Price	£100.
Meals	Food & music evenings occasionally. Pubs/restaurants 2-minute walk.
Closed	Occasionally.

Charlotte Dexter
21 Barclay Road,
Fulham,
London SW6 1EJ
Tel	+44 (0)20 7384 3390
Mobile	+44 (0)7767 420943
Email	info@barclayhouselondon.com
Web	www.barclayhouselondon.com

Entry 311   Map 22

London

London

8 Parthenia Road

Caroline, an interior designer, mixes the sophistication of the city with the feel of the countryside and her handsome big kitchen is the engine-room of the house. It leads through to a light breakfast room with doors onto a pretty brick garden with chairs and table – hope for fine days. The house is long and thin, Fulham style, and reaches up to a big sloping-ceilinged bedroom in the eaves, cosy, sunny and bright. A remarkably quiet place to stay in an accessible part of town, near the King's Road with all its antique and designer shops, and Chelsea Football ground.

Tube: Parsons Green, 4-minute walk. Parking £17.60 per day in street (9am-5pm), free on Sunday. Bus: 22, 2-minute walk.

22 Marville Road

Smart railings help a pink rose climb, orange lilies add a touch of colour, and breakfast is in the pretty back garden on sunny days. Ben, the spaniel, and Christine – music lover, traveller, rower – make you feel at home. Your big light-filled bedroom is high up in the eaves and comes in elegant French grey with comfortable beds, crisp linen, pretty lamps, a smart bathroom and a chaise longue for lounging and reading. The house is friendly with treasures from Christine's travels and gentle music at breakfast; there's a baby grand to play too. Restaurants and shops are a stroll away and the Boat Race down the river.

At Fulham Rd junc. with Parson's Green Lane, down Kelvedon Rd. Cross Bishop Rd into Homestead Rd; 1st left into Marville Rd. Tube: Parsons Green.

Rooms	1 twin/double.
Price	£100-£140. Singles from £85.
Meals	Continental breakfast. Restaurants nearby.
Closed	Rarely.

Rooms	1 twin/double.
Price	£95. Singles from £80.
Meals	Continental breakfast. Pubs/restaurants nearby.
Closed	Rarely.

Caroline & George Docker
8 Parthenia Road,
Fulham,
London SW6 4BD
Tel   +44 (0)20 7384 1165
Email   dockercaroline@gmail.com

Christine Drake
22 Marville Road,
Fulham,
London SW6 7BD
Tel   +44 (0)20 7381 3205
Email   christine.drake@btinternet.com
Web   www.londonguestsathome.com

Entry 312   Map 22

Entry 313   Map 22

London

Chiswick B&B

In a suburb of London long favoured by artists is a neat brick Victorian house framed by a beautiful maple; inside is a stylish and contemporary home. Warm gentle Ragini – life coach and English teacher – welcomes you in. Find cream marble floors, a fabulous kitchen, Indian art on the walls and the scent of fresh lilies. All feels spacious, generous and calm, and there's a sweet garden behind. Bedrooms are upstairs: fresh, snug, with waffle robes and goose down; breakfast is vegetarian and delicious. Chiswick House, Kew and the river are wonderfully close, and the 94 bus whisks you straight to Piccadilly!

Tube: Turnham Green, 5-minute walk; across park, right on street with red post box.

Rooms	3: 1 double; 2 doubles sharing bath.
Price	£100–£130. Singles £85.
Meals	Dinner £30. Pubs/restaurants 5-minute walk.
Closed	Rarely.

Ragini Annan
Chiswick B&B,
Chiswick,
London W4 1JG
Mobile   +44 (0)7973 327662
Email   reservations@chiswickbandb.com
Web   www.chiswickbandb.com

Entry 314   Map 22

London

31 Rowan Road

Terrific value for money in Brook Green. Two private studios: one under the eaves (a big comfy bed, a window seat, a deep cast-iron bath from which you can gaze at the birds), the other larger and more contemporary in style, on the lower ground floor, with its own wisteria-clad entrance. Continental breakfast is popped into your fridge the night before. Or do proper B&B and join in with family life in a pink bedroom with books and hats (there's a spacious teenager's bedroom, too), then take breakfast in the pretty conservatory with Vicky and Edmund. There's a garden full of blossom and super restaurants close by.

Tube: Hammersmith. Off-street parking £20 a day.

Rooms	4: 2 doubles sharing bath/shower; 2 studios, each with twin/double, bath/shower & kitchenette. Extra bed available.
Price	£65–£120. Singles £65–£100. Extra person £15.
Meals	Continental breakfast. Pubs/restaurants 2 minutes.
Closed	Occasionally.

Vicky & Edmund Sixsmith
31 Rowan Road,
Brook Green, Hammersmith,
London W6 7DT
Tel   +44 (0)20 8748 0930
Mobile   +44 (0)7966 829359
Email   vickysixsmith@me.com
Web   www.abetterwaytostay.co.uk

Entry 315   Map 22

London

101 Abbotsbury Road

The area is one of London's most desirable and Sunny's family home is opposite the borough's loveliest park, with open-air opera in summer. The top floor is for visitors. Warm, homely bedrooms are in gentle beiges and greens, with pale carpets, white duvets, pelmeted windows and a pretty dressing table for the double. The bathroom, marble-tiled and sky-lit, shines. You are well placed for Kensington High Street, Olympia, Notting Hill, Portobello Market, Kensington Gardens, the Albert Hall, Knightsbridge and Piccadilly! Relax, unwind, feel free to come and go.

Over sixes welcome. Tube: Holland Park, 7-minute walk. Off-street parking sometimes available.

Rooms	2: 1 double, 1 single, sharing bath.
Price	£110. Singles from £55.
Meals	Continental breakfast. Pubs/restaurants 5-minute walk.
Closed	Occasionally.

Sunny Murray
101 Abbotsbury Road,
Holland Park,
London W14 8EP
Tel   +44 (0)20 7602 0179
Mobile +44 (0)7768 362562
Email   sunny.murray@googlemail.com

Entry 316   Map 22

London

1 Peel Street

Pretty, gabled and surprisingly quiet with central London on your doorstep. Fascinating old maps, photos from Susie and Trevor's world travels and objets d'art all create an unusual and elegant feel. The top floor is all yours: the bedroom is full of character, framed by the slanting angles of the roof and soothingly decorated in neutral shades; the shelf above the snug-looking bed is crammed with interesting reads. Breakfast is at a table overlooking the patio: organic bread, pastries, fruit and excellent coffee. Just a stroll to good tapas, wine bars, Hyde Park and Notting Hill. Hop on a bus or tube to explore further.

Rooms	1 double with separate bath/shower.
Price	£115. Singles £85.
Meals	Continental breakfast. Pubs/restaurants 2-minute walk.
Closed	Occasionally.

Susan & Trevor Laws
1 Peel Street,
Kensington,
London W8 7PA
Tel   +44 (0)20 7792 8361
Mobile +44 (0)7776 140060
Email   susan@susielaws.co.uk

Entry 317   Map 22

London

The Roost

The immaculate pale blue-painted front door sets the tone for this large and lofty Victorian home. This is boutique B&B and you get smart hotel-standard rooms at a fraction of the price. The furniture is excellent: fine family pieces and clever Liz's handsome finds. There is a conservatory for continental breakfast, a delightful Parson Russell dog and art everywhere. Liz, a former fashion pattern cutter and dancer, is a natural and lovely hostess. The Roost is brilliantly positioned for whizzing into town, yet here you have a lovely park, an irresistible bakery, great restaurants and a farmers' market on Sundays. Marvellous.

Rooms	3 doubles.
Price	£100–£120. Singles £85–£105.
Meals	Pubs/restaurants 5-minute walk.
Closed	Rarely.

Liz Crosland
The Roost,
37 Lynton Road, Queen's Park,
London NW6 6BE
Tel   +44 (0)20 7625 6770
Mobile +44 (0)7967 354477
Email   liz@boutiquebandblondon.com
Web   www.boutiquebandblondon.com

Entry 318   Map 22

London

30 King Henry's Road

Shops, restaurants and sublime views of Primrose Hill are a five-minute stroll from this interesting 1860s house; walls are covered in a lifetime collection of maps, drawings and watercolours. Your room on the top floor has a comfortable brass bed, a sisal floor, fine pieces of furniture, a wall of books, digital TV and a smart new bathroom. Breakfast on homemade bread and jams, bagels, croissants, yogurts and fresh fruit salad in the large kitchen/dining room with a big open fire and garden views. There's open-air theatre in Regent's Park in summer; Carole and Ted know London well and will happily advise.

Minimum two nights weekends. Tube: Chalk Farm, 5-minute walk. Free parking at weekends, ticket parking nearby.

Rooms	1 double.
Price	£120. Singles £110.
Meals	Pubs/restaurants 2-minute walk.
Closed	Occasionally.

Carole & Ted Cox
30 King Henry's Road,
Primrose Hill,
London NW3 3RP
Tel   +44 (0)20 7483 2871
Mobile +44 (0)7976 389350
Email   carole.l.cox@gmail.com

Entry 319   Map 22

London

66 Camden Square

A modern, architect designed house made of African teak, brick and glass. Climb wooden stairs under a glazed pyramid to light-filled, Japanese-style bedrooms with low platform beds, modern chairs and private sitting room/study. Sue and Rodger have travelled widely so there are pictures, photographs and ethnic pieces everywhere – and a burst of colour from Peckam the parrot. Share their lovely open-plan dining space overlooking a verdant bird-filled courtyard at breakfast – a delicious start to the day. Cool Camden's bustling market is close, along with theatres, restaurants, bars and zoo.

Min. two nights at w/ends. Children over eight welcome. Tube: Camden Town or Kentish Town. Parking free at weekends; meters during week. Ten mins by taxi or 20-min walk from St Pancras.

Rooms	2: 1 double; 1 single sharing bath (let to same party only).
Price	£100–£110. Singles £60–£80.
Meals	Pubs/restaurants nearby.
Closed	Occasionally.

Sue & Rodger Davis
66 Camden Square,
Camden Town,
London NW1 9XD
Tel   +44 (0)20 7485 4622
Email   rodgerdavis@btopenworld.com

Entry 320   Map 22

London

Arlington Avenue

This 1848 townhouse is a real find – from here you can follow the canal up to Islington. Inside you find a world of books and art; immaculate bedrooms (the double very spacious) are colourful and filled with pictures, etchings and pretty furniture, with views over several gardens to the back. The grey marble shared guest bathroom is two flights down, but if you don't mind that, you've struck gold. Shop locally, eat picnic suppers in the red and gold dining room, chill drinks in the fridge. You help yourself to breakfast in a lemon coloured country style kitchen; this is laissez-faire B&B and fantastic value.

Tube: Angel & Old Street (15-minute walk). Buses: 5 minutes to stops for City, St Pauls, Tate Modern. Limited parking (by arrangement).

Rooms	2: 1 double, 1 single sharing bath.
Price	£55–£70. Singles £45–£65.
Meals	Pubs/restaurants 100 yds.
Closed	Rarely.

Thomas Blaikie
Arlington Avenue,
Islington,
London N1 7AX
Mobile +44 (0)7711 265183
Email   thomas@arlingtonavenue.co.uk
Web   www.arlingtonavenue.co.uk

Entry 321   Map 22

London

26 Florence Street

There's a dramatic vibrancy to Valerie's home, just off Upper Street with its restaurants, and right by the Almeida and Sadler's Wells theatres. The Victorian house is stuffed with oriental, French and Italian pieces; the basement bedroom is filled with light and character. A feast of beautiful scenes and stories, Valerie's interior design merits applause; walls and doors are ragged, sponged and stencilled in the colourful style of the Bloomsbury set; the conservatory has John Soane perspectives and there's a spacious sitting room for guests. Breakfast? You can take it at the delightful Carluccio's close by.

Minimum stay two nights.

Rooms	1 double with separate shower (extra single available, so occasional share).
Price	£120. Singles £95.
Meals	Breakfast not included; juice, milk, fruit, tea/coffee available. Cafés 5-minute walk.
Closed	Occasionally.

Valerie Rossmore
26 Florence Street,
Islington,
London N1 2FW

Tel	+44 (0)20 7359 5293 (please email if after 6pm)
Email	valerie@valerierossmore.co.uk
Web	www.valerierossmore.co.uk

Entry 322 Map 22

London

Russell's

Be in the thick of edgy, vibrant, multi-cultural London in this bright pink Victorian terraced house bang on the high street. Lovely Annette gives you imaginative, well-sourced breakfasts: try mushrooms cooked in truffle oil. You enjoy a chic guest sitting room with vintage furniture, a friendly whippet called Reggie, interesting book shelves and a steel and glass table. Lovely uncluttered bedrooms (those overlooking the garden are quieter) have good art and some great 60s and 70s pieces. Bathrooms are neatly tiled and have powerful showers. A 20-minute walk to the Olympic Stadium – but near Hackney Marshes with grazing cows!

Rooms	6: 2 doubles, 1 twin/double, 1 single all en suite; 1 double, 1 twin/double sharing bath.
Price	£75–£115. Singles from £75.
Meals	Pubs/restaurants 5-minute walk.
Closed	Rarely.

Annette Russell
Russell's,
123 Chatsworth Road,
Clapton,
London E5 0LA

Mobile	+44 (0)7976 669906
Email	annette@russellsofclapton.com
Web	www.russellsofclapton.com

Entry 323 Map 4

London

Fleet River Bakery Rooms

Meet real Londoners, not tides of tourists, in the streets of this vibrant, historic, very central part of town. Your handsome, city-sharp studio is above the bustling bakery/café: nip downstairs for delicious complimentary breakfast and coffee. You have an ample kitchen cum living area with a shiny wooden floor, a sofa, and a seriously comfortable bed – all good-looking in a refreshingly frill-free way, and surprisingly quiet. People-watch through the tall windows, cook up some local market produce or head out for a bundle of good restaurants – Covent Garden, Bloomsbury and the West End are all an easy walk.

Tube: Holborn; left from the main exit, down Kingsway, 2nd lane on left (Twyford Place). House on right at the end (corner of Twyford Place & Gate St).

Rooms	4 studios: 3 doubles, 1 twin. Each with kitchenette.
Price	£115. Singles £84.
Meals	Lunch in café downstairs, from £6.50. Packed lunch £7.50.
Closed	Rarely.

Lucy Clapp
Fleet River Bakery Rooms,
71 Lincoln's Inn Fields, Holborn,
London WC2A 3JF

Tel	+44 (0)20 7691 1457
Mobile	+44 (0)7966 267401
Email	rooms@fleetriverbakery.com
Web	www.fleetriverbakery.com

Entry 324   Map 22

London

26 Montefiore Street

Step off a quiet street into a hall of rich golds and a charming, elegant and comfortable bolthole. There's a little bird-filled garden where you can breakfast in summer: an organic spread with homemade jams and bread. This house is brimful of books – your bedroom too. Find white linen on a good handmade mattress, dressing gowns and, down steps, a fresh chic bathroom with fluffy towels and bath oils. No sitting room but there are wicker chairs in a corner of the library/dining room facing the pretty garden. Walk to Battersea Arts Centre and Battersea Park with its festivals and art fairs; not far from Chelsea Flower Show too.

Bus: 77, 87, 137 & 452. Tube: Clapham Common. Train: Queenstown Rd & Battersea Park. Parking: day pass £5, 9.30am-5.30pm; free evenings & weekends.

Rooms	1 double with separate bath/shower (1 child single in attached study).
Price	£110-£115. Singles £80. Study £50.
Meals	Restaurants 300 yds.
Closed	Occasionally.

D Porter
26 Montefiore Street,
Battersea,
London SW8 3TL

Tel	+44 (0)20 7720 0939
Email	bedandbreakfast.london.sw8@gmail.com

Entry 325   Map 22

London

20 St Philip Street

Come to retreat from the frenzy of city life. In the 1890 Victorian cottage all is peaceful and calm and Barbara looks after you beautifully. The dining room, with the odd oriental piece from past travels, is where you have your full English breakfast – unusual for London – and across the hall is the elegant sitting room, with gilt-framed mirrors, sumptuous curtains, and a piano. Upstairs is a bright and restful bedroom with pretty linen and a cloud of goose down. The large, sparkling bathroom next door is all yours – fabulous. Nothing has been overlooked and the tiny courtyard garden is a summer oasis.

Train: 6-min Waterloo, 3-min Victoria. Bus: 137, 452 (Sloane Sq) & 156 (Vauxhall). Tube: 10 mins. Parking: £2 per hour or £10 day, 9.30am-5.30pm (free at weekends).

Rooms	1 double with separate bath & shower.
Price	£110. Singles £80.
Meals	Pubs/restaurants 200 yds.
Closed	Occasionally.

Barbara Graham
20 St Philip Street,
Battersea,
London SW8 3SL

Tel +44 (0)20 7498 9967
Email stay@bed-breakfast-battersea.co.uk
Web www.bed-breakfast-battersea.co.uk

Entry 326 Map 22

London

The Glebe House

Surely one of London's most villagey spots? Find a pretty Georgian house snuggling up to the church, a community pottery and beehives and allotments in a walled garden. Alix has weaved her magic into every corner of her home. The sitting room, with velvet and linen sofas on toasty stone floors, was once an archway for horses and carriages; now it's a lofty space with huge doors onto a courtyard. Your bed is antique, your room deeply peaceful, the bathroom bright with white Metro brick tiles. Help yourself to a continental breakfast of cereal, fruit, and artisan breads in the funky kitchen. Alix, son and puppy are a delight.

Rooms	2: 1 double sharing family bathroom; 1 double sharing bathroom (let to same party only).
Price	£110. Singles £80.
Meals	Continental breakfast. Pubs/restaurants 0.2 miles.
Closed	Rarely.

Alix Bateman
The Glebe House,
Clapham Old Town,
London SW4 0DZ

Tel +44 (0)20 7720 3844
Web www.theglebehouselondon.com

Entry 327 Map 22

London

38 Killieser Avenue

On a quiet leafy street, country-house chic in South London. Philip and Winkle have filled their elegant Victorian townhouse with stunning fabrics, sunny colours and treasures from far-flung travels. The house glows, the garden is ravishing, breakfasts are delicious (so are the scones – book a cream tea course!) and bedrooms are spacious: fine linen, lambswool throws, waffle robes, the scent of roses. Few people do things with as much natural good humour as Winkle, whose passions are cooking, gardening and garden history (tours can be arranged). Transport is close and you can be in Victoria in 15 minutes.

Garden tours & afternoon tea. Minimum two nights at weekends. Balham tube 15-min walk.

Rooms	2: 1 twin; 1 single with separate bath.
Price	£105–£110. Singles from £85.
Meals	Dinner £30–£35.
Closed	Occasionally.

Winkle Haworth
38 Killieser Avenue,
Streatham Hill,
London SW2 4NT

Tel	+44 (0)20 8671 4196
Email	winklehaworth@hotmail.com
Web	www.thegardenbedandbreakfast.com

Entry 328   Map 22

London

28 Old Devonshire Road

In a quiet part of Balham – close to leafy common, tube and train – are Georgina's lovely home and award-winning garden. Enjoy breakfast under the pear tree, or at the long wooden table in the dining room, with a marble fireplace and a friend's watercolours. You have the top floor to yourself: a sunny, cosy bedroom, with city views, a TV, lots of books; a big bathroom too, with a fab shower and comforting waffle robes to pad about in. Georgina lays on a special breakfast and all sorts of thoughtful extras. She loves to chat (speaks French and Italian too) really knows her London and will help plan your stay.

Minimum two nights. 8-min walk from Balham, mainline and tube. Visitors' parking permits available £7 per day.

Rooms	1 double.
Price	£95. Singles £75.
Meals	Pubs/restaurants 500 yds.
Closed	Rarely.

Georgina Ivor
28 Old Devonshire Road,
Balham,
London SW12 9RB

Tel	+44 (0)20 8673 7179
Mobile	+44 (0)7941 960199
Email	georgina@balhambandb.co.uk
Web	www.balhambandb.co.uk

Entry 329   Map 22

London

108 Streathbourne Road

It's a handsome house in a conservation area that manages to be both elegant and cosy. The cream-coloured double bedroom has an armchair, a writing desk, pretty curtains and a big comfy walnut bed; the twin is light and airy. The dining room overlooks a secluded terrace and garden and there are newspapers at breakfast. You can eat in – David, who works in the wine trade, always puts a bottle on the table – or out, at one of the trendy new restaurants in Balham. A friendly city base on a quiet, tree-lined street – maximum comfort, delicious food and good value for London. Delightful.

Min. two nights. Tube: Tooting Bec 7-minute walk. 319 bus from Sloane Square. Free parking weekends, otherwise meters or £7 daily permit.

Rooms	2: 1 double, 1 twin.
Price	£90–£100. Singles £80–£85.
Meals	Dinner £35.
	Restaurants 5-minute walk.
Closed	Occasionally.

Mary & David Hodges
108 Streathbourne Road,
Balham,
London SW17 8QY
Tel   +44 (0)20 8767 6931
Email   davidandmaryhodges@gmail.com
Web   www.southwestlondonbandb.co.uk

Entry 330   Map 22

London

The Coach House

A rare privacy: you have your own coach house, separated from the Notts' home by a stylish terracotta-potted courtyard with Indian sandstone paving and various fruit trees (peach, pear, nectarine). Breakfast in your own sunny kitchen, or let Meena treat you to a full English in hers (she makes great porridge, too). The lovely big attic bedroom has beams, cream curtains, rugs on polished wood floors; the brick-walled ground-floor twin is pleasant and airy; both look over the peaceful garden. Urban but bucolic – just perfect as a romantic retreat, or a family getaway.

Minimum three nights; two nights Jan & Feb.

Rooms	Coach House: 1 family room for 2-3;
	1 twin with separate shower.
	Same-party bookings only.
Price	£110. £190 for whole coach house.
Meals	Pub/restaurant 200 yds.
Closed	Occasionally.

Meena & Harley Nott
The Coach House,
2 Tunley Road, Balham,
London SW17 7QJ
Tel   +44 (0)20 8772 1939
Email   coachhouse@chslondon.com
Web   www.coachhouse.chslondon.com

Entry 331   Map 22

London

The Rising Sun

Step from the grass of Wimbledon Common and into this relaxed artists' home, a splendid 18th-century former inn fronted by a lovely walled garden. Expect a big welcome from Carol and two rescue dogs before being led upstairs, passing John in his studio. The guest room showcases their work – her landscapes above wrought-iron bedsteads and John's Italian watercolours – to an elegant palette of greys and birdsong from the garden. Then there's the breakfast room with its 1730s King George fireplace and morning light streaming from French windows onto John's portraits; Carol's breakfasts are pretty wonderful too.

Rooms	1 twin.
Price	£110. Singles £80.
Meals	Pubs/restaurants 0.2 miles.
Closed	Rarely.

Carol & John Whittall
The Rising Sun,
22a West Side Common,
Wimbledon,
London SW19 4UF
Tel   +44 (0)20 8946 3949
Mobile +44 (0)7815 286551
Email   stay@risingsunbandb.co.uk
Web   www.risingsunbandb.co.uk

Entry 332   Map 22

London

113 Pepys Road

This Victorian terraced house overlooks the first landscaped park of its kind in south-east London; the pretty garden, designed by David's father, is graced with majestic magnolias. Find a quirky mix of classic British furniture and oriental antiques. Picking up from his Chinese mother Anne, David has now taken on the B&B (helped by his housekeeper) and breakfast can be English or oriental. It's a convivial, lived-in home full of family portraits, batiks and books; the Chinese 'Peony' room downstairs has a huge bed, bamboo blinds, kimonos for the bathroom. A short walk to buses and tubes... and blissfully quiet for London.

Rooms	3: 1 double, 1 twin/double; 1 twin with separate bath.
Price	£110. Singles £85.
Meals	Restaurant 0.5 miles.
Closed	Rarely.

David Marten
113 Pepys Road,
New Cross,
London SE14 5SE
Tel   +44 (0)20 7639 1060
Email davidmarten@pepysroad.com
Web   www.pepysroad.com

Entry 333   Map 22

London

16 St Alfege Passage

The peaceful approach is along the passage between the Hawksmoor church and its graveyard, away from Greenwich hubbub. At the end of the lane is a 'cottage' set about with greenery, lamp posts and benches; inside, a cup of tea and flapjack await you in the eccentrically furnished (stuffed cat on dentist chair, huge parasol) sitting room. Bedrooms are cosy and colourful, with double beds (not huge) that positively encourage intimacy. Breakfast – delicious – is in the basement, another engagingly furnished room awash with character. Robert, an actor, is easy, funny, chatty – and has created an unusual and attractive place.

Three-min walk from Greenwich train & Docklands Light Railway station or Cutty Sark DLR station. Parking free from 5pm (6pm Sundays) to 9am.

Rooms	3: 1 double, 1 four-poster, 1 single.
Price	£90–£125. Singles from £80.
Meals	Pubs/restaurants 2-minute walk.
Closed	Rarely.

Nicholas Mesure & Robert Gray
16 St Alfege Passage,
Greenwich,
London SE10 9JS
Tel   +44 (0)20 8853 4337
Email   info@st-alfeges.co.uk
Web   www.st-alfeges.co.uk

Entry 334   Map 22

Norfolk

The Old Rectory

A stately place indeed: a venerable English rectory replete with period furniture, art, history, well-bred hosts (he shoots, she rides) and, in the expansive grounds, a ruined chapel, lake, croquet lawn and pool. Breakfast is served on the terrace in summer. You dine by candlelight on local game and the kitchen garden's offerings, then settle in the Georgian drawing room by the rocking horse. Sleep in the Coach House where plush beds have beautiful linen, warm throws and beaded cushions; dogs can stay in the stables. A rare chance to experience the best of British country life.

Riding & shooting can be arranged.

Rooms	Coach House: 1 double, 1 twin/double, 1 twin.
Price	£85–£105. Singles £65–£85.
Meals	Dinner, 2 courses, £25; 3 courses, £35. Pub 1 mile. Restaurant 5 miles.
Closed	Rarely.

Veronica de Lotbiniere
The Old Rectory,
Ferry Road,
King's Lynn, Oxborough,
Norfolk PE33 9PT
Tel   +44 (0)1366 328962
Mobile   +44 (0)7769 687599
Email   onky.del@btinternet.com
Web   www.oldrectoryoxboroughbandb.co.uk

Entry 335   Map 9

Norfolk

The Merchants House

The oak four-poster – a beauty – came with the house. Part of the building (1400) is the oldest in Wells; in those days, the merchant could bring his boats up to the door. Liz and Dennis know the history, and happily share it. Inside is friendly and inviting: the mahogany shines, bathrooms sparkle, there are books to borrow and pretty sash windows overlook salt marshes. Breakfasts are a treat: homemade bread and jams, local produce and flowers on the table. As for Wells, it's on the famous Coastal Path, has a quay bustling with boats and 16 miles of sands. Birdwatch by day, dine out at night – easy when you're in the centre.

Minimum stay two nights in July & August.

Rooms	2: 1 double; 1 four-poster with separate bath/shower.
Price	£85–£95. Singles £65.
Meals	Pubs/restaurants 300 yds.
Closed	Rarely.

Elizabeth & Dennis Woods
The Merchants House,
47 Freeman Street,
Wells-next-the-Sea,
Norfolk NR23 1BQ

Tel	+44 (0)1328 711877
Mobile	+44 (0)7816 632742
Email	denniswoods@talktalk.net
Web	www.the-merchants-house.co.uk

Entry 336   Map 10

Norfolk

Holly Lodge

The whole place radiates a lavish attention to detail, from the spoilingly comfortable beds to the complimentary bottle of wine. It's perfect for those who love their privacy: these three snug guest 'cottages' have their own entrances as well as smart iron bedsteads and rugs on stone tiles, neat little shower rooms and tapestry-seat chairs, and books, music and TVs. Enjoy the Mediterranean garden, the handsome conservatory and the utter peace; Holt and historic Little Walsingham are nearby. Your hosts are delightful: ex-restaurateur Jeremy who cooks enthusiastically, ethically and with panache, and Canadian-raised Gill.

Rooms	3 cottages for 2.
Price	£90–£120. Singles £70–£100
Meals	Dinner, 3 courses with wine, £19.50. Pubs/restaurants 1 mile.
Closed	Rarely.

Jeremy Bolam
Holly Lodge,
Thursford Green,
Norfolk NR21 0AS

Tel	+44 (0)1328 878465
Email	info@hollylodgeguesthouse.co.uk
Web	www.hollylodgeguesthouse.co.uk

Entry 337   Map 10

Green Farm House

Sun streams in through the French windows of your own chic garden room – make yourself at home. Find books, DVDs, rugs on slate floors, watercolours and pots of flowers, and a comfy sofa by the wood-burner; if you're peckish there are tea and biscuits too. Sleep peacefully in well-dressed bedrooms with smart bathrooms, one with a shower, one with a bath. Lucy's house is next door and breakfast is across the garden in her conservatory: enjoy local sausages, bacon and eggs, toast with free-range eggs, homemade marmalade and muesli. Friendly Lucy can arrange sailing; it's heaven for walkers, cyclists and birdwatchers too.

1 Leicester Meadows

Up among 13 acres of wild meadow and woodland – not another building in sight. It's all so relaxed and unhurried: barn owls roosting in the outhouse, hens strutting, geese pottering up from the pond. The 19th-century cottages have been imaginatively restored; Bob was an architect, Sara an art teacher, and both are immensely friendly and helpful. Polished wood and old brick are topped with bright rugs; paintings and ceramics engage the eye; bedrooms have flowers and colourful covers. Hop downstairs for a superb breakfast at the big convivial table: rare-breed bacon, homemade jams and bread, fruits from the kitchen garden.

Rooms	1 double. Garden Room: 1 double.	Rooms	2: 1 double & sitting room; 1 twin/double.
Price	£80–£100.	Price	£70. Singles from £60.
Meals	Pub within 2 miles.	Meals	Supper from £20. Pub 1 mile.
Closed	Rarely.	Closed	Rarely.

	Lucy Jupe Green Farm House, Balls Lane, Thursford, Fakenham, Norfolk NR21 0BX		**Bob & Sara Freakley** 1 Leicester Meadows, South Creake, Fakenham, Norfolk NR21 9NZ
Tel	+44 (0)1328 878507		
Mobile	+44 (0)7768 542645	Tel	+44 (0)1328 823533
Email	ljupe@nnv.org.uk	Email	rf@freakley.com
Web	www.nnv.org.uk	Web	www.leicestermeadows.com

Entry 338   Map 10

Entry 339   Map 10

Norfolk

Bagthorpe Hall

Ten minutes from Burnham Market, yet here you are immersed in peaceful countryside. Tid is a pioneer of organic farming and the stunning 700 acres include a woodland snowdrop walk. Gina's passions are music, dance and gardens and she organises open days and concerts for charity. Theirs is a large, elegant house with a fascinating hall mural chronicling their family life; bedrooms – one with a tiny en suite shower room – have big comfy beds and lovely views. Breakfasts are delicious with local sausages and bacon, homemade jams and raspberries from the garden. Birdwatching, cycling and walking are all around.

Stabling available.

Rooms	3: 1 double; 1 double, 1 twin each with separate shower.
Price	£80. Singles £50.
Meals	Pubs/restaurants 2 miles.
Closed	Rarely.

Gina & Tid Morton
Bagthorpe Hall,
Bagthorpe, Bircham,
King's Lynn,
Norfolk PE31 6QY
Tel   +44 (0)1485 578528
Mobile +44 (0)7979 746591
Email   dgmorton@hotmail.com
Web   www.bagthorpehall.co.uk

Entry 340   Map 10

Norfolk

Bagthorpe Treehouse

Gina and Tid at Bagthorpe Hall loved their safari travels in Africa, and were captivated by the idea of living outdoors – in comfort and surrounded by nature. So the spot for their treehouse has been carefully chosen, under a holm oak in a small copse. With its king-size four-poster and huge copper bathtub it is a luxurious and romantic retreat. You even get an oven and hob, and the two single bunks enable children over eight to come too. Breakfast hampers – generous and delicious – can be ordered. What fun to eat in on the veranda and survey the wildlife on your 'Norfolk safari'!'

Children over eight welcome. Minimum two nights. Book through Sawday's Canopy & Stars online or by phone.

Rooms	Treehouse (1 double, 2 bunks for children).
Price	Treehouse £215–£260.
Meals	Breakfast hamper for 2, £15. Pubs/restaurants 2 miles.
Closed	Never.

Sawday's Canopy & Stars
Bagthorpe Treehouse,
Bagthorpe Hall, Bircham,
King's Lynn,
Norfolk PE31 6QY
Tel   +44 (0)1275 395447
Email enquiries@canopyandstars.co.uk
Web   www.canopyandstars.co.uk/
          bagthorpetreehouse

Entry 341   Map 10

Norfolk

The Close

A large, creeper-clad, Victorian house in the middle of the village, with a smooth lawn, mature trees, curved herbaceous border and a stream (source of the river Wensum). Bedrooms, one with a garden view, are large, light and airy, with a mix of antique and contemporary furniture, flowers, comfortable sofas with floral cushions; shower rooms are spotlessly tiled. You breakfast on home-baked bread and the local butcher's finest at a huge mahogany table in the dining room. Val and Rory know their patch well, so do ask: this is wonderful walking countryside and you are near the coast; Sandringham and Houghton, too.

Rooms	2 doubles.
Price	£85–£90. Singles £70.
Meals	Pub/restaurant 200 yds.
Closed	Rarely.

	Valerie McGouran
	The Close,
	Station Road, East Rudham,
	King's Lynn,
	Norfolk PE31 8SU
Tel	+44 (0)1485 528925
Email	rorymcgouran@hotmail.com
Web	www.closenorfolk.com

Entry 342   Map 10

Norfolk

Meadow House

Handmade oak banisters, period furniture: this new-build is beautifully traditional. Breakfast is served in the lovely large drawing room, where you find a warm, sociable atmosphere with squashy sofas and comfy chairs for anytime use. One bedroom is cosy and chintzy, the other is larger and more neutral; brand-new bathrooms gleam. Amanda knows B&B, does it well, and plans to grow vegetables once her land is tamed. There are footpaths from the door and plenty to see, starting with Walpole's Houghton Hall, a short walk. A bucolic setting for a profoundly comfortable stay, perfect for country enthusiasts.

Rooms	2 twins/doubles.
Price	£70. Singles from £40.
Meals	Packed lunch £5-£7.
	Pub 9-minute walk.
Closed	Rarely.

	Amanda Case
	Meadow House,
	Harpley, King's Lynn,
	Norfolk PE31 6TU
Tel	+44 (0)1485 520240
Mobile	+44 (0)7890 037134
Email	amandacase@amandacase.plus.com
Web	www.meadowhousebandb.co.uk

Entry 343   Map 10

Norfolk

Tudor Lodgings

A treasured family home on the site of Castle Acre's medieval defences, with dogs, ducks and views of the lovely Nar valley. A cosy guest sitting room leads to the ancient, dark-beamed dining room hung with portraits, where you breakfast on good things home-made and local; do try a Swaffham Sizzler. Cottagey bedrooms are cream-carpeted and have coordinated fabrics, attractive wildlife prints and small shower rooms. Julia is passionate about garden history, Gus is a keen fisherman; both know their history and horses. Peddars Way runs close by and you're not far from the coast – or the village pub!

Rooms	2 twins.
Price	£75. Singles £55.
Meals	Pub within walking distance.
Closed	Rarely.

Julia Stafford–Allen
Tudor Lodgings,
Castle Acre, King's Lynn,
Norfolk PE32 2AN

Tel	+44 (0)1760 755334
Email	jstaffordallen@btinternet.com
Web	www.tudorlodgings.co.uk

Entry 344 Map 10

Norfolk

Litcham Hall

For the whole of the 19th century this was Litcham's doctor's house; the Hall is still at the centre of the community. The big-windowed guest bedrooms look onto stunning gardens with yew hedges, a lily pond and herbaceous borders. This is a thoroughly English home with elegant proportions – the hall, drawing room and dining room are gracious and beautifully furnished, and there's a large sitting room for guests. The garden fills the breakfast table with soft fruit in season and John and Hermione are friendly and most helpful. Close to Fakenham, Burnham Market and the coast.

Children & pets by arrangement.

Rooms	3: 2 doubles;
	1 twin with separate bath.
Price	£70–£90. Singles by arrangement.
Meals	Pub in village & 5 miles.
Closed	Christmas.

John & Hermione Birkbeck
Litcham Hall,
Litcham, King's Lynn,
Norfolk PE32 2QQ

Tel	+44 (0)1328 701389
Email	hermionebirkbeck@hotmail.com
Web	www.litchamhall.co.uk

Entry 345 Map 10

Norfolk

Carrick's at Castle Farm

This warm-bricked farmhouse is up a long drive and surrounded by 720 acres; John's family have lived here since the 1920s. He and Jean are passionate about conservation and the protection of wildlife, and here you have absolute quiet – for bird-watching, fishing or walking. Return to the drawing room with its open fire, books, and decanter of sherry. Your friendly hosts give you coffee and cake, or wine, when you arrive, and bedrooms are light and luxurious with pretty fabrics and homemade biscuits. Breakfasts and candlelit dinners are delicious, and the garden leads to a footpath alongside the river.

Rooms	4: 1 double, 2 twins/doubles; 1 double with separate bath.
Price	£95. Singles £65.
Meals	Dinner, 3 courses, £30. BYO. Pub 0.5 miles.
Closed	Rarely.

Jean Wright
Carrick's at Castle Farm,
Castle Farm,
Swanton Morley,
Dereham,
Norfolk NR20 4JT
Tel   +44 (0)1362 638302
Email   jean@castlefarm-swanton.co.uk
Web   www.carricksatcastlefarm.co.uk

Entry 346   Map 10

Norfolk

Norfolk Courtyard

Walk straight in through French windows to your own, underfloor-heated room in the courtyard; privacy from the main house where young and friendly Simon and Catherine live. The rooms are decorated in soft colours, mattresses are perfect, cotton sheets are smooth and your handsome bathroom has limestone tiles – all rather luxurious. There's a welcome tea tray and a fridge to cool a bottle; help yourself to continental breakfast in the old, beamed barn next door with French iron chairs, croissants, crumpets, homemade jams and muesli. Very civilised! Stunning walks await on the coast.

Minimum stay two nights high season weekends.

Rooms	4: 3 doubles, 1 twin.
Price	£80–£90. Singles from £60.
Meals	Pub/restaurant 0.5 miles.
Closed	Rarely.

Simon & Catherine Davis
Norfolk Courtyard,
Westfield Farm, Foxley Road,
Foulsham, Dereham,
Norfolk NR20 5RH
Tel   +44 (0)1362 683333
Mobile +44 (0)7969 611510
Email   info@norfolkcourtyard.co.uk
Web   www.norfolkcourtyard.co.uk

Entry 347   Map 10

Burgh Parva Hall

Sunlight bathes the Norfolk longhouse on sunny afternoons; the welcome from the Heals is as warm. The listed house is all that remains of the old village of Burgh Parva, deserted after the Great Plague. It's an inviting, handsome home... old furniture, rugs, books, pictures and Magnet the terrier-daschund. Large guest bedrooms face the sunsets and the garden flat makes a delightful hideaway, especially in summer. Breakfast eggs come from the garden hens, vegetables and fruits are home-grown, fresh fish is locally sourced and the game may have been shot by William: settle down by the fire and tuck in!

Self-catering available in the Garden Flat.

Cleat House

A fantastic welcome in a peaceful street, a short walk from town and beach. This attractive late-Victorian seaside villa, built for a London merchant, has been sumptuously renovated inside. Bedrooms have original fireplaces and sash windows, upbeat fabrics and original art, and a warm inviting mix of antique and traditional. The guest sitting room comes with an honesty bar, games, books, DVDs and guides – set off for Holkham or Sandringham! Rob and Linda greet you with homemade treats and serve a tasty breakfast at separate tables – try Linda's hot dish of the day. You're beautifully cared for here.

Minimum two nights at weekends.

Rooms	1 double; 1 twin with separate bath. Garden Flat: 1 twin.
Price	£70–£90. Singles £45–£55.
Meals	Dinner £24. BYO. Pub/restaurant 4 miles.
Closed	Rarely.

Rooms	3: 2 suites; 1 suite with separate bath.
Price	£85–£130. Singles £70–£100.
Meals	Pubs/restaurants within 0.5 miles.
Closed	Occasionally.

Judy & William Heal
Burgh Parva Hall,
Melton Constable,
Norfolk NR24 2PU
Tel   +44 (0)1263 862569
Email   judyheal@dsl.pipex.com

Rob & Linda Ownsworth
Cleat House,
7 Montague Road, Sheringham,
Norfolk NR26 8LN
Tel   +44 (0)1263 822765
Mobile   +44 (0)7557 356952
Email   roblinda@cleathouse.co.uk
Web   www.cleathouse.co.uk

Entry 348   Map 10

Entry 349   Map 10

Norfolk

Plumstead Hall Farmhouse

Percy and Emma's large farmhouse has a gently bustling family feel, and you are made to feel at home as soon as you step onto the lovely old Norfolk pamments in the hall. The bedrooms, up higgledy-piggledy stairs, have feather duvets and pretty covers, green views and a huge bathroom; the second room with a sloping ceiling is simpler. Breakfast is a relaxed, do-it-yourself affair on the mini stove: eggs, bacon, cereals, breads and jams, all locally sourced and eaten in the guest dining room. The north Norfolk beaches are close and there are historic homes to visit. Birdwatchers, walkers and cyclists will be happy as Larry.

Rooms	2 doubles sharing bath (let to same party only).
Price	£80. Singles £60.
Meals	Dinner, 2 courses, £15. Pub/restaurant 5 miles.
Closed	Rarely.

Percy & Emma Stilwell
Plumstead Hall Farmhouse,
Northfield Lane, Plumstead,
Norwich,
Norfolk NR11 7PT

Tel	+44 (0)1263 577660
Email	plumsteadhall@gmail.com
Web	www.plumsteadhallfarmhouse.co.uk

Entry 350   Map 10

Norfolk

Stable Cottage

Sarah's home is set in the grounds of Heydon, one of Norfolk's finest Elizabethan houses. In the Dutch-gabled stable block, fronted by Cromwell's Oak, is her cottage – fresh, sunny and enchanting. Each room is touched by her warm personality and love of beautiful things: seagrass floors, crisp linen and pretty china; the cosy sitting room is set with tea and biscuits for your arrival. Bedrooms are cottagey and immaculate; bathrooms have baskets of treats. Sarah serves a delicious breakfast with golden eggs from her hens, homemade marmalade and garden fruit. Thursford is close and you're 20 minutes from the coast.

Minimum stay two nights at weekends.

Rooms	2 twins/doubles.
Price	£90. Singles from £50.
Meals	Pub 1 mile.
Closed	Christmas.

Sarah Bulwer-Long
Stable Cottage,
Heydon Hall, Heydon,
Norwich,
Norfolk NR11 6RE

Tel	+44 (0)1263 587343
Mobile	+44 (0)7780 998742
Web	www.heydon-bb.co.uk

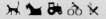

Entry 351   Map 10

Norfolk

Norfolk

Tuttington Hall

A sweeping drive brings you to this grand yet homely 16th-century house. The wide hall feels welcoming, with rugs on polished wood and a beautiful rocking horse; scones or cakes wait by the drawing room fire. Gardens brim with borders, fruit trees and an impressive vegetable patch. David and Andra are keen cooks: dinner is a convivial affair, served in the garden room or in the candlelit period dining room. Breakfast includes homemade bread and jams, eggs from the hens, home-grown tomatoes. Traditional bedrooms have luxurious beds, tea trays and books. Visit Norwich for theatre, galleries, cathedral; the coast is close.

The Buttery

Down a farm track, a treasure: your own thatch-and-flint octagonal dairy house perfectly restored by local craftsmen and as neat as a new pin. You get a jacuzzi bath, a little kitchen and a fridge stocked with delicious bacon and ground coffee so you can breakfast when you want; take it to the sun terrace in good weather. The sitting room is terracotta-tiled and has a music system, a warming fire and a sofabed for those who don't want to tackle the steep wooden stair to the snug bedroom on the mezzanine. You can play a game of tennis, and walk from the door into peaceful parkland and woods. Lovely!

Min. two nights at weekends.

Rooms	3: 1 twin/double, 1 single. Wing: 1 family room (1 twin/double, 1 twin, interconnecting bath).
Price	£120. Family room £100-£150. Singles from £50.
Meals	Dinner, 3 courses, £32.50. Pubs/restaurants 3 miles.
Closed	Rarely.

Rooms	Cottage: 1 double, sitting room & small kitchen.
Price	£80-£100.
Meals	Pub 10-minute walk.
Closed	Rarely.

Andra & David Papworth
Tuttington Hall,
Tuttington,
Norwich,
Norfolk NR11 6TL
Tel   +44 (0)1263 733417
Email david@tuttingtonhall.co.uk
Web   www.tuttingtonhall.co.uk

Deborah Meynell
The Buttery,
Berry Hall, Honingham,
Norwich,
Norfolk NR9 5AX
Tel   +44 (0)1603 880541
Email thebuttery@paston.co.uk
Web   www.thebuttery.biz

Entry 352   Map 10

Entry 353   Map 10

Norfolk

Sallowfield Cottage

In a beautifully remote part of Norfolk is a hospitable house crammed with treasures: gorgeous prints and paintings, polished family pieces, leather fender seats by the drawing room fire. One bedroom, not huge but handsome, has a Regency-style canopied bed and decoration to suit the house (1850); another room is on the ground floor. Drift into the garden to find hedged rooms and a jungly pond with a jetty on which you breakfast (deliciously): magical in spring and summer. Caroline gives you the best, her lovely lurchers add to the charm, and if you have friends locally she can do lunch for up to ten.

Over nines welcome.

Rooms	3: 1 double, 1 twin; 1 double with separate bath.
Price	£80. Singles £50.
Meals	Lunch £15. Dinner from £25. Pub 2.5 miles.
Closed	Christmas & New Year.

Caroline Musker
Sallowfield Cottage,
Wattlefield, Wymondham,
Norwich,
Norfolk NR18 9NX

Tel	+44 (0)1953 605086
Mobile	+44 (0)7778 316616
Email	caroline.musker@tesco.net
Web	www.sallowfieldcottage.co.uk

Entry 354   Map 10

Norfolk

The Grove

A 15-minute stroll to the centre, but tucked down a tree-lined drive, this grand 1840s building once housed staff from the Colman's mustard factory. Tony and Sue are passionate about good food and delight in welcoming guests to their perfectly restored home. A staggering choice of goodies at breakfast includes lemon pancakes, locally smoked bacon, award-winning sausages and homemade bread. Walls are covered in interesting art, views through large sash windows are garden green, and each warm boutique-hotel style bedroom (all on the first floor) has an immaculate bathroom with a roll top bath. Spoiling.

Rooms	3 doubles.
Price	£85-£105. Singles £75-£90.
Meals	Pubs/restaurants within walking distance.
Closed	Rarely.

Tony Hamm
The Grove,
59 Bracondale,
Norwich,
Norfolk NR1 2AT

Tel	+44 (0)1603 622053
Mobile	+44 (0)7811 064705
Email	thegrovenorwich@live.co.uk
Web	www.thegrovenorwich.co.uk

Entry 355   Map 10

Norfolk

Washingford House

Tall octagonal chimney stacks and a Georgian façade give the house a stately air. In fact, it's the friendliest of places to stay and Paris gives you a delicious, locally sourced breakfast including plenty of fresh fruit. The house, originally Tudor, is a delightful mix of old and new. Large light-filled bedrooms have loads of good books and views over the four-acre garden, a favourite haunt for local birds. Bergh Apton is a conservation village seven miles from Norwich and you are in the heart of it; perfect for cycling, boat trips on the Norfolk Broads and the twelve Wherryman's Way circular walks.

Rooms	2: 1 twin/double; 1 single with separate bath.
Price	£65-£85. Singles £35-£50.
Meals	Pubs/restaurants 4-6 miles.
Closed	Christmas.

Paris & Nigel Back
Washingford House,
Cookes Road,
Bergh Apton, Norwich,
Norfolk NR15 1AA

Tel	+44 (0)1508 550924
Mobile	+44 (0)7900 683617
Email	parisb@waitrose.com
Web	www.washingford.com

Entry 356   Map 10

Norfolk

Sloley Hall

A grand and gracious yellow-brick Georgian house with formal gardens, tree-studded parkland and glorious views from every window. It has also been beautifully renovated, with flagstoned floors, Persian rugs, gleaming circular tables and vases of garden-grown flowers. Your hosts are delightful – Barbara and Simon were married here and are easy-going and helpful. A huge light-flooded dining room is perfect for breakfast; the drawing room is comfy and uncluttered with a marble fireplace and long views. Bedrooms are large and elegant with sumptuous bed linen; generous bathrooms glow with warmth.

Child bed available. Minimum two nights at bank holidays.

Rooms	3: 1 suite; 1 double with separate bath; 1 double with separate shower.
Price	£75-£90. Singles from £50.
Meals	Pubs/restaurants 2-4 miles.
Closed	Rarely.

Barbara Gorton
Sloley Hall,
Sloley,
Norwich,
Norfolk NR12 8HA

Tel	+44 (0)1692 538582
Mobile	+44 (0)7748 152079
Email	babsgorton@hotmail.com
Web	www.sloleyhall.com

Entry 357   Map 10

Norfolk

Sutton Hall

Sweep up a gravel drive to a red-brick Victorian country house, in quiet parkland near the Norfolk Broads and coast. Sue serves eggs freshly laid by running hens, tomatoes from the kitchen garden, and knobbly apples from an orchard where deer and ducks roam free... breakfast on the terrace, or in a chandelier'd dining room with bay windows to the morning sun. Rooms are in keeping with the home's comfortable elegance – tall sash windows, a four-poster, fireplace, power showers, an extra bed for children; a Chinese screen adorns the high-ceilinged sitting room. Spend the day on the Broads with the binoculars.

Rooms	2 doubles. Extra child bed and cot.
Price	£90–£120. Singles £70–£90.
Meals	Pubs/restaurant 1.5 miles.
Closed	Rarely.

Sue Berry
Sutton Hall,
Hall Road, Sutton,
Norwich,
Norfolk NR12 9RX

Tel	+44 (0)1692 584888
Mobile	+44 (0)7977 575788
Email	enquiries@suttonhallnorfolk.co.uk
Web	www.suttonhallnorfolk.co.uk

Entry 358   Map 10

Norfolk

The Old Rectory

Conservation farmland all around; acres of wild heathland busy with woodpeckers and owls; the coast two miles away. Relax in the spacious drawing room of this handsome 17th-century rectory and friendly family home, set in four acres of grounds. Fiona loves to cook and bakes her bread daily, food is delicious, seasonal and locally sourced, jams are homemade. Comfortable bedrooms have *objets* from diplomatic postings and the spacious suite comes with mahogany furniture and armchairs so you can settle in with a book. Super views, friendly dogs, tennis in the garden and masses of space.

Rooms	2: 1 suite; 1 double with separate bath & shower.
Price	£60–£65. Suite £65–£75. Singles £40.
Meals	Dinner from £20. Pubs 2 miles.
Closed	Rarely.

Peter & Fiona Black
The Old Rectory,
Ridlington,
Norfolk NR28 9NZ

Tel	+44 (0)1692 650247
Mobile	+44 (0)7774 599911
Email	blacks7@email.com
Web	www.oldrectorynorthnorfolk.co.uk

Entry 359   Map 10

Norfolk

Home Farmhouse

A big yellow Jacobean farmhouse that stands in a couple of deeply rural acres. John and Anne rebuilt the house, removing the front wall to refit seasoned oak. Outside, birdsong fills the air; inside, the drawing-room fire crackles with gusto, and you can pick up the daily papers and sink into a sofa. John, a military historian, cooks breakfast (eggs from the resident hens, apple juice from local orchards), while Anne whisks up delicious dinners. Smart bedrooms are wonderfully comfortable with crisp linen, fresh flowers and interesting books. There are stables for horses and secure bike storage, too.

Rooms	2: 1 double, 1 twin/double.
Price	£100. Singles £50.
Meals	Dinner, 2 courses with cheese, £22.
Closed	Rarely.

Anne & John Smales
Home Farmhouse,
Letton, Thetford,
Norfolk IP25 7PS

Tel	+44 (0)1362 820502
Mobile	+44 (0)7730 398744
Email	anne@homefarmhouseletton.co.uk
Web	www.homefarmhouseletton.co.uk

Entry 360 Map 10

Norfolk

College Farm

Katharine is a natural at making guests feel like friends. Her beautiful farmhouse tucks itself away on the edge of the village and the big friendly kitchen is filled with delicious smells of home baking. Meals are served by the large wood-burner in the grand Jacobean dining room, filled with good antiques, period furnishings and cosy places to sit; food is home-grown, seasonal and local. Sleep well in charming bedrooms with smooth linen, pretty furniture and garden views; bathrooms are small and simple. A fascinating area teeming with pingos, wildlife, old churches… and glorious antique shops.

Children over 12 welcome.

Rooms	3: 2 twins/doubles; 1 twin/double with separate bath.
Price	£80. Singles £40.
Meals	Dinner from £20. Pub 1 mile.
Closed	Rarely.

Katharine Wolstenholme
College Farm,
Thompson, Thetford,
Norfolk IP24 1QG

Tel	+44 (0)1953 483318
Email	info@collegefarmnorfolk.co.uk
Web	www.collegefarmnorfolk.co.uk

Entry 361 Map 10

Northamptonshire

Bridge Cottage

A truly peaceful place, yet only a few miles from Peterborough. Sip a glass of wine on the decking down by the Willowbrook; beautiful countryside envelops you, the cattle doze, kingfishers flash by and you may see a red kite (borrow some binoculars). Inside find pretty bedrooms with sloping ceilings, the purest cotton sheets and proper blankets; bathrooms are thickly towelled and full of lovely lotions and bubbles. Breakfast is local and scrumptious and served in the friendliest kitchen facing that heavenly view, there's a tranquil conservatory for a quiet read, and Judy and Rod are brilliant hosts. A hidden gem.

Rooms	3: 1 double, 1 twin; 1 double with separate bath.
Price	£80–£85. Singles £47.50–£60.
Meals	Pub/restaurant 500 yds.
Closed	Christmas.

Judy Young
Bridge Cottage,
Oundle Road, Woodnewton,
Peterborough,
Northamptonshire PE8 5EG

Tel	+44 (0)1780 470860
Mobile	+44 (0)7979 644864
Email	enquiries@bridgecottage.net
Web	www.bridgecottage.net

Entry 362   Map 9

Northamptonshire

The Old House

Northamptonshire is the county of spires and squires. And here, on the through-road of this fascinating medieval town, is a listed squire's house – once home to a merchant who traded in the marketplace opposite. Enter the heavy oak door and step back 400 years. William, courteous, hospitable and renovating with aplomb, is full of plans. Facing the courtyard at the back (furnished for summery breakfasts and aperitifs) are the quietest rooms; all have sumptuous fabrics and wallpapers, dramatic touches and divine beds. Delightfully quirky, spanking new bathrooms with roll top tubs are as special as all the rest.

Rooms	3: 2 doubles, 1 twin/double.
Price	£65. Singles £50.
Meals	Pubs/restaurants 150 yds.
Closed	Rarely.

William Evans
The Old House,
5 Market Square,
Higham Ferrers,
Rushden,
Northamptonshire NN10 8BP

Tel	+44 (0)1933 314006
Email	theoldhousehighamferrers@gmail.com
Web	www.theoldhousehighamferrers.co.uk

Entry 363   Map 9

Northamptonshire

Colledges House

Huge attention to comfort here, and a house full of laughter. Liz clearly derives pleasure from sharing her 300-year-old stone thatched cottage, immaculate garden, conservatory and converted barn with guests. Sumptuous bedrooms have deep mattresses with fine linen, sparkling bathrooms are a good size. The house is full of interesting things: a Jacobean trunk, a Bechstein piano, mirrors and pictures, pretty china, bright fabrics, a beautiful bureau. Cordon Bleu dinners are elegant affairs – and great fun. Stroll around the conservation village of Staverton – delightful.

Children over eight & babes in arms welcome.

Rooms	4: 1 single; 1 double with separate bath. Cottage: 1 double, 1 twin.
Price	£95–£99. Singles from £68.
Meals	Dinner, 3 courses, £35. Pub 4-minute walk.
Closed	Rarely.

Liz Jarrett
Colledges House,
Oakham Lane,
Staverton, Daventry,
Northamptonshire NN11 6JQ
Tel   +44 (0)1327 702737
Mobile   +44 (0)7710 794112
Email   liz@colledgeshouse.co.uk
Web   www.colledgeshouse.co.uk

Entry 364   Map 8

Northamptonshire

Staverton Hall

Through impressive iron gates to a grand house in a spectacular setting with masses of room, and friendly owners Rupert and Serena who have young children of their own; they love having families to stay. Relaxed breakfasts (and dinner) at flexible times are served at one table; all is local and delicious. Large, light bedrooms and super-modern shared bathrooms are upstairs, have good views and feel private. Relax in the huge, creamy-yellow guest sitting room with sash windows, log fire, board games and comfy sofas; there's also a heated pool, a play area, acres of garden, and the pub a walk away. Family heaven.

Horses and pets welcome.

Rooms	4: 3 doubles, 1 single, all sharing 2 bathrooms.
Price	£90. Singles £50. One party sharing 3 rooms £200
Meals	Dinner, 3 courses, £30 (min. 4). Pub 3-minute walk.
Closed	Rarely.

Serena Frost
Staverton Hall,
Manor Road,
Staverton,
Daventry,
Northamptonshire NN11 6JD
Tel   +44 (0)1327 878296
Email   serena@stavertonhall.co.uk
Web   www.stavertonhall.co.uk

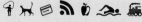

Entry 365   Map 8

Northamptonshire

The Vyne

Weighed down by wisteria, this 16th-century cottage rests in a honey-hued conservation village on the cusp of Oxfordshire. Beams and wonky lines abound; rooms are filled with good antiques and eclectic art. The twin overlooking the garden is enchanting, tucked under the rafters, its beds decorated in willow-pattern chintz, its walls glinting with gilded frames; the double has a Georgian four-poster and a sampler-decorated bathroom that's a quick flit next door. Warm and charming, Imogen not only works in publishing but is a contented gardener and Cordon Bleu cook – enjoy supper in her sunny secluded garden.

Babies welcome.

Rooms	2: 1 twin; 1 four-poster with separate bath.
Price	£80. Singles from £45.
Meals	Supper £20. Dinner £30. BYO. Pub 2-minute walk.
Closed	Christmas & New Year.

Imogen Butler
The Vyne,
High Street, Eydon,
Daventry,
Northamptonshire NN11 3PP
Tel   +44 (0)1327 264886
Mobile   +44 (0)7974 801475
Email   imogen@ibutler2.wanadoo.co.uk

🐱 🐾 🚂 ✕

Entry 366   Map 8

Northamptonshire

The Coach House

Sunlight and garden flowers fill this unusual, and welcoming, rosy-brick home. The former coach house and stables have become three luxurious light-filled rooms wrapped round a grassed and paved courtyard, an enchanting spot for breakfast in summer. Sarah's eye for colour shows in the design of her gardens, and her furnishings too – an appealing mix of modern and traditional. She gives you a big welcome, and a tasty breakfast too. Perfect for tennis – there's a court in the garden – and visits to Silverstone, Stowe, Bletchley Park and Warwick Castle... if you can bear to leave!

Rooms	3: 1 double, 1 twin, 1 family room.
Price	£80–£90. Family room £90–£100. £120 during Grand Prix & Motor Sport weekends. Singles £65.
Meals	Packed lunch on request. Pub/restaurant within 5 miles.
Closed	Rarely.

Sarah Baker Baker
The Coach House,
Duncote, Towcester,
Northamptonshire NN12 8AQ
Tel   +44 (0)1327 352855
Mobile   +44 (0)7875 215705
Email   sarahbb54@gmail.com
Web   www.thecoachhouseduncote.co.uk

🚶 🐾 📶 🐱 🚂

Entry 367   Map 8

Northumberland

Matfen High House

Bring the wellies – and jumpers! You are 25 miles from the border and the walking is a joy. Struan and Jenny are good company, love sporting pursuits and will advise on where to eat locally (and drive you there if needed). The sturdy stone house of 1735 is a lived-in, happily shabby-chic kind of place: the en suite bedrooms have fine fabrics and pictures, bathrooms are well-kept and the drawing room promises books and choice pieces. Enjoy local bacon and sausages at breakfast, with Struan's marmalade and bread warm from the oven. The countryside is stunning, Hadrian's Wall and the great castles (Alnwick, Bamburgh) beckon.

Rooms	4: 1 double, 1 twin; 1 double, 1 twin sharing bath.
Price	£60–£75. Singles £40.
Meals	Packed lunch £4.50. Restaurant 2 miles.
Closed	Rarely.

Struan & Jenny Wilson
Matfen High House,
Matfen,
Corbridge,
Northumberland NE20 0RG
Tel   +44 (0)1661 886592
Email   struan@struan.enterprise-plc.com
Web   www.matfenhighhouse.co.uk

Entry 368   Map 12

Northumberland

The Hermitage

A magical setting, three miles from Hadrian's wall, in a house full of friendship and comfort. Through ancient woodland, up the drive, over the burn and there it is: big, beautiful and Georgian. Interiors are comfortable country-house, full of warmth and charm; bedrooms, carpeted, spacious and delightful, are furnished with antiques, paintings and superb beds; bathrooms have roll top baths. Outside are lovely lawns, a walled garden, wildlife, and breakfasts on the terrace in summer. Katie – who was born in this house – looks after you brilliantly.

Guests back by 11pm please. Over sevens & babes in arms welcome.

Rooms	3: 1 double, 1 twin; 1 twin with separate bath.
Price	£85–£90. Singles from £55.
Meals	Pub 2 miles.
Closed	October-February.

Simon & Katie Stewart
The Hermitage,
Swinburne,
Hexham,
Northumberland NE48 4DG
Tel   +44 (0)1434 681248
Mobile   +44 (0)7708 016297
Email   katie.stewart@themeet.co.uk

Entry 369   Map 16

Northumberland

Shieldhall

The guest rooms are in the charming 18th-century farm buildings, each with its own entrance. Stephen and his sons make and restore furniture and rooms are named after the wood used within: Elm, Oak, Mahogany, Pine. Bathrooms are spacious, there's a beautiful sitting room/library full of books, and you pop across the courtyard for meals in the main house – once home to the family of Capability Brown. Celia, and daughter Sarah, are friendly and attentive and love cooking; ingredients are often organic or locally sourced. There's also a secret bar and a small but interesting wine list. Peaceful, hospitable B&B – with fine views.

Northumberland

Thistleyhaugh

The family thrives on hard work and humour, and if Enid's not the perfect B&B hostess, she's a close contender. Her passions are pictures, cooking and people, and certainly you eat well – local farm eggs at breakfast and their beef at dinner. Choose any of the five large, lovely bedrooms and stay the week; they are awash with old paintings, silk fabrics and crisp linen. Wake refreshed and nip downstairs, past the log fire, to a laden and sociable table, head off afterwards to find 720 acres of organic farmland and a few million more of the Cheviots beyond. Wonderful hosts, a glorious region, a happy house.

Rooms	3: 1 double, 1 twin, 1 four-poster.		Rooms	5: 3 doubles, 1 twin, 1 single.
Price	£80. Singles £60.		Price	£90. Singles £60-£85.
Meals	Dinner, 4 courses, £28. Pub 7 miles.		Meals	Dinner, 3 courses, £25. Pub/restaurant 2 miles.
Closed	Rarely.		Closed	Christmas, New Year & January.

	Celia & Stephen Robinson-Gay			Henry & Enid Nelless
	Shieldhall,			Thistleyhaugh,
	Wallington, Morpeth,			Longhorsley, Morpeth,
	Northumberland NE61 4AQ			Northumberland NE65 8RG
Tel	+44 (0)1830 540387		Tel	+44 (0)1665 570629
Email	stay@shieldhallguesthouse.co.uk		Email	thistleyhaugh@hotmail.com
Web	www.shieldhallguesthouse.co.uk		Web	www.thistleyhaugh.co.uk

Entry 370   Map 16

Entry 371   Map 16

Northumberland

East Hepple Farmhouse

In the farmhouse sitting room, a wood-burner blazes away in winter. The double, too, has a sitting room, with an original cast-iron range and shelves groaning with books – bibliophile heaven. The peace is so deep in the Coquet valley that you may sleep until the whiff of sizzling local bacon hits your nostrils. Beds are firm, old pine pieces pretty, pillows feathery soft and views over the river to the Simonside hills abundant. Joan and Brian are expert at looking after you, will drive you to dinner and guide you the next day to beaches, Cragside, Alnwick Castle and fabulous walks. To stay is a treat.

Fishing can be arranged.

Rooms	2: 1 double & sitting room, 1 twin (usually let to same party only).
Price	£70-£75. Singles £55-£60.
Meals	Packed lunch £5. Pubs/restaurants 2.5 miles.
Closed	Rarely.

Joan & Brian Storey
East Hepple Farmhouse,
Hepple, Rothbury,
Northumberland NE65 7LH
Tel   +44 (0)1669 640221
Email   joanstorey@coquetdale.net
Web   www.easthepplefarm.co.uk

Entry 372   Map 16

Northumberland

Alnham Farm

Delve deep into the glorious sheep-dotted hills and valleys of the Northumberland National Park to find Jenny's handsome Georgian farmhouse and a dollop of urban chic in bedrooms and bathrooms. Walkers will be in heaven: set off with a tummy full of farmhouse porridge, home-reared sausages and bacon or a smashing Craster kipper. Spot whirling buzzards, the elusive red squirrel, otters if you are lucky; return to the crispest linen, gleaming mahogany, fresh flowers, and a power shower or a soak in a freestanding tub (bubbles and lotions provided). Castles, deep dunes and long white beaches are an easy drive.

Rooms	2: 1 double; 1 twin/double with separate bathroom.
Price	£85. Singles £55.
Meals	Pub/restaurant 7 miles.
Closed	December-March.

Jenny Sordy
Alnham Farm,
Alnwick,
Northumberland NE66 4TJ
Tel   +44 (0)1669 630210
Email   jenny@alnhamfarm.co.uk
Web   www.alnhamfarm.co.uk

Entry 373   Map 16

Courtyard Garden

In the county town of Northumberland, with its grand castle and innovative gardens, step directly off the pavement and enter a courtyard surrounded by shrubs and pretty pots; sit out here on sunny days and sip a glass of something cool. Bedrooms (one overlooking the church, the other the garden) are traditional and immaculate; bathrooms, one with a roll top bath, have original wooden floors, thick towels. Friendly Maureen gives you breakfast in the comfortable sitting room at a round Georgian table underneath the window. Explore the town on foot, stride along white beaches, discover more castles; history is all around you.

Rooms	2: 1 double, 1 twin/double.
Price	£80–£90. Singles from £60.
Meals	Pub/restaurant within 300 yds.
Closed	Rarely.

	Maureen Mason
	Courtyard Garden,
	10 Prudhoe Street,
	Alnwick,
	Northumberland NE66 1UW
Tel	+44 (0)1665 603393
Email	maureenpeter10@btinternet.com
Web	www.courtyardgarden-alnwick.com

Entry 374   Map 16

Bilton Barns

A solidly good farmhouse B&B whose lifeblood is still farming. The Jacksons know every inch of the countryside and coast that surrounds their 1715 home; it's a pretty spot. They farm 400 acres of mixed arable land that sweeps down to the coast yet always have time for guests. Dorothy creates an easy and sociable atmosphere with welcoming pots of tea and convivial breakfasts — all delicious and locally sourced. Comfortable, smartly done bedrooms are traditional with a contemporary feel, the conservatory is huge and filled with sofas and chairs and there's an airy guests' sitting room with an open fire and views to the sea.

Rooms	3: 1 double, 1 twin, 1 four-poster.
Price	£78–£85. Singles £40–£65.
Meals	Packed lunch £4–£6.
	Pub/restaurant 2 miles.
Closed	Christmas & New Year.

	Brian & Dorothy Jackson
	Bilton Barns,
	Alnmouth, Alnwick,
	Northumberland NE66 2TB
Tel	+44 (0)1665 830427
Mobile	+44 (0)7939 262028
Email	dorothy@biltonbarns.com
Web	www.biltonbarns.com

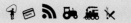

Entry 375   Map 16

Northumberland

Redfoot Lea

Prepare to be thoroughly spoiled. This fine renovation of an old farmsteading lies just off the A1 up a quiet lane — perfect for touring the county or a great stopover. Amiable Philippa gives you a super south-facing sitting room and ground-floor bedrooms with comfortable beds, crisp linen, fluffy bathrobes and heated floors; bathrooms are smart and spotless. You breakfast at a large table in the magnificent open-plan hall, scented with glorious flower arrangements; enjoy freshly squeezed orange juice, homemade compotes, local produce, excellent coffee. A short hop from Alnwick Castle and gardens, and stunning beaches.

Rooms	2: 1 double, 1 suite.
Price	£85–£95. Singles £65.
Meals	Pubs/restaurants 0.25 miles.
Closed	Rarely.

Philippa Bell
Redfoot Lea,
Greensfield Moor Farm, Alnwick,
Northumberland NE66 2HH
Tel +44 (0)1665 603891
Mobile +44 (0)7870 586214
Email info@redfootlea.co.uk
Web www.redfootlea.co.uk

Entry 376   Map 16

Northumberland

Old Rectory Howick

Christine and David's house on the edge of the village is surrounded by fields and woods, and is only minutes from the beautiful Northumberland coast, a designated AONB. Breakfasts are hearty; Craster kippers from down the road, eggs from Erica, Sylvia and Ella. Scamper about with wide beaches, stunning castles, rugged walks, golf courses and Holy Island, return to a cosy sitting room with a wood-burner. Sleep well in large, airy bedrooms with bouncy new mattresses, chintzy fabrics, top-of-the-range cotton sheets, warm showers and white towels. Wander the peaceful garden, there's a tree house and a croquet lawn.

Rooms	4: 2 doubles; 1 family suite with separate bathroom, 1 twin each with separate bathroom.
Price	£75–£95. Suite £140–£160. Singles £65–£75.
Meals	Pubs/restaurants 2 miles.
Closed	December/January.

Christine & David Jackson
Old Rectory Howick,
Howick, Alnwick,
Northumberland NE66 3LE
Tel +44 (0)1665 577590
Mobile +44 (0)7879 681753
Email stay@oldrectoryhowick.co.uk
Web www.oldrectoryhowick.co.uk

Entry 377   Map 16

Northumberland

Broome

In a coastal village with access to miles of sandy beaches, a totally surprising one-storey house, an Aladdin's cave of beautiful things. The garden room is its hub and has a country cottage feel; enjoy breakfasts here of locally smoked kippers, award-winning Bamburgh Bangers and home-cured bacon from the village. There's also a courtyard for breakfast in the sun. Bedrooms, in their own wing, come with fresh flowers and good books, and a cheerful sitting/dining room just for you. Mary, welcoming and amusing, greets you with delicious homemade cake. Make the most of her knowledge: she knows the area inside out.

Rooms	2: 1 double, 1 twin sharing bath/shower (let to same party only).
Price	£100-£110. Singles £60-£70.
Meals	Pubs/restaurants 2-minute walk.
Closed	November-March.

Mary Dixon
Broome,
22 Ingram Road, Bamburgh,
Northumberland NE69 7BT
Tel   +44 (0)1668 214287
Mobile   +44 (0)7956 013409
Email   mdixon4394@aol.com

Entry 378   Map 16

Northumberland

Laundry Cottage

History lovers, peace seekers and observers of nature will mellow further in this glorious spot overlooking the Cheviot hills. On arrival enjoy cake and tea with the evening sun – in the sun room, or in the garden on warm days. Douse yourself in one of Ginia's hiker's breakfasts, stride through iron age forts and the remains of Saxon palaces or visit long white beaches; return to Welsh slate floors, wood-burners, good home cooking, feather and down on deep comfy mattresses and fluffy towels. The feel is light and airy, Peter and Ginia are amiable hosts and the super garden is filled with roses in summer.

Rooms	2: 1 double, 1 twin.
Price	£70. Singles £45.
Meals	Dinner £17-£21. Pub/restaurant 5 miles.
Closed	December-March.

Peter & Ginia Gadsdon
Laundry Cottage,
East Horton, Wooler,
Northumberland NE71 6EZ
Tel   +44 (0)1668 215383
Email   peter@gadsdon.me.uk
Web   www.laundry-cottage-bnb.co.uk

Entry 379   Map 16

Northumberland

Chain Bridge House

Overlooking an idyllic stretch of the river Tweed is the last house in England – Scotland is 100 yards away across the magnificent Union Chain Bridge. In the sitting room: a log fire and books galore. In the bedrooms: goose down duvets and a fresh, airy feel. Livvy, a professional cook, is an active supporter of the Slow Food movement and local producers. Visit the neighbouring honey farm, glorious Bamburgh, Holy Island, the Farnes, or the unspoilt borders beyond: return to a revolving summerhouse in the garden for tea. Children and dogs get a generous welcome in this delightful family home.

Children over two welcome.

Rooms	2: 1 double, 1 twin.
Price	£90-£95. Singles £60-£65.
Meals	Dinner £30. Supper £15. Packed lunch from £7.50. Pubs/restaurants 5-7 miles.
Closed	Rarely.

Livvy Cawthorn
Chain Bridge House,
Horncliffe, Berwick-upon-Tweed,
Northumberland TD15 2XT
Tel   +44 (0)1289 382541
Email info@chainbridgehouse.co.uk
Web   www.chainbridgehouse.co.uk

Entry 380   Map 16

Northumberland

West Coates

Slip through the gates of this Victorian townhouse and you're in the country. Two acres of leafy gardens, with pretty spots to relax, belie the closeness of Berwick's centre. From the lofty ceilings and sash windows to the soft colours, paintings and gleaming furniture, the house has a calm, ordered elegance. Bedrooms have antiques and garden views; one has a roll top bath; fruit, homemade cakes, flowers welcome you. Warm, friendly Karen is a stunning cook, inventively using local produce and spoiling you; she runs a cookery school here too. The coastline is stunning and there are castles and country houses galore to visit.

Rooms	2 twins/doubles.
Price	£90-£100. Singles from £60.
Meals	Dinner £35. Pub/restaurant 15-minute walk.
Closed	December/January.

Karen Brown
West Coates, 30 Castle Terrace,
Berwick-upon-Tweed,
Northumberland TD15 1NZ
Tel   +44 (0)1289 309666
Mobile +44 (0)7814 281973
Email   westcoatesbandb@gmail.com
Web   www.westcoates.co.uk

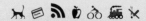

Entry 381   Map 16

Nottinghamshire

Willoughby House

Past the village pub, through a gate, this three-storey brick farmhouse reflects its owners' skilful interior design. The house brims with tokens of its 18th century past, like meat hooks in the scullery-turned-sitting room, but feels ever so smart. Bedrooms are large and comfortable: climb up to Harry's room with its brass bed and toy soldiers over the fireplace; Edward's and George's share raftered loft space and a swish bathroom. Sarah rustles up delicious breakfast in a dining room embraced by poppy red walls and shutters. Stroll round the little village; Georgian towns Southwell and Newark are close.

Nottinghamshire

Compton House

Two minutes from Newark's antique shops and old market, seek out this terraced Georgian townhouse where the mayor once lived. Naturally elegant, and overlooking Fountain Gardens, the sunny drawing room has an open fire; Lisa has filled the place with lovely personal touches. Rooms are named after friends, from plush red-gold Judy's room to Harry's bijou single; the best is Cooper's, with a four-poster bed, a roll top bath through a draped archway and a wall hand-painted by a local artist. Pad down to the sunny basement for Lisa's feast of a breakfast. Hotel comforts but a truly homely feel.

Dogs by arrangement.

Rooms	5: 3 twins/doubles, 1 double; 1 double with separate bath/shower.
Price	£85–£105. Singles £65–£75.
Meals	Dinner for special occasions. Packed lunch £7.50. Pub 3-minute walk.
Closed	Rarely.

Rooms	7: 2 doubles, 2 twins, 1 twin/double, 1 four-poster; 1 single with separate shower.
Price	£95–£125. Singles from £50.
Meals	Packed lunch £6. Buffet lunch £15. Dinner, 2 courses, from £25. Pub/restaurant 0.5 miles.
Closed	Christmas.

	Andrew & Sarah Nesbitt Willoughby House, Main Street, Norwell, Newark, Nottinghamshire NG23 6JN
Tel	+44 (0)1636 636266
Mobile	+44 (0)7789 965352
Email	willoughbybandb@aol.com
Web	www.willoughbyhousebandb.co.uk

	Lisa Holloway Compton House, 117 Baldertongate, Newark, Nottinghamshire NG24 1RY
Tel	+44 (0)1636 708670
Mobile	+44 (0)7817 446485
Email	info@comptonhousenewark.com
Web	www.comptonhousenewark.com

Entry 382   Map 9

Entry 383   Map 9

Oxfordshire

Uplands House

Come to be spoiled at this 'farmhouse' built in 1875 for the Earl of Jersey's farm manager. Renovated by a talented couple, it's elegant and sumptuously furnished; expect large light bedrooms, crisp linen, thick towels and long bucolic views from the Orangery where you have tea and cake. Relax here with a book as the sounds and scents of the pretty garden waft by, or chat to charming Poppy while she creates delicious dinner – a convivial occasion enjoyed with your hosts. Breakfast is Graham's domain – try smoked salmon with scrambled eggs and red caviar. You're well placed for exploring but you'll find it hard to leave.

Oxfordshire

Gower's Close

All the nooks, crannies and beams you'd expect from an ancient thatched cottage in a Cotswold village... and more besides: good food, lively conversation and lots of inside information about gardens to visit. Judith is a keen gardener who writes books on the subject (her passion for plants is evident from her own glorious garden) and her style and intelligence are reflected in her home. Pretty, south-facing and full of sunlight, the sitting room opens onto the garden and terrace. Bedrooms are light, charming and cottagey; the twin is at garden level. A thoroughly relaxing place to stay.

Minimum two nights at weekends.

Rooms	3: 1 double, 1 twin/double, 1 four-poster.
Price	£100-£180. Singles £65-£95.
Meals	Dinner, 2-4 courses, £20-£30. Pub 1.25 miles.
Closed	Rarely.

Rooms	2: 1 double, 1 twin.
Price	£80-£85. Singles £50.
Meals	Dinner, 4 courses, £28 (min. 4 people). Pub/restaurant 100 yds.
Closed	Christmas & New Year.

Poppy Cooksey & Graham Paul
Uplands House,
Upton, Banbury,
Oxfordshire OX15 6HJ

Tel	+44 (0)1295 678663
Mobile	+44 (0)7836 535538
Email	poppy@cotswolds-uplands.co.uk
Web	www.cotswolds-uplands.co.uk

Judith Hitching & John Marshall
Gower's Close,
Sibford Gower, Banbury,
Oxfordshire OX15 5RW

Tel	+44 (0)1295 780348
Mobile	+44 (0)7776 231588
Email	judith@gowersclose.co.uk
Web	www.gowersclose.co.uk

Entry 384   Map 8

Entry 385   Map 8

Oxfordshire

Buttslade House

Choose between a gorgeous ground-floor retreat across the courtyard, or a very pretty twin in the 17th-century farmhouse with barns and stables. The guest sitting room is a clever melody of ancient and contemporary styles: Spanish art, antique sofas, velvet cushions. Beds have seriously good mattresses, feather and down pillows and crisp white linen; bathrooms are smart and sparkling – one with a Victorian roll top. Diana is lovely and will pamper you or leave you, there's a blissful garden to stroll through, breakfast is a feast of fruits and homemade bread and it's a hop to the village pub. A fun and stylish treat.

Rooms	2: 1 double; 1 twin with separate bath.
Price	£80-£85. Singles £50.
Meals	Dinner, 3 courses, £25. Lunch £7. Pub 100 yds.
Closed	Rarely.

Diana Thompson
Buttslade House,
Temple Mill Road,
Sibford Gower,
Banbury,
Oxfordshire OX15 5RX
Tel   +44 (0)1295 788818
Email   diana@buttsladehouse.co.uk
Web   www.buttsladehouse.co.uk

Oxfordshire

Minehill House

Wind your way up the farm track to the top of a beautiful hill and you arrive at a gorgeous family farmhouse with views for miles and young, energetic Hester to care for you. Children will adore the ping-pong table and the trampoline; their parents will enjoy the gleaming old flagstones, vibrant contemporary oils, wood-burning stove and seriously sophisticated food. Rest well in the big double room with its gloriously comfortable bed, verdant leafy wallpaper and stunning views, and a cubby-hole door to extra twin beds; bathrooms are sparklingly clean and spacious. Bracing walks start straight from the door.

Rooms	1 double/family room.
Price	£95-£135. Family £135. Singles from £50.
Meals	Dinner, 3 courses, £35. Supper £20. BYO. Packed lunch available. Pubs 1-5 miles.
Closed	Christmas & New Year.

Hester & Ed Sale
Minehill House,
Lower Brailes,
Banbury,
Oxfordshire OX15 5BJ
Tel   +44 (0)1608 685594
Mobile   +44 (0)7890 266441
Email   hester@minehillhouse.co.uk
Web   www.minehillhouse.co.uk

Oxfordshire

Home Farmhouse

This 400-year-old house is charming, with low ceilings, inglenook fireplaces and winding stairs. All rooms are faded and brimming with character: the drawing room is elegant and beamed and pretty bedrooms are decorated with antiques and old-fashioned chintz. Comfortable beds have good mattresses and traditional blankets; bathrooms are small and a little dated. Enjoy independence in the simple barn room with its mixture of time-worn furniture and own entrance up old stone steps. The family's travels are evident all over and it's all so laid-back you'll find it hard to leave. The dogs are delightful too – Samson and Goliath.

Rooms	3: 1 double, 1 twin/double. Barn: 1 twin/double.
Price	£88. Singles £58.
Meals	Dinner £28. Supper £20 (min. 4 people). Pub 100 yds.
Closed	Christmas.

Rosemary & Nigel Grove-White
Home Farmhouse,
Charlton,
Banbury,
Oxfordshire OX17 3DR
Tel   +44 (0)1295 811683
Mobile +44 (0)7795 207000
Email   grovewhite@lineone.net
Web   www.homefarmhouse.co.uk

Entry 388   Map 8

Oxfordshire

The Old Post House

Great natural charm in the 17th-century Old Post House, where shiny flagstones, rich dark wood and mullion windows combine with warm fabrics, deep sofas and handsome furniture. Bedrooms are big, with antique wardrobes, oak headboards and a comforting old-fashioned feel. The walled gardens are lovely – rich with espaliered fruit trees, and with a pool for sunny evenings. Christine, a well-travelled ex-pat, has an innate sense of hospitality; her breakfasts are delicious. There's village traffic but your sleep should be sound. Deddington is delightful – and you will love Harry the friendly terrier too!

Children over 12 welcome.

Rooms	3: 1 twin/double; 1 double with separate bath; 1 four-poster with separate shower.
Price	£90. Singles £65.
Meals	Occasional dinner. Pubs/restaurants in village.
Closed	Rarely.

Christine Blenntoft
The Old Post House,
New Street,
Deddington,
Oxfordshire OX15 0SP
Tel   +44 (0)1869 338978
Mobile +44 (0)7713 631092
Email   kblenntoft@aol.com
Web   www.oldposthouse.co.uk

Entry 389   Map 8

Oxfordshire

Rectory Farm

A general sense of peaceful order pervades at this solid, big house set in a manicured lawn. Inside find large, light bedrooms, floral and feminine, with bold chintz bed covers, draped kidney-shaped dressing tables, thick mattresses; some have garden views, others face the farm buildings. Sink into comfy sofas flanking a huge fireplace in the drawing room, breakfast on local bacon and sausage with free-range eggs, stroll the pretty garden, or grab a rod and try your luck on one of the trout lakes. Elizabeth knows her patch well; walkers can borrow maps, and she can point the way to lovely shops for the dedicated.

Rooms	3: 1 double, 1 twin/double; 1 twin/double with separate bath.
Price	£92–£100. Singles £65–£75.
Meals	Pub/restaurant 1.5 miles.
Closed	December/January.

Elizabeth Colston
Rectory Farm,
Salford, Chipping Norton,
Oxfordshire OX7 5YY

Tel	+44 (0)1608 643209
Mobile	+44 (0)7866 834208
Email	enquiries@rectoryfarm.info
Web	www.rectoryfarm.info

Entry 390   Map 8

Oxfordshire

York House

On a country road between villages, surrounded by open garden, lake and trees, is this freshly painted and peaceful house. Its old cottage heart has become a delicious low-ceilinged sitting room with a log fire; new and 'deceptively spacious' is the rest. Ewa, warm, fun and full of good taste, has made it all delightful with swagged curtains, gold embossed antique books, delicate china, ancestral pieces and elegant glass. Bedrooms are comfortable, pretty and traditional. There are stately houses and gardens to visit and gastropubs to try, but if you've come with a party and decide to dine in, Ewa's cooking is a joy.

Owner can collect from pub.

Rooms	4: 2 doubles; 1 twin, 1 double sharing bath. Extra double available.
Price	£100–£130.
Meals	Dinner £40 (min. 8). BYO. Pubs within 2 miles.
Closed	Never.

Ewa Lewis
York House,
Kingham, Chipping Norton,
Oxfordshire OX7 6UL

Tel	+44 (0)1608 659341
Mobile	+44 (0)7747 784830
Email	ewa.lewis2@virgin.net
Web	www.cotswolds-yorkhouse-bandb.co.uk

Entry 391   Map 8

Oxfordshire

Upper Court Farm

In a quiet, gently hilly spot in the Cotswolds, the super smart Edwardian farmhouse comes with groomed gardens, 30 acres of grassland for Chloë's horses and woodland walks. A dressage rider, she and Tim are interesting hosts and their home is laden with good quality fabrics, country art and family pieces. Charming bedrooms (on the top floor) have madly comfy beds, TVs, smart drenching showers; there's a cosy sitting room too. Tim's a foodie and breakfast is generous and local; people come for miles for Slatters, an organic shop in the village. Relax in the rose garden with a drink or tea and cakes – two sweet dogs will join you.

Children over eight welcome.

Rooms	2: 1 twin/double; 1 double with separate shower.
Price	£80–£100. Singles £70–£100. £10 supplement for one-night stays weekends March–Sept.
Meals	Pub 200 yds & 3 miles, café 5-minute walk.
Closed	Rarely.

Chloë Robson
Upper Court Farm,
Mill End, Chadlington,
Chipping Norton,
Oxfordshire OX7 3NY

Tel	+44 (0)1608 676296
Mobile	+44 (0)7717 571792
Email	chloe.uppercourt@gmail.com
Web	www.uppercourtfarm.co.uk

Entry 392   Map 8

Oxfordshire

Manor Farm

An attractive old farmhouse dating from the 17th century with a warm friendly atmosphere. Jeannette and Andrew are generous hosts; Andrew built his own heating system, which runs on pallets and linseed straw – now he's finished a four-seater plane! Elegant, light bedrooms with garden views have pretty lamps and fabrics, sofas and comfortable beds. Wake for a full English served around a big table in an immaculate kitchen: homemade bread, eggs from the hens. There's a wood-burner in the snug sitting room, the garden has a pond and lots of birds, the little village is peaceful and Oxford is a half hour drive.

Rooms	3: 2 doubles, 1 twin.
Price	£85–£90. Singles £40–£50.
Meals	Pubs/restaurants 3 miles.
Closed	Rarely.

Andrew & Jeannette Collett
Manor Farm,
Main Street, Poundon,
Bicester,
Oxfordshire OX27 9BB

Tel	+44 (0)1869 277212
Mobile	+44 (0)7974 753772
Email	ajcollett@live.co.uk
Web	www.manorfarmpoundon.co.uk

Entry 393   Map 8

Oxfordshire

Oxford University

Oxford at your fingertips – at a fair price. In the city's ancient heart are Wadham and Keble; in leafy North Oxford is small friendly St Hugh's. Keble's sleeping quarters, functional though a good size, stand in stark contrast to the neo-gothic grandeur of its dining hall – pure Hogwarts! Wadham's hall, medieval, soaring, is yet more glorious – with top breakfasts. Its student-simple bedrooms are reached via crenellated cloisters and lovely walled gardens; ask for a room facing the beautiful quad. At St Hugh's: three residences (one historic), a student bar, romantic gardens and a 15-minute walk into town.

23 colleges in total.

Rooms	1237: 52 doubles, 1052 singles, 121 twins, 12 family rooms for 3-4.
Price	£60–£120. Family rooms £85–£150. Singles £30–£75.
Meals	Breakfast included. Keble: occasional supper £10.20. Restaurants 2-15 minutes' walk.
Closed	Mid-Jan to mid-March; May/June; Oct/Nov; Christmas. A few rooms available throughout year.

University Rooms
Oxford University,
Oxford,
Oxfordshire
Web   www.oxfordrooms.co.uk

Entry 394   Map 8

Oxfordshire

Willow Cottage

You are a short step from a village with an excellent pub (return across fields with a torch). Or treat yourself to dinner at Le Manoir aux Quat'Saisons. Katrina's delicious thatched cottage sits down a quiet lane. Through your own entrance find a guest dining room with armchairs by the old range, interesting prints and paintings, an eclectic mix of antiques and contemporary furniture. Bedrooms are warm, comfortable and stylish with views over the garden; shower rooms (not huge) are deeply smart. Breakfast, unhurried and bristling with local produce, sets walkers up for the Chiltern Way and the Ridgeway.

Rooms	2 doubles.
Price	£90. Singles £60.
Meals	Pubs/restaurants 0.5 miles.
Closed	Rarely.

Katrina Sheldon
Willow Cottage,
Denton, Oxford,
Oxfordshire OX44 9JG
Tel   +44 (0)1865 874728
Email katrinasheldon@aol.com
Web   www.willowcottage.info

Entry 395   Map 8

Oxfordshire

Manor Farmhouse

Helen and John radiate pleasure and good humour in this old Cotswold stone farmhouse, once part of the Blenheim estate (a short walk down the lane). Find comfortable, traditional living with good prints and paintings, venerable furniture and nothing cluttered or overdone. Shallow, curvy, 18th-century stairs lead up to the two pretty doubles in a completely private wing of the house. Breakfast is by the stone fireplace and ancient dresser. On warm days have tea in a sheltered corner by the fig tree and pots, and wander in the lovely garden. The pretty Cotswolds surround you, and the village is quiet yet close to Oxford.

Minimum two nights unless both rooms booked together.

Rooms	2 doubles sharing shower (let to same party only).
Price	£80–£90. Singles from £70.
Meals	Pub within walking distance.
Closed	Christmas.

Helen Stevenson
Manor Farmhouse,
Manor Road, Bladon,
Woodstock,
Oxfordshire OX20 1RU

Tel	+44 (0)1993 812168
Email	helstevenson@hotmail.com
Web	www.oxtowns.co.uk/woodstock/manor-farmhouse/

Entry 396   Map 8

Oxfordshire

Rectory Farm

Come for the happy relaxed vibe, and Mary Anne's welcome with tea and homemade shortbread. There's a wood-burner in the guest sitting room, and bedrooms have beautiful arched mullion windows. The huge twin with ornate plasterwork overlooks the garden and church, the pretty double is cosier and both have good showers and big fluffy towels. Wake for an excellent Aga breakfast with eggs from the hens, garden and hedgerow compotes, home or locally produced bacon and homemade jams. A herd of Red Ruby Devon cattle are Robert's pride and joy; the family have farmed for generations and you can buy the beef. It's a treat to stay.

Minimum two nights at weekends & high season.

Rooms	2: 1 double, 1 twin.
Price	£86–£88. Singles £64.
Meals	Pub 2-minute walk.
Closed	Mid-December to mid-January.

Mary Anne Florey
Rectory Farm,
Northmoor, Witney,
Oxfordshire OX29 5SX

Tel	+44 (0)1865 300207
Mobile	+44 (0)7974 102198
Email	pj.florey@farmline.com
Web	www.oxtowns.co.uk/rectoryfarm

Entry 397   Map 8

Oxfordshire

Oxfordshire

Lowbarrow

Swoop through wooden electric gates to find newly planted young trees, a soft, creamy Cotswold stone house and horses in the paddock. Walk straight in to travertine tiles in an enormous hall, a real fire in the book-filled drawing room with squishy sofas and gorgeous fabrics, bedrooms that will lull, state of the art bathrooms. Nothing is mean, all is generous and big; views soar through sash windows. Philippa gives you proper sausages, bread and eggs from the community shop, pretty china, delicious suppers. Wander the gardens, play tennis, swim in the pool, explore the Cotswolds on foot or for retail therapy. Live the dream.

Horse stabling available, £15 per night. Well-behaved dogs can stay in boot room.

Star Cottage

Classic Cotswolds – from the cottagey stone walls to the flower-bright garden – and swaths of open countryside for cyclists and walkers. Step inside to hand-sewn fabrics, cute lampshades, country furniture, fresh flowers and calm, pretty bedrooms: Sally delights in details. She and Peter, a plant biologist, love their winding stone-walled garden with its herbs, climbers and medlar tree; its jelly appears at breakfast, alongside smoked haddock and local sausage. The pub (yards away) offers dinner, Burford market town is a ten-minute walk, Cheltenham and Oxford a half-hour drive. Or kind Peter will fetch from the station.

Ask about private Cotswold tours.

Rooms	3: 2 doubles, 1 twin.
Price	£110-£135. Singles £80.
Meals	Dinner, 2-3 courses, £22-£30. Pubs 1 mile.
Closed	Rarely.

Rooms	3: 1 double, 1 family room. Barn: 1 family room & kitchen.
Price	£80-£110. Singles £70-£80.
Meals	Pubs/restaurants within walking distance.
Closed	Rarely.

Philippa Grace
Lowbarrow,
The Ridings, Leafield,
Witney,
Oxfordshire OX29 9NH

Tel	+44 (0)1993 878825
Mobile	+44 (0)7712 880738
Email	philippa@lowbarrow.com
Web	www.lowbarrow.com

Peter & Sally Wyatt
Star Cottage,
Meadow Lane, Fulbrook,
Burford,
Oxfordshire OX18 4BW

Tel	+44 (0)1993 822032
Email	wyattpeter@btconnect.com
Web	www.burfordbedandbreakfast.co.uk

Entry 398   Map 8

Entry 399   Map 8

Oxfordshire

Fox House

In idyllic stonewalled little Holwell is a big stylish house on a corner – the old village school. Welcoming Susan, who is in the antiques business, gives you two super sitting rooms (one with a friendly wood-burner, the other with a barn window and a heated flagstone floor), and three immaculately cosy bedrooms (one double downstairs) and serves delectable breakfasts on pretty blue china and jams and juices from the orchard. The garden is open and leads to pasture and horses, the countryside is delicious in every season and footpaths radiate from the door. The Cotswolds at its finest!

Special rates for parties of four or more.

Rooms	3: 1 double; 1 twin, 1 double sharing bath (let to same party only).
Price	£90-£125. Singles from £75.
Meals	Dinner, 3 courses, £25. Pubs/restaurants 2 miles.
Closed	Rarely.

	Susan Blacker
	Fox House,
	Holwell,
	Burford,
	Oxfordshire OX18 4JS
Tel	+44 (0)1993 823409
Email	foxhouse-rooms@btconnect.com
Web	www.foxhouse-rooms.co.uk

Entry 400   Map 8

Oxfordshire

Crown Cottage

In a history-rich village, a welcoming home with a remarkable feel. Deirdre, gentle, artistic, well-travelled, treats you to summer tea in the garden up the alley, and breakfast with fresh fruit compotes and Wallingford sausages in the Aga-warm kitchen. Sleep like a log in lovely peaceful bedrooms, one with an ancient oak casement window overlooking the courtyard of the (former) Crown Inn. Charm lies in sloping floors, sash windows and wide stairs; art, books and an open fire; and a big traditional bathroom to share. Step outside to find narrow winding streets, a very special abbey, and a bus to the dreaming spires.

Rooms	2 doubles sharing bath.
Price	£70. Singles £45-£50.
Meals	Pubs within walking distance.
Closed	October-February.

	Deirdre Wollaston
	Crown Cottage,
	52 High Street,
	Dorchester-on-Thames,
	Wallingford,
	Oxfordshire OX10 7HN
Tel	+44 (0)1865 341584
Web	www.crowncottage.net

Entry 401   Map 4

Oxfordshire

Fyfield Manor

A fabulous house in Oxfordshire (once owned by Simon de Montfort) with vast water gardens and a water wheel for eco underfloor heating. The Browns have added solar panels too. From the grand wood-panelled hall enter a beamed dining room with high-backed chairs, brass rubbings, wood-burner and pretty 12th-century arch; breakfast on eggs from the hens, garden fruit, organic bacon. Charming bedrooms have views, slippers and comfy sofas. Oxford Park & Ride is nearby, there's walking from the door and delightful Christine has wangled you a free glass of wine in the local pub if you walk or cycle to get there! Superb.

Over tens welcome. No shoes to be worn in bedrooms - slippers provided.

Rooms	2: 1 twin/double; 1 family room with sofabed & separate bath.
Price	£80-£90. Singles £60-£70. Family room £20 extra per person.
Meals	Pubs within 1 mile.
Closed	Rarely.

Christine Brown
Fyfield Manor,
Benson,
Wallingford,
Oxfordshire OX10 6HA
Tel   +44 (0)1491 835184
Email chris_fyfield@hotmail.co.uk
Web   www.fyfieldmanor.co.uk

Entry 402   Map 4

Rutland

Old Hall Coach House

A rare and special setting; the grounds of the house meet the edge of Rutland Water, with far-reaching lake and church views. Inside: high ceilings, stone archways, antiques and a conservatory overlooking a stunning garden and croquet lawn. Comfortable bedrooms are traditional (the double has a brand new bathroom, the twin glorious views from both windows.) Wake for an Aga-cooked spread of home-laid eggs, homemade marmalade – and sausages on Sundays. Rutland is a mini-Cotswolds of stone villages and gentle hills; Georgian Stamford, Burghley House and Belvoir Castle are all near. Cecilie is a well-travelled, interesting host.

Minimum stay two nights at weekends.

Rooms	2: 1 double; 1 twin with separate bath.
Price	£90. Singles from £40.
Meals	Dinner £30. Pub/restaurant 5-minute walk.
Closed	Occasionally.

Cecilie Ingoldby
Old Hall Coach House,
31 Weston Road, Edith Weston,
Oakham, Rutland LE15 8HQ
Tel   +44 (0)1780 721504
Mobile +44 (0)7767 678267
Email   cecilieingoldby@aol.com
Web   www.oldhallcoachhouse.co.uk

Entry 403   Map 9

Rutland

Old Rectory

Jane Austen fans will swoon. This elegant 1740s village house was used as Mr Collins's 'humble abode' by the BBC: you breakfast in the beautiful dining room that was 'Mr Collins's hall', and you can sleep in 'Miss Bennett's bedroom'. Victoria is wonderful – feisty, fun and gregarious – and looks after you beautifully with White Company linen in chintzy old-fashioned bedrooms, a log fire in the drawing room, fruit from the lovely garden, homemade jams and Aga-cooked local bacon and eggs. Guests love it here. You are near to some pleasant market towns and good walking and riding country. Don't forget the smelling salts!

Rooms	2: 1 double, 1 twin.
Price	£85. Singles £45.
Meals	Pubs within 3 miles.
Closed	Rarely.

	Victoria Owen
	Old Rectory,
	Teigh, Oakham,
	Rutland LE15 7RT
Tel	+44 (0)1572 787681
Mobile	+44 (0)7717 223678
Email	torowen@btinternet.com
Web	www.teighbedandbreakfast.co.uk

Entry 404   Map 9

Shropshire

Tybroughton Hall

Off a winding country lane, surrounded by 40 acres of grassland, find a pretty white listed farmhouse and a wonderful welcome from Daisy, her family and two dear dogs. Step into the hallway with its polished antique table and bright garden flowers and you know you've made the right choice: this is a house to unwind in. After a day's hiking or biking, bliss to return to bedrooms cosy and comfortable – the traditional double with its country view or the large lovely twin. Breakfasts are worth getting up for: Tim makes the preserves, bees make the honey, hens lay the eggs and the pigs (five beauties!) provide the bacon.

Rooms	2: 1 double; 1 twin with separate bath.
Price	£80–£100. Singles £50–£65.
Meals	Dinner £20–£25. Pub 4 miles.
Closed	Rarely.

	Daisy Woodhead
	Tybroughton Hall,
	Tybroughton, Whitchurch,
	Shropshire SY13 3BB
Tel	+44 (0)1948 780726
Mobile	+44 (0)7850 395885
Email	daisy.woodhead@btinternet.com
Web	www.tybroughtonhall-bedandbreakfast.co.uk

Entry 405   Map 7

Shropshire

Iscoyd Park

Ten generations have left their mark on this country estate, and none more so than Phil and Susie. You sleep in the Victorian stables, freshly transformed into light-filled bedrooms sparkling with modern art and mirrors, warmed by underfloor heating and with lovely bathrooms; from goose down duvets to handmade soaps, every detail is top drawer and you'll feel nicely independent. Bookshelves line a fire-warmed sitting room, fresh flowers brighten polished antiques. The scent of lavender accompanies morning strolls down a tree-lined avenue into the park. Return to home-laid eggs and convivial chat with this delightful family.

Minimum two nights.

Shropshire

The Isle

History buffs and nature lovers rejoice. You drive through lion-topped stone pillars to a house built in 1682 (then extended) that stands in 800 acres enfolded by the river Severn. Charming Ros and Edward are down-to-earth and hands-on: eggs, bacon, ham, vegetables, and logs, come from the estate. Flop in front of a huge fire in the drawing room, homely with family antiques, big rug, magazines strewn on large tables. Peaceful bedrooms are large and light with pocket-sprung memory mattresses and snazzy upmarket bathrooms. Walk, fish, ride (there's a livery stable on site) and lap up the views – they're sublime.

Rooms	The Stable Yard: 2 doubles.
Price	£130.
Meals	Continental breakfast in room/full cooked breakfast in house. Pubs/restaurants 5 miles.
Closed	Rarely.

Rooms	3: 2 doubles; 1 twin with separate bath.
Price	£75-£95. Singles £50-£60.
Meals	Packed lunch £5. Dinner £20. Pub/restaurant 4.3 miles.
Closed	Rarely.

| | Philip & Susie Godsal
Iscoyd Park,
Whitchurch,
Shropshire SY13 3AT |
|---|---|
| Tel | +44 (0)1948 780785 |
| Email | info@iscoydpark.com |
| Web | www.iscoydpark.com |

| | Ros & Edward Tate
The Isle,
Bicton, Shrewsbury,
Shropshire SY3 8EE |
|---|---|
| Mobile | +44 (0)7776 257286 |
| Email | ros@isleestate.co.uk |
| Web | www.the-isle-estate.co.uk |

Entry 406   Map 7

Entry 407   Map 7

Shropshire

Hardwick House

On a quiet street in the heart of Shrewsbury, this fine Georgian house has been in Lucy's family for generations. The dining room (oak panelling, a huge fireplace) is a lovely space to breakfast on locally sourced produce and homemade bread; vases of garden flowers are dotted all around this cheerful family home. Bedrooms are traditional and comfortable with pretty china tea cups; bathrooms are old-fashioned. The walled garden is fabulous; take tea in an 18th-century summerhouse. Birthplace of Darwin, this is a fascinating historic town; walk to the abbey, castle, theatre, festivals and great shops. Lucy is delightful.

Rooms	2 twins/doubles. (Adjoining twin available to form a suite.)
Price	£80–£95. Singles £55–£65.
Meals	Pubs/restaurants 150 yds.
Closed	Christmas & New Year.

Lucy Whitaker
Hardwick House,
12 St John's Hill, Shrewsbury,
Shropshire SY1 1JJ

Tel	+44 (0)1743 350165
Email	gilesandlucy@btinternet.com
Web	www.hardwickhouseshrewsbury.co.uk

Entry 408   Map 7

Shropshire

Whitton Hall

Down a long private drive with fields on either side is a lovely 18th-century farmhouse, elegant but not intimidating, with a sense of timelessness. A large open hallway with a warming fire is a comfortable, peaceful space for relaxing with a book. You breakfast in the dining room, on local muesli, bread, marmalades and jams, milk from their Jersey cows, soft fruit from their garden, sausages and bacon from down the road. Up a stunning staircase are peaceful, light and large bedrooms, with graceful, country house furniture and long views to glorious gardens. Unwind in the peace.

Over 12s welcome.

Rooms	2: 1 double with separate bathroom, 1 twin/double with separate shower.
Price	£85–£90. Singles from £50.
Meals	Supper £10–£20. Packed lunch available. Restaurant 1.5 miles.
Closed	Christmas & New Year.

Christopher & Gill Halliday
& Kate Boscawen
Whitton Hall,
Westbury, Shrewsbury,
Shropshire SY5 9RD

Tel	+44 (0)1743 884270
Mobile	+44 (0)7974 689629
Email	accommodation@whittonhall.com
Web	www.whittonhall.co.uk

Entry 409   Map 7

Shropshire

Brimford House

Beautifully tucked under the Breidden Hills, farm and Georgian farmhouse have been in the Dawson family for four generations. Views stretch all the way to the Severn; the simple garden does not try to compete. Bedrooms are spotless and fresh: a half-tester with rope-twist columns and Sanderson fabrics, a twin with Victorian wrought-iron bedsteads, a double with a brass bed, a big bathroom with a roll top bath. Liz serves you farm eggs and homemade preserves at breakfast, and there's a food pub just down the road. Sheep and cattle outdoors, a lovely black lab in, and wildlife walks from the door. Good value.

Rooms	3: 2 doubles, 1 twin.
Price	£65-£75. Singles £40-£60.
Meals	Packed lunch £4.50. Pub 3-minute walk.
Closed	Rarely.

Liz Dawson
Brimford House,
Criggion, Shrewsbury,
Shropshire SY5 9AU
Tel   +44 (0)1938 570235
Mobile   +44 (0)7801 100848
Email   info@brimford.co.uk
Web   www.brimford.co.uk

Entry 410   Map 7

Shropshire

Lawley House

A lovely calm sense of the continuity of history and family life emanates from this large, comfortable Victorian home. Jackie and Jim are delightful hosts and great fun. Bedrooms welcome you with flowers, books, duck down pillows – and stupendous views of the Stretton Hills, even from bed. Tuck into a generous breakfast in the dining room, elegant with family portraits and a grand piano you are welcome to play. Enjoy long hilltop views from the spectacular conservatory or the garden – lush with lupins, sweet peas, delphiniums and 50 types of rose that bloom in profusion. A charming and friendly place.

Over 12s welcome. One-night weekend stay, small extra charge.

Rooms	3: 2 doubles, 1 twin/double.
Price	£60-£80. Singles £40-£55.
Meals	Pub/restaurant 1.5 miles.
Closed	Christmas & New Year.

Jackie & Jim Scarratt
Lawley House,
Smethcott, Church Stretton,
Shropshire SY6 6NX
Tel   +44 (0)1694 751236
Mobile   +44 (0)7980 331792
Email   jscarratt@onetel.com
Web   www.lawleyhouse.co.uk

Entry 411   Map 7

Shropshire

Clun Farm House

These young relaxed owners make a great team. Susan gives you homemade marmalade and freshly-laid eggs for breakfast; Anthony helps you discover the secrets of the village and the heavenly hills. Both are enthusiastic collectors of country artefacts and have filled their listed 15th-century farmhouse with eye-catching things; the cowboy's saddle by the old range echoes Susan's roots. Bedrooms have aged and oiled floorboards, fun florals and bold walls; bathrooms are small and simple. Walk Offa's Dyke and the Shropshire Way; return to rescue hens wandering the garden, a cosy wood-burner and a warm smile. Good value.

Rooms	2: 1 double with extra bunk room; 1 twin/double with separate shower.
Price	£80. Singles by arrangement.
Meals	Packed lunch £4. Pubs/restaurants nearby.
Closed	Occasionally.

Anthony & Susan Whitfield
Clun Farm House,
High Street, Clun,
Craven Arms,
Shropshire SY7 8JB

Tel	+44 (0)1588 640432
Mobile	+44 (0)7885 261391
Email	anthonyswhitfield0158@btinternet.com
Web	www.clunfarmhouse.co.uk

Entry 412   Map 7

Shropshire

Hopton House

Karen looks after her guests wonderfully and even runs courses on how to do B&B! Unwind in this fresh and uplifting converted granary with old beams, high ceilings and a sun-filled dining/sitting room overlooking the hills. The bedroom above has its own balcony; those in the barn, one up, one down, each with its own entrance, are as enticing: beautifully dressed beds, silent fridges, good lighting, homemade cakes. Bathrooms have deep baths (and showers) — from one you can lie back and gaze at the stars. Karen's breakfasts promise Ludlow sausages, home-laid eggs, fine jams and homemade marmalade.

Rooms	3: 1 double. Barn: 2 doubles.
Price	£110-£120.
Meals	Restaurant 3 miles.
Closed	19-27 December.

Karen Thorne
Hopton House,
Hopton Heath,
Craven Arms,
Shropshire SY7 0QD

Tel	+44 (0)1547 530885
Email	info@shropshirebreakfast.co.uk
Web	www.shropshirebreakfast.co.uk

Entry 413   Map 7

Shropshire

The Birches Mill

Just as a mill should be, tucked in the nook of a postcard valley. It ended Gill and Andrew's search for a refuge from the city, and it's a treat to share its seclusion and beauty; all you hear is the river. Fresh breezy bedrooms in the 17th-century part have elegant brass beds, goose down duvets and fine linen – one keeps the original long roll top bath – while the new stone and oak extension blends beautifully and has become a big attractive twin. Happy hens provide the breakfast eggs. Gill and Andrew are affable hosts in a stunning valley of meadowland and woods.

Children over 12 welcome.

Rooms	3: 1 double, 1 twin; 1 double with separate bath.
Price	£84–£95. Singles by arrangement.
Meals	Packed lunch £6. Pub 3 miles.
Closed	November–March.

Gill Della Casa & Andrew Farmer
The Birches Mill,
Clun,
Shropshire SY7 8NL
Tel   +44 (0)1588 640409
Email   birchesmill@btinternet.com
Web   www.birchesmill.co.uk

Entry 414   Map 7

Shropshire

Lower Buckton Country House

You are spoiled here in house-party style; Carolyn – passionate about Slow Food – and Henry, are born entertainers. Kick off with homemade cake in the drawing room with its oil paintings, antique furniture and old rugs; return for delicious nibbles when the lamps and wood-burner are flickering. Dine well at a huge oak table (home-reared pork, local cheeses, dreamy puddings), then nestle into the best linen and the softest pillows; bedrooms feel wonderfully restful. This is laid-back B&B: paddle in the stream, admire the stunning views, find a quiet spot with a good book. Great fun!

Self-catering in Millstream Camp (shepherd's hut) available.

Rooms	3: 2 doubles; 1 twin/double with separate bath.
Price	£100.
Meals	Dinner, 4 courses, £35. BYO wine. Pub/restaurant 4 miles.
Closed	Rarely.

Henry & Carolyn Chesshire
Lower Buckton Country House,
Buckton, Leintwardine,
Shropshire SY7 0JU
Tel   +44 (0)1547 540532
Mobile +44 (0)7960 273865
Email   carolyn@lowerbuckton.co.uk
Web   www.lowerbuckton.co.uk

Entry 415   Map 7

Shropshire

Millstream Camp

A homely site in a foodie's paradise, this rustic, ramshackle set-up on the old millstream makes a lovely escape. The shepherd's hut serves as your sleeping quarters and the tipi, decked with old Indian saris, campaign trunks and a lacquered table, is your day space. Take it slow and get back to basics: lower a tin bucket into the water to chill a bottle of white, heat your bathwater over the fire (or use the outdoor gas shower) and don't be put off by the compost loo! Up at the house: breakfasts, dinners and cookery courses. The village of Leintwardine is a lovely half hour walk away along the riverside; the Sun Inn is a must.

Minimum two nights. Book through Sawday's Canopy & Stars online or by phone.

Rooms	Shepherd's hut for 2 with outdoor gas shower & compost loo.
Price	£80–£100.
Meals	BYO breakfast, or in house, £15. Dinner, 4 courses, £35. BYO wine. Pub/restaurant 4 miles.
Closed	October–March.

Sawday's Canopy & Stars
Millstream Camp,
Lower Buckton Country House,
Buckton, Leintwardine,
Shropshire SY7 0JU

Tel	+44 (0)1275 395447
Email	enquiries@canopyandstars.co.uk
Web	www.canopyandstars.co.uk/millstreamcamp

Entry 416   Map 7

Shropshire

Upper Buckton

You can't help being bowled over by the beautiful setting and the grandeur of the place. In lush gardens that slope peacefully down to millstream, meadows and river, this Georgian house, complete with heronry and point-to-point course, stands on a motte and bailey site. Convivial dinners, preceded by drinks in the drawing room, are delicious: Yvonne's cooking using local produce is upmarket and creative, Hayden's wine list is a treat. Retire to large bedrooms with huge beds made to perfection (proper blankets, lovely linen). Marvellous for walkers returning from a day in the glorious Welsh Borders.

Children by arrangement.

Rooms	3: 1 double, 1 twin/double; 1 twin/double with separate bath.
Price	£96–£110. Singles £63–£70.
Meals	Dinner, 4 courses, £30. Pub/restaurant 2 miles.
Closed	Rarely.

Hayden & Yvonne Lloyd
Upper Buckton,
Leintwardine,
Craven Arms,
Ludlow,
Shropshire SY7 0JU

Tel	+44 (0)1547 540634
Email	ghlloydco@btconnect.com
Web	www.upperbuckton.co.uk

Entry 417   Map 7

Shropshire

Walford Court

Come for a break from clock-watching and a spot of fresh air. Large bedrooms delight with the comfiest mattresses on king-size beds, scented candles, antiques, books, games and double-end roll top baths – one under a west facing window. Aga-cooked breakfasts include eggs from "the ladies of the orchard"; candlelit dinners may be served outside on fine evenings. Wander through apple, plum and pear trees, find a motte and bailey, strike out for a long hike. Craig and Debbie are thoughtful and hugely keen on wildlife (you get binoculars) and this is the perfect place to bring a special person – and a bottle of champagne.

Older children by arrangement.

Rooms	3: 1 double; 2 doubles each with sitting room.
Price	£95. Singles £85.
Meals	Dinner, 2-3 courses, £25-£31. Cold platters. Packed lunch available. Pubs/restaurants 1-3 miles.
Closed	Christmas & Boxing Day.

Debbie & Craig Fraser
Walford Court,
Walford, Leintwardine,
Ludlow,
Shropshire SY7 0JT
Tel   +44 (0)1547 540570
Email info@romanticbreak.com
Web   www.romanticbreak.com

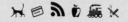

Entry 418   Map 7

Shropshire

35 Lower Broad Street

You're almost at the bottom of the town, near the river and the bridge. Elaine's terraced Georgian cottage is spotless and cosy; her office doubles as a sitting area for guests with leather armchairs and desk space for workaholics. Upstairs are two good-sized doubles with a country crisp feel, king-size beds and a pretty blue and white bathroom. Walkers, shoppers, antique- and book-hunters can fill up on a superb breakfast of homemade potato scones, black pudding, organic eggs and good coffee before striding out to explore. This is excellent value, comfortable B&B and can be enjoyed without a car. Perfect for two couples.

Rooms	2: 1 double & sitting room; 1 double sharing bath (let to same party only).
Price	£75. Singles £45.
Meals	Pubs/restaurants 100 yds.
Closed	Rarely.

Elaine Downs
35 Lower Broad Street,
Ludlow,
Shropshire SY8 1PH
Tel   +44 (0)1584 876912
Mobile +44 (0)7980 037576
Email a.downs@tesco.net
Web   www.ludlowbedandbreakfast.blogspot.com

Entry 419   Map 7

Shropshire

Rosecroft

A pretty, quiet, traditional house with charming owners, well-proportioned rooms, an elegant sitting room and not a trace of pomposity. Breakfasts are huge enough to set you up for the day: Pimhill organic muesli, smoked or unsmoked local bacon, black pudding, delicious jams. The garden is a delight to stroll through – in summer you can picnic here – while serious walkers are close to the Welsh borders. Bedrooms and bathrooms are polished to perfection; there are fresh flowers, plenty of interesting books, home-baked cakes when you arrive. The village has a super pub and Ludlow is close by.

Children over 12 welcome.

Rooms	2: 1 double; 1 double with separate bath.
Price	£80. Singles £55-£60.
Meals	Packed lunch £4. Pub 200 yds.
Closed	Rarely.

Gail Benson
Rosecroft,
Orleton,
Ludlow,
Shropshire SY8 4HN
Tel +44 (0)1568 780565
Email gailanddavid@rosecroftorleton.co.uk
Web www.rosecroftbedandbreakfast.co.uk

Entry 420 Map 7

Shropshire

Timberstone Bed & Breakfast

The house is young and engaging – as are Tracey and Alex, new generation B&Bers. Come for charming bedrooms – two snug under the eaves, two in the smart oak-floored extension – roll top baths, pretty fabrics, thick white cotton, beams galore... and reflexology or a sauna in the garden studios; Tracey, once in catering, is a reflexologist. In the warm guest sitting/dining room find art, books, comfortable sofas and glass doors onto the terrace. Breakfasts are special with croissants and local eggs and bacon; suppers are delicious too, or you can head off to Ludlow and its clutch of Michelin stars.

Children welcome. Whole house available for self-catering.

Rooms	5: 2 doubles, 1 family room, 1 double with sofabed. Summerhouse: 1 double (summer only).
Price	£90-£100. Singles £50-£90.
Meals	Dinner, 3 courses, £25. Pubs/restaurants 5 miles.
Closed	Rarely.

Tracey Baylis & Alex Read
Timberstone Bed & Breakfast,
Clee Stanton, Ludlow,
Shropshire SY8 3EL
Tel +44 (0)1584 823519
Mobile +44 (0)7905 967263
Email timberstone1@hotmail.com
Web www.timberstoneludlow.co.uk

Entry 421 Map 7

Shropshire

The Old Rectory

With its own spring water, horses, dogs and slow pace this Georgian rectory is comfortable country living at its best. Izzy and Andy are charming and interesting and give you scones and tea by the fire in a drawing room full of family photos, plump sofas and books. Elegant bedrooms have fluffy hot water bottles; smart bathrooms have scented lotions in pretty bottles, robes and slippers. Candlelit dinner will often be fish or game with garden vegetables; breakfast is local and leisurely with homemade granola and jams. There's a bootroom for muddy feet and paws, stabling and seven acres to roam.

Pets sleep in bootroom.

Rooms	3: 1 double, 1 twin/double; 1 double with separate bathroom.
Price	£80-£120. Singles from £65.
Meals	Dinner, 3 courses, £30. Packed lunch £10. Pubs 1.25-4 miles.
Closed	Rarely.

	Isabel Barnard
	The Old Rectory,
	Wheathill, Ludlow,
	Bridgnorth,
	Shropshire WV16 6QT
Tel	+44 (0)1746 787209
Email	enquiries@theoldrectorywheathill.com
Web	www.theoldrectorywheathill.com

Entry 422   Map 7

Shropshire

Church Farm

In a walled garden with flowing lawns, borders, pond and trees is this smartly renovated, church-side farmhouse. Friendly Chris and Allison share a love of gardening and are full of plans for their B&B. They give you an invitingly low-beamed sitting room with sofas, books and wood-burner, antique tables topped with pretty things, and ancestors on the walls. Big cream-carpeted bedrooms are immaculate with good mattresses, feather duvets and double-lined floral curtains at windows that frame long Shropshire views. Gorgeous walks abound and Ironbridge is close – birthplace of the Industrial Revolution.

Rooms	3: 1 double, 1 twin, 1 twin/double.
Price	£75. Singles £55.
Meals	Pubs/restaurants across the road.
Closed	Rarely.

	Chris & Allison Kwiatkowski
	Church Farm,
	Hall Lane, Kemberton,
	Shifnal,
	Shropshire TF11 9LQ
Tel	+44 (0)1952 586907
Email	info@churchfarmshropshire.com
Web	www.churchfarmshropshire.com

Entry 423   Map 8

Somerset

The Old Priory

The 12th-century priory leans against its church, with a rustic gate, an enchanting garden, a tumble of flowers. Both house and hostess are dignified, unpretentious and friendly. Here are old oak tables, flagstones, wood panelling, higgledy-piggledy corridors and large bedrooms filled with family antiques. But an ancient English house in a sweet Somerset village needs a touch of pepper and cosmopolitan Jane adds her own special flair with eccentric touches here and there, and books and Horace the dog for company. Peaceful spots and scents in the garden, Dunster Castle above on the hill and walks from the door.

Rooms	3: 1 twin, 1 four-poster; 1 double with separate shower.
Price	£90-£100. Singles by arrangement.
Meals	Pubs/restaurants 5-minute walk.
Closed	Christmas.

Jane Forshaw
The Old Priory,
Priory Green,
Dunster,
Somerset TA24 6RY
Tel   +44 (0)1643 821540
Web   www.theoldpriory-dunster.co.uk

Entry 424   Map 2

Somerset

Higher Orchard

A little lane tumbles down to the centre of lovely old Dunster. The village is a two-minute walk, yet here you have open views of fields, sheep and sea. Exmoor footpaths start behind the house and Janet encourages explorers, by bike or on foot: ever helpful and kind, she is a local who knows the patch well. The 1860s house keeps its Victorian features, bedrooms are quiet and simple and the double has a view to Blue Anchor Bay and Dunster castle and church. All is homely, with stripped pine, cream curtains, fresh flowers, garden fruit and home-laid eggs for breakfast.

Children & pets by arrangement.

Rooms	3: 1 double, 2 twins/doubles.
Price	£70. Singles from £35.
Meals	Packed lunch from £3.50. Restaurants 2-minute walk.
Closed	Christmas.

Janet Lamacraft
Higher Orchard,
30 St George's Street, Dunster,
Somerset TA24 6RS
Tel   +44 (0)1643 821915
Mobile   +44 (0)7896 464420
Email   lamacraft@higherorchard.fsnet.co.uk
Web   www.higherorchard-dunster.co.uk

Entry 425   Map 2

Somerset

Glen Lodge

Come for the food and Meryl and David's comfy open house vibe. Their sheltered, secluded Victorian home is spacious, comfortable and surrounded by high banks of woodland. Enjoy delicious meals with an American slant using local venison, lamb, honey, cheeses and fish; they grow fruit and veg, make jams and serve tea and cakes every day – perfect brownies! Polished oak floors are dotted with oriental rugs and log fires burn. Wander the 21 acres, play croquet, sip a sunset drink on the terrace overlooking the wide bay. Exmoor and popular Porlock are on the doorstep; sandy beaches, harbours and boat trips will keep you happy too.

Rooms	5: 3 doubles; 1 double, 1 twin, each with separate bath.
Price	£90-£95. Singles £60.
Meals	Dinner, 3 courses, £30. Supper £20. Packed lunch £8. Pub/restaurant 0.5 miles.
Closed	Rarely.

	Meryl Salter
	Glen Lodge,
	Hawkcombe, Porlock,
	Somerset TA24 8LN
Tel	+44 (0)1643 863371
Mobile	+44 (0)7786 118933
Email	glenlodge@gmail.com
Web	www.glenlodge.net

Entry 426   Map 2

Somerset

North Wheddon Farm

Pootle through the vibrant green patchwork of Exmoor National Park and bowl down a pitted track to land in Blyton-esque bliss – a classic Somerset farmyard, crackling with geese and hens, round which is the gentleman farmer's house. Bedrooms are airy and comfortable with grand views, books, fresh flowers and small, but neat-as-a-pin bathrooms. Bring children and they will be in heaven, with eggs to collect and pigs to pat, or come just for yourself and a bit of indulgence. Food is 'River Cottage' style and much is home-reared, the walking is fabulous for miles and kind Rachael sends you off with a thermos of tea.

Rooms	2: 1 double, 1 twin/double.
Price	£75-£80. Singles £38.50.
Meals	Cold packed lunch £7.50-£9.75. Pub 0.25 miles.
Closed	Rarely.

	Rachael Abraham
	North Wheddon Farm,
	Wheddon Cross,
	Somerset TA24 7EX
Tel	+44 (0)1643 841791
Email	rachael@go-exmoor.co.uk
Web	www.northwheddonfarm.co.uk

Entry 427   Map 2

Somerset

West Liscombe

Down deep Devon lanes, then up, up, up to the remote farmhouse encircled by footpaths and bridle paths, breezes and green views. Heaven! Inside is comfy, cheery, chintzy and English to the core. Deborah, true country lady and Cordon Bleu cook, was born to do B&B and welcomes all. The grandfather clock tick-tocks in the sitting room, the silver shines, the log-burner glows, and the guest bedrooms, with books, great beds and posies of flowers, are well-groomed and inviting. Sheep roam the drive, the garden stretches down the valley, Exmoor is 600 yards, the sea is 11 miles.

Rooms	2: 1 double;
	1 twin with separate bath.
Price	£75. Singles £45.
Meals	Lunch £7.50. Dinner £20.
	Pub 5 miles.
Closed	Rarely.

Robert & Deborah Connell
West Liscombe,
Waddicombe,
Dulverton,
Somerset TA22 9RX
Tel   +44 (0)1398 341282
Email   deborahconnell@btinternet.com

Entry 428   Map 2

Somerset

Cider Barn

Set back from the lane is a newly converted and refurbished barn. Elm boards have been removed for heated oak floors, fine old proportions remain, Louise's stunning living quarters spread under the beams and the bedrooms lie privately below on the ground floor. There's a sunny guest sitting room leading onto the garden, and delightful Louise, Cordon Bleu trained, serves breakfast at a long table by the wood-burner. You can walk through fields to the river or the hills, book an Indian head massage, stroll to the pub for supper. Bedrooms, one opening to the courtyard, are airy and peaceful with modern fabrics and cream walls. Lovely.

Rooms	2: 1 double, 1 twin/double.
Price	£70-£80. Singles £40-£45
Meals	Pub 1 mile.
Closed	Rarely.

Louise Bancroft
Cider Barn,
Runnington, Wellington,
Somerset TA21 0QW
Tel   +44 (0)1823 665533
Email   louisegaddon@btinternet.com
Web   www.runningtonciderbarn.co.uk

Entry 429   Map 2

Somerset

29 Strawberry Bank

Henrietta's eye for design is evident in this beautifully renovated 19th-century cottage. Squashy sofas, ethnic baskets, pictures from her travels and garden views... best enjoyed over local or organic sausages and double yolkers (not guaranteed!). You're close to the centre of a charming market town, yet within minutes of the countryside; see it from your bedroom window. Pour yourself a cup of tea from floral china, pad across golden boards, clamber into a huge bed with a dramatic quilt. Delightful Henrietta is happy for you to share her sitting room with wood-burner, and her sunny secluded garden – perfect for a sundowner.

Rooms	1 double.
Price	£85.
Meals	Dinner, 3 courses, £25.
	Pubs/restaurants 5-minute walk.
Closed	Rarely.

	Henrietta Van den Bergh
	29 Strawberry Bank,
	High Street,
	Ilminster,
	Somerset TA19 9AW
Tel	+44 (0)1460 54394
Mobile	+44 (0)7973 838452
Email	info@hvdbphoto.com

Entry 430   Map 2

Somerset

Causeway Cottage

Robert and Lesley are ex-restaurateurs, so guests heap praise on their food, most of which is sourced from a local butcher and fishmonger; charming Lesley is an author, runs cookery courses and once taught at Prue Leith's. This is the perfect, pretty Somerset cottage, with an apple orchard and views to the church across a cottage garden and a field. The bedrooms are light, restful and have a country-style simplicity with their green check bedspreads, white walls and antique pine furniture; guests have their own comfortable sitting room. Easy access to the M5 yet with a rural feel. Very special.

Children over ten welcome.

Rooms	3: 1 double, 2 twins.
Price	£78-£85. Singles by arrangement.
Meals	Supper from £25.
	Pub/restaurant 0.75 miles.
Closed	Christmas.

	Lesley & Robert Orr
	Causeway Cottage,
	West Buckland, Taunton,
	Somerset TA21 9JZ
Tel	+44 (0)1823 663458
Mobile	+44 (0)7703 412827
Email	causewaybb@talktalk.net
Web	www.causewaycottage.co.uk

Entry 431   Map 2

Somerset

Bashfords Farmhouse

A feeling of warmth and happiness pervades this exquisite 17th-century farmhouse in the Quantock hills. The Ritchies love doing B&B – even after over 20 years! – and interiors have a homely feel with well-framed prints, natural fabrics, comfortable sofas, and a sitting room with inglenook, sofas and books. Bedrooms are pretty, fresh and large and look over the cobbled courtyard or open fields. Charles and Jane couldn't be nicer, know about local walks (the Macmillan Way runs by) and love to cook: local meat and game, tarte tatin, homemade bread and jams. A delightful garden rambles up the hill; the pub is just a minute away.

Rooms	3: 1 twin/double; 1 twin/double with separate bath; 1 twin/double with separate shower.
Price	£75. Singles £45.
Meals	Dinner £27.50. Supper £22.50. Pub 75 yds.
Closed	Rarely.

Charles & Jane Ritchie
Bashfords Farmhouse,
West Bagborough,
Taunton,
Somerset TA4 3EF
Tel   +44 (0)1823 432015
Email   info@bashfordsfarmhouse.co.uk
Web   www.bashfordsfarmhouse.co.uk

Entry 432   Map 2

Somerset

Parsonage Farm

The Quantock Hills are wonderful for walking and cycling, with the Coleridge Way starting down the lane. In this 17th-century farmhouse relaxed hosts give you easy comfort with quarry floors, books, a cosy log-fired sitting room and spacious bedrooms with tranquil country views. Suki, from Vermont, has turned a stable into a studio – her pots and paintings add charm to the décor. Breakfast by the fire is a feast: homemade bread and jam, eggs from the hens, juice from the orchard, porridge and pancakes with maple syrup. Relax in the beautiful walled kitchen garden; there's an outdoor wood-fired pizza oven too!

Over twos welcome.

Rooms	3: 1 double, 1 twin/double (both with extra sofabed); 1 double with separate bathroom.
Price	£65-£85. Singles £50-£70.
Meals	Supper £11. Dinner, 2-3 courses, £20-£25. Pub/restaurant 1 mile.
Closed	Christmas day.

Susan Lilienthal
Parsonage Farm,
Over Stowey, Nether Stowey,
Somerset TA5 1HA
Tel   +44 (0)1278 733237
Mobile   +44 (0)7928 368836
Email   suki@parsonfarm.co.uk
Web   www.parsonfarm.co.uk

Entry 433   Map 2

Blackmore Farm

Come for atmosphere and architecture: the Grade I-listed manor-farmhouse is remarkable. Medieval stone, soaring beams, ecclesiastical windows, giant logs blazing in the Great Hall. Ann and Ian look after guests and busy dairy farm with equal enthusiasm. Furnishings are comfortable, décor is rich, bedrooms are cavernous and the oak-panelled suite (with secret stairway) takes up an entire floor. The rooms in the stables are simpler with green oak and wide doorways. Breakfast is generous and organic and eaten at the 20-foot polished table in baronial splendour. Visit the calves in the dairy and don't miss the excellent farm shop.

Huntstile Organic Farm

Catapult yourself into country life in the foothills of the Quantocks; make that connection between the rolling green hills, the idyllic munching animals and the delicious, organic food on your plate; here it is understood. Lizzie and John buzz with energy in this gorgeous old house with Jacobean panelling and huge walk-in fireplaces, two sitting rooms, sweet and cosy rustic bedrooms, a café, and a restaurant serving their own meat, eggs and vegetables. House parties, weddings, team building, a stone circle for hand-fasting ceremonies – all come under Lizzie's happy and efficient umbrella. And there are woodlands to roam.

Rooms	5: 1 double, 1 four-poster, 1 suite. Courtyard stables: 1 double, 1 twin.
Price	£100. Singles £50.
Meals	Occasional dinner for parties. Pubs/restaurants 5-minute walk.
Closed	Rarely.

Rooms	12: 7 doubles, 3 family rooms. Apartment: 1 double, 1 twin & sitting room.
Price	£60–£150. Family rooms £85–£150. Singles from £55–£60.
Meals	Dinner, 3 courses, £22.50–£27. Packed lunch from £6.50. Pub/restaurant 3 miles.
Closed	22 December–7 January.

	Ann Dyer
	Blackmore Farm,
	Cannington,
	Bridgwater,
	Somerset TA5 2NE
Tel	+44 (0)1278 653442
Email	dyerfarm@aol.com
Web	www.dyerfarm.co.uk

	Lizzie Myers
	Huntstile Organic Farm,
	Goathurst,
	Bridgwater,
	Somerset TA5 2DQ
Tel	+44 (0)1278 662358
Email	huntstile@live.co.uk
Web	www.huntstileorganicfarm.co.uk

Somerset

Pool House

Step into the generous hall, where a quirky gull made of driftwood greets you. Paul and Tricia's house has a friendly heart and you feel instantly at home. All is gleaming and artistic: bedrooms have gorgeous fabrics, garden posies, the best linen, and a chaise longue or easy chairs; en suite bathrooms are tiny but perfect; the dining room is elegant with a glass-topped table and a regal horse sculpture. Sun yourself in the sweet garden; the pool (tucked between barn and pool house) provides a sheltered spot with a Mediterranean vibe. Head out for walks, music festivals, Glastonbury… then back to a fire-warmed drawing room.

Minimum two nights at weekends.

Rooms	3: 2 doubles; 1 double with separate bath & shower.
Price	£100-£120. Singles £88-£108.
Meals	Pubs within 5 miles.
Closed	Occasionally.

Paul & Tricia Canham
Pool House,
4 Higher Road, Woolavington,
Bridgwater,
Somerset TA7 8DY

Tel   +44 (0)1278 683756
Email enquiries@poolhousewoolavington.co.uk
Web   www.poolhousewoolavington.com

Entry 436   Map 2

Somerset

Church House

Feel happy in this warm Georgian rectory with sweeping views over gardens, seaside homes and the dramatic Bristol channel. Tony and Jane are great fun, enormously generous and love what they do. Bedrooms are large, pristine and indulgent with goose down duvets as soft as a cloud, swish modern bathrooms, huge towels and thoughtful extras like fluffy hot water bottles and scrumptious biscuits. Breakfasts are a grand feast of eggs from their hens, organic sausages and homemade preserves, all served on delightful china at a long mahogany table. Take the whole house and be cosseted – great for large gatherings.

Rooms	5: 4 doubles, 1 twin.
Price	£85. Singles from £65.
Meals	Pubs 400 yds.
Closed	Rarely.

Jane & Tony Chapman
Church House,
27 Kewstoke Road, Kewstoke,
Weston-super-Mare,
Somerset BS22 9YD

Tel   +44 (0)1934 633185
Email churchhouse@kewstoke.net
Web   www.churchhousekewstoke.co.uk

Entry 437   Map 2

Somerset

Stonebridge

A country house with scrumptious food, a friendly black labrador and croquet on the lawn. When their daughters flew the nest, Liz and Richard opened an independent wing of their listed house: perfect for families and couples. You have two pretty bedrooms (one up, one down) with country furniture and super bathrooms. In winter, a wood-burner keeps your little sitting room cosy; in summer, laze in a sea of flowers. You feast on local eggs, homemade bread and delicious dinners with garden veg. Just off the village road, it's close to Bristol airport, the M5 and Wells. And with hosts this friendly you can't go wrong.

Rooms	2: 1 double, 1 twin/double.
Price	£75-£80. Singles £45-£50.
Meals	Dinner, 2-3 courses, £19-£24. Pub 2 miles.
Closed	Christmas.

	Richard & Liz Annesley
	Stonebridge,
	Wolvershill Road,
	Banwell,
	Somerset BS29 6DR
Tel	+44 (0)1934 823518
Email	liz.annesley@talktalk.net
Web	www.stonebridgebandb.co.uk

Entry 438   Map 3

Somerset

Barton Drove Cottage

Come for the views – on a clear day you can see the Black Mountains. The pretty cottage extension is tucked into the hill so the first-floor drawing room opens directly to the terrace. All is polished and spotless: beautiful big bedrooms have patterned rugs on soft carpets, goose down and crisp linen, fresh flowers; bathrooms gleam; one loo has a view. Charming Sarah gives you bacon and sausages from Mendip pigs, eggs from her hens, soft fruit from the garden and maybe pheasant casserole for supper. Roe deer in the field, primroses in the woods, wonderful walking on Wavering Down, and a real welcome for children.

Rooms	2: 1 double; 1 twin with separate bath.
Price	£70. Singles £35.
Meals	Dinner from £17.50. Packed lunch £5. Pub 1 mile.
Closed	Rarely.

	Sarah Gunn
	Barton Drove Cottage,
	Winscombe Hill, Winscombe,
	Somerset BS25 1DJ
Tel	+44 (0)1934 842373
Mobile	+44 (0)7736 417363
Email	sarahgunn2000@hotmail.com
Web	www.bartondrovecottage.com

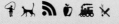

Entry 439   Map 3

Somerset

Burrington Farm

High in the Mendips, Ros and Barry's 15th-century longhouse is blissfully rural, yet Bristol, Bath and Wells are close. Their wonderful house glows: rugs and flagstones, books, burnished beams, paintings and fine old furniture. Guests have a cosy sitting room and bedrooms are charming; you'll need to be nimble to negotiate ancient steps and stairs. For those who prefer a bit more privacy there's a lovely family room in a separate green oak barn – stunningly converted and with views over the enchanting garden. Wake for a locally sourced breakfast round a big table. A friendly, relaxed and special place.

Airport pick-up available.

Rooms	4: 1 double; 1 double, 1 twin sharing bath (let to same party only). Garden Room: 1 family room.
Price	£80–£120. Singles £65.
Meals	Pub 10-minute walk.
Closed	Christmas.

Barry & Ros Smith
Burrington Farm,
Burrington,
Somerset BS40 7AD
Tel   +44 (0)1761 462127
Mobile   +44 (0)7825 237144
Email   unwind@burringtonfarm.co.uk
Web   www.unwindatburringtonfarm.co.uk

Entry 440   Map 3

Somerset

Harptree Court

A gorgeous Georgian house that has been in Charles' family for generations. Inside all is elegant and grand, but this is very much a family home; there's a welcoming log fire in the hall and Charles and Linda are charming and relaxed. The interior gleams with flowers, art and polished wood, and the dining room looks onto the beautiful garden; warm, sunny bedrooms have delicate fabrics, china pieces and antiques, and bathrooms sparkle. An excellent breakfast of garden fruits, local honey and sausages sets you up for a walk in the grounds: acres of parkland with ponds, an ancient bridge, carpets of spring flowers. A peaceful delight.

Rooms	4: 3 doubles, 1 twin/double.
Price	£130. Singles £80.
Meals	Pub 300 yds.
Closed	December/January.

Linda & Charles Hill
Harptree Court,
East Harptree, Bristol,
Somerset BS40 6AA
Tel   +44 (0)1761 221729
Mobile   +44 (0)7970 165576
Email   bandb@harptreecourt.co.uk
Web   www.harptreecourt.co.uk

Entry 441   Map 3

Harptree Court Treehouse & Yurt

Up the stairs and across the walkway above the laurel, the sumptuous Harptree Court Treehouse awaits in all its leafy glory in the grounds of Harptree Court. Reaching new heights for luxury camping, it's a spectacular suite in the treetops, where you can soak in style in a copper bath or catch the sunset from the veranda. Down below is the lavish Yurt, with its own claw-foot tub and furniture to fit its curves. Linda and Charles will leave you welcome treats of homemade lemon cake, local eggs, bacon, sausages and more (both spaces have superb kitchens) or you can order breakfast at the house – if you can bear to leave!

Min. two nights in treehouse; min. three nights in yurt. Book through Sawday's Canopy & Stars online or by phone.

The Post House

Four centuries old, this was Chewton Mendip's post office; now it's a delightful home with a sunny feel. Smiling, stylish Karen loves meeting new people – make the most of her and John's knowledge of Bath, Bristol and Wells. After a day's exploring, return to fresh, lovely bedrooms and bathrooms; the suite, limewashed, oak-floored, pretty and private, has a handy fridge. Huge flagstones cover the oldest part downstairs, there's a big stone fireplace in the Old Bakery Cottage and the odd low beam; pale walls display charming sketches from an artist friend, much of the furniture is French country, and a Gallic-rustic mood prevails.

Rooms	Treehouse for 2. Yurt for 2.
Price	Treehouse £250-£325.
	Yurt £115-£190.
Meals	Breakfast hamper included.
	Breakfast in house, £12.50.
	Pub 300 yds.
Closed	Never.

Rooms	3: 1 double; 1 suite & sitting room.
	Old Bakery Cottage: 1 double.
Price	£80-£90. Suite £95-£110.
	Cottage £100-£120.
Meals	Pub 0.5 miles.
Closed	Rarely.

	Sawday's Canopy & Stars
	Harptree Court Treehouse & Yurt,
	Harptree Court, East Harptree,
	Bristol, Somerset BS40 6AA
Tel	+44 (0)1275 395447
Email	enquiries@canopyandstars.co.uk
Web	www.canopyandstars.co.uk/
	harptreecourt

	Karen Price
	The Post House,
	Bath Way, Chewton Mendip,
	Wells,
	Somerset BA3 4NS
Tel	+44 (0)1761 241704
Email	info@theposthousebandb.co.uk
Web	www.theposthousebandb.co.uk

Somerset

Beryl

A lofty, mullioned, low-windowed home – yet bright and devoid of Victorian gloom. Every bedroom has a talking point – an extravagantly draped four-poster, an original bath clad in mahogany reached by a tiny private stair, and arch-doorway rooms in the attic with a 'gothic revival' feel. Holly and her gentle staff serve delicious breakfasts in the sunny dining room, and drinks in the richly elegant drawing room. The antiques are remarkable, and there's a jewellery boutique in the Coach House. The old walled garden is full of roses, ancient figs and espaliered apples; the wonders of Wells lie just below.

Stairlift to first floor.

Rooms	11: 4 doubles, 2 twins/doubles, 2 twins, 2 family rooms, all en suite; 1 double with separate bathroom.
Price	£90-£150. Family room £120-£190. Singles £75-£95.
Meals	Pubs/restaurants within 1 mile. Kitchenette available.
Closed	Christmas.

Holly Nowell
Beryl,
Hawkers Lane,
Wells,
Somerset BA5 3JP
Tel   +44 (0)1749 678738
Email   stay@beryl-wells.co.uk
Web   www.beryl-wells.co.uk

Entry 444   Map 3

Somerset

Stoberry House

Super swish B&B in this old coach house surrounded by 26 acres of parkland, but within walking distance of Wells; Frances has thought of everything and has oodles of local knowledge. Bedrooms are sumptuous and differently styled; two are in the main house, and there's one little love nest in a richly clad studio. Bathrooms are vamped up and spacious. There is a huge choice at breakfast: fresh fruit, porridge, boiled eggs with soldiers, prunes and berries, ham and salami, pancakes with grilled bacon, whatever you desire. Work it off with a stroll around the gorgeous gardens: the scents, sculptures and views are fantastic.

Rooms	3: 1 double, 1 twin/double. Studio: 1 double & sitting room.
Price	£90-£155. Singles £65-£135.
Meals	Supplement for cooked breakfast. Pubs/restaurants 0.5 miles.
Closed	Rarely.

Frances Young
Stoberry House,
Stoberry Park,
Wells,
Somerset BA5 3LD
Tel   +44 (0)1749 672906
Email   stay@stoberry-park.co.uk
Web   www.stoberry-park.co.uk

Entry 445   Map 3

Somerset

Coach House

Take a glass of wine to your private courtyard and absorb the peace; or picnic in the gardens. In the hamlet of Dulcote, a mile from Wells, is your own two-storey coach house flooded with light, full of character and the latest mod cons. Downstairs, a black and white zebra theme plays; upstairs, white walls, crisp linen, high beams, a glimpse of Wells Cathedral and views that reach to the Mendips. Friendly Chumba the dog greets you and your (well-behaved) waggy friend. Karen leaves eggs from her hens and other goodies in your fridge so you can breakfast in your jim-jams. A delightful B&B for nature lovers and dog-walkers.

Well-behaved dogs by arrangement.

Rooms	Coach House: 1 double, 1 twin & sitting/dining room, sofabeds, kitchen, shower. Same-party bookings only.
Price	£95. Singles £90. Whole house £155 per night.
Meals	Pubs within 2 miles.
Closed	Rarely.

Karen Smallwood
Coach House,
Little Fountains, Dulcote,
Wells,
Somerset BA5 3NU

Tel	+44 (0)1749 678777
Mobile	+44 (0)7789 778880
Email	stay@littlefountains.co.uk
Web	www.littlefountains.co.uk

Entry 446 Map 3

Somerset

Hillview Cottage

Catherine is a wonderful host: warm-spirited, cultured and humorous. She knows the area well, and is happy to show you around Wells Cathedral – she's an official guide. This is a comfy tea-and-cakes family home with rugs on wooden floors and antique quilts. Bedrooms have a French feel, the bathroom an armchair for chatting and there's a friendly sitting room with an open fire. The stunning vaulted breakfast room has huge beams, an old Welsh dresser with hand painted mugs, a cheerful red Aga, a wood-burner to sit by and glorious views; breakfasts are superb. Guests love it here; excellent value too.

Self-catering in Garden Studio.

Rooms	2: 1 twin/double, 1 twin sharing bath (let to same party only).
Price	£70. Singles £35-£40.
Meals	Pubs 5-minute walk.
Closed	Rarely.

Michael & Catherine Hay
Hillview Cottage,
Paradise Lane, Croscombe,
Wells,
Somerset BA5 3RN

Tel	+44 (0)1749 343526
Mobile	+44 (0)7801 666146
Email	cathyhay@yahoo.co.uk
Web	www.hillviewcottage.me.uk

Entry 447 Map 3

Somerset

Upper Crannel Farm Barn

Your views, across sheep and the lush flat Levels, reach to both Glastonbury and Wells; birds wing across a vast, silent sky. Phoebe has created a magical place: up you climb to the first floor of the barn, into a huge sitting room with a vast medieval painted fireplace. Each room is a work of art, with stacks of it on the walls – the kitchen is handsome and seductive, the bedroom is generous and richly clad. Breakfast will be left for you to cook when you want, you can walk across fields to climb Glastonbury Tor and Wells is just five miles. This house is a treat, and Phoebe is too.

Minimum stay two nights. .

Rooms	Barn: 1 double with sitting room & kitchen. Extra bedrooms available in the barn and main house
Price	£120.
Meals	Pubs/restaurants 2.5 miles.
Closed	Rarely.

Phoebe Judah
Upper Cranel Farm Barn,
Glastonbury,
Somerset BA6 9AD
Tel   +44 (0)1458 831758
Email   phoebe.judah@btinternet.com

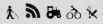

Entry 448   Map 3

Somerset

Chindit House

Inside this light, elegant Arts and Crafts mansion you will find fine architectural features, charming furniture, fresh flowers, vibrant paintings and compelling sculptures. There are long views over garden and town from the living and dining rooms; opulent bedrooms have serious mattresses, good art, thick curtains and sleek, contemporary bathrooms. Felicity, an art consultant who holds exhibitions here, is easy-going and fun and gives you an organic and locally sourced breakfast with speciality breads. You are a short hop from Glastonbury with its lively mix of exotic independent shops and cafés; Wells is not far.

Rooms	4: 2 doubles; 2 singles with shared bath (let to same party only).
Price	£100-£125. Singles £70-£85.
Meals	Pubs/restaurants 5-minute walk.
Closed	Rarely.

Felicity Wright
Chindit House,
23 Wells Road, Glastonbury,
Somerset BA6 9DN
Tel   +44 (0)1458 830404
Mobile   +44 (0)7812 077175
Email   enquiries@chindit-house.co.uk
Web   www.chindit-house.co.uk

Entry 449   Map 3

Somerset

Westbrook House

David is an interior designer; Keith a garden designer – hence this blend of good taste and style in a revamped 1870s house with acres of beautiful grounds blending seamlessly with open countryside. Wander through a young orchard, spot unusual plants, sit on stone benches or a sunny patio. Inside, every object has a story (your hosts are full of smiles and stories too): tapestries from India, a mirrored cabinet from an officer's mess, ornate brass lanterns. Light floods into the dining room as you breakfast on local treats – all the while absorbing the peace of this tranquil hamlet, where cows amble down the lane.

Rooms	3: 1 double, 1 twin; 1 double with separate bath.
Price	£100. Singles £65-£80.
Meals	Dinner £30. Pub/restaurant 4 miles.
Closed	Rarely.

Keith Anderson & David Mendel
Westbrook House,
West Bradley,
Glastonbury,
Somerset BA6 8LS
Tel +44 (0)1458 850604
Email mail@westbrook-bed-breakfast.co.uk
Web www.westbrook-bed-breakfast.co.uk

Entry 450 Map 3

Somerset

The Lynch Country House

Peace and privacy at this immaculate Regency house in a Somerset valley. First-floor bedrooms are traditionally grand, attic rooms are smaller but pretty; those in the coach house have a more modern feel. Rich colours prevail, fabrics are flowery and linen best Irish. You'll feel as warm as toast and beautifully looked after. A stone staircase goes right to the top where the observatory lets in cascading light; the flagged hall, high ceilings, long windows and private tables at breakfast create a country-house hotel feel. The lovely garden has black swans on a lake, hundreds of trees and a terrace from which to drink it all in.

Rooms	8: 1 double, 1 four-poster, 1 twin/double; 1 double with separate bath). Extra single beds. Coach house: 2 doubles, 2 twins/doubles.
Price	£80-£115. Singles £65-£80.
Meals	Pubs 5-minute walk.
Closed	Rarely.

Mike McKenzie
The Lynch Country House,
4 Behind Berry,
Somerton,
Somerset TA11 7PD
Tel +44 (0)1458 272316
Email enquiries@thelynchcountryhouse.co.uk
Web www.thelynchcountryhouse.co.uk

Entry 451 Map 3

Somerset

Lower Severalls Farmhouse

This is one for garden lovers, with a number of gardens in the area and three acres here: lovely lawns and curving borders, bulbs, wildflowers and hidden hostas, a 'dogwood basket', a nursery on site. The guest suites are in the stable block behind the beautiful old farmhouse – two up, one down, refurbished to a very high standard with bathrooms shiny and smart. Breakfast is served beneath dark aged beams in the mullioned house: Mike enjoys the cooking, Mary is passionate about the garden, and the pigs and the chickens roam free. For dinner: a mill hotel across the road and a super pub in Hinton St George.

Rooms	Stables: 3 suites (2 with kitchenettes). Extra family room available.
Price	£85-£140. Singles £65.
Meals	Restaurant within walking distance.
Closed	Rarely.

Mary Pring & Mike Wycherley
Lower Severalls Farmhouse,
Lower Severalls,
Crewkerne,
Somerset TA18 7NX
Tel   +44 (0)1460 73234
Email   mary@lowerseveralls.co.uk
Web   www.lowerseveralls.co.uk

Entry 452   Map 3

Somerset

Barwick Farm House

A 17th-century farmhouse sitting in ten acres of organically managed land dotted with hens, horses and Dorset sheep. Charming Angela and Robin have limewashed the walls in vibrant colours, restored ancient elm boards and exposed sandstone fireplace lintels, in a house full of open fires, books and flowers. Roomy bedrooms have good cotton sheets, comfortable beds and a mishmash of styles; one bathroom, painted bubble-gum pink, has a freestanding bath and views over fields. Wake to birdsong and the sizzle of good local bacon; excellent walking and cycling start from the door and there are gardens to visit.

Rooms	3: 1 double, 1 twin/double; 1 double with separate bathroom.
Price	£70-£80. Singles from £50.
Meals	'Early Bird' packed breakfasts also available. Restaurant 100 yds.
Closed	Rarely.

Angela Nicoll
Barwick Farm House,
Barwick, Yeovil,
Somerset BA22 9TD
Tel   +44 (0)1935 410779
Mobile   +44 (0)7967 385307
Email   info@barwickfarmhouse.co.uk
Web   www.barwickfarmhouse.co.uk

Entry 453   Map 3

Somerset

Yarlington House

A mellow Georgian manor surrounded by impressive parkland, romantic rose gardens, apple tree pergola and laburnum walk. Your hosts are friendly and flexible, artists with an eye for quirky detail; Carolyn's embroideries are everywhere. Something to astound at every turn: fine copies of 18th-century wallpapers, elegant antiques, statues with hats atop and tremendous art. Traditional bedrooms with glorious garden views and proper 50s bathrooms have a faded charm. Enjoy a full English breakfast, grape juice from the glasshouse vines, log fires and lovely local walks. Surprising, unique.

Yarlington Yurt

In the grounds of dignified Yarlington House, the equally refined Yarlington Yurt is tucked behind the walled garden (where there's an honesty box for fruit and veg in season). Decorated in a style described as 'late 18th-century with French influence,' with a twin-bedded pod curtained off from the double, it comes decked with rugs, lamps, and paintings, and fairy lights set in the canopy; the compost loo is a dash outside. The wood-burner belts out the heat, while next door's pavilion with kitchen and shower room is fully plumbed-in. Cook here, or head up to the house for breakfast by arrangement.

Min. three nights. Book through Sawday's Canopy & Stars online or by phone.

Rooms	2: 1 double, 1 twin.
Price	£140. Singles £70.
Meals	Pubs/restaurants within 0.5 miles.
Closed	25 July-23 August.

Rooms	Yurt for 4 with separate shower & compost loo.
Price	£99-£165.
Meals	BYO breakfast, or in house, £10. Pubs/restaurants within 0.5 miles.
Closed	November-April.

Carolyn & Charles de Salis
Yarlington House,
Yarlington,
Wincanton,
Somerset BA9 8DY
Tel   +44 (0)1963 440344
Email   carolyn.desalis@yarlingtonhouse.com
Web   www.yarlingtonhouse.com

Sawday's Canopy & Stars
Yarlington Yurt,
Yarlington House, Wincanton,
Somerset BA9 8DY
Tel   +44 (0)1275 395447
Email   enquiries@canopyandstars.co.uk
Web   www.canopyandstars.co.uk/
yarlingtonyurt

Entry 454   Map 3

Entry 455   Map 3

Somerset

Bratton Farmhouse

A gorgeous old 1600 house around which strut hens and happy Jacob sheep. Intelligent and generous Suellen has created warm contemporary interiors and the bedrooms are a joy. One, in the main house, has oak-panelled walls, bucolic views and a vast bed with vintage French embroidered linen. Another, in a converted studio across the courtyard, gives you independence; you have your own book-filled sitting room made cosy with a wood-burner, while lovers can laze till late in a huge nest of feather and down. Good books and art surround you, breakfasts are delicious and imaginative, walks start from the door.

Somerset

Rectory Farm House

Lavinia has showered love and attention on her early Georgian house and garden in a landscape that has changed little since the 18th century. Beams, sash windows, wood fires and high ceilings are the backdrop for polished family furniture and delightfully arranged flowers. Good-sized bedrooms in restful colours have starched linen, pretty fabrics and binoculars for watching the wildlife; the beautiful, peaceful garden draws deer, badgers, foxes, hares. Breakfast is so local it could walk to the table – and includes homemade marmalade and jams. A lovely summery place – and only a mile off the A303!

Rooms	3: 2 doubles, each with separate bath/shower. Studio: 1 twin/double & sitting room.		Rooms	3: 1 double; 1 double, 1 twin/double sharing bath (let to same party only).
Price	£80–£110. Singles from £70.		Price	£100–£110. Singles from £70.
Meals	Lunch £10. Dinner, 3 courses, £28. Packed lunch £5. Pub 2 miles.		Meals	Dinner £35. Pub 0.5 miles.
Closed	Rarely.		Closed	Christmas & New Year.

	Suellen Dainty Bratton Farmhouse, Bratton Seymour, Wincanton, Somerset BA9 8BY			**Michael & Lavinia Dewar** Rectory Farm House, Charlton Musgrove, Wincanton, Somerset BA9 8ET
Tel	+44 (0)1963 32458		Tel	+44 (0)1963 34599
Mobile	+44 (0)7780 848567		Mobile	+44 (0)7775 651868
Email	sdainty52@gmail.com		Email	l.dewar@btconnect.com
Web	www.brattonfarmhouse.co.uk		Web	www.rectoryfarmhouse.com

Entry 456 Map 3   Entry 457 Map 3

Ansford Park Cottage

An old farmworker's house, modernised and freshly spruced, stands proud in verdant countryside. Long views from the clipped garden drift into the distance; warm Sue (plus cute Jack Russells) greets you. You sleep in the extension to the front of the house; one bedroom has valley views, the other has views over the Mendips. Both have comfy beds, books, homely touches and peacefulness. Breakfast is a leisurely affair of local bacon and eggs. Tramp off on an inspiring walk – Leland trail, Macmillan Way – you're spoilt for choice. Escape London by train (95 minutes) – collection from the station can be arranged.

Pets by arrangement.

Orchard Carriage

The Orchard Carriage, in use on the local branch line until the 1950s, sits in a small orchard just down from the main house; behind is a country lane. The fire is lit on arrival; the interior is beautifully and unusually furnished. Facing the raised bed are the sofa and colourful dresser where the gas hobs and the wood-burner sit. In the back: a big red freestanding bathtub (oh joy!) and a basin. The compost loo is a few metres away. After you get back from a hearty hike or a day out in Bristol and Bath, you may be able to use Zoe's wood-fired sauna. She and John, helpful and charming, can provide organic hampers – just ask.

Minimum two nights. Book through Sawday's Canopy & Stars online or by phone.

Rooms	2: 1 twin/double; 1 twin/double with separate bath.
Price	£70. Singles from £50.
Meals	Dinner £25. Packed lunch £5. Pub/restaurant 1 mile.
Closed	Christmas & rarely.

Rooms	Railway wagon for 2 with compost loo alongside.
Price	£90–£102.
Meals	BYO breakfast (hampers on request). Pub 3 miles.
Closed	November–March.

	Susan Begg
	Ansford Park Cottage,
	Ansford Park, Maggs Lane,
	Castle Cary,
	Somerset BA7 7JJ
Tel	+44 (0)1963 351066
Email	beggsusan@tiscali.co.uk
Web	www.ansfordparkcottage.co.uk

	Sawday's Canopy & Stars
	Orchard Carriage,
	Strap Lane, Bruton,
	Somerset BA10 0JW
Tel	+44 (0)1275 395447
Email	enquiries@canopyandstars.co.uk
Web	www.canopyandstars.co.uk/ orchardcarriage

Somerset

Glyde Cottages

Smell Victoria's just-baked bread as you enter this charmingly restored merchant's house – all 16th-century stone walls and aged oak beams. Relax in the guests' sitting room with its inglenook stuffed with logs, or stroll to the pub; wind your way up a spiral staircase to a beautifully rustic room with a hand-crafted bed and stripped floors. Children may venture up to the attic twin where a rocking horse waits; breakfasts are a home-cooked delight at the long wooden table. Strike out to Alfred's Tower – or opt for a plump slice of cake and croquet on the lawn. Just watch out for errant chickens!

Rooms	2: 1 double, 1 twin sharing bath (let to same party only).
Price	£85. Adjoining twin room: child £20, adult £25.
Meals	Dinner, 2 courses, £18.
Closed	Rarely.

Victoria Savage
Glyde Cottages,
Upton Noble,
Shepton Mallet,
Somerset BA4 6BA
Tel   +44 (0)1749 850230
Email   v.savage@live.com
Web   www.glydecottages.co.uk

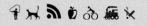

Entry 460   Map 3

Somerset

Pennard House

Splendid Pennard has been in Susie's family since the 1600s – a comfortably lived-in home with bedrooms as big as any we've seen. Discover a library and billiard room, a drawing room and dining room, and, upstairs, old-fashioned bedrooms with a mix of furniture, fine linen and beautiful views. The gardens are stunning with terraces leading on to sweeping lawns, roses, mature trees, a grass tennis court and a Victorian spring-fed swimming pool (swim with the newts!). The Georgian Coach House has been converted into a venue for weddings and conferences, and you're free to roam 60 tranquil acres of orchards, meadows and woods.

Rooms	3: 1 double, 1 twin; 1 twin/double with separate bath/shower.
Price	£120. Singles from £60.
Meals	Pub 2 miles.
Closed	Rarely.

Martin & Susie Dearden
Pennard House,
East Pennard, Shepton Mallet,
Somerset BA4 6TP
Tel   +44 (0)1749 860266
Mobile   +44 (0)7770 751357
Email   susie@pennardhouse.com
Web   www.pennardhouse.com

Entry 461   Map 3

Somerset

Broadgrove House

Head down the long, private lane and arrive at Sarah's peaceful 17th-century stone house with its pretty walled cottage garden and views to Alfred's Tower and Longleat. Inside is just as special. Beams, flagstones and inglenook fireplaces have been sensitively restored; rugs, pictures, comfy sofas and polished antiques add warmth and serenity. The twin, at the end of the house, has its own sitting room. Breakfast on homemade and farmers' market produce before exploring Stourhead, Wells, Glastonbury. Sarah, engaging, well-travelled and a great cook, looks after you warmly.

Children by arrangement.

Rooms	2: 1 twin & sitting room; 1 double with separate bath.
Price	£80-£90. Singles £60.
Meals	Pub/restaurant 1 mile.
Closed	Christmas.

Sarah Voller
Broadgrove House,
Leighton, Frome,
Somerset BA11 4PP
Tel   +44 (0)1373 836296
Mobile +44 (0)7775 918388
Email broadgrove836@tiscali.co.uk
Web   www.broadgrovehouse.co.uk

Entry 462   Map 3

Somerset

Claveys Farm

For the artistic seeker of inspiration, not those who thrill to standardised luxury. Fleur is a talented artist, Francis works for English Heritage, both have a passion for art, gardening and lively conversation. Rugs are time-worn, panelling and walls are distempered with natural pigment, bedrooms are better than simple, bathrooms old. From the Aga-warm kitchen of this lived-in, historic farmhouse come eggs from the hens, honey from the bees, oak-smoked bacon from Fleur's rare-breed pigs and homemade bread and jams. Fields, footpaths and woodland for walks, and a garden for children to adore. Bring your woolly jumpers!

Rooms	2: 1 double/family; 1 twin with separate bath (shared with owner sometimes).
Price	£75. Singles £50.
Meals	Dinner, 3 courses, £25. BYO. Packed lunch £7. Pub in village.
Closed	Rarely.

Fleur & Francis Kelly
Claveys Farm,
Mells,
Frome,
Somerset BA11 3QP
Tel   +44 (0)1373 814651
Mobile +44 (0)7968 055398
Email bandb@fleurkelly.com

Entry 463   Map 3

Somerset

Penny's Mill

The old part of Nunney village, with its small pretty streets, has a shop, a café and Rosie's gorgeous old stone millhouse down in the river valley. You are greeted warmly with tea and biscuits at a large wooden table in the kitchen, or in the drawing room upstairs with family photos, paintings and a big window looking over the millpond. Bedrooms are light and bright, painted in gentle blues and greens with a mix of antique and modern furniture; bathrooms have Molton Brown soaps and white fluffy towels. Rosie's fine breakfast sets you up for a short walk to Nunney Castle, or a yomp further afield.

Ask about cookery courses.

Rooms	3: 1 double; 1 double, 1 twin sharing shower (let to same party only).
Price	£55–£85.
Meals	Dinner £25. Pub 300 yds.
Closed	Rarely.

Rosie Davies
Penny's Mill,
Horn Street, Nunney,
Frome,
Somerset BA11 4NP
Tel   +44 (0)1373 836210
Email   stay@pennysmill.com
Web   www.stayatpennysmill.com

Entry 464 Map 3

Somerset

Old Reading Room

Mells is a treasure with its medieval centre and liberal sprinkling of charming cottages; you'll find Vicky and John's attractive house down a track in the quiet wooded valley. It's a home with a friendly feel: books, art, pots of flowers, intriguing finds from family travels, comfy sofas around the wood-burner. Beds are wrapped in fine cotton and colourful quilts; sweet bathrooms have scented candles. Come down for breakfast in the kitchen – homemade bread, eggs from happy hens – delivered by a friend on a pony! Sunny cottage garden, walks from the door, a five-minute drive to Babington House... and entertaining hosts.

Rooms	2 doubles.
Price	£85. Singles £65.
Meals	Pubs/restaurants 5-minute walk.
Closed	Rarely.

Vicky & John Macdonald
Old Reading Room,
Mells,
Frome,
Somerset BA11 3QA
Tel   +44 (0)1373 813487
Email   johnmacdonaldm@gmail.com

Entry 465 Map 3

Somerset

Flint House

Off a village lane, up a sweeping drive, is an elegant 18th-century home with a private chapel. Smart yet relaxed, it's a perfect mix: a sophisticated sitting room with low valley views, a roaring fire in the snug. Be seduced by the Mendips in your modern-classic bedroom with roll top bath; and a cosy twin for a larger party. Breakfast treats await on the summer veranda, from pancakes to poached plums. Take to the tennis court or sit under wisteria, cake in hand, and gaze on the noble garden – Jacquie is loving its restoration. Your relaxed hosts will provide dinner for you or you can pop to the local. Walks galore – and Bath irresistibly near.

Rooms	2: 1 double; 1 twin sharing shower with double (let to same party only).
Price	£60-£100. Singles £60.
Meals	Dinner, 3 courses, £20-£25. Picnic lunch £8. Afternoon tea £4. Pubs 10-minute walk.
Closed	Rarely.

	Jacquie Hamshaw Thomas
	Flint House,
	Common Lane, Holcombe,
	Bath, Somerset BA3 5DS
Tel	+44 (0)1761 232419
Mobile	+44 (0)7723 031378
Email	htsuk@btconnect.com
Web	www.flinthousebandb.co.uk

Entry 466   Map 3

Somerset

The Old Vicarage

The vicarage sits at the foot of Jack and Jill's hill in a sleepy Mendip village. Both bedrooms have goose down comfort: one has an antique French bed and limestone wet room; the sunny blue room upstairs has a freestanding roll top. Your hosts are informal and friendly and their home exudes charm: a medieval stone floor in the hall, old flagstones, carpets designed by Lizzy, flowers, wood-burners and a pretty kitchen. Hens potter, carp laze in the canal pond; breakfast when you want on a full English, garden compotes and delicious coffee. National Trust gems and splendid walking on the Colliers Way will keep you busy.

Rooms	2: 1 double & sitting room; 1 four-poster with separate wc.
Price	£90-£95.
Meals	Pub 100 yds.
Closed	Occasionally.

	Elizabeth Ashard
	The Old Vicarage,
	Church Street, Kilmersdon,
	Radstock,
	Somerset BA3 5TA
Tel	+44 (0)1761 436926
Email	lizzyashard@btinternet.com
Web	www.theoldvicaragesomerset.co.uk

Entry 467   Map 3

Staffordshire

Manor House Farm

A working rare-breed farm in an area of great beauty, a Jacobean farmhouse with oodles of history. Behind mullioned windows is a glorious interior crammed with curios and family pieces, panelled walls and wonky floors... hurl a log on the fire and watch it roar. Three rooms have four-posters; one bathroom flaunts rich red antique fabrics. Chris and Margaret are passionate hosts who serve perfect breakfasts (eggs from their own hens, sausages and bacon from their pigs and home-grown tomatoes) and give you the run of a garden resplendent with plants, vistas, tennis, croquet, two springer spaniels and one purring cat. Heaven.

Minimum two nights at weekends during high season. Children welcome.

Rooms	4: 1 double, 2 four-posters, 1 four-poster family room for 4.
Price	£64–£75. Family room £70–£95. Singles £44–£50.
Meals	Pub/restaurant 1.5 miles.
Closed	Christmas.

Chris & Margaret Ball
Manor House Farm,
Prestwood, Denstone,
Uttoxeter,
Staffordshire ST14 5DD

Tel	+44 (0)1889 590415
Mobile	+44 (0)7976 767629
Email	cmball@manorhousefarm.co.uk
Web	www.towersabovetherest.com

Entry 468   Map 8

Staffordshire

CANOPY&STARS

Secret Cloud Yurts

Derbyshire oatcakes, fresh eggs, local bacon and further treats await your arrival. These three luxurious yurts – and one Scandinavian wood cabin – stand on the edge of the wonderful wild Peaks: come for a dash of adventure. Catherine, the owner, has made each supremely comfortable, with sheepskin rugs and top bed linen; they're beautiful too, with their handmade furniture and views over the hills. Each yurt has a barbecue around which to gather in the evening, and its own compost loo. All spaces share the washroom's hot showers and basins – and you can book the cedar wood hot tub for a soak under the stars.

Minimum three nights. Book through Sawday's Canopy & Stars online or by phone.

Rooms	3 yurts for 2, 1 cabin for 2, each with own compost loo, sharing 2 showers.
Price	£75–£99.
Meals	Welcome breakfast hamper. Pubs 1 mile.
Closed	October–April.

Sawday's Canopy & Stars
Secret Cloud Yurts,
Limestone View Farm, Stoney Lane,
Cauldon,
Staffordshire ST10 3EP

Tel	+44 (0)1275 395447
Email	enquiries@canopyandstars.co.uk
Web	www.canopyandstars.co.uk /secretcloud

Entry 469   Map 8

Suffolk

Pavilion House

A conservation village surrounded by chalk grassland – famous for its flora, fauna and butterflies; marked walks are straight from this 16-year-old red-brick house. Friendly Gretta teaches cooking and you are in for a treat: homemade cake, enormous breakfasts with her own bread and jams, proper dinners or simple suppers. Sleep peacefully in traditional, comfortable bedrooms with crisp linen and TVs. There's a guest sitting room too: English comfort with an oriental feel, parquet floors, antiques, original drawings, a cosy log-burner. Wander the superb garden. Newmarket and Cambridge are close.

Child bed available.

Rooms	3: 1 double, 1 twin/double, 1 single, each with separate bath/shower.
Price	£85-£105. Singles £55-£60.
Meals	Lunch from £10. Dinner from £25. Supper from £15. BYO. Pub 1.5 miles.
Closed	Christmas.

Gretta & David Bredin
Pavilion House,
133 Station Road, Dullingham,
Newmarket,
Suffolk CB8 9UT

Tel	+44 (0)1638 508005
Mobile	+44 (0)7776 197709
Email	gretta@thereliablesauce.co.uk
Web	www.pavilionhousebandb.co.uk

Entry 470   Map 9

Suffolk

The Old Vicarage

Up the avenue of fine horse chestnut trees to find just what you'd expect from an old vicarage: a Pembroke table in the flagstoned hall, a refectory table sporting copies of *The Field*, a piano, silver pheasants, a log fire that warms the sitting room and homemade cake on arrival. The house is magnificent, with huge rooms and passageways. Comfy mattresses are dressed in old-fashioned counterpanes, and the double has hill views. Weave your way through the branches of the huge copper beech to the garden that Jane loves; she grows her own vegetables, keeps hens and cooks a fine breakfast.

Children over seven welcome.

Rooms	2: 1 double, extra single available (let to same party only); 1 twin with separate bath.
Price	£80-£90. Singles £50.
Meals	Dinner £20. BYO. Packed lunch £6. Pub 1 mile.
Closed	Christmas.

Jane Sheppard
The Old Vicarage,
Great Thurlow,
Newmarket,
Suffolk CB9 7LE

Tel	+44 (0)1440 783209
Mobile	+44 (0)7887 717429
Email	s.j.sheppard@hotmail.co.uk
Web	www.thurlowvicarage.co.uk

Entry 471   Map 9

Suffolk

The Lucy Redman Garden and B&B

Off a country lane, through an estate village, hides this immaculate, thatched, 1930s house – a gem. Lucy and Dominic are full of life and fun. Lucy is an artistic garden designer so all glows with texture and colour, and the garden is a stunner. Family antiques blend with multi-cultural pieces, there are books, paintings and pets. Choose between the cosy, ochre-walled 'Indian' room upstairs and the 'Moroccan' down, with aqua walls and vibrant Mexican tiles. Wake to eggs from the hens, plum jams from the trees, and lovely homemade marmalade. Views swoop over garden, grazing horses and miles of Suffolk countryside. A happy place!

Rooms	2: 1 double, 1 twin/double.
Price	£80. Singles £70.
Meals	Pubs/restaurants 2 miles.
Closed	Rarely.

Lucy & Dominic Watts
The Lucy Redman Garden and B&B,
6 The Village, Rushbrooke,
Bury St Edmunds,
Suffolk IP30 0ER

Tel	+44 (0)1284 386250
Mobile	+44 (0)7503 633671
Email	lucyredman7@gmail.com
Web	www.lucyredman.co.uk

Entry 472 Map 10

Suffolk

The Old Manse Barn

A large, lush loft apartment in sleepy Suffolk; this uncluttered living space of blond wood, white walls and big windows has an urban feel yet overlooks glorious countryside. Secluded from the main house, in a timber-clad barn, all is fabulous and spacious: leather sofas, glass dining table, stainless steel kitchenette. Floor lights dance off the walls, surround-sound creates mood and you can watch the stars from your bed. Homemade granola, fruits, cold meats, cheeses and fresh pastries are popped in the fridge – bliss. There's peace for romance, solitude for work, a garden to sit in and lovely Sue to suggest the best pubs.

Rooms	Apartment: 1 double & kitchenette.
Price	£80-£85.
Meals	Pubs within walking distance.
Closed	Rarely.

Sue & Ian Jones
The Old Manse Barn,
Chapel Road, Cockfield,
Bury St Edmunds,
Suffolk IP30 0HE

Tel	+44 (0)1284 828120
Mobile	+44 (0)7931 753996
Email	bookings@theoldmansebarn.co.uk
Web	www.theoldmansebarn.co.uk

Entry 473 Map 10

Suffolk

16 Bolton Street

The house, part medieval, part Tudor, rests on a quiet street within striking distance of lovely, bustling Lavenham: this is one of England's showpiece towns. Heavy beams, low doorways, books, magazines, fresh flowers and gentle hosts create a warm happy feel; steep oak stairs lead to fresh, cosy bedrooms where patchwork quilts, colourful cushions and handmade curtains abound. Gillian likes nothing better than to spoil her guests with breakfasts of local sausages and bacon, potato cakes, her special mushroom recipe, yogurt and fresh fruit. A delightful, relaxed, generous place to stay.

Minimum two nights at weekends.

Rooms	2: 1 twin/double, 1 double.
Price	£80-£90.
Meals	Pubs/restaurants within walking distance.
Closed	Rarely.

Gillian de Lucy
16 Bolton Street,
Lavenham,
Suffolk CO10 9RG
Tel   +44 (0)1787 249046
Mobile +44 (0)7747 621096
Email   gdelucy@aol.com
Web   www.guineahouse.co.uk

Entry 474   Map 10

Suffolk

Milden Hall

Generations of Hawkins have lived in this seemingly grand 16th-century hall farmhouse with its enormous sash windows and vast fireplaces. Bedrooms ranging from big to huge are elegantly old-fashioned and filled with fascinating wall hangings, maps, prints, etchings and lovely furniture. Juliet is a passionate conservationist, full of ideas for making the most of the surrounding countryside, on foot or by bike. Expect delicious home-grown bacon, sausages, bantam eggs and compotes for breakfast in the sunny living room, warmed by a wood-burner in the winter. Great fun, with a friendly, family feel.

Self-catering barn for large groups. Barn licensed for civil ceremonies & civil partnerships.

Rooms	3: 2 twins, 1 double/family room, all sharing separate bathroom & 2nd wc.
Price	£65-£90. Singles from £45.
Meals	Occasional supper from £20. BYO. Pubs/restaurants 2-3 miles.
Closed	Rarely.

Christopher & Juliet Hawkins
Milden Hall,
Milden,
Lavenham,
Suffolk CO10 9NY
Tel   +44 (0)1787 247235
Email   hawkins@thehall-milden.co.uk
Web   www.thehall-milden.co.uk

Entry 475   Map 10

Suffolk

The Old Rectory Country House

In a hamlet of thatched cottages by the Church of St Lawrence sits a handsome rectory, quietly steeped in ancient history. Find elegant proportions, family antiques and owner Frank who asks only that you feel at home. The drawing room has an honesty bar and walking maps, the garden is a delight and you can use the pool. Feel spoiled in big smart bedrooms with pretty fabrics, smooth linen and lovely views; the Stables are charming with books, a garden suite and comfy sofas. Be lazy and have continental breakfast in your room, or rouse yourself for local sausages and bacon by a log fire in the magnificent dining room. A treat.

Self-catering available in The Old Stables.

Rooms	6: 2 doubles, 1 twin/double. The Old Stables: 3 doubles, sitting/dining room & kitchen (self-catering available).
Price	£85-£200. Singles £85 (Sun-Thurs only).
Meals	Lunch & supper £15-£30, arrange in advance. Pub 1 mile.
Closed	Rarely.

Frank Lawrenson
The Old Rectory Country House,
Rectory Road, Great Waldingfield,
Lavenham, Sudbury,
Suffolk CO10 0TL

Tel	+44 (0)1787 372428
Email	info@theoldrectorycountryhouse.co.uk
Web	www.theoldrectorycountryhouse.co.uk

Entry 476   Map 10

Suffolk

Copinger Hall

The house, a stunning bay-windowed number, has been in the family since the 14th century, yet is anything but ancient in feel. At the end of a sweeping gravel drive, past the church which adjoins the garden, the much-modernised family seat is 'country smart', deeply comfortable and very much a home. Lisa is someone to whom throwing open the doors to guests brings immeasurable pleasure, a gifted and generous host. Breakfasts are around a long table in a separate dining room and you will have the use of the drawing room which looks out across the immaculate lawn and garden. Head out for Aldeburgh, Lavenham and musical Snape Maltings.

Rooms	3: 1 double, 1 twin/double; 1 double with separate bath/shower.
Price	£95. Singles £75.
Meals	Pub & restaurant within 1 mile.
Closed	Occasionally.

Lisa & Stephen Minoprio
Copinger Hall,
Brettenham Road, Buxhall,
Stowmarket,
Suffolk IP14 3DJ

Tel	+44 (0)1449 736000
Mobile	+44 (0)7775 621715
Email	lisa@copingerhall.com

Entry 477   Map 10

Suffolk

Haughley House

A timber-framed medieval manor in three acres of garden overlooking farmland. The attractive village is in a conservation area, and your hosts, the Lord of the Manor and his wife, are accomplished cooks and passionate about organic food; they produce their own beef, game, eggs, vegetables and soft fruits. Breakfast is an Aga-cooked feast of homemade bread, Suffolk cured bacon and black pudding, fresh juices and compote; delicious dinners are served in an elegant, silk-lined dining room. You'll find genuine country-house style here with tea and homemade cake on arrival, pretty wallpapers, flowers and a welcoming fire in the hall.

Suffolk

Church House

A short hop from riverside Woodbridge and musical Snape Maltings, between a conservation churchyard and a history-rich field, is something different and unusual: a customised house of gentle colours and textures, home to an architect and a designer. From the hand-carved, oak porch to the lovely wildlife garden, there's a feeling of warmth and delight. Under the eaves: two jewel-bright and comfortable bedrooms full of books and fresh flowers. In the kitchen: a big farmhouse table laid for beautiful breakfasts. And, a short walk away, "one of the best gastropubs in East Anglia". Brilliant!

Children over eight welcome.

Rooms	3: 2 doubles, 1 twin.
Price	£90–£110. Singles £60–£75.
Meals	Dinner, 3 courses, £28. Restaurants 12 miles.
Closed	Rarely.

Rooms	2: 1 twin/double; 1 twin with separate bath/shower.
Price	£70–£90. Singles £60–£70.
Meals	Pub 1 mile.
Closed	Rarely.

	Jeffrey & Caroline Bowden
	Haughley House,
	Haughley,
	Suffolk IP14 3NS
Tel	+44 (0)1449 673398
Mobile	+44 (0)7860 284722
Email	bowden@keme.co.uk
Web	www.haughleyhouse.co.uk

	Sally & Richard Pirkis
	Church House,
	Clopton,
	Woodbridge,
	Suffolk IP13 6QB
Tel	+44 (0)1473 735350
Email	sallypirkis@gmail.com
Web	www.churchhousebandbsuffolk.co.uk

Entry 478   Map 10

Entry 479   Map 10

Suffolk

Suffolk

Melton Hall

There's more than a touch of theatre to this beautiful listed house. The dining room is opulent red; the drawing room, with its delicately carved mantelpiece and comfortable sofas, has French windows to the terrace. There's a four-poster in one bedroom, an antique French bed in another and masses of fresh flowers and books. The garden includes an orchid and wildflower meadow: a designated County Wildlife Site. River walks, the coast and the Saxon burial site Sutton Hoo are close. Generous Cindy, her delightful children, little dog Poppy and cats Bea and Bubbles, all give a great welcome.

The Old Rectory

Through the front door to a generously proportioned and flagstoned hall and a smiling welcome from Christopher. Archways lead down the corridor to the library (cosy with maps, books and open fire) and a tall elegant staircase leads to spacious bedrooms, one with delightful bow windows and a view of the sea. There are sash windows and shutters, pelmets and antiques, heaps of good books. Outside: 20 acres of woodlands, meadows, paddocks, croquet lawn and vegetable garden (walled and wonderful). Walks galore on the Deben Peninsula, music at Snape Maltings; it's Suffolk at its best and peace reigns supreme.

Rooms	3: 1 double; 1 double, 1 single sharing bath.		Rooms	3: 2 doubles, 1 twin. (Extra bed available.)
Price	£115-£135. Singles from £60.		Price	£85-£115. Singles from £60.
Meals	Dinner, 1-3 courses, £19-£38. BYO. Pubs/restaurants nearby.		Meals	Dinner, 3 courses, £30. Pub 5-minute walk.
Closed	Rarely.		Closed	Occasionally.

	Lucinda de la Rue		**Christopher Langley**
	Melton Hall,		The Old Rectory,
	Woodbridge,		Alderton,
	Suffolk IP12 1PF		Woodbridge,
Tel	+44 (0)1394 388138		Suffolk IP12 3DE
Mobile	+44 (0)7775 797075	Tel	+44 (0)1394 410003
Email	cindy@meltonhall.co.uk	Email	clangley@keme.co.uk
Web	www.meltonhall.co.uk	Web	www.oldrectoryaldertonbandb.co.uk

Entry 480   Map 10

Entry 481   Map 10

Suffolk

Willow Tree Cottage

Seductively near RSPB Minsmere, medieval castles and the glorious coast, and Edwardian Southwold with its pier and sand beach. The evening sun pours into the back of this contemporary cottage with butter yellow walls; you are on the edge of the village but all is quiet with an orchard behind and a bird-filled garden for tea. No sitting room, but easy chairs in your pretty bedroom face views. Caroline is a good cook and breakfast is large (try her kedgeree). Snape Maltings, for music lovers, is just four miles away; Aldeburgh with its shingle beach, fishing boats, fun shops and good places to eat, is a short drive.

Minimum two nights at weekends.

Rooms	1 double.
Price	£68–£70. Singles £50.
Meals	Pub/restaurant 1.5 miles.
Closed	Rarely.

Caroline Youngson
Willow Tree Cottage,
3 Belvedere Close, Kelsale,
Saxmundham,
Suffolk IP17 2RS

Tel	+44 (0)1728 602161
Mobile	+44 (0)7747 624139
Email	cy@willowtreecottage.me.uk
Web	www.willowtreecottage.me.uk

Entry 482   Map 10

Suffolk

Sandpit Farm

Idyllic views of the wide Alde valley stretch from this deeply comfortable, listed farmhouse. The river borders 20 acres of beautiful meadows, orchard, gardens, tennis court, ponds and the remains of a brick-lined moat; be charmed by Susie's hens and guinea fowl too. Step inside to family antiques and portraits, easy colour schemes, beams and open fires; pretty bedrooms have every cossetting thing. Susie and her Aga will make a scrumptious breakfast of homemade and local produce and home-grown tomatoes, plus fresh fruits and juices. You're near the coast, Snape for concerts, great birdwatching, walks and cycling... bliss!

Rooms	2: 1 double, 1 twin.
Price	£65–£90. Singles from £50.
Meals	Pub/restaurant 1.5 miles.
Closed	Rarely.

Susie Marshall
Sandpit Farm,
Bruisyard,
Saxmundham,
Suffolk IP17 2EB

Tel	+44 (0)1728 663445
Email	smarshall@aldevalleybreaks.co.uk
Web	www.aldevalleybreaks.co.uk

Entry 483   Map 10

Suffolk

Hill Farm House

Close to the village yet surrounded by fields is a listed farmhouse steeped in character, with sloping floors and 400-year-old beams. Ex-restaurateur John, generous and great fun, makes scrumptious breads for breakfast and an array of jams, from hedgerow to strawberry to damson; relish it all in the delightful dining room. Stylish bedrooms, real value, are upstairs. The Oak room is huge, with a mahogany sleigh bed and a view to wildflower paddock, ducks and long pond; the Poppy room has a bathroom and its own sitting room off the landing. Utterly peaceful, perfect for unwinding – and Framlingham's fortress is close!

Rooms	2: 1 double; 1 double with separate bath/shower.
Price	£80. Singles £45-£60.
Meals	Restaurant 3.5 miles.
Closed	Christmas & New Year.

John Brown
Hill Farm House,
Redlingfield Road,
Horham, Eye,
Suffolk IP21 5ED
Tel   +44 (0)1379 388832
Email   jr@hillfarmbb.plus.com
Web   www.hillfarmbb.moonfruit.com

Entry 484   Map 10

Suffolk

Camomile Cottage

Aly and Tim's 16th-century longhouse is a feast of old beams, kilims, antiques and art. They give you homemade cake on arrival; relax in the garden or the guest lounge, kick off your shoes and enjoy a glass of wine by the log fire. Beamed bedrooms have period furnishings, goose down duvets, luxury linen, flowers and handmade chocolates; bathrooms have Molton Brown toiletries. Aly will also bring you tea in bed! Breakfast is in the garden room: cornbread toast, eggs from the hens, croissants and all sorts of cooked choices. Eye is an attractive old market town; Southwold, Bury St Edmunds and Snape Maltings are all close.

Minimum stay two nights at weekends.

Rooms	2 doubles.
Price	£99-£110. Singles £85.
Meals	Pubs/restaurants 0.5 miles.
Closed	Rarely.

Aly Kahane
Camomile Cottage,
Brome Avenue,
Eye,
Suffolk IP23 7HW
Tel   +44 (0)1379 873528
Email   aly@camomilecottage.co.uk
Web   www.camomilecottage.co.uk

Entry 485   Map 10

Suffolk

Church Farmhouse

This Elizabethan farmhouse is by the ancient thatched church in a little hamlet close to Southwold. Minsmere RSPB bird sanctuary, Snape Maltings and the coast are nearby for lovely days out. Sarah, characterful, well-travelled and entertaining, is also an excellent cook, so breakfast will be a treat with bowls of fruit, Suffolk bacon and free-range eggs; occasional candle-lit dinners are worth staying in for, too. Bedrooms have supremely comfy beds well-dressed in pure cotton. Although there is no sitting room, you can enjoy tea and cake and linger in the garden, there are flowers in every room and books galore.

Minimum two nights at weekends. Over 12s welcome.

Rooms	3: 1 double, 1 twin/double; 1 double with separate bath.
Price	£90–£100. Singles from £50.
Meals	Dinner from £28. Pubs/restaurants within 4 miles.
Closed	Christmas.

Sarah Lentaigne
Church Farmhouse,
Uggeshall, Southwold,
Suffolk NR34 8BD
Tel	+44 (0)1502 578532
Mobile	+44 (0)7748 801418
Email	sarahlentaigne@btinternet.com
Web	www.churchfarmhousesuffolk.co.uk

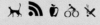

Entry 486 Map 10

Suffolk

Valley Farm

Soaps and sweeties in baskets, walking and cycle route maps on tap, DVDs to borrow: some of the personal touches you'll find at this delightfully unpretentious B&B. The soft brick farmhouse in a lovely corner of Suffolk sits in two acres of new landscaped garden, with a play area for children, a field for kite flying and a wonderful indoor solar-heated pool, shared with the self-catering guests. You get jams from their fruits for breakfast – Jackie and Andrew have a passion for real food – and two friendly and comfortable carpeted bedrooms, each with a spotless shower room.

Minimum stay two nights at weekends.

Rooms	2: 1 double, 1 family room for 3–4.
Price	£80–£100. Family room £80–£120.
Meals	Pub 0.4 miles.
Closed	Rarely.

Jackie Circus
Valley Farm,
Bungay Road, Holton,
Halesworth,
Suffolk IP19 8LY
Tel	+44 (0)1986 874521
Email	mail@valleyfarmholton.co.uk
Web	www.valleyfarmholton.co.uk

Entry 487 Map 10

Surrey

Swallow Barn

A squash court, coach house and stables, once belonging to next-door's manor, have become a home of old-fashioned charm. Full of family memories, and run very well by Joan, this B&B is excellently placed for Windsor, Wisley, Brooklands and Hampton Court; close to both airports too. Lovely trees in the garden, fields and woods beyond, a paddock and a swimming pool... total tranquillity, and you can walk to the pub. None of the bedrooms is huge but the beds are firm, the garden views are pretty and the downstairs double has its own sitting room. Breakfasts are both generous and scrumptious.

Children over eight welcome.

Rooms	3: 1 double & sitting room; 1 twin with separate shower. Apple Store: 1 twin.
Price	£80–£90. Singles from £45.
Meals	Pub/restaurant 0.75 miles.
Closed	Rarely.

Joan Carey
Swallow Barn,
Milford Green, Chobham,
Woking,
Surrey GU24 8AU

Tel	+44 (0)1276 856030
Mobile	+44 (0)7768 972904
Email	swallowbarn@web-hq.com
Web	www.swallow-barn.co.uk

Entry 488   Map 4

Surrey

Lower Easing Farmhouse

A homely place with a lovely walled garden and super hosts; Gillian, who speaks French, German and Spanish, welcomes people from all over the world. The house, 16th to 19th century, has exposed timbers, books and bold colours. The dining room is red; the guest sitting room – with open fire and fascinating artefacts from around the world – is big enough for a small company meeting, or a wedding group. Your hosts, who are great fun, run an efficient and caring ship. In the walled garden, sipping tea, the distant rumble of the A3 reminds you how well placed you are for Gatwick and Heathrow.

Rooms	4: 1 twin/double; 1 twin/double with separate bath/shower; 2 singles sharing shower.
Price	£80–£90. Singles from £50.
Meals	Pub 300 yds.
Closed	Occasionally.

David & Gillian Swinburn
Lower Easing Farmhouse,
Lower Easing,
Godalming,
Surrey GU7 2QF

Tel	+44 (0)1483 421436
Email	davidswinburn@hotmail.com

Entry 489   Map 4

Surrey

Hambledon House

Through an old ornate iron gate, up a sweeping drive in rolling parkland and... enter another world. With an Elizabethan core and Victorian additions, Vanessa's house is a unique celebration of the Arts and Crafts movement. It's been in her family for generations and the restoration, with a marvellous Italian slant, is well underway. Find rooms of pure opulence with regal beds and bags of character, fabulous bathrooms, art, antiques, vast fireplaces, stunning stained glass, an orangery for breakfasts and a wonderful garden with a long reflecting pond. Vanessa is great fun and you're free to wander everywhere. Magical.

Rooms	3 doubles.
Price	£110-£130. Singles £75.
Meals	Dinner, 3 courses, £30. Catering for house parties. Pubs/restaurants 10-minute walk.
Closed	Rarely.

Vanessa Rhode
Hambledon House,
Vann Lane, Hambledon,
Godalming,
Surrey GU8 4HW
Tel   +44 (0)1428 683815
Mobile   +44 (0)7768 645500
Email   vanessaswarbreck@yahoo.co.uk
Web   www.hambledonhouse.com

Entry 490   Map 4

Surrey

The Dovecote at Greenaway

An enchanting cottage in an idyllic corner of Chiddingfold. People return time and again – for the house (1545), the garden with dovecote, vegetables, flowers and hens, the glowing interiors, and Sheila and John. The sitting room is inviting with rich colours and textures, and the turning oak staircase leads to bedrooms that are cosy and sumptuous at the same time. Bathrooms are bliss, with deep roll top tubs. Come for gorgeous countryside and walks on the Greensand Way... who would guess London and the airports were so close? Delightful B&B; guests are full of praise.

Rooms	3: 1 double; 1 double, 1 twin sharing bath.
Price	£110-£115. Singles £75.
Meals	Pubs 300 yds.
Closed	Rarely.

Sheila & John Marsh
The Dovecote at Greenaway,
Pickhurst Road,
Chiddingfold,
Surrey GU8 4TS
Tel   +44 (0)1428 682920
Email   jfmarsh@btinternet.com
Web   www.bedandbreakfastchiddingfold.co.uk

Entry 491   Map 4

Surrey

Colliers Farm

Acres of grounds and a restored 17th-century farmhouse with all the trimmings will make you want to stay. Step into a hallway with a welcoming wood-burner; Marina rustles up tea and cake (delicious brownies!) on flowery china – served outside with the roses and roaming hens in summer. Pastel walls blend with soaring beams, stained glass and vases of flowers. Luxurious bedrooms come with TVs, DVDs, iPod docks and tip-top bathrooms; one is downstairs, all have comfy armchairs. Breakfast in the elegant dining room is a local spread with homemade compotes, bread and marmalade. Trips to Goodwood, Guildford and Chichester are easy.

Rooms	3: 2 doubles, 1 twin.
Price	£110-£160. Singles from £75.
Meals	Pubs/restaurants 0.25 miles.
Closed	Rarely.

Marina Shellard
Colliers Farm,
Midhurst Road, Fernhurst,
Haslemere,
Surrey GU27 3EX
Tel   +44 (0)1428 652265
Email   info@colliersfarm.co.uk
Web   www.colliersfarm.co.uk

Entry 492   Map 4

Surrey

Blackbrook House

A large Victorian house sitting in lawns and garden and with a wide gravel drive; this has a rural feel but you are less than two miles from the centre of Dorking. Emma and Rae, both easy-going, give you a super little sitting room with a hidden TV and space to make a cup of tea; both bedrooms are spacious, smart and feminine with floral fabrics, deep pocket sprung mattresses and good linen, bathrooms are tip-top. Breakfast is beautifully presented with cereals and fruit or the full Monty. Walk it off over lawns, shrubs and woods – or strike out further over National Trust land.

Rooms	2: 1 double, 1 suite.
Price	£90-£100. Suite £95-£115. Singles from £60.
Meals	Pub 0.5 miles.
Closed	Christmas & New Year.

Emma & Rae Burdon
Blackbrook House,
Blackbrook, Dorking,
Surrey RH5 4DS
Tel   +44 (0)1306 888898
Mobile   +44 (0)7880 723512
Email   blackbrookbb@btinternet.com
Web   www.surreybandb.co.uk

Entry 493   Map 4

Surrey

South Lodge

The beautiful Surrey Hills surround this smart home overlooking the village green. Paul and Joanna's house gets the sun all day and has a country chic feel. They look after you well, and give you tea and cake on arrival, three cosy, pretty bedrooms in the eaves and locally sourced and homemade treats at breakfast. Joanna's catering business is run from the house so there are always people coming and going – this is a fun place to stay with a lovely friendly feel. Hop next door for a tasty supper at The Grumpy Mole (popular so you need to book). Handy for Gatwick, too – it's a 15-minute drive.

Sussex

Church Gate

Janie greets you with afternoon tea in the big conservatory extension of her 1930s house, and rustles up a superb continental breakfast under the vine in summer – home-baked muffins if you're lucky! The garden is dreamy and the guest quarters are in the garden cottage, a high-quality new build with a spectacular flagstoned living area downstairs, a delightful understated décor and two fresh bedrooms above; bathrooms come beautifully stocked. Set off for Chichester with its theatre and shops, walk to pretty Itchenor and West Wittering beach, come home for a spot of tennis and a drink on your own terrace.

Usually minimum two nights.

Rooms	3: 2 doubles; 1 twin with separate bath.
Price	£95. Singles £85.
Meals	Evening meal by arrangement. Pub next door.
Closed	Christmas.

Rooms	Cottage: 1 double, 1 twin & sitting room.
Price	£90–£135. Singles from £70.
Meals	Continental breakfast. Pub within 0.5 miles.
Closed	Often in the winter months.

	Joanna Rowlands
	South Lodge,
	Brockham Green, Brockham,
	Betchworth,
	Surrey RH3 7JS
Tel	+44 (0)1737 843883
Email	bookings@brockhambandb.com
Web	www.brockhambandb.com

	Janie Impey
	Church Gate,
	Itchenor,
	Chichester,
	Sussex PO20 7DL
Tel	+44 (0)1243 514700
Email	janie.allen@btinternet.com
Web	www.chichesterbandb.co.uk

Entry 494   Map 4

Entry 495   Map 4

Sussex

Itchenor Park House

The Duke of Richmond reportedly built Itchenor Park for his French mistress in 1783; it's a listed Georgian house in beautiful formal gardens on a 700-acre farmed estate. It is remote and utterly peaceful, and a path across the fields brings you to Chichester harbour for boat trips and sailing bustle. There are great walks to the beach, too, and around the village. You stay in a cosy self-contained apartment in the wing with your own sitting room, kitchenette and wood-burner. And you may enjoy the lovely little walled garden, sheltered from the winds. Susie leaves you breakfast to have at your leisure.

Rooms	Apartment: 1 double & sofabed & kitchenette.
Price	£100–£150. Singles from £80.
Meals	Breakfast in fridge. Pub 5-minute walk. Restaurants 5 minute drive.
Closed	Rarely.

Susie Green
Itchenor Park House,
Itchenor, Chichester,
Sussex PO20 7DN

Tel	+44 (0)1243 512221
Mobile	+44 (0)7718 902768
Email	susie@itchenorpark.co.uk
Web	www.itchenorpark.co.uk

Entry 496   Map 4

Sussex

The Old Manor House

Wild flowers in jugs, old wooden floors and beams, pretty cottagey curtains: Judy's manor house near Chichester has bags of character and she is friendly and kind. Originally constructed round a big central fireplace, the rooms are all refreshingly simple allowing features to shine. Sweet bedrooms up steep stairs have seagrass floors, limed furniture, gentle colours and warm bathrooms. Enjoy delicious breakfasts by the wood-burner in the dining room: fresh fruit smoothies and an organic full English. Great for horse racing, castle visiting, sailing, theatre and festivals; fantastic walks on the south downs, too. Lovely.

Rooms	2 doubles.
Price	£95.
Meals	Pub/restaurant 500 yds.
Closed	Christmas.

Judy Wolstenholme
The Old Manor House,
Westergate Street, Westergate,
Chichester,
Sussex PO20 3QZ

Tel	+44 (0)1243 544489
Email	judy@veryoldmanorhouse.com
Web	veryoldmanorhouse.com

Entry 497   Map 4

Sussex

Seabeach House

Sitting sleepily behind its white gate this pretty stone cottage is surrounded by the Sussex Downs National Park. Throughout Francesca's friendly home her love of folk art, rich oils, antiques and hand-painted pieces adds zest. Comfy cottagey bedrooms are on the ground floor; wake to local sausages and eggs, garden tomatoes, homemade jams with croissants and brioche. Francesca loves cooking, and dinner, with home-grown veg, is good too. Explore garden and fields, admire wide views from a pretty terrace and chat to Popeye the dog. There's art, theatre and sailing in Chichester, the castle in Arundel, and events galore at Goodwood.

Rooms	Annexe: 1 double, 1 twin sharing bath (let to same party only).
Price	£85–£150. Singles £75.
Meals	Dinner, 3 courses, £25. BYO. Pub 1 mile.
Closed	Rarely.

Francesca Emmet
Seabeach House,
Selhurst Park, Halnaker,
Chichester,
Sussex PO18 0LX
Tel   +44 (0)1243 537944
Email   francescaemmet@hotmail.co.uk
Web   www.bandbatseabeachhouse.co.uk

Entry 498   Map 4

Sussex

West Marden Farmhouse

Bowl down a gentle valley in the South Downs to this 16th-century farmhouse with beautiful Sussex granaries and barn; the Edney family has farmed the land for generations. Your delightful, helpful hosts, who are committed to the environment, give guests a sitting/dining room with a huge old fireplace, comfortable sofas, flowers, oak floor and French windows to the garden. Find beamed bedrooms with a luxurious feel and thoughtful touches; fabulous bathrooms (freestanding baths, swish showers) burst with gorgeous Ren toiletries. Breakfasts are delicious, the walking is great and Goodwood is a 20-minute drive.

Minimum two nights at weekends & April-Oct.

Rooms	2 doubles.
Price	£115.
Meals	Pub 75 yds.
Closed	Occasionally.

Carole Edney
West Marden Farmhouse,
West Marden,
Chichester,
Sussex PO18 9ES
Tel   +44 (0)2392 631761
Email   info@westmardenfarm.com
Web   www.westmardenfarmhousebandb.co.uk

Entry 499   Map 4

Sussex

Fitzlea Farmhouse

A wooded track leads to the beautiful, mellow, 17th-century farmhouse with tall chimneys and a cluster of overgrown outbuildings – a sensational house in a breathtaking setting. Wood-panelled walls and ancient oak beams, a vast open fireplace, mullioned windows and deep sofas create a mood of relaxed country charm. Maggie gives you a delicious locally sourced breakfast in her Aga-warm kitchen; in spring, the scent of bluebells wafts through open doors. A winding staircase leads to comfortable timbered bedrooms which overlook fields, rolling lawns and woodland where you can stroll in peace.

Children by arrangement.

Sussex

Woolbeding Cottage

Come for an idyllic, tucked-away cottage, gorgeous bedrooms, breakfasts worth getting out of bed for, the prettiest garden and the friendliest of owners. Generous Clare gives you a bright sitting room filled with books, deep sofas, natural fabrics and a whacking great fire. The barn bedroom feels more private with its own entrance and terrace but both are large, lovely and view-filled, and bathrooms are full of character. Food is taken seriously, breakfasts are homemade, delicious and vast, and you can have a light supper too. Scamper around the South Downs straight from the door. Cowdray and Goodwood are close.

Minimum two nights.

Rooms	2 doubles.
Price	£98–£110. Singles £69.
Meals	Light supper £18. Packed lunch £10. Pub/restaurant 1.5 miles.
Closed	Rarely.

STOP PRESS
NO LONGER DOING B&B

Clare Devereux
Woolbeding Cottage,
Bepton, Midhurst,
Sussex GU29 0LY
Tel   +44 (0)1730 816620
Email   bookings@woolbedingcottage.co.uk
Web   www.woolbedingcottage.co.uk

Riverhill Lodge

Views and more views over the South Downs National Park from this handsome red-brick house with early Georgian origins. A sunny, airy sitting room with open fire and elegant cream and pink sofas looks onto the well-planted garden, and you breakfast on homemade bread, eggs from local hens and smoked bacon in the cosy terracotta-coloured dining room. Peaceful bedrooms are in pale, neutral colours, with fresh fabrics and deep mattresses; bathrooms are sleekly up-to-date and as warm as toast, with the thickest towels. Walk from the house for miles. There are good pubs nearby and the friendly Leavers provide masses of info.

The Shepherd's Return

Lizzie's dream has been realised in her West Sussex country garden an hour from London: welcome to her sweet shepherd's hut. Simply decorated in soft colours with red gingham curtains, it's in perfect keeping with its South Downs setting, and is lit and heated by solar and wood fuel. The shower and bath are up at the cottage; so, for the moment, is the loo. Lizzie, who spoils you with tea and cake on arrival, keeps everything as local and as natural as possible, from the sheepskin hot water bottle and the merino wool bedding and organic ticking sheets to the beautiful organic breakfast hamper that arrives every morning.

Minimum two nights. Book through Sawday's Canopy & Stars online or by phone.

Rooms	2: 1 double, 1 twin/double.
Price	£85–£125. Singles £70–£75.
Meals	Pub 0.75 miles.
Closed	Christmas & occasionally Easter.

Rooms	Shepherd's hut for 2; bathroom & wc in the house.
Price	£100–£120.
Meals	Continental breakfast hamper included.
Closed	Never.

	Christopher & Jenny Leaver
	Riverhill Lodge,
	Riverhill, Fittleworth,
	Petworth, Pulborough,
	Sussex RH20 1JY
Tel	+44 (0)1798 343872
Email	bookings@riverhilllodge.co.uk
Web	www.riverhilllodge.co.uk

	Sawday's Canopy & Stars
	The Shepherd's Return,
	Sutton End, Pulborough,
	Sussex RH20 1PY
Tel	+44 (0)1275 395447
Email	enquiries@canopyandstars.co.uk
Web	www.canopyandstars.co.uk/
	shepherdsreturn

Entry 502   Map 4

Entry 503   Map 4

Sussex

Stream Cottage

One of Sussex's prettiest villages, an endearing 1587 thatched cottage, the cheeriest hosts and a breakfast menu including blueberry pancakes, smoked salmon, homemade plum compote and, for the very hungry, 'The Famous Amberley Monty'! Through a private door and up a narrow staircase find your own sweet sitting room with comfy sofa and chair, lots of books and a charming bedroom with plenty of space and dual aspect low windows overlooking the garden. Your sparkling bathroom is downstairs (robes are provided) with big bottles of Cowshed potions and a sleek bath for resting weary limbs. Arundel and the South Downs await.

Rooms	1 double with separate bath & sitting room.
Price	£90. Singles £70.
Meals	Pubs in village.
Closed	Christmas & occasionally.

Mike & Janet Wright
Stream Cottage,
The Square, Amberley,
Arundel,
Sussex BN18 9SR
Tel   +44 (0)1798 831266
Email   janet@streamcottage.co.uk
Web   www.streamcottage.co.uk

Entry 504   Map 4

Sussex

The Hyde Granary

A 1,000-acre estate, where roe deer roam and the odd buzzard circles above. The granary stands at the end of a one-mile drive, alongside a coach house and clock tower, in the shadow of the big house. Airy interiors are just the ticket: timber frames, exposed walls, beams in the dining room and a drying room for walkers. Bedrooms are uncluttered and have a country feel: one has a claw-foot bath, the other is in the eaves. Margot, a homeopath, can realign your back after a long journey, and does super breakfasts. There's a small garden for sundowners in summer, you can walk to the village and Gatwick is close.

Rooms	2: 1 double; 1 double with separate bath/shower.
Price	£80. Singles £60.
Meals	Pub 1.7 miles.
Closed	Christmas & New Year.

Margot Barton
The Hyde Granary,
The Hyde, London Road,
Handcross, Haywards Heath,
Sussex RH17 6EZ
Tel   +44 (0)1444 401930
Email   margot@thehydegranary.com
Web   www.thehydegranary.com

Entry 505   Map 4

Sussex

Mayes Park Lodge

It's nicely private here, up a bird-filled lane, and you stay in a stunning converted dairy near to where charming owners James and Hannah live. Two super bedrooms are filled with cleverly sourced furniture – if you fall in love with anything you can buy it and take it home! Beds are deeply comfy, linen is crisp, fabrics are luxurious and the bathroom is immaculate with underfloor heating. It's all on one floor with a lovely shared sitting/dining room; a delicious organic breakfast is served in the kitchen – apples from the orchard, home laid eggs. Good pubs and restaurants are near; perfect for friends.

Sussex

Ocklynge Manor

On top of a peaceful hill, a short stroll from Eastbourne, find tip-top B&B in an 18th-century house with an interesting history – ask Wendy! Now it is her home, and you will be treated to home-baked bread, delicious tea time cakes and scrummy jams – on fine days you can take it outside. Creamy carpeted, bright and sunny bedrooms, all with views over the lovely walled garden, create a mood of relaxed indulgence and are full of thoughtful touches: dressing gowns, DVDs, your own fridge. Breakfasts are superb: this is a very spoiling, nurturing place.

Rooms	The Old Dairy: 2 doubles sharing bathroom & sitting room.
Price	£105-£120. Singles £90-£105.
Meals	Supper £15-£25. Pub 1 mile.
Closed	Rarely.

Rooms	3: 1 twin, 1 suite for 3; 1 double with separate shower.
Price	£90. Singles from £50.
Meals	Pub 5-minute walk.
Closed	Rarely.

	Hannah Clapshaw
	Mayes Park Lodge,
	Mayes Lane, Warnham,
	Horsham,
	Sussex RH12 3SG
Tel	+44 (0)1403 218879
Mobile	+44 (0)7976 846810
Email	enquiries@mayespark.com
Web	www.mayespark.com

	Wendy Dugdill
	Ocklynge Manor,
	Mill Road,
	Eastbourne,
	Sussex BN21 2PG
Tel	+44 (0)1323 734121
Mobile	+44 (0)7979 627172
Email	ocklyngemanor@hotmail.com
Web	www.ocklyngemanor.co.uk

Entry 506   Map 4

Entry 507   Map 5

Sussex

Hailsham Grange

Come for elegance and ease. Noel looks after you very well in his lovely Queen 'Mary Anne' home. No standing on ceremony here, despite the décor: classic English touched with chinoiserie in perfect keeping with the house; all is luxurious and special. Busts on pillars, delicious fabrics, books galore and bedrooms a treat: a sunny double, a romantic four-poster, smart suites. Summery breakfasts are served on the flagged terrace, marmalades and jams on a silver salver. The town garden, with its box parterre and gothic summerhouse, is an equal joy. Close by are gardens to visit, Glyndebourne, the sea and South Downs National Park.

Minimum two nights on bank holidays.

Rooms	4: 1 double. 1 four-poster. Coach house: 2 suites.
Price	£100-£110. Singles from £70.
Meals	Pub/restaurant 300 yds.
Closed	Rarely.

Noel Thompson
Hailsham Grange,
Hailsham,
Sussex BN27 1BL
Tel   +44 (0)1323 844248
Email   noel@hgrange.co.uk
Web   www.hailshamgrange.co.uk

Entry 508   Map 5

Sussex

Globe Place

A listed 17th-century house beside the church in a tiny village, ten minutes from Glyndebourne. Alison – a former chef to the Beatles – is a great cook and can provide you with a delicious and generous hamper, and tables and chairs too. Willie is a former rackets champion who gives tennis coaching; there's a court in the large, pretty garden, and a pool. Relax by the inglenook fire in the drawing room after a walk on the Cuckoo Trail or the South Downs, then settle down to a great supper – local fish, maybe, with home-grown vegetables. An easy-going, fun and informal household.

Children over 12 welcome.

Rooms	6: 2 doubles, 1 twin, each with separate bath; 2 singles sharing baths (let to same party only). Cottage: 1 twin/double with sitting room.
Price	£85-£110. Singles £50.
Meals	Dinner £30. BYO wine. Hamper £35. Pub 10-minute drive.
Closed	Christmas.

Alison & Willie Boone
Globe Place,
Hellingly,
Sussex BN27 4EY
Tel   +44 (0)1323 844276
Mobile +44 (0)7870 957608
Email   stay@globeplace.co.uk
Web   www.globeplace.co.uk

Entry 509   Map 5

Sussex

Netherwood Lodge

The scent of fresh flowers and a smattering of chintz over calm uncluttered interiors will please you. Engaging Margaret is a mine of local knowledge and offers you peaceful, cosy, ground-floor bedrooms beautifully dressed with wool carpets, designer interlined curtains, luxurious bed linens and gloriously comfortable beds. Enjoy an award-winning breakfast overlooking the garden (it's stunning); all is homemade or locally sourced. Then set off to discover this beautiful corner of East Sussex – ideal for walking, visiting National Trust houses and gardens and, of course, Glyndebourne.

Rooms	2: 1 twin; 1 double with separate bath.
Price	£100–£120. Singles from £80.
Meals	Pub/restaurant 0.75 miles.
Closed	Rarely.

Margaret Clarke
Netherwood Lodge,
Muddles Green, Chiddingly,
Lewes,
Sussex BN8 6HS
Tel   +44 (0)1825 872512
Email   netherwoodlodge@hotmail.com
Web   www.netherwoodlodge.co.uk

Entry 510   Map 5

Sussex

Old Whyly

Breakfast in a light-filled, chinoiserie dining room – there's an effortless elegance to this manor house, once home to one of King Charles's Cavaliers. Bedrooms are atmospheric, one in French style. The treats continue outside with a beautiful flower garden annually replenished with 5,000 tulips, a lake and orchard, a swimming pool and a tennis court – fabulous. Dine under the pergola in summer: food is a passion and Sarah's menus are adventurous with a modern slant. Glyndebourne is close so make a party of it and take a divine 'pink' hamper, with a table and chairs or a blanket included. Sheer bliss.

Rooms	4: 2 twins/doubles; 2 twins/doubles with separate bath.
Price	£95–£140. Singles by arrangement.
Meals	Dinner, 3 courses, £32.50. Hampers £35. Pub/restaurant 0.5 miles.
Closed	Rarely.

Sarah Burgoyne
Old Whyly,
London Road,
East Hoathly,
Sussex BN8 6EL
Tel   +44 (0)1825 840216
Email   stay@oldwhyly.co.uk
Web   www.oldwhyly.co.uk

Entry 511   Map 5

Sussex

Walnut Cottage

Christine's cottage – one of two tucked down a pretty lane – has a beautiful country-house feel. Bedrooms tempt with chocolates, flowers and comfy beds. Rise for a delicious breakfast: homemade yogurt and granola, coddled eggs with cream and nutmeg, or sausages from a nearby farm. Christine uses local seasonal produce; autumn dinners can feature game or venison. On arrival enjoy tea and homemade biscuits in an elegant sitting room; the garden, with views towards the South Downs, has a lovely terrace for al fresco meals. Days out include the Cuckoo Trail, Glyndebourne and Rudyard Kipling's house.

Over 12s welcome.

Rooms	2: 1 double; 1 double with separate bath.
Price	£70–£80. Singles £60–£70.
Meals	Dinner from £25. BYO. Pub 3 miles.
Closed	Rarely.

Christine Jermyn
Walnut Cottage,
Hanging Birch Lane, Horam,
Heathfield,
Sussex TN21 0PE

Tel	+44 (0)1435 812781
Email	info@walnutcottagesussex.com
Web	www.walnutcottagesussex.com

Entry 512   Map 5

Sussex

Thimbles

Enter the characterful hallway of this higgledy-piggledy house and fall under the spell of its charm. Imagine family antiques, pictures, plates, just-picked flowers and duvets as soft as a cloud: a timeless elegance, a fresh country style. Feast your eyes on the garden, six gentle acres that rise to fantastic views… a hammock, 89 varieties of roses, humming honey bees, a lake with an island (for barbecues!), a long lazy swing. Breakfasts and suppers are a dream: eggs from the hens, bacon from the pigs, jams from a jewel of a kitchen garden. Vicki, her family and Lottie the Irish terrier are the icing on the cake.

Minimum two nights on bank holidays.

Rooms	2: 1 suite (extra bed available); 1 single sharing bathroom (let to same party only).
Price	£80–£90. Singles £45–£75. Extra bed £30.
Meals	Dinner, 1-3 courses, £12.50–£21.50. Lunch £12.50. Pub 1 mile.
Closed	Rarely.

Vicki Wood
Thimbles,
New Pond Hill, Cross in Hand,
Heathfield,
Sussex TN21 0NB

Tel	+44 (0)1435 860745
Mobile	+44 (0)7960 588447
Email	vicki.simonwood@btinternet.com
Web	www.thimblesbedandbreakfast.co.uk

Entry 513   Map 5

Sussex

Longbourn

Through the gates and down the drive to a big Victorian house in 12 lovingly nurtured acres. Longbourn is a smallholding with conservation flocks of sheep, pigs and fowl, and a farm shop on site – hence the exceptional breakfasts! (Fresh croissants too.) As for the house, it is large, light, immaculate and a perfect showcase for a fascinating collection of military lithographs. Big bedrooms, one opening to veranda and garden, have deep carpets and elegant wallpapers; the guests' drawing room is equally grand. Roland and Jane, she an ex-costume designer, are completely charming and love to share their home.

Minimum two nights in high season.

Rooms	2: 1 double; 1 double with separate bath.
Price	£120-£140. Singles £70-£105.
Meals	Pubs/restaurants within 5 miles.
Closed	Rarely.

	Jane Horton
	Longbourn,
	Burwash Road, Broad Oak,
	Heathfield,
	Sussex TN21 8XG
Tel	+44 (0)1435 882070
Email	jane@overthestile.com
Web	www.longbourn1895.co.uk

Entry 514   Map 5

Sussex

The Cloudesley

One mile from the sea, a remarkable house full of beautiful things. Shahriar – photographer, holistic therapist, Chelsea gold-medal winner – has created an artistic bolthole: books, African masks, an honesty bar, chic bedrooms and two sitting rooms that double as art galleries. You are looked after with great kindness. Shahriar has a couple of treatment rooms where, in cahoots with local therapists, he offers massage, shiatsu and reiki. You breakfast on exotic fruits, Armagnac omelettes, or the full cooked works; in summer on a bamboo terrace. Don't miss Derek Jarman's cottage at Dungeness or St Clement's for great food.

Minimum two nights at weekends. Whole house available. Children over six welcome.

Rooms	5: 4 doubles, 1 twin.
Price	£75-£135. Extra bed £25.
Meals	Pubs/restaurants 5-minute drive.
Closed	Rarely.

	Shahriar Mazandi
	The Cloudesley,
	7 Cloudesley Road,
	St Leonards-on-Sea,
	Sussex TN37 6JN
Mobile	+44 (0)7507 000148
Email	info@thecloudesley.co.uk
Web	www.thecloudesley.co.uk

Entry 515   Map 5

Sussex

Appletree Cottage

An enviable position facing south for this old hung-tile farmer's cottage, covered in roses, jasmine and wisteria; views are over farmland towards the coast at Fairlight Glen. Jane will treat you to tea and cake when you arrive – either before a warming fire in the drawing room, or in the garden in summer. Bedrooms are sunny, spacious, quiet and traditional, one with gorgeous garden views. Breakfast well on apple juice from their own apples, homemade jams and marmalade, local bacon and sausages. Perfect for walkers with a footpath at the front gate; birdwatchers will be happy too, and you are near the steam railway at Bodiam.

Minimum two nights at weekends May-Sept. Children over eight welcome.

Rooms	3: 1 twin; 1 double, 1 single each with separate bath.
Price	£80. Singles £50.
Meals	Pub/restaurant 0.5 miles.
Closed	Rarely.

Jane & Hugh Willing
Appletree Cottage,
Beacon Lane, Staplecross,
Battle, Robertsbridge,
Sussex TN32 5QP

Tel	+44 (0)1580 831724
Mobile	+44 (0)7914 658861
Email	appletree.cottage@hotmail.co.uk
Web	www.appletreecottage.co

Entry 516   Map 5

Sussex

Swan House

Effortless style drifts through the beamed rooms of this boutiquey B&B in a 1490s bakery, from a roaring inglenook fireplace to an honesty bar in a mock bookcase – all run by relaxed creative hosts Brendan and Lionel. Bedrooms hold surprises: Elizabethan frescoes, an old pulley for bags of flour, a window seat, seashell mosaics and handmade soaps. Step out into lively Old Hastings, wander down to see fishing boats tucked in for the night or find an antiques bargain. Seagulls herald the new day: pick a morning paper; breakfast like kings on organic croissants and local kippers (dinners also on request). Unique.

Rooms	4: 3 doubles, 1 suite.
Price	£120-£150. Suite £115-£145. Singles £80-£120.
Meals	Restaurants 2-minute walk.
Closed	Christmas.

Brendan McDonagh
Swan House,
1 Hill Street,
Hastings,
Sussex TN34 3HU

Tel	+44 (0)1424 430014
Email	res@swanhousehastings.co.uk
Web	www.swanhousehastings.co.uk

Entry 517   Map 5

Sussex

Coromandel House

A glorious farmhouse with a duck pond, brick and weatherboard outbuildings, flouncing flower beds and charming Lisette, a garden designer from London. Large bedrooms have big wide floor boards and inviting beds, decorative gates for headboards, reclaimed windows for mirrors and a delicious rusticity. Bathrooms could appear in *Country Living* (and have!); views are green from every window. Outside are acre of lawns, a wildflower garden, hens and handsome Berkshire pigs; organic breakfasts are outstanding. A bucolic retreat ten minutes from Rye, in rolling Sussex hills: open the door and walk for miles.

Rooms	2: 1 double, 1 twin/double. (Extra child bed available.)
Price	£90–£115. Child £20.
Meals	Pub 1 mile.
Closed	Rarely.

	Lisette Pleasance
	Coromandel House,
	Boonshill Farm, Grove Lane,
	Iden, Rye,
	Sussex TN31 7QA
Tel	+44 (0)1797 280533
Email	boonshillfarm@yahoo.co.uk
Web	www.boonshillfarm.co.uk

Entry 518 Map 5

Warwickshire

Park Farm House

Fronted by a circular drive, the warm red-brick farmhouse is listed and old – it dates from 1655. Linda is friendly and welcoming, a genuine B&B pro, giving you an immaculate guest sitting room filled with pretty family pieces. The bedrooms sport comfortable mattresses, mahogany or brass beds, blankets on request, bathrobes, flowers and magazines; bathrooms are a little dated but spotless. A haven of rest from the motorway (morning hum only) this is in the heart of a working farm yet hugely convenient for Birmingham, Warwick, Stratford and Coventry. You may get their own beef at dinner and the vegetables are home-grown.

Rooms	2: 1 double, 1 twin.
Price	£79–£82. Singles from £48.
Meals	Dinner, 3 courses, from £25. Supper £19. Pub/restaurant 1.5 miles.
Closed	Rarely.

	Linda Grindal
	Park Farm House,
	Barnacle, Shilton,
	Coventry,
	Warwickshire CV7 9LG
Tel	+44 (0)2476 612628
Web	www.parkfarmguesthouse.co.uk

Entry 519 Map 8

Warwickshire

Hardingwood House

Close to Birmingham and the NEC and with a theatrical, Tudor feel. Denise, warm and delightful, spoils guests with big bedrooms, dressing rooms, good linen and deep gold-tapped baths. There are books, flowers, antique clocks and plush sofas; a wood-burner warms the sitting room; dark timbers and reds and pinks abound. The 1737 barn is immaculate inside and out: the kitchen gives onto a stunning patio, while bedrooms have views to garden or fields. Breakfast is delicious: homemade bread and muesli, local sausages, bacon and jams. A convivial, happy place with much rural charm – guests love it here!

Minimum two nights at weekends. Children over 12 welcome.

Rooms	3: 1 double, 2 twins.
Price	£85. Singles from £65.
Meals	Pub 20-minute drive.
Closed	Rarely.

Denise Owen
Hardingwood House,
Hardingwood Lane,
Fillongley,
Coventry,
Warwickshire CV7 8EL
Tel   +44 (0)1676 542579
Mobile +44 (0)7713 153320
Email   denise@hardingwoodhouse.fsnet.co.uk

🐾 🔊 ♿ ✕

Entry 520   Map 8

Warwickshire

Mows Hill Farm

From the chocolate labradors in the flagstoned kitchen to the cattle munching in their stalls, this late-Victorian farmhouse is a proper working farm of 1,300 acres that has been in the family for generations. Lynda and Edward give you an elegant and comfortable sitting and dining room with field views, loads of books and magazines, family portraits and an open fire. Breakfast on homemade bread and jams, fruit salad, home-reared bacon, just-laid eggs – in the conservatory looking onto the garden in the summer. Bedrooms have cotton sheets, armchairs for flopping and cosy bathrobes. A warm, family home.

Children over ten welcome.

Rooms	2: 1 twin/double; 1 double with separate bath.
Price	£80–£90. Singles from £60.
Meals	Pub/restaurant 3 miles.
Closed	Rarely.

Lynda Muntz
Mows Hill Farm,
Mows Hill Road, Kemps Green,
Tanworth in Arden,
Warwickshire B94 5PP
Tel   +44 (0)1564 784312
Mobile +44 (0)7919 542501
Email   mowshill@farmline.com
Web   www.b-and-bmowshill.co.uk

🐾 🔊 🚜 🚂 ✕

Entry 521   Map 8

Warwickshire

Austons Down

A fine modern country house with splendid views of the rural Vale of Arden. Your hosts are generous and chatty and look after you well. Their comfortable and relaxed family home has an elegant, light-filled sitting room complete with antiques, fabulous marquetry and open fire; bedrooms are fresh and traditional, bathrooms immaculate. Breakfast on homemade bread, compotes, a continental spread or full English. Admire Jacob sheep on the farm, relax in the terraced gardens. Plenty to visit nearby too: Warwick Castle, Stratford, National Trust properties, classic car museums... and the Monarch's Way is on the doorstep.

Rooms	3: 1 double, 2 twins/doubles.
Price	£90–£120. Singles £65 (Mon–Thurs).
Meals	Supper from £15. Dinner from £30.
	Pubs/restaurants 1 mile.
Closed	Rarely.

Lucy Horner
Austons Down,
Saddlebow Lane,
Claverdon,
Warwickshire CV35 8PQ

Tel	+44 (0)1926 842068
Mobile	+44 (0)7767 657352
Email	lmh@austonsdown.com
Web	www.austonsdown.com

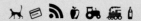

Entry 522   Map 8

Warwickshire

Marston House

A generous feel pervades this lovely family home; Kim's big friendly kitchen is the hub of the house. She and John are easy-going and kind and there's no standing on ceremony. Feel welcomed with tea on arrival, delicious breakfasts, oodles of interesting facts about what to do in the area. The house, with solar electricity, is big and sunny; old rugs cover parquet floors, soft sofas tumble with cushions, sash windows look onto the smart garden packed with birds and borders. Bedrooms are roomy, traditional and supremely comfortable. A special, peaceful place with a big heart, great walks from the door and Silverstone a short hop.

Rooms	2: 1 twin/double with separate bath;
	1 twin/double with separate shower.
Price	£90–£110. Singles from £70.
Meals	Supper, 3 courses, £29.50.
	Dinner £35 (min. 4).
	Pub 5-minute walk.
Closed	Occasionally in winter.

Kim & John Mahon
Marston House,
Byfield Road, Priors Marston,
Southam,
Warwickshire CV47 7RP

Tel	+44 (0)1327 260297
Mobile	+44 (0)7813 831028
Email	kim@mahonand.co.uk
Web	www.ivabestbandb.co.uk

Entry 523   Map 8

Warwickshire

Warwickshire

Shrewley Pools Farm

A charming, eccentric home and fabulous for families, with space to play and animals to see: sheep, bantams and pigs. A fragrant, romantic garden with a blossoming orchard and a fascinating house (1640), all low ceilings, aged floors and steep stairs. Timbered passages lead to large, pretty, sunny bedrooms (all with electric blankets) with leaded windows and polished wooden floors and a family room with everything needed for a baby. In a farmhouse dining room Cathy serves sausages, bacon, and eggs from the farm, can do gluten-free breakfasts and is happy to do teas for children. Buy a day ticket and fish in the lake.

Machado Gallery

Artists and artisans have lived in this red-brick village house since 1746 – and it has never looked finer. Sue, a well-travelled sculptor and designer, has spent many happy years filling her home with art and natural light: skylights gulp sunshine into the fire-warmed sitting room; carved Russian windows frame daylight; bedrooms – one with a private patio, another a Juliet balcony – have pretty linen and super bathrooms. Wake to espresso and homemade bread, then sit out by the garden pond or browse the studio gallery. The village pubs are close; Warwick, the Cotswolds and Stratford-on-Avon beckon.

Families welcome if booking all rooms for two or more nights.

Rooms	2: 1 family room, 1 twin.
Price	£65. Family room £70 for 2, £110 for 3. Singles from £50.
Meals	Packed lunch £5. Child's high tea £5. Pub/restaurant 1.5 miles.
Closed	Christmas.

Rooms	3: 2 doubles, 1 twin/double.
Price	£75-£115. Singles from £70.
Meals	Clotted cream tea £6.50 (order on booking). Pub 50 yds, restaurant 100 yds.
Closed	December-January.

Cathy Dodd
Shrewley Pools Farm,
Five Ways Road, Haseley,
Warwick,
Warwickshire CV35 7HB

Tel   +44 (0)1926 484315
Mobile +44 (0)7818 280681
Email   cathydodd@hotmail.co.uk
Web   www.shrewleypoolsfarm.co.uk

Sue Machado
Machado Gallery,
9 Wellesbourne Road, Barford,
Warwick,
Warwickshire CV35 8EL

Tel   +44 (0)1926 624061
Mobile +44 (0)7715 109609
Email   machadogallery@barford.org.uk
Web   www.machadogallery.co.uk

Entry 524   Map 8

Entry 525   Map 8

Warwickshire

Oxbourne House

Hard to believe the house is so young, with all its beamed ceilings, fireplaces and antiques. Bedrooms are fresh, crisp, cosy and cared for, the family room with an 'in the attic' feel; lighting is soft, beds excellent, bath and shower rooms attractive and warm, and the views are far-reaching. In the garden: tennis, sculpture and Graeme's rambler-bedecked pergola. Wake to birdsong and eggs from the hens; on peaceful summer nights, watch the dipping sun. Posy and Graeme are hugely likeable and welcoming, and an excellent village pub is down the road. A most comforting place to stay.

Dogs by arrangement.

Rooms	3: 1 double, 1 family room; 1 twin/double with separate bath.
Price	£75–£95. Family room £85–£135. Singles from £55.
Meals	Dinner from £20. Pub 5-minute walk.
Closed	Rarely.

Graeme & Posy McDonald
Oxbourne House,
Oxhill, Warwick,
Warwickshire CV35 0RA

Tel	+44 (0)1295 688202
Mobile	+44 (0)7753 661353
Email	graememcdonald@msn.com
Web	www.oxbournehouse.com

Entry 526   Map 8

Warwickshire

The Old Manor House

An attractive 16th-century manor house with beautiful landscaped gardens sweeping down to the river Stour. The beamed double has oak furniture and a big bathroom; the newly decorated twins (one in a private wing) are simply lovely. There is a large and elegant drawing and dining room whose antiques, contemporary art and open fire are for visitors to share. Jane prepares first-class breakfasts, and in warm weather you can have tea on the terrace: pots of tulips in spring, old scented roses in summer, meadow land beyond. A comfortable, lived-in family house with Stratford and the theatre close by.

Children over seven welcome.

Rooms	2: 1 double, 2 twin/doubles, each with separate bath.
Price	£90–£110. Singles £50–£65.
Meals	Restaurants nearby.
Closed	Rarely.

Jane Pusey
The Old Manor House,
Halford, Shipston-on-Stour,
Warwickshire CV36 5BT

Tel	+44 (0)1789 740264
Mobile	+44 (0)7786 467916
Email	info@oldmanor-halford.co.uk
Web	www.oldmanor-halford.co.uk

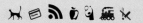

Entry 527   Map 8

Warwickshire

Upper Larkstoke

A gorgeous Cotswold house lost in its own valley with views that stretch for miles; bluebells carpet the wood in spring, you can walk across fields to the pub in summer. Rupert and Laurie, an Anglo-American partnership, spent two years refurbishing from top to toe. Outside, find smart lawns, beds of lavender and a sun-trapping terrace. Inside, beautiful colours and chic fabrics mix with golden stone and open fires. Bedrooms are crisply elegant with fine linen, French beds, beautiful views; one has a magnificent private bathroom. Laurie whisks up Cordon Bleu breakfasts and Stratford is close for all things Shakespeare.

Rooms	3: 2 doubles; 1 double with separate bath.
Price	£100–£175.
Meals	Pub 2 miles.
Closed	Rarely.

Laurie Bell
Upper Larkstoke,
Admington,
Shipston-on-Stour,
Warwickshire CV36 4JH
Mobile   +44 (0)7811 160218
Email   welcome@upperlarkstoke.co.uk
Web   www.upperlarkstoke.co.uk

Entry 528   Map 8

Warwickshire

Stamford Hall

Soft hills and lines of poplars bring you to the high, pretty red-brick Georgian house with a smart hornbeam hedge. James, whose art decorates the walls, and Alice look after you impeccably but without fuss. You have a generous sitting room overlooking the garden, with gleaming furniture, early estate and garden etchings, and pastel blue sofas. Peaceful bedrooms are on the second floor and both have charm: soft wool tartan rugs on comfy beds, calming colours, attractive fabrics, restful outlooks. Wake to home-baked soda bread and Alice's full English; walk it off in open countryside or head for Stratford.

Rooms	2: 1 double, 1 twin.
Price	£85. Singles £60.
Meals	Pub 1 mile.
Closed	Christmas & occasionally.

James & Alice Kerr
Stamford Hall,
Fosse Way, Ettington,
Stratford-upon-Avon,
Warwickshire CV37 7PA
Tel   +44 (0)1789 740239
Email   jk@jameskerr.co.uk
Web   www.stamfordhall.co.uk

Entry 529   Map 8

Warwickshire

Sequoia House

A riverside stroll along the old tramway path brings you to the centre of Stratford. Step into the handsome hallway of this impeccable Victorian house to find high ceilings, deep bays, generous landings and a homely sitting room. The Evanses downsized from the hotel they used to run here, and are happy to treat just a few guests: trouser presses (yes!) and piles of towels mingle with fine old furniture in immaculate bedrooms; two have Swan Theatre views. Hotel touches, a lovely warm welcome, Jean's cake on arrival and homemade preserves at breakfast. Park off road – or leave the car at home.

Rooms	4 doubles.
Price	£125. Singles £85.
Meals	Pub/restaurant 100 yds.
Closed	Christmas & New Year.

Jean & Philip Evans
Sequoia House,
51 Shipston Road,
Stratford-upon-Avon,
Warwickshire CV37 7LN

Tel	+44 (0)1789 268852
Mobile	+44 (0)7833 727914
Email	info@sequoia-house.co.uk
Web	www.sequoia-house.co.uk

Entry 530   Map 8

Warwickshire

Cross o' th' Hill Farm

Stratford is a 12-minute walk by footpath across a field, and from the veranda you can see the church where Shakespeare is buried. The farm predates medieval Stratford with later additions to the house in 1860, though it has an earlier Georgian feel. All is chic, spacious and full of light with deco chandeliers, floor to ceiling sash windows, large uncluttered bedrooms and contemporary bathrooms. Wake to bird song, play the baby grand piano, enjoy croquet on the lawn and picnic in the gardens and orchards. Decima grew up here; she and David are charming hosts and passionate about art and architecture.

Rooms	3: 2 doubles; 1 double with separate bath/shower.
Price	£90-£96. Singles £65-£68.
Meals	Pubs/restaurants 15-minute walk.
Closed	20 December-23 February.

Decima Noble
Cross o' th' Hill Farm,
Clifford Lane,
Stratford-upon-Avon,
Warwickshire CV37 8HP

Tel	+44 (0)1789 204738
Mobile	+44 (0)7973 971067
Email	decimanoble@hotmail.com
Web	www.cross-o-th-hill-farm.com

Entry 531   Map 8

Warwickshire

Salford Farm House

Beautiful within, handsome without. Thanks to subtle colours, oak beams and lovely old pieces, Jane has achieved a seductive combination of comfort and style. A flagstoned hallway and an old rocking horse, ticking clocks, beeswax, fresh flowers: this house is well-loved. Jane was a ballet dancer, Richard has green fingers and runs a fruit farm and farm shop nearby – you may expect meat and game from the Ragley Estate and delicious fruits in season. Bedrooms have a soft, warm elegance and flat-screen TVs, bathrooms are spotless and welcoming, views are to garden or fields. Wholly delightful.

Rooms	2 twins/doubles.
Price	£90. Singles £55.
Meals	Dinner £28. Restaurant 2.5 miles.
Closed	Rarely.

Jane & Richard Beach
Salford Farm House,
Salford Priors,
Evesham,
Warwickshire WR11 8XN
Tel   +44 (0)1386 870000
Email   salfordfarmhouse@aol.com
Web   www.salfordfarmhouse.co.uk

Entry 532   Map 8

Wiltshire

Park Farm House

Pass endless fields of gambolling lambs to a patchwork of paddocks and horses – the setting is bucolic. This former stud manager's house has had a warm, inviting facelift; Laura Ashley meets taupe polka-dots and blue gingham in the big stylish bedroom, and the bathroom is a flit across the landing. Bright, engaging Sarah is a keen rider and a talented cook, so there are homemade breads and preserves at breakfast, and the finest Wiltshire bacon. Jasper, enthusiastic conservationist and historian, has spent years researching the history of the estate: arm yourself with an OS map for 7,000 acres of heaven.

Rooms	1 family room with separate bath.
Price	£75. Singles £55. Divan bed £20.
Meals	Pubs/restaurants 1 mile.
Closed	Rarely.

Sarah & Jasper Humphreys
Park Farm House,
Tollard Royal,
Salisbury,
Wiltshire SP5 5PU
Tel   +44 (0)1725 553134
Email   jasper.humphreys@kcl.ac.uk
Web   www.bandbtollardroyal.co.uk

Entry 533   Map 3

Wiltshire

Brook House

The minute you pull up in the drive you know you're in for a treat. Henry Lamb lived in this Georgian house, Evelyn Waugh came to visit, now it's the home of delightful Kate who gives you local sausages and homemade bread at breakfast. You'll love her farmhouse kitchen with its long cheerful table, the guest sitting room with its open log fire, and the beautiful, luxurious bedrooms, one with a balcony for the view. Gaze on with a glass of wine: the garden with its gorgeous planting and river running through, the visiting ducks, resident hens, the water meadows beyond. The village is charming, Salisbury is close.

Rooms	2: 1 double, 1 twin/double.
Price	£85–£95. Singles £50–£55.
Meals	Pub 3-minute walk.
Closed	Rarely.

Kate Seal
Brook House,
Homington Road, Coombe Bissett,
Salisbury,
Wiltshire SP5 4LR

Tel	+44 (0)1722 718242
Mobile	+44 (0)7595 509937
Email	info@brookhousesalisbury.com
Web	www.brookhousesalisbury.com

Entry 534   Map 3

Wiltshire

Old Stoke

As pretty as thatched cottages come. This lovely old farmhouse is edged by an AONB filled with birdsong and wildlife, yet you are close to Salisbury. Guests have a book-filled sitting room with Dorset cream walls and pretty chairs and sofas to collapse onto: upstairs are fresh bedrooms with bright fabrics on headboards and window cushions, feathery beds and sparkling bathrooms. Tracie is charming and cooks well: good wholesome food using eggs from the hens and home veg; stroll down the fecund garden for tea and her delicious flapjacks or cake in the summerhouse. A meadow and river lie beyond.

Over eights welcome.

Rooms	2: 1 twin/double; 1 double with separate bath.
Price	£65–£75. Singles from £45.
Meals	Dinner £17.50–£22.50. Packed lunch £6. Pub 1 mile.
Closed	December–February.

Tracie Pickford
Old Stoke,
Stoke Farthing,
Broad Chalke,
Salisbury,
Wiltshire SP5 5ED

Tel	+44 (0)1722 780513
Email	stay@oldstoke.co.uk
Web	www.oldstoke.co.uk

Entry 535   Map 3

Wiltshire

Dowtys

A beautifully converted Victorian dairy farm with fabulous views over the Nadder valley. Peaceful, private, stylish bedrooms, one on the ground floor, have original beams, antiques and big Vi-Spring beds; bathrooms are perfect. The sunny guest sitting room has a contemporary feel too, with its wood-burner and sliding doors to the garden. Have a delicious breakfast in the old milking parlour, now the dining room, or on the terrace, sit beneath the espaliered limes in the lovely garden, dip into the National Trust woods. Footpaths start from the gate and your charming hosts will help you with all your plans.

Rooms	3: 1 double & sitting room; 1 double, 1 twin each with separate bath/shower.
Price	£78-£95. Singles from £60.
Meals	Packed lunch on request. Pub 0.25 miles.
Closed	Christmas & New Year.

Di & Willi Verdon-Smith
Dowtys,
Dowtys Lane,
Dinton,
Salisbury,
Wiltshire SP3 5ES
Tel   +44 (0)1722 716886
Email   dowtys.bb@gmail.com
Web   www.dowtysbedandbreakfast.co.uk

Entry 536   Map 3

Wiltshire

The Mill House

In a tranquil village next to the river is a house surrounded by water meadows and wilderness garden. Roses ramble, marsh orchids bloom and butterflies shimmer. This 12-acre labour of love is the creation of ever-charming Diana and her son Michael. Their home, the time-worn 18th-century miller's house, is packed with country clutter – porcelain, foxes' brushes, ancestral photographs above the fire – while bedrooms are quaint and flowery, with firm comfy beds; organic breakfasts are served at small tables. Diana has lived here for many many years, and has been doing B&B for at least 27 of them!

Children over six welcome.

Rooms	5: 3 doubles, 1 family room; 1 twin with separate bath.
Price	£100. Family room £100. Singles from £65.
Meals	Pub 5-minute walk.
Closed	Rarely.

Diana Gifford Mead & Michael Mertenson
The Mill House,
Berwick St James,
Salisbury,
Wiltshire SP3 4TS
Tel   +44 (0)1722 790331
Web   www.millhouse.org.uk

Entry 537   Map 3

Wiltshire

The Duck Yard

Independence with your own terrace, entrance and sitting room. Peace too, at the end of the lane; find a charming and colourful cottage garden, a summerhouse and free-ranging hens. Harriet makes wedding cakes, looks after guests well and cheerfully rustles up fine meals at short notice; breakfasts feature delicious homemade bread. Your carpeted bedroom and aquamarine bathroom are tucked under the eaves; below is the sitting room, cosy with wood-burner, books and old squashy sofas, leading to a sunny terrace. Good for walkers: maps are supplied and you may even borrow a dog.

Reflexology available: book in advance.

Rooms	1 twin/double & sitting room.
Price	£70–£80. Singles £55.
Meals	Dinner, 3 courses, £25. Packed lunch £7. Pub 2 miles.
Closed	Christmas & New Year.

Harriet & Peter Combes
The Duck Yard,
Sandhills Road, Dinton,
Salisbury,
Wiltshire SP3 5ER
Tel +44 (0)1722 716495
Mobile +44 (0)7729 777436
Email harriet.combes@googlemail.com

Entry 538   Map 3

Wiltshire

Ridgewood Park

The parkland around this mellow house is alive with bluebells, buzzards and beds of lavender. Simon and his friendly dogs will greet you; step inside to relaxing rooms, family photos, antiques and open fires. Your big double is on the third floor, and there's a single bed in the eaves across the landing for a child. A locally sourced breakfast (including organic seeded bread from the vicar sometimes!) is served in the sunny yellow dining room, or outside overlooking the wooded valley. Stourhead and Stonehenge are close, and you're right on the edge of the Wessex Ridgeway — you can walk, cycle and ride from the house.

Rooms	2: 1 double, 1 single sharing bath.
Price	£70–£80. Singles £35–£40.
Meals	Pub 1.5 miles.
Closed	Rarely.

Simon & Louise Sturdy
Ridgewood Park,
Hindon Lane, East Knoyle,
Salisbury,
Wiltshire SP3 6BB
Tel +44 (0)1747 830472
Email stay@ridgewoodpark.co.uk
Web www.ridgewoodpark.co.uk

Entry 539   Map 3

Wiltshire

Deverill End

Colourful gardens surround this comfortable house, and fantastic views of the Wiltshire downs and Wylye valley, fields of horses and tall steeple stretch as far as the eye can see. Sim and Joy are well-travelled and friendly; their sunny sitting room, warmed by a wood-burner, is full of books, art and African treasures. Comfortable bedrooms are all downstairs: soft colours, posies of flowers, little shower rooms. In the kitchen or dining room is where you feast on eggs and fruits from the garden, homemade jams and home-grown tomatoes in season – they used to grow 300 acres of them in Africa! Bath and Salisbury are an easy hop.

Over tens welcome.

Oaklands

A comfortable townhouse, a south-facing garden, two dear dogs and a lovely old Silver Cross pram sitting under the stairs. It was the first house in Warminster to have a bathroom; these have multiplied since and the interiors have had a makeover – no wonder this delightful, spacious 1880s house has been in the family forever. Andrew and Carolyn, relaxed and charming, serve delicious breakfasts in the lovely, light-suffused conservatory at the drawing room end. Bedrooms, desirable and welcoming, overlook churchyard, lawns and trees; find soft colours, cosy bathrooms, family antiques. Restaurants are a stroll.

Rooms	3: 2 doubles, 1 twin.
Price	£70–£75. Singles £60–£70.
Meals	Pubs/restaurants 5-10 minutes walk.
Closed	Rarely.

Rooms	3: 1 double; 1 double, 1 twin/double sharing bath (let to same party only). Child bed available.
Price	£65–£85. Singles from £55.
Meals	Occasional dinner (min. 4 guests). Pub/restaurant 0.5 miles.
Closed	Christmas & rarely.

	Joy Greathead
	Deverill End,
	Deverill Road, Sutton Veny,
	Warminster,
	Wiltshire BA12 7BY
Tel	+44 (0)1985 840356
Email	deverillend@gmail.com
Web	www.deverillend.co.uk

	Carolyn & Andrew Lewis
	Oaklands,
	88 Boreham Road, Warminster,
	Wiltshire BA12 9JW
Tel	+44 (0)1985 215532
Mobile	+44 (0)7850 158302
Email	apl1944@yahoo.co.uk
Web	www.stayatoaklands.co.uk

Entry 540   Map 3

Entry 541   Map 3

Wiltshire

The Limes

Through the electric gates, past the gravelled car park and the pretty, box-edged front garden and you arrive at the middle part of a 1620 house divided into three. The beams, stone mullions and leaded windows are charming, and Ellodie is an exceptional hostess. Immaculate, comfortable bedrooms have pretty curtains and fresh flowers, smart bathrooms have good soaps and thick towels, logs glow in the grate, and breakfasts promise delicious Wiltshire bacon, prunes soaked in orange juice and organic bread. You are on the main road leading out of Melksham – catch the bus to Bath from right outside the door.

Rooms	3: 2 twins/doubles, 1 single.
Price	£85-£90. Singles £55-£60.
Meals	Pub 1.5 miles.
Closed	Rarely.

Ellodie van der Wulp
The Limes,
Shurnhold House, Shurnhold,
Melksham,
Wiltshire SN12 8DG
Tel	+44 (0)1225 790627
Mobile	+44 (0)7974 366892
Email	eevanderwulp@gmail.com

Entry 542   Map 3

Wiltshire

Glebe House

The rogues' gallery of photographs up the stairs says it all: Glebe House is quirky and fun. Friendly Ginny spoils you rotten with pressed linen and sociable dinners served on Wedgwood china. Charming, cosy and comfortable are the bedrooms, one with an Indian theme; delightful is the drawing room with its landscape oils, Bechstein piano and a large rug from Jaipur; settle into the sofa and roast away by the fire. Breads, marmalades and jams are homemade, beautiful woodland fills the valley, the cottage garden, alive with birds, wraps around the house and Mr Biggles – the grey parrot – chats by the Aga.

Rooms	2: 1 double, 1 twin.
Price	£80-£85. Singles £45-£55.
Meals	Dinner, 3 courses, from £25 (BYO). Pub 4 miles.
Closed	Christmas.

Ginny Scrope
Glebe House,
Chittoe, Chippenham,
Wiltshire SN15 2EL
Tel	+44 (0)1380 850864
Mobile	+44 (0)7767 608841
Email	ginnyscrope@gmail.com
Web	www.glebehouse-chittoe.co.uk

Entry 543   Map 3

Wiltshire

Wiltshire

Manor Farm

Farmyard heaven in the Cotswolds. A 17th-century manor farmhouse in 550 arable acres; horses in the paddock, dozing dogs in the yard, tumbling blooms outside the door and a perfectly tended village, with duck pond, a short walk. Beautiful bedrooms are softly lit, with muted colours, plump goose down pillows and the crispest linen. Breakfast in front of the fire is a banquet of delights, tea among the roses is a treat, thanks to charming, welcoming Victoria; she will arrange a table for dinner at the pub too. This is the postcard England of dreams, with Castle Combe, Lacock, grand walking and gardens to visit.

Over 12s welcome.

Dauntsey Park House

Be awed by history here. Parts of the house – like the grand dining room where you breakfast – date from Elizabethan times; the stunning summer drawing room is Edwardian. Both rooms are yours to use. Emma and her Italian husband have four young children and a flair for matching new with old: a striking glass chandelier sets off the sturdy oak table beneath; a turbine keeps the house in hot water. Up a wide staircase, two wallpapered bedrooms with views to the river are huge and comfortable with a self-indulgent feel (one has a thunderbox loo!). St James the Great church with its 14th-century doom board is in the garden. Lovely.

Rooms	3: 2 doubles; 1 twin with separate bath.	Rooms	2: 1 double, 1 twin.
Price	£84. Singles from £46.	Price	£120. Singles £75.
Meals	Pub nearby.	Meals	Pubs/restaurants in village.
Closed	Rarely.	Closed	Rarely.

Victoria Lippiatt-Onslow
Manor Farm,
Alderton, Chippenham,
Wiltshire SN14 6NL

Tel +44 (0)1666 840271
Mobile +44 (0)7721 415824
Email victoria.lippiatt@btinternet.com
Web www.themanorfarm.co.uk

Emma Amati
Dauntsey Park House,
Dauntsey,
Chippenham,
Wiltshire SN15 4HT

Tel +44 (0)1249 721777
Email enquiries@dauntseyparkhouse.co.uk
Web www.dauntseyparkhouse.co.uk

Entry 544   Map 3

Entry 545   Map 3

Wiltshire

Bridges Court

You're in the heart of the village with its small shop, friendly pub and the Melvilles' lovely 18th-century farmhouse. They havn't lived here long but it's so homely you'd never tell. Dogs wander, horses whinny, there's a beautiful garden with a Kiftsgate rose and a swimming pool for sunny days. On the second floor, off a corridor filled with paintings, are three florally inspired bedrooms: comfortable, bright and spacious with views to the village green. Breakfast leisurely on all things local at the long table in a dining room filled with silver and china. And there's a pleasant guests' sitting room to relax in.

Rooms	3: 1 double, 1 twin; 1 double with separate bath.
Price	£80-£90. Singles £60. (Discount for 3 nights or more, excluding Badminton w/e.)
Meals	Pub in village.
Closed	Rarely.

	Fiona Melville
	Bridges Court,
	Luckington,
	Wiltshire SN14 6NT
Tel	+44 (0)1666 840215
Mobile	+44 (0)7711 816839
Email	fionamelville2003@yahoo.co.uk
Web	www.bridgescourt.co.uk

Entry 546   Map 3

Wiltshire

Bullocks Horn Cottage

Up a country lane is this hidden-away house which the delightful Legges have turned into a haven of peace. Liz loves fabrics and flowers and mixes them with flair, Colin has painted a mural for the conservatory, bright with plants and wicker sofa. Super bedrooms, both twins, have lovely views; the sitting room has a log fire, fine antiques, big comfy sofas, and the garden is so special it's appeared in magazines. Organic veg and herbs from the garden and local seasonal food make an appearance at dinner which, on balmy nights, you may eat under the arbour, covered in climbing roses and jasmine.

Children over five welcome.

Rooms	2: 1 twin; 1 twin/double with separate bath/shower.
Price	£90. Singles from £45.
Meals	Dinner £20-£25. BYO. Pub 1.5 miles.
Closed	Christmas.

	Colin & Liz Legge
	Bullocks Horn Cottage,
	Charlton,
	Malmesbury,
	Wiltshire SN16 9DZ
Tel	+44 (0)1666 577600
Email	bullockshorn@clara.co.uk
Web	www.bullockshorn.co.uk

Entry 547   Map 3

Wiltshire

Overtown Manor

It's just a few miles from the centre of Swindon, but this listed manor house is still part of a working farm, tucked into quiet countryside. Feel swish in an elegant, duck-egg blue drawing room with ornate plaster work, marble fireplace and lofty sash windows overlooking gardens and pool. You'll eat like a lord in the impressive dining room: Nancy is a chef and chooses locally sourced or home-grown produce. Large light bedrooms are classic country-house style, with views; bathrooms are smart, tiled in stone and heated to perfection. Explore quaint villages and stone circles, try clay pigeon shooting; all is possible.

Rooms	4: 2 doubles, 2 twins/doubles.
Price	£100-£125. Singles £65-£90.
Meals	Pub within 5 miles.
Closed	Rarely.

Nancy Lawson
Overtown Manor,
Wroughton, Swindon,
Wiltshire SN4 0SH

Tel	+44 (0)1793 814737
Mobile	+44 (0)7887 597090
Email	nancy@overtownmanor.co.uk
Web	www.overtownmanor.co.uk

Entry 548   Map 3

Wiltshire

Copes Cottage

Sarah's pretty thatched cottage has far-reaching views over the Vale of Pewsey. Admire the gardens, with wildflower meadow and orchard, and step into her friendly Aga kitchen for tea and cake. Breakfast is in a dining room full of warm colours, flowers, books, glowing lamps and blue and white china. You have a choice of bedrooms – one with beams, antique bed and adjoining space for children, the other more modern and airy; the rustic sitting room is in a converted barn with comfy sofas and table tennis. Set out for forest and downland walks, ancient monuments, Salisbury Cathedral; there are crop circles to find in summer.

Rooms	2: 1 double (with extra double room, let to same party only); 1 double with separate bath/shower.
Price	£80. Singles £50.
Meals	Pub/restaurant 3 miles.
Closed	Rarely.

Sarah Townsend-Rose
Copes Cottage,
Harris Lane, Easton Royal,
Pewsey,
Wiltshire SN9 5LX

Tel	+44 (0)1672 810427
Email	copescottage@live.co.uk
Web	www.copescottage.co.uk

Entry 549   Map 3

Wiltshire

Honeypot Cottage

Honeypot sits in the middle of a terrace of pretty slate-topped cottages overlooking the Kennet & Avon canal. Nicola has created three floors of artistic, easy living. Bedrooms (up steep stairs) are chic and sunny, the top-floor one with a balcony for stargazing, both with garden posies and views of swans gliding by. The shared bathroom is made for lingering in: music, candles, scented things. Breakfast (homemade bread and jams) is in the gorgeous Aga kitchen, or out in the summerhouse with wonderful views over Pewsey Vale. Nicola is friendly and relaxed and you can have the whole house to yourself if you want – a romantic treat.

Minimum two nights. Whole house self-catering option available.

Rooms	2 doubles sharing bath.
Price	£125-£137. B&B for 4: £225-£247.
Meals	Pub/café within 1.5 miles.
Closed	Rarely.

	Robert Carpenter Turner
	Honeypot Cottage,
	Honeystreet, Pewsey,
	Wiltshire SN9 5PU
Tel	+44 (0)1672 852265
Email	info@honeystreet.biz
Web	www.honeystreet.biz

Entry 550   Map 3

Wiltshire

Rushall Manor

A gorgeous country house – and Caroline is a treat of a host. The dining room shines with glass, antiques and family portraits; a particularly impressive admiral gazes benignly down as you tuck into breakfast: local eggs and sausages, and jams from the orchard. The harmonious sitting room has comfy sofas, books and games; pretty bedrooms have perfect mattresses and linen (and, from one, fantastic views up to Salisbury Plain); bathrooms come with cast-iron baths, scented soaps and lashings of hot water. Stonehenge and Salisbury are nearby, walks are good, and Caroline holds the village fête in her delightful garden.

Grounds available for weddings.

Rooms	3: 1 twin; 1 double, 1 twin, both with separate bath.
Price	£100. Singles £60.
Meals	Dinner £30. Pubs 1 mile.
Closed	Rarely.

	Caroline Larken
	Rushall Manor,
	Rushall, Pewsey,
	Wiltshire SN9 6EG
Tel	+44 (0)1980 630301
Email	bandb@rushallmanor.com
Web	www.rushallmanor.com

Entry 551   Map 3

Wiltshire

Westcourt Farm

Rozzie and Jonny left London to restore a medieval, Grade II* cruck truss hall house (beautifully) amid wildflower meadows, hedgerows, ponds and geese. Delightful people, they love to cook and can spoil you rotten. Rooms are well decorated, crisp yet traditional, the country furniture is charming and the architecture fascinating. Bedrooms have comfortable beds and fine linen, bathrooms are spot-on; there's a lovely light drawing room and a barn for meetings and parties too. Encircled by footpaths and fields, Westcourt is the oldest house in a perfect village, two minutes from a rather good pub.

Worcestershire

Harrowfields

Tucked just off the high street is a compact cottage that's massively comfortable and stylish too: contemporary colours and old beams, great books and a homely feel. Your bedroom is large enough to lounge in with a good sofa, an antique brass bed, crisp linen and a cosy wood-burner; the spoiling continues in a shower room with comfy robes. Susie and Adam (who cooks) are natural and charming, hens cluck around the delightful garden, breakfast is local and seasonal, you can walk for miles or just to the pub. Romantic couples will be in heaven; uncork the wine, light the fire, turn up the music.

Minimum stay two nights high season weekends.

Rooms	2: 1 twin, 1 double.
Price	£80. Singles £50.
Meals	Pub/restaurant in village.
Closed	Rarely.

Rooms	1 double.
Price	£80. Singles from £60.
Meals	Pubs in village.
Closed	Rarely.

Jonny & Rozzie Buxton
Westcourt Farm,
Shalbourne, Marlborough,
Wiltshire SN8 3QE
Tel   +44 (0)1672 871399
Email   rozzieb@btinternet.com
Web   www.westcourtfarm.com

Susie Alington & Adam Stanford
Harrowfields,
Cotheridge Lane, Eckington,
Worcestershire WR10 3BA
Tel   +44 (0)1386 751053
Email   susie@harrowfields.co.uk
Web   www.harrowfields.co.uk

Entry 552   Map 3

Entry 553   Map 8

Worcestershire

The Birches

Thoughtful Katharine is attentive; Edward puts you at ease humming a jolly tune. Come and go as you please from this self-contained annexe, spotless and contemporary. French windows lead to a pretty terrace, then to a charming garden opening to fields and views of the Malverns. Though the house is easily accessible, the tranquillity is sublime; plenty of spots to sit and ponder the view back to the timber-framed house. Hens pottering on the lawn lay eggs for breakfast, served – in your room – with local bacon and sausages, and bread from Ledbury's baker. Wander further for abundant leafy walks and lovely Regency Malvern.

Rooms	1 double.
Price	£80. Singles £60.
Meals	Pub/restaurant 0.3 miles.
Closed	Rarely.

Katharine Litchfield
The Birches,
Birts Street, Birtsmorton,
Malvern,
Worcestershire WR13 6AW
Tel   +44 (0)1684 833821
Mobile +44 (0)7875 458441
Email   katharine-thebirches@hotmail.co.uk
Web   www.the-birchesbedandbreakfast.co.uk

Entry 554   Map 8

Worcestershire

Bidders Croft

Completely rebuilt in 1995 from 200-year-old bricks, this solid house has oak-framed loggias and an enormous conservatory where you eat overlooking the garden, orchard, newly planted vineyard and the Malvern Hills. Traditional bedrooms with mirror-fronted wardrobes and dressing tables are warm and comfortable; bathrooms shine. Bill and Charlotte give you a log fire, books and magazines in the drawing room and an Aga-cooked breakfast with home-produced eggs and fruits. There is a large terrace overlooking lawns and an ornamental pond; the hills beckon walkers, the views soar and the Malvern theatres are a short drive.

Children over 12 welcome.

Rooms	2: 1 twin with separate bath; 1 double with separate shower.
Price	£85-£95. Singles £50-£55.
Meals	Pub/restaurant 250 yds.
Closed	Christmas & New Year.

Bill & Charlotte Carver
Bidders Croft,
Welland,
Malvern,
Worcestershire WR13 6LN
Tel   +44 (0)1684 592179
Email carvers@bidderscroft.com
Web   www.bidderscroft.com

Entry 555   Map 8

Worcestershire

Old Country Farm & The Lighthouse

Ella's passion for this tranquil place – and conservation of its wildlife – is infectious. She's keen on home-grown and local food too so breakfast is delicious. Dating from the 1400s, the farm is a delightful rambling medley: russet stone and colour-washed brick, huge convivial round table by the Aga, rugs on polished floors. The sitting room has wood-burner, piano and books, and you sleep soundly in pretty, cottagey bedrooms: lovely linen, garden flowers. In winter you stay in The Lighthouse, down the lane: an inspired green-oak retreat with soaring beams, snug library, comfy downstairs bedrooms and roses in the garden. Magical.

Old Country Farm available in summer. The Lighthouse available in winter: 2 doubles.

Rooms	3: 1 double; 1 double with separate bath; 1 double with separate shower.
Price	£65-£90. Singles £35-£55.
Meals	Pubs/restaurants 3 miles.
Closed	Rarely.

Ella Grace Quincy
Old Country Farm & The Lighthouse,
Mathon,
Malvern,
Worcestershire WR13 5PS
Tel   +44 (0)1886 880867
Email   ella@oldcountryhouse.co.uk
Web   www.oldcountryhouse.co.uk

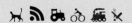

Entry 556   Map 8

Worcestershire

The Old Rectory

The listed 18th-century rectory has taken on a new lease of life, thanks to welcoming Claire (and John and two spaniels) whose ethos is flexibility and whose generosity spreads far. Relax in the library, the breakfast room, the garden full of birds, the grand red drawing room that overlooks Elgar country. Beautiful bedrooms are sumptuously furnished with old and new pieces, fluffy bathrobes and feather duvets, artisan biscuits and Malvern spring water. Claire is an inspired cook: breakfasts, beautifully sourced, are a treat, and candlelit dinners are amazing. Bliss for walkers, foodies, romantics, and all who love the Malverns.

Rooms	4: 3 doubles, 1 twin/double.
Price	£130-£150. Singles £100.
Meals	Dinner £37.50. Pubs/restaurants 1 mile.
Closed	Rarely.

Claire Dawkins
The Old Rectory,
Rectory Lane, Cradley,
Malvern,
Worcestershire WR13 5LQ
Tel   +44 (0)1886 880109
Mobile   +44 (0)7920 801701
Email   oldrectorycradley@btinternet.com
Web   www.oldrectorycradley.com

Entry 557   Map 8

Yorkshire

Broomhead

High in the ancient county of Hallamshire, surrounded by curlews, skylarks and 6,000 acres of National Park, is the renovated stable block of Broomhead Hall. This warm, light, contemporary conversion is home to a lovely young family, passionate about the land and their responsibility for it. After a day of trout fishing or picnicking beside Ewden Beck, bliss to come home to cosy soothing bedrooms with beds heaped with pillows and breathtaking views. A fire-warmed snug rammed with books, a huge oil painting of the grouse moor up high, eggs from their hens and home-baked bread at breakfast: it's fabulous.

Rooms	2 twins/doubles.
Price	£100. Singles £80.
Meals	Packed lunch £8. Pub/restaurant 2.5 miles.
Closed	Rarely.

Catherine Rimington Wilson
Broomhead,
Bolsterstone, Sheffield,
Yorkshire S36 4ZA

Tel	+44 (0)1142 882161
Mobile	+44 (0)7706 483346
Email	catherine_heaton@yahoo.co.uk
Web	www.broomheadestate.co.uk

Entry 558   Map 12

Yorkshire

Sunnybank

A Victorian gentleman's residence just a short walk up the hill from the centre of bustling *Last of the Summer Wine* Holmfirth, still with its working Picturedrome cinema (touring bands too), arts and folk festivals, restaurants and shops. Attentive hosts look after you when the Whites are away. Peaceful bedrooms have a mix of contemporary, Art Nouveau and Art Deco pieces, caramel cream velvets and silks, spoiling bathrooms and lovely valley or garden views. A full choice Yorkshire breakfast will set you up for a lazy stroll round the charming gardens, or a brisk yomp through rural bliss.

Minimum two nights at weekends.

Rooms	3: 2 doubles; 1 twin/double (with extra single bed).
Price	£65–£140. Singles from £55.
Meals	Dinner, 3 courses, £25. Dinner, 2 courses, £20. Packed lunch £12. Pubs/restaurants 500 yds.
Closed	Rarely.

Peter & Anne White
Sunnybank,
78 Upperthong Lane,
Holmfirth,
Yorkshire HD9 3BQ

Tel	+44 (0)1484 684065
Email	info@sunnybankguesthouse.co.uk
Web	www.sunnybankguesthouse.co.uk

Entry 559   Map 12

Yorkshire

Thurst House Farm

This solid Pennine farmhouse, its stone mullion windows denoting 17th-century origins, is English to the core. Your warm, gracious hosts give guests a cosy and carpeted sitting room with an open fire in winter; bedrooms are equally generous, with inviting brass beds, lovely antique linen and fresh flowers. Outside: clucking hens, two friendly sheep and a hammock in a garden with beautiful views. Tuck into homemade bread, marmalade and jams at breakfast, and good traditional English dinners, too – just the thing for walkers who've trekked the Calderdale or the Pennine Way.

Over eights welcome.

Rooms	2: 1 double, 1 family room.
Price	£80. Singles by arrangement.
Meals	Dinner, 4 courses, £25 (BYO). Packed lunch £5. Restaurants within 0.5 miles.
Closed	Christmas & New Year.

David & Judith Marriott
Thurst House Farm,
Soyland, Ripponden,
Sowerby Bridge, Yorkshire HX6 4NN

Tel	+44 (0)1422 822820
Mobile	+44 (0)7759 619043
Email	judith@thursthousefarm.co.uk
Web	www.thursthousefarm.co.uk

Entry 560   Map 12

Yorkshire

Field House

You drive over bridge and beck to this listed, 1713 farmhouse – expect comfort, homeliness and open fires. Pat and Geoff love showing guests their hens, horses, goats and lambs, and will tell you about the 14 circular walks or lend you a torch so you can find the pub across the fields! Ramblers and dog walkers will be in heaven – step out of the front door, past the lovely walled garden and you're in rolling, Brontë countryside. Good big bedrooms are in farmhouse style, one bathroom has a roll top bath. Geoff's breakfasts are generous in the finest Yorkshire manner.

Minimum two night stay in summer. Cot & highchair available.

Rooms	3: 1 double (with extra single bed), 1 twin/double; 1 family room with separate bath/shower.
Price	£70–£78. Family room £68–£74. Singles £45.
Meals	Packed lunch available. Pub/restaurant 200 yds.
Closed	Rarely.

Pat & Geoff Horrocks-Taylor
Field House,
Staups Lane, Stump Cross,
Halifax, Yorkshire HX3 6XX

Tel	+44 (0)1422 355457
Mobile	+44 (0)7729 996482
Email	stayatfieldhouse@yahoo.co.uk
Web	www.fieldhouse-bb.co.uk

Entry 561   Map 12

Yorkshire

Ponden House

Bump your way up the farm track to Brenda's sturdy house, high on the Pennine Way. The spring water makes wonderful tea, the ginger scones are delicious and the house hums with interest and artistic touches. Comfy sofas are jollied up with throws, there are homespun rugs and hangings, paintings, plants and a piano. Feed the hens, plonk your boots by the Aga, chat with your lovely leisurely hostess as she turns out fab home cooking; food is a passion. Bedrooms are exuberant, comfortable and cosy, it's great for walkers and there's a hot tub under the stars (bookable by groups in advance). Good value with a relaxed, homely feel.

Rooms	3: 2 doubles; 1 twin with separate bath (occasionally sharing bath with family).
Price	£70–£75. Singles from £45.
Meals	Dinner, 3 courses, £18. BYO. Packed lunch £6. Pub/restaurant 1 mile.
Closed	Rarely.

Brenda Taylor
Ponden House,
Stanbury,
Haworth,
Yorkshire BD22 0HR
Tel   +44 (0)1535 644154
Email   bjt@pondenhouse.co.uk
Web   www.pondenhouse.co.uk

Entry 562   Map 12

Yorkshire

Ellerbeck House

Walk from the door of this beautifully restored country house, or head west to the Lakes, east to the Dales, north to Scotland. Period rooms display exquisite antiques and Harriet's artistic touch: sofas and curtains in dark pink and cream, Persian rugs on shiny oak floors, marble fireplaces, stained glass in the stairwell, huge sash windows overlooking the lawn. One window holds the breakfast table – full Cumbrian, at flexible times. Outside, a courtyard for sitting out with the birds and the breeze. It's all so pretty, as is this bucolic – yet accessible – spot near Kirkby Lonsdale, Settle, and Kendal of Mint Cake fame.

Rooms	2: 1 double; 1 double with separate bath. Extra single room available (let to same party only).
Price	£90. Singles £45–£55.
Meals	Pubs/restaurants 2 miles.
Closed	Rarely.

Harriet Sharp
Ellerbeck House,
Westhouse, Ingleton,
Carnforth,
Yorkshire LA6 3NH
Tel   +44 (0)15242 41872
Email   harrietnsharp@gmail.com
Web   www.ellerbeckhouse.co.uk

Entry 563   Map 12

Yorkshire

Brandymires

The Wensleydale hills lie framed through the windows of the time-warp bedrooms; no TV, no fuss, just calm. In the middle of the National Park, this is a glorious spot for walkers. Gail and Ann bake their own bread, make jams and marmalade, and their delicious well-priced dinners, served at your own table, are prepared with fresh local produce. Both bedrooms, not in their first flush of youth, have lush views and private bathrooms; one has a four-poster. If you're arriving by car, take the 'over-the-top' road from Buckden to Hawes – stunning. A friendly, characterful place.

Over eights welcome.

Rooms	2: 1 twin, 1 four-poster, each with separate bath. One room only per floor can be let, on request.
Price	£60. Singles £35.
Meals	Dinner, 4 courses, £21 (not Thursday). Pubs/restaurant 5-minute walk.
Closed	November-February.

Gail Ainley & Ann Macdonald
Brandymires,
Muker Road,
Hawes,
Yorkshire DL8 3PR
Tel +44 (0)1969 667482

Entry 564   Map 12

Yorkshire

Low Mill

Off the village green this handsome historic mill in the Dales keeps many of its original features. The huge beamed guest sitting room has a roaring fire, and the old waterwheel is working! Friendly relaxed Neil and Jane have restored their home, then filled it with interesting art, quirky sculpture, flowers and vintage gems. Bedrooms have tip-top linen and luxurious throws; bathrooms are fabulous. Eat well at separate tables on all things local and home-grown: bacon, pancakes, homemade bread; and for dinner, perhaps Yorkshire ham or herby lamb. The pretty riverside garden is perfect for chilling with a glass of wine.

Rooms	3: 2 doubles, 1 suite.
Price	£90-£160. 25% discount for singles.
Meals	Dinner, 2-3 courses, £17.50-£22.50. Pubs 5-minute drive.
Closed	Rarely.

Neil McNair
Low Mill,
Bainbridge, Leyburn,
Yorkshire DL8 3EF
Tel +44 (0)1969 650553
Email lowmillguesthouse@gmail.com
Web www.lowmillguesthouse.co.uk

Entry 565   Map 12

Yorkshire

Waterford House

Middleham Castle – northern stronghold of Richard III – stands around the corner from this attractive Georgian house. Martin and Anne are great hosts and their house is full of beautiful things: clocks everywhere, polished chests, vintage luggage, interesting art. There's an open fire in the sitting room, claret walls in the dining room – and delicious breakfasts from Anne. Pretty bedrooms (one up steep stairs) have bags of comfort: four-posters, decanters of sherry, homemade cakes. Middleham is a racing village with 14 stable yards – horses clop by in the morning on their way to the gallops. Bring hiking boots and unravel the Dales.

Rooms	4: 2 doubles, 1 four-poster; 1 four-poster (with extra single).
Price	£98-£135. Singles from £85.
Meals	Four pubs & Bistro within 200 yds (£19, 2 courses).
Closed	Christmas & January.

	Martin Cade & Anne Parkinson Cade
	Waterford House,
	Kirkgate, Middleham, Leyburn,
	Yorkshire DL8 4PG
Tel	+44 (0)1969 622090
Email	info@waterfordhousehotel.co.uk
Web	www.waterfordhousehotel.co.uk

Entry 566   Map 12

Yorkshire

Manor House

It's the handsomest house in the village. Annie – warm, intelligent, fun – invites you in to spacious interiors elegantly painted and artfully cluttered. Tall shuttered windows and a big open fire, candles in glass sconces and heaps of flowers, soft wool carpets and charming fabrics: a genuinely relaxing family home. Bedroom are a treat, one with green views on two sides and a bathroom with a French country feel; fittings are vintage but spotless. Stride the Dales or discover Georgian Richmond, a hop away; return to a simple delicious supper, with veg from the garden and eggs from the hens.

Rooms	2: 1 double; 1 twin/double with separate bath.
Price	£95. Singles £80.
Meals	Supper, 2 courses, £20. BYO. Pubs 1 mile.
Closed	Christmas.

	Annabel Burchnall
	Manor House,
	Middle Street,
	Gayles,
	Richmond,
	Yorkshire DL11 7JF
Tel	+44 (0)1833 621578
Email	annieburchnall@hotmail.com

Entry 567   Map 12

Yorkshire

Cliffe Hall

What remains is the Victorian section of an earlier mansion, added by Richard's family in 1858. Inside is a beautifully proportioned and charming family home: huge reception rooms, plasterwork ceilings, acres of sofas, family portraits, floor to ceiling shelves of books. Bedrooms are large, sunny, traditional and uncontrived, bathrooms carpeted and twin beds super-comfy; large windows look onto the glorious grounds that run down to the river Tees. Breakfast on local organic bread and eggs and seasonal fruit from the garden. A special place with a soft, timeless grandeur and a big welcome.

Rooms	2 twins/doubles, each with separate bath.
Price	£90. Singles £50.
Meals	Pub 1 mile.
Closed	Rarely.

Caroline & Richard Wilson
Cliffe Hall,
Piercebridge,
Darlington,
Yorkshire DL2 3SR
Tel   +44 (0)1325 374322
Mobile   +44 (0)7785 756380
Email   petal@cliffehall.co.uk

Entry 568   Map 12

Yorkshire

Lovesome Hill Farm

Who could resist home-reared lamb followed by apple crumble cake? This is a working farm and the Pearsons the warmest people imaginable; even in the mayhem of the lambing season they greet you with delicious cakes and Yorkshire tea. Their farmhouse is as unpretentious as they are: chequered tablecloths, cosy bedrooms (four in the old granary, one in the cottage) with garden and hill views, and a Victorian-style sitting room. Wake to tasty breakfasts of home-laid eggs and homemade bread and jams. You have easy access to the A167 and are brilliantly placed for the Moors and Dales. Good for walkers, families, business people.

Rooms	5: 1 twin, 1 double, 1 family room, 1 single. Gate Cottage: 1 double.
Price	£80-£84. Family room £80-£110. Singles £42-£55. Gate Cottage: £84-£90.
Meals	Dinner, 2 courses, £18-£25. BYO. Packed lunch £5. Pub 4 miles.
Closed	Rarely.

John & Mary Pearson
Lovesome Hill Farm,
Lovesome Hill,
Northallerton,
Yorkshire DL6 2PB
Tel   +44 (0)1609 772311
Email   lovesomehillfarm@btinternet.com
Web   www.lovesomehillfarm.co.uk

Entry 569   Map 12

Yorkshire

Mill Close

Country-house B&B in a tranquil spot among fields and woodland; spacious, luxurious and with your own entrance through a flower-filled conservatory. Beds are large and comfortable, there's a grand four-poster with a spa bath, lovely linen and sconces for flickering candle light. Be spoiled by handmade chocolates, fluffy robes, even your own 'quiet' fridge. An elegant, pretty blue and cream sitting room has an open fire – but you are between the National Park and the Dales so walks are a must. Start with one of Patricia's famous breakfasts: bacon and sausages from the farm, smoked haddock or salmon, homemade jams. Bliss.

Rooms	3: 2 twins/doubles, 1 four-poster.
Price	£80–£95. Singles £45–£65.
Meals	Pubs/restaurants 2 miles.
Closed	Christmas & New Year.

Patricia Knox
Mill Close,
Patrick Brompton,
Bedale,
Yorkshire DL8 1JY
Tel   +44 (0)1677 450257
Email   pat@millclose.co.uk
Web   www.millclose.co.uk

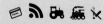

Yorkshire

Low Sutton

Judi's biscuits are a sweet welcome, Steve has a twinkle in his eye: they're B&B pros. Wood fires in the vast dining/sitting room and cosy snug burn fuel from their own copse; good insulation and underfloor heating keep the homely rooms comfy. Curl up in a soft white robe with a book, or wallow in the sparkling bathrooms – one is solar-heated (more greenie points!). There are six acres to explore with ponies, sheep, dogs and chickens; taste the fruit keen cook Judi jams up for breakfast and expect good dinners with veggies from the garden. Country delights from abbeys to markets are in easy reach.

Rooms	2 doubles.
Price	£75. Singles £50.
Meals	Packed lunch £5. Dinner £25.
	Pub/restaurant 1.5 miles.
Closed	Rarely.

Judi Smith
Low Sutton,
Masham, Ripon,
Yorkshire HG4 4PB
Tel   +44 (0)1765 688565
Mobile +44 (0)7821 600521
Email   info@lowsutton.co.uk
Web   www.lowsutton.co.uk

Yorkshire

Firs Farm

The landscape is rural and rolling, the lanes are narrow and quiet, and Healey is pretty-as-a-picture: mellow York stone, smart gardens and immaculate paintwork on every house. Richard and Sarah, relaxed and genial, offer homemade cakes and coffee when you arrive and the cosy feel of their home makes you feel instantly at ease. Enjoy a sitting room with an open fire and fabulous fabrics, fresh and cottagey bedrooms with spotted upholstered windows seats, and vases of flowers in every corner. There are great views from the lovely walled garden, acres to roam, wonderful walking, and tip-top towns to visit all around.

Children over ten welcome.

Rooms	2: 1 double, 1 twin/double with separate bath/shower.
Price	£75–£90. Singles £60.
Meals	Packed lunch £7. Pubs/restaurants 1 mile.
Closed	Christmas & New Year.

Richard & Sarah Townsend
Firs Farm,
Healey,
Ripon,
Yorkshire HG4 4LH
Tel   +44 (0)1765 688910
Email   sarah@firsfarmbandb.co.uk
Web   www.firsfarmbandb.co.uk

Entry 572   Map 12

Yorkshire

Mallard Grange

Perfect farmhouse B&B. Hens, cats, sheepdogs wander the garden, an ancient apple tree leans against the wall, guests unwind and feel part of the family. Enter the rambling, deep-shuttered 16th-century farmhouse, cosy with well-loved family pieces, and feel at peace with the world. Breakfast is generous – homemade muffins, poached pears with cinnamon, a sizzling full Monty. A winding steep stair leads to big, friendly bedrooms, two cheerful others await in the converted 18th-century smithy, and Maggie's enthusiasm for this glorious area is as genuine as her love of doing B&B. It's a gem!

Minimum two nights at weekends.

Rooms	4: 2 twins/doubles. Old Blacksmith's Shop & Carthouse: 2 twins/doubles.
Price	£80–£100. Singles from £70.
Meals	Pubs/restaurants 10-minute drive.
Closed	Christmas & New Year.

Maggie Johnson
Mallard Grange,
Aldfield, Ripon,
Yorkshire HG4 3BE
Tel   +44 (0)1765 620242
Mobile +44 (0)7720 295918
Email   maggie@mallardgrange.co.uk
Web   www.mallardgrange.co.uk

Entry 573   Map 12

Yorkshire

Laverton Hall

The hall is a beauty, even on a dull day, and the village is a dream. Half an hour from Harrogate find space, beauty, history (it's 400 years old), three walled gardens and comfort in great measure: beloved antiques, a rocking horse in the hall, feather pillows, thick white towels, and sumptuous breakfasts followed by delightful Rachel's Cordon Bleu dinner: we loved the pheasant casserole. The sunny guest sitting room is elegant and charming, the cream and white twin and the snug little single have long views to the river. The area is rich with abbeys and great houses, and then there are the glorious Dales to be explored.

Rooms	2: 1 twin/double, 1 single.
Price	£95. Singles £60.
Meals	Dinner, 3 courses, £28. Pubs/restaurants 2 miles.
Closed	Christmas.

Rachel Wilson
Laverton Hall,
Laverton, Ripon,
Yorkshire HG4 3SX

Tel	+44 (0)1765 650274
Mobile	+44 (0)7711 086385
Email	rachel.k.wilson@hotmail.co.uk
Web	www.lavertonhall.co.uk

Entry 574   Map 12

Yorkshire

Carlton House

Quietly tucked into a corner of the sedate green, a short stride from the pub, lies a stylishly renovated 18th-century farmhouse. The old wash house, tractor shed and stable have become airy, chic, characterful rooms with beams and fabulous bathrooms. In summer, pull up a chair in a pretty yard with hanging baskets or find a tranquil spot in the charmingly secret garden. The dining room with open fire is a delight, so linger over a breakfast of delicious local produce, then set off for market towns, dales and moors. There's a big-hearted family feel here — Denise's oat and raisin crunchies and soda bread are to die for! Lovely.

Rooms	Outbuildings: 2 doubles, 1 twin/double.
Price	£68-£85. Singles from £50.
Meals	Pub/restaurant 2-minute walk.
Closed	Rarely.

Denise & David Mason
Carlton House,
Sandhutton,
Thirsk,
Yorkshire YO7 4RW

Tel	+44 (0)1845 587381
Email	info@carltonbarns.co.uk
Web	www.carltonbarns.co.uk

Entry 575   Map 12

Yorkshire

The Old Rectory

Once the residence of the Bishops of Whitby this elegant rectory has a comfortable lived-in air. Both Turner and Ruskin stayed here and probably enjoyed as much good conversation and comfort as you will. Bedrooms are pretty, traditional and with grand views; the drawing room is classic country house with a fine Venetian window and an enticing window-seat. The graceful, deep pink dining room looks south over a large garden of redwood and walnut trees — some are 300 years old. Caroline will give you a generous breakfast; wander at will to find an orchard, tennis court and croquet lawn.

Children over three welcome.

Rooms	2: 1 double with separate bath & dressing room; 1 twin/double with separate bath and shower.
Price	£70–£74. Singles from £45.
Meals	Pub/restaurant opposite.
Closed	Rarely.

Tim & Caroline O'Connor-Fenton
The Old Rectory,
South Kilvington, Thirsk,
Yorkshire YO7 2NL

Tel	+44 (0)1845 526153
Mobile	+44 (0)7981 329764
Email	ocfenton@talktalk.net
Web	www.oldrectorythirsk.co.uk

Entry 576   Map 12

Yorkshire

Shallowdale House

Phillip and Anton have a true affection for their guests so you will be treated royally. Sumptuous bedrooms dazzle in yellows, blues and limes, acres of curtains frame wide views over the Howardian Hills, bathrooms are immaculate. You breakfast on the absolute best; fresh fruit compotes, dry-cured bacon, homemade bread. Admire the amazing garden, then walk off in any direction straight from the house. Return to a cosily elegant drawing room with a fire in winter, and an enticing library. Dinner is a real treat — coffee and chocolates before you crawl up to bed? Bliss.

Children over 12 welcome. Minimum two nights at weekends.

Rooms	3: 2 twins/doubles; 1 double with separate bath/shower.
Price	£110–£135. Singles £90–£105.
Meals	Dinner, 4 courses, £39.50. Pub 0.5 miles.
Closed	Christmas & New Year.

Anton van der Horst & Phillip Gill
Shallowdale House,
West End,
Ampleforth,
Yorkshire YO62 4DY

Tel	+44 (0)1439 788325
Email	stay@shallowdalehouse.co.uk
Web	www.shallowdalehouse.co.uk

Entry 577   Map 12

Yorkshire

Cundall Lodge Farm

Ancient chestnuts, crunchy drive, sheep grazing, hens free-ranging. This four-square Georgian farmhouse could be straight out of Central Casting. Homely rooms of damask sofa, comfy armchairs and bright wallpapers have views to Sutton Bank's White Horse or the river Swale, spotless bedrooms are inviting – family furnishings, fresh flowers, Roberts radios – and tea and oven-fresh cakes welcome you. This is a working farm and the breakfast table groans with free-range eggs, homemade jams and local bacon. The garden and river walks guarantee peace, and David and Caroline are generous and delightful.

Children over 14 welcome.

Rooms	3: 2 doubles, 1 twin/double.
Price	£80–£95.
Meals	Packed lunch £7.
	Pubs/restaurants 2 miles.
Closed	Christmas & January.

Caroline Barker
Cundall Lodge Farm,
Cundall, York,
Yorkshire YO61 2RN

Tel	+44 (0)1423 360203
Mobile	+44 (0)7773 494260
Email	enquiries@cundall-lodgefarm.co.uk
Web	www.cundall-lodgefarm.co.uk

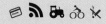

Entry 578   Map 12

Yorkshire

Poppleton House

Down a driveway off Main Street, through restored gates, to a wonderful red-brick Georgian house and a big welcome from Kathleen. Inside is graceful, stately, spacious and light: elegant breakfasts at a mahogany table and flowers in every room – Kathleen arranges flowers professionally. Luxuriate in pale wool carpeting and heritage colours, cornicing, pelmets and chandeliers, silver-framed photos and a grand piano. Everything feels relaxed in this peaceful grown-up place, and that includes the bedrooms. Behind: an acre of garden, with secret corners and pathways. Beyond: York, its river walks and its Minster, a bus ride away.

Minimum two nights at weekends.

Rooms	3: 2 doubles; 1 double with
	separate bath/shower.
Price	£80–£115. Singles £50–£68.
Meals	Pubs/restaurants in village & in
	York, 4 miles.
Closed	Christmas & New Year.

Kathleen Doggett
Poppleton House,
3 Main Street, Nether Poppleton,
York,
Yorkshire YO26 6HS

Tel	+44 (0)1904 781160
Email	info@poppletonhouse.co.uk
Web	www.bbyork.co.uk

Entry 579   Map 12

Yorkshire

The Chantry

The Chantry is a listed building in a village setting, lived in by Diana and Nigel – warm, humorous and engaging. A member of the Slow Food movement in York, and half Lebanese by birth, Diana reflects her culture in her cooking; her big ramshackle kitchen is the heart of this house. Bedrooms have space and high ceilings and an old-fashioned décor while bathrooms are swisher; the mood is comfy, warm, authentic, historic, and ever so gently eccentric. Pull yourself away from the suntrap terrace and sally forth into town: York, history-rich, is a sturdy walk (or a 20-minute bike ride) away.

Rooms	2: 1 double, 1 twin.
Price	£85. Singles from £60.
Meals	Dinner £25. Pubs 200 yards, restaurant 0.5 miles.
Closed	Rarely.

Diana Naish
The Chantry,
Chantry Lane, Bishopthorpe,
York,
Yorkshire YO23 2QF

Tel	+44 (0)1904 709767
Mobile	+44 (0)7850 912203
Email	diananaish@athomecatering.freeserve.co.uk

Entry 580   Map 12

Yorkshire

Corner Farm

Tea and home-baked cakes on arrival: you get a lovely welcome here! This peaceful farmhouse is so well insulated it's snug and warm even on the coldest day. With York so close and stunning estates nearby, this is a cosy nest from which to explore the area – or just the good village pub. Bathrooms are swish and bedrooms are light, fresh and comfortable: cast-iron beds, fine sheets, cute satin cushions. There are six acres to roam, and Tim and Sharon give you freshly pressed apple juice from the orchard, home-laid eggs and local produce for breakfast; the dining room is charming with vintage crockery and pots of flowers.

Rooms	2: 1 double, 1 twin.
Price	£80. Singles £55.
Meals	Packed lunch £4. Pub 100 yds.
Closed	Rarely.

Sharon Stevens
Corner Farm,
Low Catton, York,
Yorkshire YO41 1EA

Tel	+44 (0)1759 373911
Mobile	+44 (0)7711 440796
Email	cornerfarmyork@gmail.com
Web	www.cornerfarmyork.co.uk

Entry 581   Map 13

Yorkshire

The Mount House

A dollop of stylish fun in the rolling Howardian Hills (an AONB), Kathryn and Nick's redesigned village house is light, airy and filled with gorgeous things – from good antiques to splashy modern art and fresh flowers. The ground-floor twin with white cast-iron beds has its own cosy book-filled sitting room; the sunny upstairs double has views across the roof tops to open countryside. Kathryn, an excellent cook, will spoil you at breakfast – supper too, if you wish – sometimes in the pretty garden. Discover Castle Howard, Nunnington Hall, old market towns and great walking; only 20 minutes from York too. Super.

Friends of guests welcome for meals.

Rooms	3: 1 double; 1 twin & sitting room; 1 double with separate bath.
Price	£80-£130. Singles from £60.
Meals	Dinner, 2-4 courses, £25-£35. BYO. Pub/restaurant 200 yds.
Closed	Rarely.

	Kathryn Hill
	The Mount House,
	Terrington, York,
	Yorkshire YO60 6QB
Tel	+44 (0)1653 648206
Mobile	+44 (0)7780 536937
Email	mount.house@clayfox.co.uk
Web	www.howardianhillsbandb.co.uk

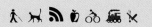

Entry 582   Map 13

Yorkshire

Hunters Hill

The moors lie behind this elegant farmhouse, five yards from the National Park, in farmland and woodland with fine views; the position is marvellous and you can walk from the door. The house is full of light and flowers; bedrooms are pretty but not overly grand, and look onto valley or church. The lovely lived-in drawing room displays comfortable old sofas, paintings and fine furniture; rich colours, hunting prints and candles at dinner create a warm and cosy feel. The family has poured a good deal of affection into this tranquil house and the result is a home that's happy, charming and remarkably easy to relax in… Wonderful.

Rooms	2: 1 double; 1 twin/double with separate bathroom.
Price	£90. Singles from £65.
Meals	Dinner, 3 courses, £35. Pub/restaurant 10-minute walk.
Closed	Rarely.

	Jane Otter
	Hunters Hill,
	Sinnington,
	York,
	Yorkshire YO62 6SF
Tel	+44 (0)1751 431196
Email	ejorr@tiscali.co.uk

Entry 583   Map 13

Yorkshire

Habton House Farm

Mellow stone, smart painted windows and a warm relaxed greeting from Lucy and James: a good start! You breakfast well here too, on home-produced sausages, bacon, eggs and jams, all delicious, at a big table in an elegant dining room. There are two cosy sitting rooms with wood fires to choose from, and the smartly done bedrooms have a pleasing medley of modern and vintage pieces, views of hill and river and immaculate bathrooms. Visit the pigs, fish for brown trout in the river, hire a bike; further afield are the North Yorks Moors and the coast. A tasty supper at the local pub is an added bonus.

Over eights welcome.

Rooms	4: 3 doubles, 1 twin/double.
Price	£85–£110. Singles £55–£75
Meals	Pub 0.5 miles.
Closed	January.

Lucy Haxton
Habton House Farm,
Little Habton, Malton,
Yorkshire YO17 6UA
Tel   +44 (0)1653 669707
Mobile +44 (0)7876 433351
Email   habtonhouse@gmail.com
Web   www.habtonhouse.co.uk

Entry 584   Map 13

Yorkshire

West View Cottage

In a village packed with thatched houses is Valerie's – gorgeous, 17th-century and fronted by cottage flowers, with a bench at the side to take advantage of the views; they reach for miles. The hall is high-raftered with a stunning chandelier, the little dining room has exquisite oak panelling; there's no sitting room but a sofa in your bedroom, reached via the patio, beautifully self-contained. Find an ornate brass bed and a funky shower-room – comfortable luxury in an unusual space. History and abbeys abound, the North York Moors lie across the field, and bright friendly Valerie knows the area inside out.

Rooms	1 double.
Price	£80–£100. Singles £65.
Meals	Pubs/restaurants 2 miles.
Closed	Rarely.

Valerie Lack
West View Cottage,
Pockley, Helmsley,
Yorkshire YO62 7TE
Tel   +44 (0)1439 770526
Email   westview.cottage@btinternet.com
Web   www.westviewcottage.info

Entry 585   Map 13

Yorkshire

Brickfields Farm

Down a long peaceful track, but a stone's throw from bustling Kirkbymoorside, is this walker's paradise. Friendly Janet sends you off to the North Yorks Moors with maps and information, and a tasty breakfast, served at separate tables in the conservatory overlooking guinea fowl and sheep. Bedrooms, one in the house and others in the barn or converted cow shed, are lovely: a French vintage four-poster, antiques, heavy curtains, sprung mattresses, flowers, a hidden fridge. All have stunning views over the fields. Bathrooms have big open showers, thick towels and plenty of lotions. Come to be pampered.

Unsuitable for children.

Rooms	7: 1 twin. Barn: 4 suites. Cow shed: 1 suite, 1 four-poster suite.
Price	£95-£130.
Meals	Pub/restaurant 1 mile.
Closed	Rarely.

Sheila Trousdale Ward & Neil Ward
Brickfields Farm,
Kirkby Mills, Kirkbymoorside,
Yorkshire YO62 6NS
Tel   +44 (0)1751 433074
Email   bookings@brickfieldsfarm.co.uk
Web   www.brickfieldsfarm.co.uk

Entry 586   Map 13

Yorkshire

Low Farm

The first thing you see is the amazing view – it's a jaw-dropper! This handsome old farmhouse in the heart of the North Yorks Moors National Park will relax you from the moment you step in – a warm home where Linda welcomes with tea and homemade cake. Fresh comfortable bedrooms have far-reaching views and immaculate en suite bathrooms. In the morning, feast on freshly squeezed juice and homemade jam, Whitby kippers or the full works, all sourced locally; the polished table in the cosy dining room is set with pretty china and flowers. Castle Howard is a hop, the walks are fabulous and you can stroll to the village bistro.

Rooms	2: 1 double, 1 twin.
Price	£90-£110. Singles £55-£65.
Meals	Packed lunch available. Pub 0.25 miles.
Closed	Rarely.

Linda & Andrew Dagg
Low Farm,
Rosedale Abbey, Pickering,
Yorkshire YO18 8SE
Tel   +44 (0)1751 417003
Email   adagg@moorsweb.co.uk
Web   www.lowfarmrosedale.co.uk

Entry 587   Map 13

Yorkshire

Rectory Farmhouse

Walk from the door straight onto the North Yorkshire Moors; it's a brisk 30-minute stride across fields to the Steam Railway. Michael and Heather have been here since 1997 – along with dogs, horses, a flock of sheep and bountiful hens. Cosy old-fashioned bedrooms have pine furniture, fluffy robes and flowery fabrics. You can relax in front of the log fire, or enjoy homemade cakes and tea or sherry in the guest lounge. Tuck into a hearty breakfast in the dining room; proper Yorkshire dinner too – or it's a short stroll across the green to the pub. Good value – and superb for walking, biking and riding.

Minimum two nights. Over eights welcome

Rooms	4: 1 double, 1 twin. Apartment: 1 double, 1 twin sharing bath (same party only).
Price	£70–£80. Singles from £50.
Meals	Dinner, 2 courses, £15. BYO. Pub in village.
Closed	Christmas & New Year.

Michael & Heather Holt
Rectory Farmhouse,
Levisham, Pickering,
Yorkshire YO18 7NL
Tel   +44 (0)1751 460304
Mobile   +44 (0)7971 625898
Email   info@rectoryfarmlevisham.co.uk
Web   www.rectoryfarmlevisham.co.uk

Entry 588   Map 13

Yorkshire

Union Place

A listed Adam Georgian townhouse – elegance epitomised. Lofty well-proportioned rooms with polished floors and cornices and fireplaces intact are delightfully dotted with sophisticated, quirky *objets*: bead-and-embroidery lampshades and chandeliers, bone china, a small mirrored Indian ceramic child's dress – and your urbane host Richard's accomplished paintings. Bedrooms, one painted duck egg blue, one green with floral wallpaper, are beautiful, with lots of lace and fine linen; the claw-foot roll top in the shared bathroom cuts a dash. Breakfast is unbeatable… then it's off to explore the North York Moors. Superb.

Rooms	2 doubles sharing bath.
Price	£65–£70.
Meals	Pubs/restaurants within walking distance.
Closed	Christmas.

Richard & Jane Pottas
Union Place,
9 Upgang Lane,
Whitby,
Yorkshire YO21 3DT
Tel   +44 (0)1947 605501
Email   pottas1@btinternet.com
Web   www.unionplacewhitby.co.uk

Entry 589   Map 13

Yorkshire

Thorpe Hall

Arrive and listen: nothing, bar the wind in the trees and the odd seagull. The eye gathers glimmering sea and mighty headland, the final edge of the moors... are there still smugglers? This old listed house smells of polish and flowers, the drawing room breathes history. Angelique, a delight, has furnished it all, including TV-free bedrooms, with an eclectic mix of old and new and some fun (a framed transport caff poster in the breakfast room). She's hung contemporary art on ancient walls and has made a veg patch with young Phoebe. David helps out with simple breakfast when he's not globetrotting. The very opposite of stuffy.

Rooms	8: 3 doubles, 1 twin; 4 doubles sharing separate bath & shower rooms.
Price	£70-£90.
Meals	Pub within 0.25 miles.
Closed	Usually Christmas & January.

	Angelique Russell
	Thorpe Hall,
	Middlewood Lane,
	Fylingthorpe,
	Whitby,
	Yorkshire YO22 4TT
Tel	+44 (0)1947 880667
Email	thorpehall@gmail.com
Web	www.thorpe-hall.co.uk

Entry 590   Map 13

Yorkshire

Holly Croft

Huge kindness and thoughtful touches (hot water bottles, lifts to the pub, cake and tea on arrival) make this special. The décor is in Edwardian style, the rooms are scented with flowers and polish, the clock ticks, the comforts are indisputable. The double has a textured silk headboard with matching curtains, there are bathrobes in fitted wardrobes, big showers and generous breakfasts – own jams, Yorkshire teas, kippers if you choose – served at the gleaming mahogany table. After a bracing cliff-top walk return to a homely open-fired sitting room overlooking the lovely garden. Wonderful Whitby is 20 minutes away.

Minimum two nights at weekends during summer.

Rooms	2: 1 twin/double; 1 double with separate bath.
Price	£85-£95. Singles £55-£60.
Meals	Dinner (4+ only), £25. Pub 600 yds.
Closed	Rarely.

	John & Christine Goodall
	Holly Croft,
	28 Station Road, Scalby,
	Scarborough,
	Yorkshire YO13 0QA
Tel	+44 (0)1723 375376
Mobile	+44 (0)7759 429706
Email	christine.goodall@tesco.net
Web	www.holly-croft.co.uk

Entry 591   Map 13

Yorkshire

The Wold Cottage

Drive through mature trees, and a proper entrance with signs, to a listed Georgian manor house in 300 glorious acres; tea awaits in the guest sitting room. The graceful dining room has heart-lifting views across the landscaped gardens, and there are many original features: fanlights, high ceilings, broad staircases. Bedrooms are sumptuous, traditional, with thoughtful extras: chocolates, biscuits, monogrammed waffle robes. You are warmed by straw bale heating, and an award-winning breakfast sets you up for a day of discovery; visit RSPB Bempton Cliffs, and the Wolds that have inspired David Hockney.

Rooms	6: 2 doubles, 2 twins. Barn: 1 four-poster, 1 family room.
Price	£100-£120. Singles £60-£75.
Meals	Supper £25. Wine from £12.95.
Closed	Rarely.

Derek & Katrina Gray
The Wold Cottage,
Wold Newton,
Driffield,
Yorkshire YO25 3HL

Tel	+44 (0)1262 470696
Mobile	+44 (0)7811 203336
Email	katrina@woldcottage.com
Web	www.woldcottage.com

Entry 592 Map 13

Yorkshire

Village Farm

Tucked behind houses and shops, this was once the village farm with land stretching to the coast. Now the one-storey buildings overlooking a courtyard are large bedrooms in gorgeous colours with luxurious touches. Chrysta, who moved from London, is living her dream and looks after you well: baths are deep, beds crisply comfortable, heating is underfoot. Delicious breakfasts are served at wooden tables in a cheerful light room with a contemporary feel; dinner is candlelit and locally sourced. Stride the cliffs, watch birds at Flamborough Head or make for Spurn Point – remote and lovely.

Rooms	3: 1 double, 1 twin/double, 1 family room for 4.
Price	£80. Family room £95. Singles £60. Half-board option (dinner, 2 courses) £110 p.p. Dogs £5.
Meals	Dinner, 2-3 courses, £18-£22. Pubs/restaurants within 20 yds.
Closed	Rarely.

Chrysta Newman
Village Farm,
Back Street,
Skipsea,
Driffield,
Yorkshire YO25 8SW

Tel	+44 (0)1262 468479
Email	villagefarmskipsea@yahoo.com
Web	www.villagefarmskipsea.co.uk

Entry 593 Map 13

Channel Islands

Guernsey

Seabreeze

Maggie's house – the most southern on Guernsey – comes with enormous views: Herm and Sark glistening in the water under a vast sky. The breakfast terrace is hard to beat, there are sofas in the conservatory, cliff-top paths for fabulous walks, a beach for picnics in summer. The house started life as HQ for French pilots flying seaplanes in WWI; these days warm, rustic interiors make for a great island base. It's not grand, just very welcoming with rooms that hit the spot: pretty linen, bathrobes, super showers, fresh flowers. You can hire bikes locally, then spin up the lane to a top island restaurant. Brilliant.

Rooms	3: 1 twin/double; 1 twin/double & kitchen; 1 double (extra single bed).
Price	£70–£95. Reduction for single occupancy £25 per night.
Meals	Pubs/restaurants 500 yds & 0.5 miles.
Closed	Rarely.

	Maggie Talbot-Cull
	Seabreeze,
	La Moye Lane, Route de Jerbourg,
	St Martin,
	Guernsey GY4 6BN
Tel	+44 (0)1481 237929
Email	seabreeze-guernsey@mail.com
Web	www.guernseybandb.com

Entry 594   Map 4

Scotland

Aberdeenshire

Lynturk Home Farm

The stunning drawing room, with pier-glass mirror, baby grand and enveloping sofas, is reason enough to come; the food, served in a candlelit, deep-sage dining room, is delicious, with produce from the farm. You're treated as friends here and your hosts are delightful. It's peaceful, too, on the Aberdeenshire Castle Trail. The handsome farmhouse has been in the family since 1762 and you can roam the surrounding, rolling, 300 acres. Inside: flowers, polished furniture, Persian rugs, family portraits and supremely comfortable bedrooms. "A blissful haven," says a guest.

Fishing, shooting & golf breaks.

Rooms	3: 1 double, 2 twins/doubles.
Price	£90. Singles £50.
Meals	Dinner, 4 courses, £30. Pub 1 mile.
Closed	Rarely.

John & Veronica Evans-Freke
Lynturk Home Farm,
Alford,
Aberdeenshire AB33 8HU
Tel   +44 (0)1975 562504
Mobile   +44 (0)7773 389793
Email   lynturk@hotmail.com

Entry 595 Map 19

Aberdeenshire

Balwarren

Thirty acres at the end of a farm track, a field of Highland cattle, mixed woodland, ancient dykes, a wildlife pond, a herb garden, and a burn you may follow down the hill. Hazel and James, warm, friendly, quietly passionate about green issues, came to croft 25 years ago and the whole place is a delight: cathedral roof, shiny wooden floors, cashmere blankets, wood-burning stove, green views. Enjoy superb breakfasts and dinners: eggs from their hens, homemade marmalade and jams, beef from their cattle. A beautiful, uplifting and peaceful place in glorious countryside.

Rooms	2: 1 twin, 1 double.
Price	£75-£85. Singles £50.
Meals	Dinner, 3 courses, £25. Afternoon tea £4. Pub/restaurant 10 miles.
Closed	Rarely.

Hazel & James Watt
Balwarren,
Ordiquhill, Banff,
Aberdeenshire AB45 2HR
Tel   +44 (0)1466 751688
Email   balwarrenbedandbreakfast@gmail.com
Web   www.balwarren.com

Entry 596 Map 19

Aberdeenshire

West Mains Steading

Spot red kites and white hare from the big garden, as you relish the long peaceful views. This converted farm steading on what was the Castle Fraser estate has had a smart renovation. Anne welcomes you with home baking, brings wonderful breakfasts to an elegant polished table and helps you plan your day: enjoy castles, stone circles, fishing and golf. Return to books, games, a piano, warmth, spaciousness and light, and soft-carpeted bedrooms in a separate wing. There are firm mattresses, huge wardrobes, and dressing gowns for quick dashes to private bathrooms, replete with heated rails for towels and lots of lovely smellies.

Rooms	2: 1 double, 1 twin/double, each with separate bath.
Price	£80. Singles £50.
Meals	Restaurant 10-minute walk.
Closed	Rarely.

Anne Harrison
West Mains Steading,
Castle Fraser, Kemnay,
Inverurie,
Aberdeenshire AB51 7JS

Tel	+44 (0)1330 833351
Email	info@westmainssteading.co.uk
Web	www.westmainssteading.co.uk

Entry 597   Map 19

Angus

Newtonmill House

The house and grounds are in perfect order; the owners are warm, charming and discreet. This is a little-known part of Scotland, with glens and gardens to discover; fishing villages, golf courses and deserted beaches, too. Return to a cup of tea in the sitting room or summerhouse, a wander in the lovely walled garden, and a marvellous supper of local produce; Rose grows interesting varieties of potato and her hens' eggs make a great hollandaise! Upstairs are crisp sheets, soft blankets, feather pillows, flowers, homemade fruit cake and warm sparkling bathrooms with thick towels. Let this home envelop you in its warm embrace.

Dogs by arrangement.

Rooms	2: 1 twin; 1 double with separate bath.
Price	£100-£120. Singles from £70.
Meals	Dinner, £28-£36. BYO. Packed lunch £10. Pub 3 miles.
Closed	Christmas.

Rose & Stephen Rickman
Newtonmill House,
Brechin,
Angus DD9 7PZ

Tel	+44 (0)1356 622533
Mobile	+44 (0)7793 169482
Email	rrickman@srickman.co.uk
Web	www.newtonmillhouse.co.uk

Entry 598   Map 19

Argyll & Bute – Isle of Arran

Hawthorn Cottage

The most southerly of the Scottish islands, Arran is splendid for nature lovers. When you've worn yourselves out you can flop in Fiona's low, whitewashed cottage. It's up a bumpy track and far from smart but brimming with reality. The cottage is split in two: you get one end with a bedroom (up a rusty spiral stair), a bathroom and a sitting room (downstairs) and a small kitchen area: find hotchpotch furniture, original old bath, frayed rugs, a piano, a cosy wood-burner to sit by and electric storage heating for chilly days. Fiona leaves your continental breakfast hanging on the door. Will not suit boutique hotel lovers one iota!

Rooms	1 twin/double with separate bath & kitchenette.
Price	£50.
Meals	Continental breakfast. Pub/restaurant 2 miles.
Closed	Rarely.

Fiona Mackenzie
Hawthorn Cottage,
Brodick,
Isle of Arran,
Argyll & Bute KA27 8DF
Tel   +44 (0)1770 302534
Email   fionamackenzie569@btinternet.com
Web   www.hawthorn-cottage.eu

Entry 599   Map 14

Argyll & Bute

Melfort House

Enter a wild landscape of hidden glens, ancient woods and rivers that tumble to a blue sea. Find a big beautiful house with views straight down the loch, aglow with exquisite fabrics and polished antiques, fine oak floors, paintings and prints. Bedrooms have upholstered beds in soft plaids, delicious colours, superb views and handmade chocolates; bathrooms have huge towels and locally made soaps. Yvonne and Matthew are brilliant at looking after you: breakfasts of Stornoway black pudding, chilli omelettes, tattie scones, kedgeree. Sally forth with boots or bikes, come home to a dram and a roaring log fire. Argyll at its finest.

Rooms	3: 2 twins/doubles, 1 suite.
Price	£95-£125. Singles from £70. Sofabed £15.
Meals	Dinner, 3 courses, from £32. Packed lunch £10. Pub/restaurant 400 yds.
Closed	Rarely.

Yvonne & Matthew Anderson
Melfort House,
Kilmelford, Oban,
Argyll & Bute PA34 4XD
Tel   +44 (0)1852 200326
Mobile +44 (0)7795 438106
Email   relax@melforthouse.co.uk
Web   www.melforthouse.co.uk

Entry 600   Map 14

Glenmore

An easy-going, traditional country house with no need to stand on ceremony. Built in the 1800s but with later 1930s additions setting the style, find solid oak doors and floors, red-pine panelling, Art Deco pieces and a unique carved staircase. Alasdair's family has been here for 150 years and many family antiques remain. One of the huge doubles can be arranged as a suite to include a single room and a sofabed; bath and basins are chunky 30s style with chrome plumbing. From the organic garden and the house there are magnificent views of Loch Melfort with its bobbing boats; you're free to come and go as you please.

Rooms	2: 1 family room; 1 double with separate bath/shower.
Price	£85-£100. Family room £95-£170. Singles £50-£65.
Meals	Pub 0.5 miles, restaurant 1.5 miles.
Closed	Christmas & New Year.

Melissa & Alasdair Oatts
Glenmore,
Kilmelford, Oban,
Argyll & Bute PA34 4XA

Tel	+44 (0)1852 200314
Mobile	+44 (0)7786 340468
Email	oatts@glenmore22.fsnet.co.uk
Web	www.glenmorecountryhouse.co.uk

Entry 601   Map 17

Greystones

A baronial mansion built for the owner of a diamond mine. He clearly liked a good view — a five-mile sweep across Oban bay lands on the Isle of Mull. Inside, bright white interiors soak up the light, while coolly uncluttered bedrooms have chic bathrooms and well-dressed beds. One has a turret with armchairs looking out to sea, another has a vast walk-in shower, three have the view. You breakfast downstairs on honey-drenched porridge while watching boats come and go on the water. There's a sitting room with smart sofas, a list of local restaurants, a library of DVDs. Castles and gardens wait, as do ferries to far-flung islands.

Minimum two nights in bigger rooms.

Rooms	5: 4 doubles, 1 suite.
Price	£110-£145. Suite £160. Singles from £80.
Meals	Pubs/restaurants 5-minute walk.
Closed	Rarely.

Mark & Suzanne McPhillips
Greystones,
13 Dalriach Road,
Oban,
Argyll & Bute PA34 5EQ

Tel	+44 (0)1631 358653
Email	stay@greystonesoban.co.uk
Web	www.greystonesoban.co.uk

Entry 602   Map 17

Argyll & Bute

Ardtorna

Come for perfect comfort and uninterrupted views of loch and mountain. These thoughtful, professional hosts are happy to share their new, open-plan, eco-friendly house where contemporary Scandinavian and Art Deco styles are cleverly blended with homely warmth. Sink into a bedroom with a wall of glass for those views; each has a wet room or spa bath with Molton Brown treats. Flowers and jauntily coloured coffee pots decorate the oak table in the stunning dining room, and food is home-baked and delicious. Argyll brims with historic sites and walks; return to watch the sun go down over the Morvern hills. Fabulous.

Rooms	4 twins/doubles.
Price	£150-£200. Singles from £125.
Meals	Room service supper £10-£20. Pub/restaurant 3 miles.
Closed	Rarely.

Karen O'Byrne
Ardtorna,
Mill Farm, Barcaldine,
Oban,
Argyll & Bute PA37 1SE

Tel	+44 (0)1631 720125
Mobile	+44 (0)7867 785524
Email	info@ardtorna.co.uk
Web	www.ardtorna.co.uk

Entry 603   Map 17

Argyll & Bute – Isle of Mull

Ardnacross Farm

This Aberdeen Angus cattle farm borders Mull's stunning coastline, where eagles, whales, red deer and otters leap, swoop, breach and soar. Rory and Penelope are warm and friendly, their farmhouse wonderfully homely: the dining room has a huge antique table and open fire; your bedroom (up private stairs) has a pretty patterned bedspread and floral curtains. The Scottish breakfast with Ardnacross eggs and porridge is hearty. Tobermory has everything from very good fish and chips and pleasant restaurants to an excellent theatre and festival; you can catch a boat trip to Iona or Staffa too. A beautiful slice of island Scotland.

Rooms	1 double.
Price	£75.
Meals	Pubs/restaurants 5 miles.
Closed	Christmas & New Year.

Rory & Penelope Forrester
Ardnacross Farm,
Aros,
Isle of Mull,
Argyll & Bute PA72 6JS

Tel	+44 (0)1680 300262
Email	enquiries@ardnacross.com
Web	www.holidaycottages-mull.co.uk

Entry 604   Map 17

Argyll & Bute – Isle of Mull

HotelForTwo

For friends or for two: your own stone cottage sitting in the middle of a row of jaunty colours. The door opens to Julia, who makes you feel immediately at home; an ex-foreign correspondent, she has oodles of panache and an easy charm. Her home is intimate, cosy, filled with tapestries, antiques, chintzy sofas, curious artwork and a tousle of books; bedrooms (one up, one down) come in cottage chic with gorgeous bed linen. Julia lives in a bothy at the top of the garden, so the house is all yours with delicious meals all provided too. The bay bursts with boats and Mull is a treat: wildlife, whale tours, castles, good eating.

Self-catering available.

Rooms	2: 1 double; 1 double with separate bath (let to same party only).
Price	£80.
Meals	Dinner £35. Afternoon tea £12.50. Packed lunch £15. Restaurants 15-minute walk.
Closed	Winter.

	Julia Watson
	HotelForTwo,
	5 Argyll Terrace, Tobermory,
	Isle of Mull,
	Argyll & Bute PA75 6PB
Mobile	+44 (0)7990 940562
Email	watson.julia@gmail.com
Web	www.hotelfortwo.co.uk

Entry 605 Map 17

Argyll & Bute

Meall Mo Chridhe

Caring owners, exquisite food and a welcome sight, surrounded by the savage beauty of Britain's most westerly village. The warm ochre walls of this listed Georgian manse peep through wooded gardens across the Sound to Mull. Rooms are beautiful – French antiques, a wood stove, roll top baths – but it's the food that draws most to this far-flung spot. What David magics from his 45-acre smallholding (a bit of everything that grows, grunts, bleats or quacks) Stella transforms into feasts. Dine on spiced mackerel, minted lamb, hazelnut meringue; and duck eggs at breakfast. A gem buried in spectacular, wild walking country.

Rooms	3 doubles.
Price	£103–£204. Singles £51.50–£102.
Meals	Dinner from £37. Pub 0.25 miles.
Closed	Rarely.

	Stella & David Cash
	Meall Mo Chridhe,
	Kilchoan, Acharacle,
	Argyll & Bute PH36 4LH
Tel	+44 (0)1972 510238
Mobile	+44 (0)7730 100639
Email	enquiries@westcoastscotland.co.uk
Web	www.westcoastscotland.co.uk

Entry 606 Map 17

Ayrshire

Heughmill

Acres of fields and lawn with free-range hens that kindly donate for breakfast and views to the sea. The house is just as good, surrounded by old stone farm buildings, with climbing roses and a small burn tumbling through. Inside, a lovely country home with tapestries in an airy hall, open fire in the sitting room and a terrace that sits under a vast sky. Country-house bedrooms with delightful art are stylishly homely. Two have the view, others come with claw-foot bath or an old armoire. Your hosts are relaxed and entertaining – Julia sculpts, Mungo cooks breakfast on the Aga, rural Ayrshire awaits.

Ayrshire

The Pits

We're often staggered by the ingenuity of our owners. What may be seen by some as a rather unprepossessing stretch of land alongside a rubble-strewn wattle and daub hovel is now a unique B&B. The rigorous minimalism of the build was such that Kevin McCloud started sniffing about but felt that it was perhaps too avant-garde. Luxuries are scant – the yellow bowl (just seen) has cunningly been pressed into service as a bath and outside privy. But breakfast is a feast: warm croissants, homemade jams and granola, fresh fruit and organic sausages but there is a catch – it's BYO. One of our more 'Special' finds.

Rooms	3: 2 twins/doubles, 1 twin.
Price	£65–£80. Singles on request.
Meals	Pubs/restaurants within 2 miles.
Closed	Christmas & New Year.

Rooms	Unlikely.
Price	Owner pays you.
Meals	Let's hope not.
Closed	No, open to the skies.

	Mungo & Julia Tulloch
	Heughmill,
	Craigie, Kilmarnock,
	Ayrshire KA1 5NQ
Tel	+44 (0)1563 860389
Email	mungotulloch@hotmail.com
Web	www.stayprestwick.com

	Tony Bwoke
	The Pits,
	Sticks and Stones,
	Ayrshire
Web	www.ohnopleaseno.com

Entry 607   Map 14

Entry 608   Map 14

Dumfries & Galloway

The House on the Shore

Impossible not to be wowed by this incredible shoreline setting with views across the Solway Firth. The 1,250-acre estate has been in Jamie's family for generations; he and Sheri are excellent hosts and love their dower house with its rich and varied woodland and wildlife, formal gardens and stupendous views. Grand but with a family feel, this is old country house style at its best with rugs on polished floors, paintings, open fires and fresh flowers. The farm produces its own meat, an enormous walled kitchen garden is being restored, and a peach tree fruits abundantly; you'll eat well. Very special.

Rooms	2: 1 double, 1 twin.
Price	£90–£100. Singles £60–£80.
Meals	Dinner, 3 courses, £25. BYO. Pub/restaurant 2 miles.
Closed	Rarely.

	Jamie & Sheri Blackett
	The House on the Shore,
	Arbigland, Kirkbean,
	Dumfries,
	Dumfries & Galloway DG2 8BQ
Tel	+44 (0)1387 880717
Email	sheri@arbigland.com
Web	www.arbiglandestate.co.uk

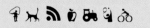

Entry 609   Map 11

Dumfries & Galloway

Chipperkyle

This beautiful Scottish-Georgian family home has not a hint of formality, and the sociable Dicksons put you at your ease. Your sitting and dining rooms connect through a large arch; there are gloriously comfortable sofas, family pictures, rugs on wooden floors, masses of books and a constant log fire. Upstairs: good linen, striped walls, thick curtains, armchairs and windows with views – this wonderful house just gets better and better. There are 200 acres, dogs, cats, donkeys and hens (children can collect the eggs!), and you can walk, play golf, watch birds, visit gardens, sail or cycle – all in magnificent countryside.

Minimum two nights at weekends (May-Sept, bank holidays).

Rooms	2: 1 double; 1 twin with separate bath/shower. (Cot available.)
Price	£100. Discounts for children.
Meals	Occasional dinner available for groups. Pub 3 miles.
Closed	Christmas.

	Willie & Catriona Dickson
	Chipperkyle,
	Kirkpatrick Durham, Castle Douglas,
	Dumfries & Galloway DG7 3EY
Tel	+44 (0)1556 650223
Mobile	+44 (0)7917 730009
Email	special_place@chipperkyle.co.uk
Web	www.chipperkyle.co.uk

Entry 610   Map 11

Dumfries & Galloway

Chlenry Farmhouse

Handsome in its glen; a traditional family farmhouse full of old-fashioned comfort with charming, well-travelled owners and friendly dogs. In peaceful bedrooms with leafy views, solid antiques jostle with photos, flowers, bowls of fruit, and magazines on country matters. There are capacious bath tubs, robes – and suppers for walkers with the Southern Upland Way passing nearby. Breakfasts are properly fortifying, evening meals can be simple or elaborate, often with game or fresh salmon. Convenient for ferries to Belfast and Larne; Galloway gardens and golf courses are close too – return to a snug sitting room with an open fire.

Rooms	3: 1 twin/double with separate bath; 1 double, 1 twin sharing bath.
Price	£80. Singles £50.
Meals	Supper £17.50. Dinner, 4 courses, £35. Packed lunch £6. Pub 1.5 miles.
Closed	Christmas, New Year, February & occasionally.

David & Ginny Wolsley Brinton
Chlenry Farmhouse,
Castle Kennedy, Stranraer,
Dumfries & Galloway DG9 8SL

Tel	+44 (0)1776 705316
Mobile	+44 (0)7704 205003
Email	wolseleybrinton@aol.com
Web	www.chlenryfarmhouse.com

Entry 611 Map 14

Dumfries & Galloway

Holmhill Country House

Among the rolling hills of Dumfries and Galloway, by the banks of the Nith, is a hidden gem of a Georgian country house. It was a favourite of philosopher Thomas Carlyle, who had his own pipe-smoking spot in the marvellously colourful garden. There are seven acres to explore, utter tranquillity, stunning views of the Keir Hills and excellent fishing. Rosie and Stewart love sharing their family home with guests, and can treat you to breakfast, and possibly dinner, by the fire in the graceful dining room. Masses of space everywhere, each room deftly combining rustic virtue with modern savoir-faire.

Rooms	2 twins/doubles.
Price	£83–£100. Singles £55–£70.
Meals	Pubs/restaurants 0.5 miles.
Closed	Christmas & New Year.

Rosie Lee
Holmhill Country House,
Thornhill,
Dumfries & Galloway DG3 4AB

Tel	+44 (0)1848 332239
Email	booking@holmhill.co.uk
Web	www.holmhill.co.uk

Entry 612 Map 15

Dumfries & Galloway

Byreburnfoot House

Tucked away down a gravelled drive on the banks of the salmon-rich Esk, this pretty Victorian forester's house combines traditional charm with modern comforts. Airy rooms and wooden floors offset antique pieces — grandfather clock, writing desk, chandeliers — within an elegant rural décor: cushioned bay windows, fashionable florals. Beds are big, the linen is trimmed and the views are sublime. Warm hosts Bill and Lorraine are keenly green-fingered, and their 1.5 acres of orchards, flower-fringed lawns and organic kitchen garden are deliciously productive. Stay a few days and become part of the scenery.

Fishing available.

Rooms	3: 2 doubles; 1 twin/double with separate bath.
Price	£90-£95. Singles £65.
Meals	Dinner, 3 courses, £30. Packed lunch from £7.50. Pub/restaurant 5 miles.
Closed	Rarely.

Bill & Lorraine Frew
Byreburnfoot House,
Canonbie,
Dumfries & Galloway DG14 0XB
Tel   +44 (0)1387 371209
Mobile   +44 (0)7764 194901
Email   enquiries@byreburnfoot.co.uk
Web   www.byreburnfoot.co.uk

Entry 613   Map 15

Dumfries & Galloway CANOPY&STARS

Harelawhill Eco Yurt

On the Scottish side of the border at Harelawhill is a rustic yurt on a working farm. Diana and Michael make (and paint) anything, and love local music: certain nights see gigs happening here. A wandering friend dropped off a yurt on her way back from Mongolia! Now it has gas hobs and a grill for knocking supper together, a big double bed and a wood-burning stove. In the house, an eco-friendly 'one shower per day' is cordially requested, and the compost loo is a step away; it's super sustainable, and great for walkers and wanderers. Good value breakfast baskets greet you in the morning — then it's off to hike the hills.

Minimum two nights at weekends and in summer. Book through Sawday's Canopy & Stars online or by phone.

Rooms	Yurt for 4; shower in house & compost loo close by.
Price	£65.
Meals	Continental breakfast hamper for two, £8. Pub within 2 miles.
Closed	November-March.

Sawday's Canopy & Stars
Harelawhill Eco Yurt,
Kiln Cottage, Canonbie,
Dumfries & Galloway DG14 0RX
Tel   +44 (0)1275 395447
Email   enquiries@canopyandstars.co.uk
Web   www.canopyandstars.co.uk/
harelawhill

Entry 614   Map 15

Dunbartonshire

Finglen House

The Campsie Hills rise behind (climb them and you can see Loch Lomond), the Fin Burn takes a two-mile tumble down the hill into the garden, and herons and wagtails can be spotted from the breakfast table. All this 40 minutes from Glasgow. Sabrina's designer flair gives an easy, graceful comfort to the whole house: good beds in stylish rooms, proper linen, French touches, eclectic art and cast-iron baths. Douglas, a documentary film maker, knows the Highlands and Islands well; he and Sabrina are fun and wonderful hosts. Plenty of walks from the door, golf courses close by too; return to a log fire in the elegant drawing room.

Rooms	2: 1 double; 1 double with separate bath.
Price	£100. Singles £55.
Meals	Pub 5-minute drive.
Closed	Christmas & New Year.

Sabrina & Douglas Campbell
Finglen House,
Campsie Glen,
Dunbartonshire G66 7AZ
Tel   +44 (0)1360 310279
Mobile   +44 (0)7774 820454
Email   sabrina.campbell@btinternet.com
Web   www.finglenhouse.com

Entry 615   Map 15

Edinburgh & the Lothians

2 Cambridge Street

A mischievous humour, tinged with historical and cultural references, alerts you to the specialness of this place, a ground-floor B&B under the lee of Edinburgh Castle, in the heart of theatre land. Find fin-de-siècle Scotland, with darkly striking colours on walls, antiques aplenty, and a captivating attention to detail. There are interactive art installations that sing and play, a line of old theatre seats up on the wall, photos and 'objets' serving startling and original purposes. Erlend and Hélène are delightful and free-spirited; Erlend, a quietly spoken (but don't be fooled) Shetlander, serves a breakfast to remember.

Rooms	2 doubles.
Price	£95-£135. Singles £90-£110.
Meals	Pubs/restaurants 1-minute walk.
Closed	Christmas.

Erlend & Hélène Clouston
2 Cambridge Street,
Edinburgh EH1 2DY
Tel   +44 (0)131 478 0005
Email   erlendc@blueyonder.co.uk
Web   www.wwwonderful.net

Entry 616   Map 15

14 Hart Street

The brightly lit Georgian house has a smart front of polished brass and glossy paint. The warm raspberry hall is lined with art, and the graceful dining room is just as inviting: decanters on the sideboard, period furniture, glowing lamps, and a welcoming home-baked something. Fresh bright bedrooms are elegant and comfortable with whisky and wine on a tray and smart, sparkling bathrooms. Wake for breakfast at a beautifully polished table, with plenty of coffee, newspapers and chat; James and Angela are easy to talk to and love having guests to stay. Perfect for a peaceful city break, and Princes Street is a five-minute walk.

24 Saxe Coburg Place

A ten-minute walk from the centre of Edinburgh, this 1827 house stands in a quiet Georgian square with a central communal garden. The three attractive bedrooms are on the garden level and are self-contained with their own entrance; find comfortable beds, good lighting, handsome antiques and a small kitchen for making tea and coffee. Bathrooms are spotless and one has Paris metro tiling in white and green. Excitingly you can nip over the road to the refurbished Victorian Baths for a swim, sauna or workout in the gym; return to a generous continental breakfast served in the little hall – or on the pretty terrace in summer.

Rooms	3: 2 doubles, 1 twin/double.		Rooms	3: 1 double, 1 twin/double, 1 single.
Price	£84–£120.		Price	£90–£130. Singles £48–£60.
Meals	Restaurants 10-minute walk.		Meals	Continental breakfast.
Closed	Rarely.			Restaurants/pubs 5-minute walk.
			Closed	Rarely.

James & Angela Wilson	**Diana McMicking**
14 Hart Street,	24 Saxe Coburg Place,
Edinburgh EH1 3RN	Edinburgh EH3 5BP
Tel +44 (0)131 557 6826	Tel +44 (0)131 315 3263
Mobile +44 (0)7795 203414	Mobile +44 (0)7979 351717
Email hartst.edin@virgin.net	Email diana@saxecoburgplace.co.uk
Web www.14hartst.com	Web www.saxecoburgplace.co.uk

7 Gloucester Place

A cantilevered staircase in walnut and mahogany, a soaring hand-painted cupola, and a classic Georgian townhouse five minutes from Princes Street. Rooms are large and immaculate, sprinkled with paintings and decorative things from travels to far-flung places, while bedrooms are comfortable, traditional and well-stocked with books and radio (and a useful Z-bed). Bag the south-facing double with its Art Deco bathroom and garden views. Naomi is relaxed and happy to chat to you about the local music and art scene, or to leave you in peace. An interesting and hospitable place to unwind, and breakfasts are delicious.

.

10 London Street

A Roman X marks this special spot: a beautiful Georgian terraced house in Edinburgh's world heritage New Town, home to descendants of Scots author John Gibson Lockhart. Step into a family home of period elegance and charming informality: accept a dram by the fire in the sash-windowed drawing room (with baby grand piano), relax at the dining table over a leisurely continental breakfast. Sleep undisturbed in 'Beauregard', with its lovely views and paintings; or 'Gibson' with its off-courtyard privacy and self-catering option. The best of Edinburgh is a stroll away, good buses zip you further afield, and at night-time all is quiet.

Rooms	3: 1 double; 1 double with separate bath; 1 double with separate shower. (Extra child beds.)
Price	£90–£120. Singles from £70.
Meals	Pubs/restaurants 300 yds.
Closed	Christmas & rarely.

Rooms	2 doubles (one with self-catering option).
Price	£100–£120.
Meals	Continental breakfast. Pub/restaurant 500 yds.
Closed	Rarely.

	Naomi Jennings
	7 Gloucester Place,
	Edinburgh EH3 6EE
Tel	+44 (0)131 225 2974
Mobile	+44 (0)7803 168106
Email	naomijennings@hotmail.com
Web	www.stayinginscotland.com

	Pippa Lockhart
	10 London Street,
	Edinburgh EH3 6NA
Tel	+44 (0)131 556 0737
Email	pippa@hjlockhart.co.uk
Web	www.londonstreetaccommodation.co.uk

Entry 619   Map 15

Entry 620   Map 15

Edinburgh & the Lothians

Edinburgh & the Lothians

Geraldsplace

Elegant Georgian New Town... so splendid and handsome it's a World Heritage Site. Welcoming, enthusiastic, charming Gerald runs a B&B on one of its finest streets. His patio basement apartment is full of character, comfort and colour. Bedrooms have cosiness, warmth, fine fabrics, excellent art... and special extras: DVDs and a book swop shelf, a laptop with fast broadband, a tea tray, a decanter of single malt whisky; bathrooms are newly done. Breakfast is a feast and mostly organic. There's a private garden opposite, an incredibly convenient location and, of course, Gerald, your brilliantly well-informed, up-to-the-minute host.

Minimum stay three nights.

22 Royal Circus

Step from an elegant cobbled crescent in Georgian New Town into another world: of Aga-cooked breakfasts, landscaped gardens and a farmhouse kitchen you're welcome to share. Well-travelled Kirsty has filled her listed, William Playfair-designed basement flat with bold reds and yellows, family art and Indian treasures. Choose the romantic Moroccan-style en suite or the larger, brighter family room. Young fruit trees and carved garden furniture dot the grounds; seasoned botanists can trot to the Botanic Garden; shoppers can walk to Princes Street through World Heritage streets of delis, cafés, restaurants. Charming!

Minimum two nights at weekends.

Rooms	2 twins/doubles.
Price	£69-£129. Additional supplement during festivals.
Meals	Restaurants within 3-minute walk.
Closed	Rarely.

Rooms	2: 1 double; 1 family room with separate bath.
Price	£89-£119. Additional supplement during festivals.
Meals	Pubs/restaurants 2-minute walk.
Closed	Christmas.

Gerald Della-Porta
Geraldsplace,
21b Abercromby Place,
Edinburgh EH3 6QE
Tel   +44 (0)131 558 7017
Mobile   +44 (0)7766 016840
Email   gerald11@geraldsplace.com
Web   www.geraldsplace.com

Kirsty MacGregor
22 Royal Circus,
Edinburgh EH3 6SS
Tel   +44 (0)1312 261303
Email   stay@22royalcircus.co.uk
Web   www.22royalcircus.co.uk

Entry 621   Map 15

Entry 622   Map 15

Edinburgh & the Lothians

Number29

You overlook the green of St Mary's Cathedral from this elegant, Georgian, West End townhouse – a stone's throw from Princes Street. Renovated with style and quirky touches, it feels grand yet friendly; Simon and Corinne welcome you into their home with charm. Ceilings are high, cornices and wooden shutters original and light floods in. The beautiful staircase is crowned by a cupola and lit at night, a wood-burner warms you in the dining room and you sleep in peaceful bedrooms with views, restful with flowers and immaculately dressed beds. Wake for a splendid, locally sourced variety of treats at breakfast. A delicious place.

Rooms	3: 1 double, 2 suites.
Price	£100–£120. Suites £110–£170. Singles from £100.
Meals	Pubs/restaurants 150 yds.
Closed	Rarely.

Simon & Corinne Rawlins
Number29,
29 Manor Place,
Edinburgh EH3 7DX
Tel   +44 (0)1312 256385
Mobile +44 (0)7780 527500
Email   info@number29edinburgh.co.uk
Web   www.number29edinburgh.co.uk

Entry 623   Map 15

Edinburgh & the Lothians

11 Belford Place

Guests love Sue's modern townhouse, quietly tucked away in a private road above the Water of Leith yet a short distance from the city. From the wooden-floored entrance a picture-lined staircase winds upward. Handsome bedrooms display china cups and floral spreads; dazzling bathrooms have Molton Brown goodies. Wake for Stornoway black pudding, kedgeree, homemade jams and delicious ginger compote at the gleaming table. Owls sometimes hoot in the pretty sloping garden, there's an outside luggage store, parking is free and art galleries and Murrayfield Stadium are nearby.

Minimum two nights in August. Children over 12 welcome.

Rooms	3: 1 double, 2 twins/doubles.
Price	£70–£120. Singles £50–£60.
Meals	Restaurants 10-minute walk.
Closed	Christmas.

Susan Kinross
11 Belford Place,
Edinburgh EH4 3DH
Tel   +44 (0)131 332 9704
Mobile +44 (0)7712 836399
Email   suekinross@blueyonder.co.uk

Entry 624   Map 15

Edinburgh & the Lothians

12 Belford Terrace

Leafy trees, a secluded garden, a stone wall and, beyond, a quiet riverside stroll. On the doorstep of the Modern Art and Dean galleries with Edinburgh's theatres and restaurants just a 15-minute walk, this Victorian end terrace, beside Leith Water, oozes an easy-going elegance, helped by Carolyn's laid-back but competent manner. Garden level bedrooms have their own entrance and are big and creamy with stripy fabrics, antiques, sofas and huge windows. (The single has a Boy's Own charm.) Carolyn spoils with crisp linen, books and biscuits and a delicious, full-works breakfast. After a day in town, relax on the sunny terrace.

Rooms	3: 1 double, 1 twin/double; 1 single with separate shower.
Price	£70–£110. Singles £40–£55.
Meals	Pub/restaurants within 10-minute walk.
Closed	Christmas.

Carolyn Crabbie
12 Belford Terrace,
Edinburgh EH4 3DQ
Tel   +44 (0)131 332 2413
Email   carolyncrabbie@blueyonder.co.uk

Edinburgh & the Lothians

Wallace's Arthouse Scotland

The apartment door swings open to a world of white walls, smooth floors, modern art, acoustic jazz, and smiling Wallace with a glass of wine — well worth the three-storey climb up this old Assembly Rooms building. Your host — New York fashion designer and arts enthusiast, Glasgow-born, not shy — has created a bright, minimalist space sprinkled with humour and casual sophistication. Bedrooms capture light and exude his inimitable style; the kitchen's narrow bar is perfect for a light breakfast. Leith is Edinburgh's earthy side with its docks and noisy street life, but fine restaurants abound and the centre is close. Memorable.

Rooms	2 doubles.
Price	£105. Singles £95.
Meals	Pubs/restaurants 10 yds.
Closed	Christmas Eve & Christmas Day.

Wallace Shaw
Wallace's Arthouse Scotland,
41-4 Constitution Street,
Edinburgh EH6 7BG
Tel   +44 (0)131 538 3320
Mobile   +44 (0)7941 343714
Email   cawallaceshaw@mac.com
Web   www.wallacesarthousescotland.com

Two Hillside Crescent

Leave your worries behind as you enter this exquisitely restored Georgian townhouse. All is peaceful, spacious and light, with an upbeat contemporary feel. Bedrooms are on the first and second floors: imagine sleek modern furniture, big beds, superb mattresses, clouds of goose down, crisp linen, and immaculate bathrooms with organic toiletries and lashings of hot water. Over a superb breakfast your charming hosts will help you get the most out of your stay. Calton Hill is across the road for the best views of the city, and you're a stroll from the start of the Royal Mile. Wonderful.

2 Fingal Place

An elegant house on a Georgian terrace. The leafy park lies opposite (look upwards to Arthur's Seat). Bustling theatres, shops and the university are a stroll away, yet this is a very quiet house. Your hostess is sometimes away so you may be looked after by a housekeeper, but when at home Gillian can help plan your trips – or cater for celebrations and graduations with lunch and dinner; it's entirely flexible. Downstairs at garden level bedrooms have mahogany antique beds, floral curtains and bathrooms with good towels. Noodle the Llasa Apso will welcome you.

Parking metered 8.30–5.30pm weekdays.

Rooms	5 twins/doubles.
Price	£115-£155.
Meals	Pubs/restaurants across the road.
Closed	Rarely.

Rooms	2: 1 twin (with single room attached), 1 twin.
Price	£90-£140. £100-£150 during Festival. Singles from £55 (from £80 during Festival).
Meals	Pubs/restaurants 100 yds.
Closed	22-27 December.

	Elaine Adams
	Two Hillside Crescent,
	Edinburgh EH7 5DY
Tel	+44 (0)131 556 4871
Email	info@twohillsidecrescent.com
Web	www.twohillsidecrescent.com

	Gillian Charlton-Meyrick
	2 Fingal Place,
	The Meadows,
	Edinburgh EH9 1JX
Tel	+44 (0)131 667 4436
Mobile	+44 (0)7880 705022
Email	gcmeyrick@fireflyuk.net
Web	www.fingalplace.co.uk

Entry 627   Map 15

Entry 628   Map 15

Edinburgh & the Lothians

1 Albert Terrace

A warm-hearted home with a lovely garden, an American hostess and a gorgeous Siamese cat. You are 20 minutes by bus from Princes Street yet the guests' sitting room overlooks pear trees and clematis and the rolling Pentland Hills. Cosy up in the winter next to a stylish log-effect wood-burner; in summer, take your morning paper onto the sunny terrace. Books, flowers, interesting art and ceramics and – you are on an old, quiet street – utter, surprising peace. Bedrooms are colourful, spacious and bright, one with an Art Deco bathroom and views over the garden. Clarissa is arty, easy, generous and loves having guests.

Rooms	3: 1 double; 1 double, 1 single sharing bath.
Price	£85. Singles £40.
Meals	Pubs/restaurants nearby.
Closed	Rarely.

Clarissa Notley
1 Albert Terrace,
Edinburgh EH10 5EA
Tel   +44 (0)131 447 4491
Email canotley@aol.com

Entry 629 Map 15

Edinburgh & the Lothians

Glebe House

A treasure of a home – and host! A perfect Georgian family house with all the well-proportioned elegance you'd expect, it is resplendent with original features – fireplaces, arched glass, long windows – that have appeared more than once in interiors magazines. Bedrooms are light and airy with pretty fabrics and lovely linen. The beach is a stone's throw away, views are leafy-green, golfers have over 21 courses to choose from. There's also a fascinating sea bird centre close by – and you are 30 minutes from Edinburgh: regular trains bring you to the foot of the castle.

Rooms	3: 1 double, 1 four-poster; 1 twin with separate bath.
Price	£120. Singles by arrangement.
Meals	Restaurants 2-minute walk.
Closed	Christmas & New Year.

Gwen & Jake Scott
Glebe House,
Law Road, North Berwick,
East Lothian EH39 4PL
Tel   +44 (0)1620 892608
Mobile +44 (0)7973 965814
Email   gwenscott@glebehouse-nb.co.uk
Web   www.glebehouse-nb.co.uk

Entry 630 Map 16

Edinburgh & the Lothians

Traprain Cottage

Beneath the big farming skies of East Lothian, martins swoop over the top of Traprain Law, while bees hum and hens potter in the garden of these carefully renovated labourers' cottages. You have independence in the oldest part, with a suite of rooms up in the eaves and a bright comfortable twin next to the cosily private sitting room: just the place to toast one's feet by the fire or hunker down with a book after a day's coastal walking or golfing. Ask Jim and Kirstie where to go over a welcome of afternoon tea, or during a traditional and local breakfast served in the kitchen, or on the terrace if the weather is fine.

Rooms	2: 1 twin with separate shower; 1 double with adjoining child twin & separate bath.
Price	£90. Singles £50. Double & adjoining twin £120 (with two children under 12).
Meals	Dinner, 2-3 courses, £22.50-£28. Pubs/restaurants 4 miles.
Closed	Christmas & New Year.

Kirstie Shearer
Traprain Cottage,
Standingstone Farm, Haddington,
East Lothian EH41 4LF
Tel +44 (0)1620 825375
Email kirstie.shearer@morham.org
Web www.trapraincottagebandb.co.uk

Entry 631   Map 16

Fife

Blair Adam

If staying in a place with genuine Adam features is special, how much more so in the Adam family home! They've been in this corner of Fife since 1733: John laid out the walled garden, son William was a prominent politician, Sir Walter Scott used to come and stay… you may be similarly inspired. The house, in a swathe of parkland and forest overlooking the hills and Loch Leven, has big, comfortable light-flooded rooms filled with intriguing contents, and superb walks from the door. The pretty bedroom is on the ground floor and you eat with your friendly hosts in the dining room, with coffee by the fire in the library after dinner.

Rooms	1 twin.
Price	£100. Singles £70.
Meals	Dinner, with wine, £25. Restaurants 5 miles.
Closed	December/January.

Keith & Elizabeth Adam
Blair Adam,
Kelty,
Fife KY4 0JF
Tel +44 (0)1383 831221
Mobile +44 (0)7986 711099
Email adamofblairadam@hotmail.com

Entry 632   Map 15

Fife

Greenlaw House

With superb views towards the Lomond Hills, Debbie's bright, warm converted farm steading will please you the moment you step in. The oak-floored sitting room has Afghan rugs, sofas around a log-burner, a grand piano, and leads to a decked area for summer sun. In all the rooms is a medley of modern and antique, and fascinating art. The ground-floor bedroom has a lovely old chest and books; the more lived-in upstairs one has the view. Debbie loves to cook: smoked salmon and scrambled eggs, porridge with cream, local honey. Falkland Palace, hunting haunt of the Stuart kings, is close; there are wonderful walks and sea eagles soar.

Rooms	2: 1 double; 1 double with separate bath.
Price	£80–£90. Singles £40–£50.
Meals	Dinner £25–£30. Restaurants 15-minute drive.
Closed	Christmas & New Year.

Debbie Butler
Greenlaw House,
Braeside, Collessie,
Cupar,
Fife KY15 7UX
Tel   +44 (0)1337 810413
Email   butlerjackson@googlemail.com
Web   www.greenlawhouse.com

Entry 633   Map 15

Fife

Kinkell

An avenue of beech trees patrolled by guinea fowl, Hebridean sheep and Highland cows leads to the house. If the sea views and salty smack of St Andrews Bay air don't get you, step inside and have your senses tickled. Your hosts are wonderful and offer you a glass of something on arrival; the elegant drawing room has two open fires, rosy sofas, a grand piano – gorgeous. Bedrooms and bathrooms are immaculate and sunny. Sandy and Frippy are great cooks and make full use of local produce. Gaze on the sea from the garden, head down to the beach, walk the wild coast. A friendly, comfortable family home.

Rooms	3 twins/doubles.
Price	£100. Singles from £55.
Meals	Dinner £30. Restaurants in St Andrews, 2 miles.
Closed	Rarely.

Sandy & Frippy Fyfe
Kinkell,
St Andrews,
Fife KY16 8PN
Tel   +44 (0)1334 472003
Mobile +44 (0)7836 746043
Email   fyfe@kinkell.com
Web   www.kinkell.com

Entry 634   Map 16+19

Glasgow

Highland

64 Partickhill Road

Be greeted by three free-range hens and Gertie the terrier on arrival at this relaxed family home. It's the bustling West End but the road is peaceful and there's a lovely big garden. Caroline and Hugh are lovers of the arts: the house is full of pictures, vintage finds and books. There are wood floors, rugs, a fire in the comfy sitting room and your bedroom is bright and spacious. Tuck into a delicious breakfast, in the conservatory, of good croissants, organic bacon and sausages, homemade bread and jams. Easy for the underground, trendy cafés and delis, museums, theatres and the university. A city treat.

The Grange

A Victorian townhouse with its toes in the country: the mountain hovers above, the loch shimmers below and the garden slopes steeply to great banks of rhododendrons. Bedrooms, the one in the turret with a sumptuous bathroom, are large, luscious, warm and inviting: crushed velvet, beautiful blankets, immaculate linen — all ooze panache. Expect decanters of sherry, ornate cornices, a Louis XV bed and a superb suite with contemporary touches. Elegant breakfasts are served at glass-topped tables; Joan's warm vivacity and love of B&B means guests keep coming back. And just a 10-minute walk into town.

Rooms	1 double. Extra twin available.	Rooms	3: 2 doubles, 1 suite.
Price	£80.	Price	£116-£130.
Meals	Packed lunch available. Pubs/restaurant 0.25 miles.	Meals	Restaurants 12-minute walk.
Closed	Occasionally.	Closed	Mid-November to March.

	Caroline Anderson		Joan & John Campbell
	64 Partickhill Road,		The Grange,
	Glasgow G11 5NB		Grange Road, Fort William,
Tel	+44 (0)141 339 1946		Highland PH33 6JF
Mobile	+44 (0)7962 144509	Tel	+44 (0)1397 705516
Email	carolineanderson64@gmail.com	Email	info@thegrange-scotland.co.uk
		Web	www.thegrange-scotland.co.uk

Entry 635   Map 15

Entry 636   Map 17

Highland

Arisaig House

Imposing Arisaig – a 19th-century industrialist's highland fantasy – sits in a walkers' paradise; the views to Skye are to die for. In former days it was a hotel; now Sarah, who has known Arisaig all her life, revels in returning house and gardens to their former glory. The sitting room is bright with Sanderson sofas, portraits and paintings and a huge open fire, and bedrooms are spacious and charming, with comfortable furniture and updated bathrooms. Lovely generous Sarah, passionate Slow Food member, serves breakfasts, high teas and dinners at the long oak table: don't miss the Stornoway black pudding!

Rooms	10: 4 twins/doubles, 6 suites.
Price	£145–£165. Singles £85.
Meals	Dinner, 3 courses, from £30. Pub/restaurant 3 miles.
Closed	Rarely.

Sarah Winnington-Ingram
Arisaig House,
Arisaig,
Highland PH39 4NR
Tel   +44 (0)1687 450730
Email   sarahwi@arisaighouse.co.uk
Web   www.arisaighouse.co.uk

Entry 637   Map 17

Highland – Isle of Skye

Napier Cottage

A beautiful house, filled with light, that floats above the Sound of Sleat with fabulous views across the water. Seals bask on local rocks, herons come in search of supper, the odd pod of minke whales passes through. The house, newly built in traditional style, is delightful: books everywhere, a wood-burner in the sitting room, afternoon tea (on the house) in the conservatory. Big bedrooms have warm colours, pretty fabrics, comfy beds, excellent bathrooms, watery views. Christine cooks tempting suppers – cheese soufflé, venison casserole, raspberry panna cotta – but Kinloch Lodge is close if you want to splash out.

Rooms	2 doubles.
Price	£90–£120. Singles from £70.
Meals	Dinner, 3 courses with wine, £35. Pub/restaurant 1 mile.
Closed	Occasionally.

Christine Jenkins & Ian Rudd
Napier Cottage,
Isleornsay, Sleat,
Isle of Skye, Highland IV43 8QX
Tel   +44 (0)1471 833460
Email   napiercottage@gmail.com
Web   www.napiercottage.co.uk

Entry 638   Map 17

Highland

The Berry

Drive through miles of spectacular landscape then bask in the final approach down a winding single-track road to Allt-Na-Subh – just five houses overlooking the loch. Joan, who is friendly and kind, prepares delicious meals in her Rayburn-warmed kitchen – the hub of this character-filled house. Inside is fresh and light with stylish bedrooms – one up, one down; the sitting room has a log fire and stunning views. Eat fish straight from the boats, pop over to Skye, stride the hills and spot golden eagles, red deer and otters. The perfect place for naturalists and artists, or those seeking solace. A hidden gem.

Minimum stay two nights.

Rooms	2: 1 double with separate shower; 1 double sharing bath with owner.
Price	£75. Singles from £45.
Meals	Dinner, 3 courses with wine, £30. Packed lunch £10. Pub 3 miles.
Closed	Rarely.

Joan Ashburner
The Berry,
Allt-Na-Subh,
Dornie,
Kyle of Lochalsh,
Highland IV40 8DZ
Tel   +44 (0)1599 588259

Highland

Aurora

The perfect spot for walkers and climbers (single-track roads, lochs, rivers and mountains) and the perfect B&B for groups: three smart, uncluttered bedrooms have flexible sleeping arrangements and spick and span shower rooms. The guest sitting room is light and airy with binoculars, books to borrow, maps and a small fridge for your wine – stay put for glorious sunsets and views to Harris. Breakfast time is generously bendy; good seasonal food is important here and you eat round a big table. There's a drying room and bike storage, but those wanting to relax will love it here too.

Minimum stay two nights. Over 12s welcome.

Rooms	3: 2 doubles, 1 triple.
Price	£76-£82. Triple £80-£86.
Meals	Dinner £8. BYO. Packed lunch £6. Pub/restaurant within 0.5 miles.
Closed	November-March.

Ann Barton
Aurora,
Shieldaig, Torridon,
Highland IV54 8XN
Tel   +44 (0)1520 755246
Email   info@aurora-bedandbreakfast.co.uk
Web   www.aurora-bedandbreakfast.co.uk

Highland

The Peatcutter's Croft

There's more beauty in a mile on the west coast than in the rest of the world put together – vast skies, soaring mountains, shimmering water, barely a soul in sight. Pauline and Seori left London to give their family the freedom to roam. Now they have a colourful cast of companions: sheep, hens, ducks, rabbits – all live here. In the adjoining byre: country simplicity, a Norwegian wood-burner, colour, texture and style. Sea eagles patrol the skies, porpoises bask in the loch, red deer come to eat the garden. This, coupled with Pauline's home cooking, makes it very hard to leave. Dogs and children are very welcome.

Rooms	Byre: 1 double & mezzanine for 2 children.
Price	Byre £70; £100 for 4. Singles from £45.
Meals	Dinner, 3 courses, £30. BYO. Pub/restaurant 30 miles.
Closed	Christmas.

Seori & Pauline Burnett
The Peatcutter's Croft,
Croft 12, Badrallach,
Dundonnell, Garve, Ullapool,
Highland IV23 2QP
Tel   +44 (0)1854 633797
Email   info@peatcutterscroft.com
Web   www.peatcutterscroft.com

Entry 641   Map 17

Highland

The Old Ferryman's House

This former ferryman's house is small, homely and lived-in, just yards from the river Spey with its spectacular mountain views. Explore the countryside or relax in the garden with a tray of tea and homemade treats; plants tumble from whisky barrels and pots and you may spot woodpeckers. The sitting room is cosy with a wood-burning stove and brimming with books (no TV). Generous Elizabeth, a keen traveller who lived in the Sudan, cooks delicious, imaginative meals: herbs and some veg from the garden, eggs from her hens, heathery honeycomb, homemade bread and jams. An unmatched spot for explorers, and very good value.

Rooms	3: 1 double, 1 twin/double, 1 single, all sharing 1 bath & 2 wcs.
Price	£70. Singles £35.
Meals	Dinner, 3 courses, £25. BYO. Packed lunch £7.50.
Closed	Occasionally in winter.

Elizabeth Matthews
The Old Ferryman's House,
Boat of Garten,
Highland PH24 3BY
Tel   +44 (0)1479 831370

Entry 642   Map 18

Highland

Rehaurie Cottage

You are steeped in history here, surrounded by woodland, castles, cairns and ancient battlefields. This 19th-century woodcutter's cottage is mercifully free of tartan; instead find clean lines, neutral colours and a contemporary feel. Spacious bedrooms are at either side of the house, one in cool greys with its own sitting room, the other in pretty rose-pink and cream with a private feel; both have sparkling, well-designed bathrooms. Sylvia and Chris, lovely people, give you an ample breakfast in the dining room which leads to a veranda; walks from the door are stunning. Discover golf courses, fishing and Highland games in Nairn.

Rooms	2: 1 double, 1 twin/double each with separate bath/shower.
Price	£85–£125. Singles from £65.
Meals	Packed lunch £7.50. Supper from £17.50. Pub 5 miles.
Closed	Rarely.

Sylvia Price
Rehaurie Cottage,
Nairn,
Highland IV12 5JD

Tel	+44 (0)1309 651322
Mobile	+44 (0)7513 974276
Email	stay@rehaurie.co.uk
Web	www.rehaurie.co.uk

Entry 643   Map 18

Highland

Craigiewood

The best of both worlds: the remoteness of the Highlands (red kites, wild goats) and Inverness just four miles away. The landscape surrounding this elegant cottage exudes a sense of ancient mystery augmented by these six acres – home to woodpeckers, roe deer and glorious roses. Inside, maps, walking sticks, two cats and a lovely, family-home feel – what you'd expect from delightful owners. Bedrooms, old-fashioned and cosy, overlook a garden reclaimed from Black Isle gorse. Gavin runs garden tours and can take you off to Inverewe, Attadale, Cawdor and Dunrobin Castle. Warm, peaceful, special.

Rooms	2 twins.
Price	£78–£95. Singles £40–£50.
Meals	Pub 2 miles.
Closed	Christmas & New Year.

Araminta & Gavin Dallmeyer
Craigiewood,
North Kessock, Inverness,
Highland IV1 3XG

Tel	+44 (0)1463 731628
Mobile	+44 (0)7831 733699
Email	2minty@craigiewood.co.uk
Web	www.craigiewood.co.uk

Entry 644   Map 18

Highland

Knockbain House

This is a well-loved farm, its environmental credentials supreme, and David and Denise are warm and interesting. A beautiful setting, too: landscaped gardens, a 700-acre farm (cows, lambs, barley) and rolling countryside stretching to Cromarty Firth. A grandfather clock ticks away time to relax, by floor-to-ceiling windows and a wood-burner in the antiques-filled sitting room; over a breakfast or dinner of home-grown foods; with a drink on the pond-side terrace; in bedrooms with fresh bathrooms and stunning views. Revel in the birds, walks and your hosts' commitment to this glorious unspoilt nature.

Babes in arms & over tens welcome.

Rooms	2: 1 double, 1 twin.
Price	£70-£90. Singles £40-£45.
Meals	Dinner, 3 courses, £25. Pubs/restaurants 1 mile.
Closed	Rarely.

David & Denise Lockett
Knockbain House,
Dingwall,
Highland IV15 9TJ
Tel	+44 (0)1349 862476
Mobile	+44 (0)7736 629838
Email	davidlockett@avnet.co.uk
Web	www.knockbainhouse.co.uk

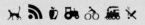

Entry 645   Map 18

Highland

Wemyss House

The peace is palpable, the setting overlooking the Cromarty Firth is stunning. Take an early morning stroll and spot buzzards, pheasants, rabbits and roe deer. The deceptively spacious house with sweeping maple floors is flooded with light and fabulous views, big bedrooms are warmly decorated with Highland rugs and tweeds, there's Christine's grand piano in the living room, Stuart's handcrafted furniture at every turn, and a sweet dog called Bella. Aga breakfasts include homemade bread, preserves and eggs from happy hens. Dinners are delicious; Christine and Stuart are wonderful hosts.

Rooms	3: 2 doubles, 1 twin.
Price	£95-£105.
Meals	Dinner £38. Restaurants 15-minute drive.
Closed	Rarely.

Christine Asher & Stuart Clifford
Wemyss House,
Bayfield, Tain,
Highland IV19 1QW
Tel	+44 (0)1862 851212
Mobile	+44 (0)7759 484709
Email	stay@wemysshouse.com
Web	www.wemysshouse.com

Entry 646   Map 18

Highland

St Callan's Manse

Fun, laughter and conversation flow in this warm and happy home. You share it with prints, paintings, antiques, sofas, amazing memorabilia, two dogs, four ducks, 10 hens and 1,200 teddy bears of every size and origin. Snug bedrooms have pretty fabrics, old armoires, flower-patterned sheets and tartan blankets; your sleep will be sound. Caroline cooks majestic breakfasts and dinners; Robert, a fund of knowledgeable anecdotes, can arrange just about anything. All this in incomparable surroundings: 60 acres of land plus glens, forests, buzzards, deer and the odd golden eagle. A gem.

Dogs by arrangement.

Rooms	2: 1 double with separate bath; 1 double with separate shower.
Price	£90. Singles £65.
Meals	Dinner, 2-4 courses, £20-£25. BYO. Pub/restaurant in village, 1.5 miles.
Closed	March & occasionally.

	Robert & Caroline Mills
	St Callan's Manse,
	Rogart,
	Highland IV28 3XE
Tel	+44 (0)1408 641363
Email	caroline@rogartsnuff.me.uk

Entry 647   Map 21

Highland

Thrumster House

A Victorian laird's house in an 8,500 acre estate. Drive south a mile to the 5,000-year-old neolithic remains of the Yarrow Archeological Trail for brochs, round houses and long cairns, then back to the big old house, "steamboat gothic" in the words of an American guest. The vaulted hall gives an ecclesiastical feel, with fires burning at both ends and a grand piano on the landing (it gets played wonderfully). Big, traditional bedrooms have mahogany dressers, brass beds, floral wallpapers, lots of books. Islay and Catherine look after guests well and conversation flows. There's woodland to wander and free trout fishing in the lochs.

Rooms	2: 1 double, 1 twin.
Price	£95. Singles £50.
Meals	Dinner, 3 courses with wine, £30.
Closed	Rarely.

	Islay & Catherine MacLeod
	Thrumster House,
	Thrumster, Wick,
	Highland KW1 5TX
Tel	+44 (0)1955 651387
Mobile	+44 (0)7840 750407
Email	cat.macleod@btinternet.com
Web	www.thrumster.co.uk

Entry 648   Map 21

Lanarkshire

Cormiston Farm

Wend your way through the soft hills of the Clyde Valley to a Georgian farmhouse in 26 acres of farmland and mature garden. Richard's a keen cook and produce from the walled garden – including delicious eggs from the quails – takes centre stage. Wonderful to retire to quiet, spacious rooms with bucolic views, stunning beds and rich fabrics; characterful Art Deco bathrooms, too. Tuck nippers up in bunks, then slip back for a snifter in front of the log fire in the sitting room. It's home from home, and licensed, too! There's untamed landscape to explore – and the children will love the friendly alpacas.

Rooms	2 doubles, each with separate bath.
Price	£86-£108. Singles £65-£81 (Extra bunk room available.)
Meals	Dinner, 4 courses, £25-£30. Supper, 2 courses, £20. Pub 2 miles.
Closed	Rarely.

Richard Philipps
Cormiston Farm,
Cormiston Road, Biggar,
Lanarkshire ML12 6NS

Tel	+44 (0)1899 221507
Email	info@cormistonfarm.com
Web	www.cormistonfarm.com

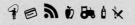

Entry 649   Map 15

Moray

Westfield House

Sweep up the drive to the grand home of an illustrious family: Macleans have lived here since 1862. Inside: polished furniture and burnished antiques, a tartan-carpeted hall, an oak stair hung with ancestral oils. John farms 500 acres and Veronica cooks sublimely; dinner is served at a long candelabra'd table, with vegetables from the vegetable garden. A winter fire crackles in the guest sitting room, old-fashioned bedrooms are inviting (plump pillows, fine linen, books, lovely views), the peace is deep. You can reach the coast easily and the walking is splendid; a historic house in a perfect setting with charming hosts.

Rooms	3: 1 twin; 1 twin with separate bath & shower; 1 single with separate bath.
Price	£90. Singles £50.
Meals	Supper, 2 courses, £20. Dinner, 3 courses, £25. Pub 3 miles.
Closed	Rarely.

John & Veronica Maclean
Westfield House,
Elgin,
Moray IV30 8XL

Tel	+44 (0)1343 547308
Email	veronica.maclean@yahoo.co.uk
Web	www.westfieldhouseelgin.co.uk

Entry 650   Map 18

Perth & Kinross

Beinn Bhracaigh

Excellent views stretch out from this Victorian villa. All the bedrooms are in relaxing creams, with duck-egg blues in throws and subtly patterned cushions propped like toast in a toast rack; TVs and fine Scottish soaps complete the Perthshire picture. Friendly hosts give you a continental breakfast in your room or a full Scottish and good coffee at separate tables in the dining room. Great fun and conviviality can be had in the evening when guests take over the honesty bar with its many wines and more than 50 whiskies. Amble to Pitlochry Theatre; discover an area rich with castles, fishing, white water rafting and walks.

Minimum two nights at weekends. Children over eight welcome.

Rooms	12: 8 doubles, 3 twins/doubles, 1 suite.
Price	£59-£103. Suite £89-£129. Singles from £49.
Meals	14 pubs/restaurants within 10-minute walk.
Closed	Rarely.

James & Kirsty Watts
Beinn Bhracaigh,
14 Higher Oakfield,
Pitlochry,
Perth & Kinross PH16 5HT
Tel   +44 (0)1796 470355
Email info@beinnbhracaigh.com
Web   www.beinnbhracaigh.com

Entry 651   Map 15+18

Perth & Kinross

Riverwood

Down the drive through woodland and bluebells, step inside and you see right through to the river Tay at the bottom of acres of grounds. Alf and Ann welcome you with fresh scones and tea. Find hotel comfort throughout with laundered linen, calm colours and state of the art bathrooms. Breakfast is in the vast dining room at separate tables: pancakes, potato rösti, smoked salmon.... spy red squirrels on the feeding table as you eat. Fish for brown trout, play golf over the road, picnic on your own river beach; gardens, castles, festivals and theatre are within reach too. Return for a full dinner – or Scottish tapas!

Rooms	5: 3 twins/doubles, 1 suite; 1 suite with separate bath/shower.
Price	£85-£100. Suites £85-£150. Singles £60-£125.
Meals	Dinner, 3 courses, £27.50. Pub 0.5 miles.
Closed	Rarely.

Ann & Alf Berry
Riverwood,
Strathtay,
Pitlochry,
Perth & Kinross PH9 0PG
Tel   +44 (0)1887 840751
Mobile +44 (0)7708 668436
Email   info@riverwoodstrathtay.com
Web   www.riverwoodstrathtay.com

Entry 652   Map 15+18

Perth & Kinross

The Steading

Hens scatter as you approach this house behind the hamlet of Tullicro – a clever fusion of modern Scottish and Scandinavian design. Built of local Aberfeldy stone, Sarah Jane's home has splendid mountain and river views. Breakfast on the loggia (when sunny) or at the picture window, on fine local and organic food (seeded breads, raspberries, smoked salmon). The upstairs bedroom has a magnificent star-gazey skylight; both rooms have the right balance of comfort and contemporary chic. Fine Scottish woollens, French linens, firm mattresses, thick towels in pristine warm-floored shower rooms. Evenings in front of that wood-burner beckon.

Minimum two nights at weekends April-Oct.

Rooms	2: 1 double, 1 twin/double.
Price	£85-£95. Singles £70.
Meals	Pub/restaurant 2 miles.
Closed	Christmas, New Year & occasionally.

Sarah Jane Burton
The Steading,
Tullicro, By Camserney, Aberfeldy,
Perth & Kinross PH15 2JG

Tel	+44 (0)1887 820718
Mobile	+44 (0)7813 066662
Email	enquiries@steadingaberfeldy.co.uk
Web	www.steadingaberfeldy.co.uk

Entry 653   Map 15+18

Perth & Kinross

Essendy House

Down a tree-lined drive blazing with colour, Tess and John's charming country house is surrounded by lochs, castles and serenity. Inside is cosy and comfortable with warm fires, flowers, porcelain, Italianate murals and an unusual collection of family artefacts. Traditionally furnished bedrooms have antiques, good linen, garden views and silk or floral touches. Enjoy hearty breakfasts and suppers in the huge dining room or family kitchen; the terrace is heaven in summer. There's lots to do: visit cathedral and theatre, walk in Macbeth's Birnam Wood, play golf, ski, fish and admire the swooping ospreys.

Rooms	2: 1 double, 1 twin.
Price	£100. Singles £50.
Meals	Packed lunch £5. Supper, 2 courses, £25. Pub/restaurant 2 miles.
Closed	Christmas & New Year; February/March.

John Monteith
Essendy House,
Blairgowrie,
Perth & Kinross PH10 6QY

Tel	+44 (0)1250 884260
Mobile	+44 (0)7841 121538
Email	johnmonteith@hotmail.com
Web	www.essendy.org

Entry 654   Map 15+18

Perth & Kinross

Perth & Kinross

Inchyra House

Sweep up through mature parkland to a gorgeous welcome from Caroline and James, and Flint the Scottish deerhound. Here is 18th-century grandeur, all grace and charm with a welcoming fire in the hall. Elegant doubles are classically decorated: 'Yellow' has the edge with lawn views but 'Blue' is gracious too, with a chaise longue and vintage lace; 'Nettle' has a charmingly old-fashioned French feel. Set off for Perth or a round of golf, return for tea and scones in front of a roaring fire in the splendid drawing room with parkland views. You'll feel beautifully at home in this relaxed house.

Pilot Panther

Dramatic Loch Voil views from your window and an award-winning hotel next door – Pilot Panther lords a stupendous spot. A classic 1950 showman's wagon, it has a main living and sleeping area (with a gleaming oven and grill) and a separate bunk room. Your loo and shower are a minute's walk away at the hotel. Great walking and stunning views around the long loch will help you work up an appetite worthy of Monachlye Mhor, a pilgrimage site for Scottish foodies. They have their own fishery, smokehouse and bakery... go on, treat yourself to some of the best food in Scotland.

Minimum two nights. Book through Sawday's Canopy & Stars online or by phone.

Rooms	3: 1 twin; 1 double, 1 twin each with separate bath.
Price	£130-£140.
Meals	Pub 0.5 miles. Restaurants 4 miles.
Closed	Christmas & New Year.

Rooms	Wagon for 4 (1 double, 2 bunks for children) with shower & wc close by.
Price	£125.
Meals	BYO breakfast, or at hotel, £12.50. Dinner £50. Sunday lunch £32.
Closed	Never.

Caroline & James Hoyer Millar
Inchyra House,
Glencarse,
Perth,
Perth & Kinross PH2 7LU
Tel   +44 (0)1738 860210
Email   caroline@hoyers.demon.co.uk
Web   www.inchyrahouse.co.uk

Sawday's Canopy & Stars
Pilot Panther,
Mhor, Balquhidder,
Perth & Kinross FK19 8PQ
Tel   +44 (0)1275 395447
Email   enquiries@canopyandstars.co.uk
Web   www.canopyandstars.co.uk/
        pilotpanther

Entry 655   Map 15

Entry 656   Map 18

Perth & Kinross

Mackeanston House

They grow their own organic fruit and vegetables in the walled garden, make their own preserves, bake their own bread. Likeable and energetic – Fiona a wine buff and talented cook, Colin a tri-lingual guide – your hosts are hospitable people whose 1690 farmhouse combines informality and luxury in peaceful, central Scotland. Light-filled bedrooms have pretty fabrics, fine antiques, TVs and homemade cake. Roomy bathrooms have robes and a radio; one has a double shower (with a seat if you wish it). Dine by the log fire in the dining room, or in the conservatory with views to Stirling Castle.

Rooms	2: 1 double, 1 twin/double.
Price	£100–£104. Singles £60–£62.
Meals	Dinner, 3 courses, £32; 4 courses, £35. Pub 1 mile.
Closed	Christmas.

Fiona & Colin Graham
Mackeanston House,
Doune, Stirling,
Perth & Kinross FK16 6AX
Tel   +44 (0)1786 850213
Mobile   +44 (0)7921 143018
Email   info@mackeanstonhouse.co.uk
Web   www.mackeanstonhouse.co.uk

Entry 657   Map 15

Perth & Kinross

Old Kippenross

What a setting! Old Kippenross rests in 150 peaceful acres of gorgeous park and woodland overlooking the river Allan – spot red squirrels and deer, herons, dippers and otters. The 15th-century house has a Georgian addition and an air of elegance and great courtesy, with its rustic white-vaulted basement, and dining and sitting rooms strewn with soft sofas and Persian rugs. Sash-windowed bedrooms are deeply comfortable, warm bathrooms are stuffed with towels. Susan and Patrick (an expert on birds of prey) are welcoming, the food is good and there's a croquet lawn in the walled garden.

Over tens welcome. Dogs by arrangement only.

Rooms	2: 1 double, 1 twin/double with adjoining single room (let to same party only.)
Price	£100–£102. Singles £65.
Meals	Dinner £30. BYO. Pub 1.5 miles.
Closed	Rarely.

Susan & Patrick Stirling-Aird
Old Kippenross,
Kippenross,
Dunblane,
Perth & Kinross FK15 0LQ
Tel   +44 (0)1786 824048
Email   kippenross@hotmail.com
Web   www.oldkippenross.co.uk

Entry 658   Map 15

Scottish Borders

Skirling House

An intriguing house with 1908 additions, impeccably maintained. The whole lovely place is imbued with the spirit of Scottish Arts & Crafts, augmented with Italianate flourishes. Colourful blankets embellish chairs; runners soften flagged floors; the carvings, wrought-ironwork and rare Florentine ceiling are sheer delight. Upstairs, superb comfort holds sway: carpets and rugs, window seats and wicker, fruit and flowers. Bob cooks the finest local produce, Isobel shares a love of Scottish contemporary art and both look after you beautifully. They've planted some 25,000 trees, and grand woodland walks start from the door.

Rooms	5: 3 doubles, 1 twin, 1 twin/double.
Price	£120–£180. Singles £60–£95.
Meals	Dinner £35.
	Pubs/restaurants 2 miles.
Closed	Christmas & January/February.

Bob & Isobel Hunter
Skirling House,
Skirling,
Biggar,
Scottish Borders ML12 6HD
Tel   +44 (0)1899 860274
Email   enquiry@skirlinghouse.com
Web   www.skirlinghouse.com

Entry 659   Map 15

Scottish Borders

Fauhope House

Near to Melrose Abbey and the glorious St Cuthbert's Walk, this solid 1890s house is immersed in bucolic bliss. Views soar to the Eildon Hills through wide windows with squashy seats; all is luxurious, elegant, fire-lit and serene with an eclectic mix of art. Bedrooms are warm with deeply coloured walls, thick chintz, pale tartan blankets and soft carpet; bathrooms are modern and pristine. Breakfast is served with smiles at a flower-laden table and overlooking those purple hills. A short walk through the garden and over a footbridge takes you to the interesting town of Melrose, with shops, restaurants and its own theatre.

Rooms	3 twins/doubles.
Price	£90–£110. Singles from £60.
Meals	Pub/restaurant 0.5 miles.
Closed	Rarely.

Ian & Sheila Robson
Fauhope House,
Gattonside, Melrose,
Scottish Borders TD6 9LY
Tel   +44 (0)1896 823184
Mobile   +44 (0)7816 346768
Email   info@fauhopehouse.com
Web   www.fauhopehouse.com

Entry 660   Map 15

Scottish Borders

Whitehouse Country House

A proud avenue of trees leads to Angela and Roger's handsome 19th-century country house in the heart of the Scottish Borders. They have been welcoming guests for over 20 years providing comfort, relaxation and great hospitality. Enjoy log fires and deep armchairs in the elegant dining and drawing rooms, traditional bedrooms with the most comfortable beds and glorious views from every room. Angela's cooking is heavenly and she uses wild salmon, game and the finest in-season local produce. Explore historic Border towns, cycle the Tweed Cycleway, walk St Cuthbert's Way – your hosts know the area well and are happy to advise.

Rooms	3: 1 double, 2 twins.
Price	£116–£130. Singles from £73.
Meals	Dinner £22–£29. Supper tray £10. Packed lunch £7. Pub 3 miles.
Closed	Rarely.

Angela & Roger Tyrer
Whitehouse Country House,
St Boswells, Melrose,
Scottish Borders TD6 0ED

Tel	+44 (0)1573 460343
Mobile	+44 (0)7877 800582
Email	stay@whitehousecountryhouse.com
Web	www.whitehousecountryhouse.com

Entry 661   Map 16

Stirling

The Moss

Rozie loves fishing and Jamie keeps bees; great hosts, they live in a charming listed house full of lovely things. Outside are 28 acres where deer prune the roses, pheasants roam and a garden seat sits with its toes in the water. Generous bedrooms await privately in their own wing and have big beds with feather pillows, books, flowers and long views to pastures and moorland. Find walking sticks (and the bell of HMS Tempest) in the porch, rugs in the hall and smart sofas in the log-fired drawing room. Breakfast comes fresh from the Aga and is served at a big oak table; walk it all off on the West Highland Way.

Rooms	3: 1 twin; 2 doubles sharing bath (2nd room let to same party only).
Price	£90. Singles £45.
Meals	Pubs/restaurants within 2 miles.
Closed	Rarely.

Jamie & Rozie Parker
The Moss,
Killearn,
Stirling G63 9LJ

Tel	+44 (0)1360 550053
Mobile	+44 (0)7787 123599
Email	themoss@freeuk.com

Entry 662   Map 15

Stirling

Stirling

Cardross

Dodge the lazy sheep on the long drive to arrive (eventually!) at a sweep of gravel and lovely old Cardross in a gorgeous setting. Bang on the enormous ancient door and either Archie or Nicola (plus labradors and lively Jack Russells) will usher you in. And what a delight it is; come here for a blast of Scottish history! Traditional big bedrooms have airiness, long views, antiques, wooden shutters, towelling robes and good linen; one bathroom has a cast-iron period bath. The drawing room is vast, the house is filled with warm character, the Orr Ewings can tell you all the history.

Over 14s welcome.

Bramble Bield

Three fairytale wagons gather at the foot of the Ochil hills, near historic Stirling and in the grounds of Powis House. Holly (green) and Rowan (red) are Gypsy bowtops; Bramley is a potter's wagon retired from the estate. All are traditionally snug and enchanting. You share the central fire pit by the hawthorn, but get your own outdoor space too. The well-stocked kitchen, shower room (eco toiletries) and compost loo (nothing to fear!) are shared between the three. Book one wagon for a relaxing break, all three for an unusual gathering. Friendly Colin and Jane leave breakfast in the Stables: Danish pastries, fresh eggs, coffee.

Minimum two nights. Book through Sawday's Canopy & Stars online or by phone.

Rooms	2: 1 twin; 1 twin with separate bath.
Price	£120. Singles £70–£75.
Meals	Occasional dinner £30. Pubs/restaurants 3-6 miles.
Closed	Christmas & New Year.

Rooms	2 gypsy caravans for 2-4, 1 wagon for 2, all sharing shower room, kitchen & compost loo.
Price	£56–£75.
Meals	Continental breakfast included. Breakfast in house, £7.50. Pub/restaurant 3 miles.
Closed	October-April.

	Sir Archie & Lady Orr Ewing
	Cardross,
	Port of Menteith,
	Kippen,
	Stirling FK8 3JY
Tel	+44 (0)1877 385223
Email	enquiries@cardrossestate.com
Web	www.cardrossestate.com

	Sawday's Canopy & Stars
	Bramble Bield,
	Powis House, Stirling,
	Stirling FK9 5PS
Tel	+44 (0)1275 395447
Email	enquiries@canopyandstars.co.uk
Web	www.canopyandstars.co.uk/ bramblebield

Entry 663   Map 15

Entry 664   Map 15

Stirling

Powis House

A sprawling 18th-century mansion with the volcanic Ochil Hills as a stunning backdrop and a colourful entrance hall of antlers and stuffed animals. Country style bedrooms invite with polished old floors, tartan throws, garden views and original bathrooms. You have a huge dining room with warming wood-burner, a guest lounge on the first floor, a sunny stone-flagged patio with places to sit and acres of estate with a woodland walk to explore. Colin and Jane are caring and interesting; Colin is a keen cook and has ghost stories galore to share. Historical Stirling is close: castle, university, festival and more.

Rooms	3: 2 doubles, 1 twin.
Price	£90–£100. Singles £65.
Meals	Dinner, 4 courses with coffee, £25. Pub/restaurant 3 miles.
Closed	Rarely.

Jane & Colin Kilgour
Powis House,
Stirling,
Stirling FK9 5PS
Tel   +44 (0)1786 460231
Email   info@powishouse.co.uk
Web   www.powishouse.co.uk

Entry 665   Map 15

Stirling

Quarter

This stately 1750s house commands views across Stirling's lush countryside and comes complete with crunching gravel drive and original ceiling dome. It was owned by the same family for generations until the Macleans took over its high ceilings, cornicing features and sash windows. Pad your way upstairs to two comfortable bedrooms and bathrooms, brightened with a pretty floral touch. Breakfast is a grand affair at a long polished table (the free-range hens providing the eggs). You are cocooned in extensive grounds, yet have easy access to Stirling, Edinburgh, Perth and Glasgow.

Rooms	2: 1 double, 1 twin/double.
Price	£100. Singles £55.
Meals	Pub/restaurant 4 miles.
Closed	Christmas.

Pippa Maclean
Quarter,
Denny,
Stirling FK6 6QZ
Tel   +44 (0)1324 825817
Email   quarterstirling@hotmail.co.uk
Web   www.quarterstirling.com

Entry 666   Map 15

Western Isles – Isle of South Uist

Kinloch

Never a dull moment here in Wegg's house and you're encouraged to feel at home. All is friendly and full of interest with gorgeous food, good company and a happy dog. The house, built in the 70s, is comfy with books, photos, easy chairs and art. Bedrooms (one downstairs) are fresh and sunny; views across the loch are enormous and sunrises spectacular. Breakfasts and dinners are wonderfully sociable occasions and Wegg loves cooking: homemade bread, eggs from his hens, barbecued freshly caught trout. Wander the woodland garden and machair, fish the loch, spot the birds… return to relax by the log fire. A special place.

Minimum two nights at weekends. Children & pets welcome.

Rooms	3: 1 twin/double; 1 twin/double, 1 single both with separate bath.
Price	£90. Singles £45.
Meals	Dinner £25. Packed lunch £5-£8. Restaurant 5 miles.
Closed	Rarely.

Wegg Kimbell
Kinloch,
Grogarry,
Isle of South Uist,
Western Isles HS8 5RR
Tel +44 (0)1870 620316
Email wegg@kinlochuist.com
Web www.kinlochuist.com

Entry 667   Map 20

Western Isles – Isle of Harris

Pairc an t-Srath

Richard and Lena's lovely home overlooks the beach at Borve – another absurdly beautiful Harris view. Inside, smart simplicity abounds: wooden floors, white walls, a peat fire, colourful art. Airy bedrooms fit the mood perfectly: trim carpets, chunky wood beds, Harris tweed throws, excellent shower rooms (there's a bathroom, too, if you want a soak). Richard crofts, Lena cooks, perhaps homemade soup, venison casserole, wet chocolate cake with raspberries. Views from the dining room tumble down hill, so expect to linger over breakfast. You'll spot otters in the loch, while the standing stones at Callanish are unmissable.

Rooms	4: 2 doubles, 1 twin, 1 single.
Price	£100. Singles £50.
Meals	Dinner, 3 courses, £35. Restaurant 3 miles, pub 7 miles.
Closed	Rarely.

Lena & Richard MacLennan
Pairc an t-Srath,
Borve,
Isle of Harris,
Western Isles HS3 3HT
Tel +44 (0)1859 550386
Email info@paircant-srath.co.uk
Web www.paircant-srath.co.uk

Entry 668   Map 20

Wales

Anglesey

Cleifiog

On a soft spring morning this could be Lake Garda. The bay view is spectacular, the masts of Beaumaris chink in the wind. Lovely Gill and gardening husband Laurie have taken over the running of this B&B and serve a delicious breakfast. Set on the coast road, all is stunning inside and out: the clear light, the scent of lilies, the smell of freshly brewed coffee. First it was a Georgian hospice, later a customs house; now the big, bright, elegant sitting room's panelling is offset by white linen sofas and pretty potted plants, and bedrooms are inviting with top-notch linen. Lap up the views and the beautiful sea air.

Rooms	3: 2 twins/doubles, 1 suite.
Price	£75–£90. Suite £90–£110.
	Singles £60–£80.
Meals	Pub/restaurant 200 yards.
Closed	Christmas & New Year.

Gill Beevers
Cleifiog,
Townsend,
Beaumaris,
Anglesey LL58 8BH
Tel +44 (0)1248 811507
Email enquiries@cleifiog.co.uk
Web www.cleifiogbandb.co.uk

Entry 669   Map 6

Carmarthenshire

Sarnau Mansion

Listed and Georgian, this handsome house has 16 acres of grounds complete with pond, well-tended walled garden and woodland with nesting red kites. Bedrooms are calm and traditionally furnished with heritage colours, art poster prints and green views; big bathrooms have plenty of hot water. The oak-floored sitting room with leather chesterfields has French windows leading onto the rhododendron lawn, the dining room has separate tables, café-style, and there's good home cooking from Cynthia. A peaceful place from which to explore beaches, castles and more – 15 minutes from the National Botanic Garden of Wales.

Children over five welcome.

Rooms	4: 2 doubles, 1 twin; 1 double with separate bath.
Price	£80–£90. Singles £50.
Meals	Dinner, 3 courses, around £25. BYO. Pub 1 mile.
Closed	Rarely.

Cynthia & David Fernihough
Sarnau Mansion,
Llysonnen Road, Bancyfelin,
Carmarthen,
Carmarthenshire SA33 5DZ
Tel +44 (0)1267 211404
Email d.fernihough@btinternet.com
Web www.sarnaumansion.co.uk

Entry 670   Map 6

Carmarthenshire

Beddyn Breakfast

You approach the blue and white china house up a solid oak driveway leading to a sweep of gingham lawn. The entrance hall is cold but full of character, with flaky pastry wallpaper and a jam-jar umbrella stand, but the rest of the property has been recently reheated. The lounge has been given a chic modern flavour with designer eggcup armchairs and Danish sofas, although the icing on the latter can be unkind to clothing. The bedrooms all have beautifully squidgy eggy-beds, plump pillows of shredded wheat and toasty duvets, but the gem is the continental suite with its Parma ham-draped watermelon bed and cafetière plunge pool.

Rooms	Spacious and plenty.
Price	£5.50 inc. tea and toast.
Meals	Surprisingly disappointing breakfast.
Closed	Seasonally, according to taste.

D P Fry
Beddyn Breakfast,
Downstairs-on-the-table,
Cumman Geddit,
Now,
Carmarthen B4 Its cold
Web   www.donteggmeon.com

Entry 671   Map 6

Carmarthenshire

Plas Alltyferin

Wisteria-wrapped and, in parts, delightfully creaky, this Georgian family house sits in 270 beautiful acres. The breakfast room has the original panelling and the bedrooms have an old-fashioned charm. Not the place for you if you like spotlessness and state-of-the-art plumbing, but the views across the ha-ha to the Norman hill fort are timelessly lovely and the welcome is heartfelt. Gerard and Charlotte are the easiest, kindest and dog-friendliest of hosts. You're close to the National Botanical and Aberglasney gardens – and, most importantly, many lovely gastropubs!

Over tens welcome.

Rooms	2: 1 twin; 1 twin with separate bath.
Price	£70–£80. Singles £40–£45.
Meals	Pubs/restaurants within 2 miles.
Closed	September & occasionally.

Charlotte & Gerard Dent
Plas Alltyferin,
Pont-ar-gothi, Nantgaredig,
Carmarthen,
Carmarthenshire SA32 7PF
Tel   +44 (0)1267 290662
Email   dent@alltyferin.co.uk
Web   www.alltyferin.co.uk

Entry 672   Map 6

Ty Cefn Tregib

Mary and John Evans have created something special in their corner of the Brecon Beacons National Park. Waterfall Yurt and Gert's Yurt, each in a private setting, are rustic, homely and enticing, while the vintage Airstream's jazzy interior is one for fans of retro. Each space has its own mains-connected 'yurtmobile' next door with a hot shower and a high-tech compost loo; the yurts each have a little kitchen. Homely breakfast baskets are good value and the Store Shed stocks provisions. Walk in lush gorges rich with waterfalls, or explore the Towy river valley; Mary and John will lend you their bikes.

Minimum two nights. Book through Sawday's Canopy & Stars online or by phone.

The Glynhir Estate

This fine old house on a Huguenot estate stands on the western edge of the Black Mountain. Outside: a waterfall, a two-acre kitchen garden, a brigade of chickens, and peacocks that patrol the grounds with panache. Inside, the house has spurned the urge to take itself too seriously and remains decidedly lived in. Find William Morris wallpaper in the dining room, lemon trees in the conservatory and old cabinets stuffed with interesting things in the sitting room. Country-house bedrooms fit the mood perfectly: smart and comfortable with excellent bathrooms. You can ride, walk, fish or visit Aberglasney Garden – just ask Katy.

Rooms	2 yurts for 2, Airstream for 2, each with separate shower & compost loo. Shared kitchen hut.
Price	£64-£74.
Meals	Continental breakfast basket for 2, £8. Pubs/restaurants 10-minute drive.
Closed	November-April.

Rooms	6: 5 doubles, 1 family room.
Price	£85. Family room £103.50. Singles £55.
Meals	Dinner from £19.25. Pubs/restaurants 2 miles.
Closed	November-March.

	Sawday's Canopy & Stars
	Ty Cefn Tregib,
	Ffairfach,
	Llandeilo,
	Carmarthenshire SA19 6TD
Tel	+44 (0)1275 395447
Email	enquiries@canopyandstars.co.uk
Web	www.canopyandstars.co.uk /tregib

	Katy Jenkins
	The Glynhir Estate,
	Glynhir Road, Llandybie,
	Ammanford,
	Carmarthenshire SA18 2TD
Tel	+44 (0)1269 850438
Mobile	+44 (0)7810 864458
Email	enquiries@theglynhirestate.com
Web	www.theglynhirestate.com

Entry 673   Map 7   Entry 674   Map 7

Ceredigion

Nantgwynfaen Organic Farm

Retired organic farmers here for over a decade, your hosts, and Gyp the sheepdog, couldn't be more welcoming. Amanda's culinary skills (using home-grown or local produce) seduce all-comers and laverbread bacon cockles are a speciality. Their 170-year-old farmhouse, sheltered by its barns (one a games room, others for self-caterers) is a friendly and unfussy place to stay with cosy, light bedrooms, spotless bathrooms, a wood-burner in the little sitting/dining room and Ken's paintings and woodwork adding to the whole. Walk straight down the valley to the river Teifi; lovely beaches are a 20-minute drive.

Lifts to the pub & babysitting.

Rooms	2: 1 double, 1 family suite for 3 (1 double, 1 single). Extra bed available for suite.
Price	£63-£70. Family suite £63-£125. Singles from £45.
Meals	Dinner, 2 courses, £15. Pubs/restaurant 1.9 miles.
Closed	Rarely.

Amanda & Ken Edwards
Nantgwynfaen Organic Farm,
Penrhiwllan Road, Croeslan,
Llandysul,
Ceredigion SA44 4SR
Tel   +44 (0)1239 851914
Email   amanda@organicfarmwales.co.uk
Web   www.organicfarmwales.co.uk

Entry 675   Map 6

Ceredigion

Broniwan

The Jacobs began farming organically here in the 70s and concentrate now on their kitchen garden – meals celebrate their success. Their cosy ivy-clad home is quietly, colourfully stylish, with books, watercolours and good local art; the attractive guest bedroom has a traditional Welsh bedspread and views to the Preseli hills. There are acres to roam and the meadow garden's pond brims with life. Carole is passionate about history and literature and can advise on days out: try the Museum of Quilts in Lampeter, or Aberglasney, an hour's drive. Do linger; this is such a rich spot.

Rooms	1 double.
Price	£76-£80. Singles £40.
Meals	Dinner £25-£30. BYO. Restaurants 7-8 miles.
Closed	Rarely.

Carole & Allen Jacobs
Broniwan,
Rhydlewis,
Llandysul,
Ceredigion SA44 5PF
Tel   +44 (0)1239 851261
Email   broniwan@btinternet.com
Web   www.broniwan.com

Entry 676   Map 6

Ceredigion

Ffynnon Fendigaid

Arrive through rolling countryside – birdsong and breeze the only sound; within moments you will be sprawled on a leather sofa admiring modern art and wondering how a little bit of Milan arrived here along with Huw and homemade cake. A place to come and pootle, with no rush; you can stay all day to stroll the fern-fringed paths through the acres of wild garden to a lake and a grand bench, or opt for hearty walking. Your bed is big, the colours are soft, the bathrooms are spotless and the food is local – try all the Welsh cheeses. Wide beaches are close by, red kites and buzzards soar above you. Pulchritudinous.

Rooms	2 doubles.
Price	£75-£77. Singles from £45.
Meals	Dinner, 2-3 courses, £20-£22. Pub 1 mile.
Closed	Rarely.

Huw Davies
Ffynnon Fendigaid,
Rhydlewis, Llandysul,
Ceredigion SA44 5SR
Tel   +44 (0)1239 851361
Mobile   +44 (0)7974 135262
Email   ffynnonf@btinternet.com
Web   www.ffynnonf.co.uk

Entry 677   Map 6

Conwy

Lympley Lodge

The solid Victorian exterior belies a surprising interior. Welcoming Patricia, a former restorer, has brought together a gorgeous collection of furniture, while her meticulous paintwork adds light and life to her seaside home. Above is the Little Orme; below, across the main coast road, the sweep of Llandudno Bay. Bedrooms strike the perfect balance between the practical and the exotic; all have crisp linen, rich fabrics, fresh flowers, lovely views. There's an elegant sitting room for guests, a stunning dining room with a Renaissance feel and breakfasts full of local and homemade produce. Wonderful.

Rooms	3: 2 doubles, 1 twin.
Price	£85. Singles £50-£55.
Meals	Pubs/restaurants 5-minute drive.
Closed	Mid-December to end January.

Patricia Richards
Lympley Lodge,
Colwyn Road, Craigside,
Llandudno,
Conwy LL30 3AL
Tel   +44 (0)1492 549304
Email   patricia@lympleylodge.co.uk
Web   www.lympleylodge.co.uk

Entry 678   Map 7

Conwy

Pengwern Country House

The steeply wooded Conwy valley snakes down to this stone and slate property set back from the road in Snowdonia National Park, and the walks are wonderful. Inside has an upbeat traditional feel: a large sitting room with tall bay windows and pictures by the Betws-y-Coed artists who once lived here. Settle with a book by the wood-burner; Gwawr and Ian are naturally friendly and treat guests as friends. Bedrooms have rough plastered walls, colourful fabrics and super bathrooms; one comes with a double-ended roll top tub and views of Lledr Valley. Breakfast on fruits, herb rösti, soda bread – superb.

Minimum stay two nights.

Rooms	3: 1 double, 1 twin/double, 1 four-poster.
Price	£72-£84. Singles from £62.
Meals	Pubs/restaurants within 1.5 miles. Packed lunch £5.50.
Closed	Christmas & New Year.

Gwawr & Ian Mowatt
Pengwern Country House,
Allt Dinas,
Betws-y-Coed,
Conwy LL24 0HF

Tel	+44 (0)1690 710480
Email	gwawr.pengwern@btopenworld.com
Web	www.snowdoniaaccommodation.co.uk

Entry 679   Map 7

Conwy

Maesmor Hall

Historic and grand, this old Welsh manor, gazing over Berwyn mountains, is surrounded by parkland, river and organically farmed acres. The furnishings and décor are classic country house with fine paintings, sculptures and china in comfortable elegant rooms; Johanna is friendly and you're welcomed as part of the family. Breakfast in the polished dining room might include scrambled eggs and pancetta, cockles and laverbread. Splash in the pool, wander outside for croquet, tennis and rose garden, chat to Truffle the labrador. Come for open-air theatre in summer, peaches from the peach house and an array of wildlife and walks.

Rooms	3: 2 doubles, 1 twin.
Price	£80-£100. Singles £60.
Meals	Pub a short walk.
Closed	Christmas & New Year.

Johanna Jackson
Maesmor Hall,
Maerdy,
Corwen,
Conwy LL21 0NS

Tel	+44 (0)1490 460411
Email	maesmorhall@aol.com
Web	www.maesmor.com

Entry 680   Map 7

Denbighshire

Plas Efenechtyd Cottage

Efenechtyd means 'place of the monks' but there's nothing spartan about Dave and Marilyn's handsome brick farmhouse. Breakfasts of local sausages, eggs from their hens, salmon fishcakes with mushrooms and homemade bread are served at a polished table in the dining room with exotic wall hangings from Vietnam and Laos. Light bedrooms have an uncluttered feel, excellent mattresses and good linen; bathrooms are warm as toast. In the pretty cottage garden: a summerhouse and Marilyn's beehive. Motor to Ruthin, with its windy streets and interesting shops, or strike out for Offa's Dyke with a packed lunch; this is stunning countryside.

Flintshire

Plas Penucha

Swing back in time with polished parquet, tidy beams, a huge Elizabethan panelled lounge with books, leather sofas and open fire – a cosy spot for Nest's dogs and for tea in winter. Plas Penucha – 'the big house on the highest point in the parish' – has been in the family for 500 years. Airy, old-fashioned bedrooms have long views across the garden to Offa's Dyke and one has a shower in the corner. The L-shaped dining room has a genuine Arts & Crafts interior; outside, rhododendrons and a rock garden flourish. There are views to the Clywdian Hills and beyond is St Asaph, with the smallest medieval cathedral in the country.

Rooms	3: 2 doubles, 1 twin.
Price	£70. Singles £50.
Meals	Packed lunch £6. Pub 1.6 miles.
Closed	Rarely.

Rooms	2: 1 double, 1 twin.
Price	£72. Singles from £36.
Meals	Dinner £19. Packed lunch £5. Pub/restaurant 2-3 miles.
Closed	Rarely.

	Dave Jones & Marilyn Jeffery
	Plas Efenechtyd Cottage,
	Efenechtyd, Ruthin,
	Denbighshire LL15 2LP
Tel	+44 (0)1824 704008
Mobile	+44 (0)7540 501009
Email	info@plas-efenechtyd-cottage.co.uk
Web	www.plas-efenechtyd-cottage.co.uk

	Nest Price
	Plas Penucha,
	Pen y Cefn Road, Caerwys,
	Mold,
	Flintshire CH7 5BH
Tel	+44 (0)1352 720210
Email	nest@plaspenucha.co.uk
Web	www.plaspenucha.co.uk

Entry 681   Map 7

Entry 682   Map 7

Gwynedd

The Slate Shed at Graig Wen

Sarah and conservationist John spent months travelling in a camper looking for their own special place and found this lovely old Welsh slate cutting mill... captivated by acres of wild woods and stunning views. You'll feel at ease as soon as you step into their eclectic modern home with its reclaimed slate and wood, cosy wood-burners, books, games, snug bedrooms (one downstairs) and superb bathrooms. Breakfast communally on local eggs and sausages, honey from the mountainside, homemade bread and granola. Hike or bike the Mawddach Trail, climb Cadair Idris, wonder at the views... and John's chocolate brownies.

Rooms	5: 4 doubles, 1 twin/double.
Price	£75–£130. Singles £65.
Meals	Packed lunch £6.50. Pub 5 miles.
Closed	Rarely.

	Sarah Heyworth
	The Slate Shed at Graig Wen,
	Arthog,
	Gwynedd LL39 1BQ
Tel	+44 (0)1341 250482
Email	hello@slateshed.co.uk
Web	www.slateshed.co.uk

Entry 683   Map 7

Gwynedd

Caerynwch

Feast your eyes on a mountain framed against brilliant skies from this Georgian home. Come for peace, space, acres of beautiful garden, woodland and burbling streams, and vast trees sheltering rhododendrons and plants collected by Andrew's botanist grandmother. Inside is unpretentious and charming with big comfy country bedrooms and those mesmerising views. Gaze at Cadair Idris from a grand-scale drawing room; cosy up in a sitting room with a wood-burner; breakfast under the gaze of the ancestors. Snowdonia and river walks beckon – and then there's the pub, a short stroll through the grounds.

Pets can sleep downstairs.

Rooms	3: 1 double; 1 double, 1 twin, both with separate bath/shower.
Price	£90. Singles £45.
Meals	Pub within 1 mile.
Closed	Rarely.

	Andrew & Hilary Richards
	Caerynwch,
	Brithdir, Dolgellau,
	Gwynedd LL40 2RF
Tel	+44 (0)1341 422263
Email	richards@torrentwalkcottages.com
Web	www.torrentwalkcottages.com

Entry 684   Map 7

Gwynedd

Gwynedd

The Old Rectory on the lake

Hike to Cadair Idris – the scenery is breathtaking. Return to a hot tub under the stars, and champagne to toast your good fortune. This lakeside B&B in southern Snowdonia is utterly spoiling and Ricky has become a chef of reputation. Slow-roast lamb shank, fillet of local salmon, a trio of Welsh ices; the menus change each day. Spacious bedrooms (one downstairs) have ever-changing views, bathrooms are sumptuous and you wake to the smell of Welsh bacon: breakfasts are to die for. Binoculars for the birds, a wonderful welcome for you, candlelit dining… it's bliss.

Minimum two nights at weekends; three on bank holidays.

Y Goeden Eirin

A little gem tucked between the sea and the mountains, an education in Welsh culture, and a great place to explore wild Snowdonia, the Llyn peninsula and the dramatic Eifl mountains. Inside presents a cosy picture: Welsh-language and English books share the shelves, paintings by contemporary Welsh artists enliven the walls, an arty 70s décor mingles with sturdy Welsh oak in the bedrooms – the one in the house the best – and all bathrooms are super. Wonderful food is served alongside the Bechstein in the beamed dining room – the welcoming, thoughtful Eluned and John have created an unusually delightful space.

Rooms	4 doubles.
Price	£120. Singles £70.
Meals	Dinner, 4 courses, £30 (not Wednesdays). Pub 4 miles.
Closed	January.

Rooms	3: 1 double. Sea and Mountain Rooms: 1 double, 1 twin.
Price	£80–£100. Singles from £60.
Meals	Dinner, 4 courses, £28. Wine from £14. Packed lunch £12. Pub/restaurant 0.75 miles.
Closed	Christmas, New Year & occasionally.

	Ricky Francis
	The Old Rectory on the lake, Talyllyn, Gwynedd LL36 9AJ
Tel	+44 (0)1654 782225
Email	enquiries@rectoryonthelake.co.uk
Web	www.rectoryonthelake.co.uk

	John & Eluned Rowlands
	Y Goeden Eirin, Dolydd, Caernarfon, Gwynedd LL54 7EF
Tel	+44 (0)1286 830942
Mobile	+44 (0)7708 491234
Email	john_rowlands@tiscali.co.uk
Web	www.ygoedeneirin.co.uk

Entry 685   Map 7

Entry 686   Map 6

Monmouthshire

Penpergwm Lodge

On the edge of the Brecon Beacons, a large and lovely Edwardian house. Breakfast round the mahogany table, relax by the fire in the sitting room with books to read and piano to play. The Boyles have been here for years and pour much of their energy into three beautiful acres of parterre and potager, orchard and flowers. Bedrooms are gloriously traditional – ancestral portraits, embroidered bed covers, big windows, good chintz – with garden views; bathrooms are a skip across the landing. A pool and tennis for the sporty, two summer houses for the dreamy, a good pub you can walk to. Splendid, old-fashioned B&B.

Rooms	2 twins, each with separate bath.
Price	£75. Singles £45.
Meals	Pub within walking distance.
Closed	Rarely.

Catriona Boyle
Penpergwm Lodge,
Penpergwm, Abergavenny,
Monmouthshire NP7 9AS
Tel   +44 (0)1873 840208
Email   boyle@penpergwm.co.uk
Web   www.penplants.com

Entry 687   Map 7

Monmouthshire

Myrtle Cottage

The family has found a slice of heaven in Llandogo. You're in the heart of their home and little Elsie, George and Alicia make terrific hosts. Bedrooms have a private balcony or French windows leading to the garden, and lovely wide views across the Wye Valley. Breakfasts in the conservatory are scrumptious. Tori bakes fabulous breads, cakes and waffles, and you could find yourself lingering all day for the wood-fired pizzas and Ed's microbrewery beers. Hike up and down the river, visit the pub at Brockweir, drop in on the brewery – we recommend Humpty's Fuddle!

Rooms	2 doubles sharing bath with family.
Price	£70. Singles £50.
Meals	Supper by arrangement, £12.50–£30. Monthly pizza evenings. Picnics & lunches £7.50–£25. Pubs/restaurants 3 miles.
Closed	Rarely.

Edward & Tori Biggs
Myrtle Cottage,
Llandogo, Monmouth,
Monmouthshire NP25 4TP
Mobile   +44 (0)7824 663550
Email   shop@meadowfarm.org.uk

Entry 688   Map 7

Monmouthshire

Upper Red House

Head down the lane into deepest Monmouthshire and the meadows, orchards and woodland of Teona's organic farm. There are six ponds and miles of bushy hedges; bees, ponies, peafowl and wildlife flourish. The 17th-century house, restored from dereliction, has lovely views, flagstones and oak, limewashed walls and a magical feel. Up steep stairs are rustic bedrooms with beams, lots of books, no TV; the attic rooms get the best views of all. Bathrooms are simple, one has a huge old roll top tub. After a good vegetarian breakfast at the long kitchen table take a farm tour, explore Offa's Dyke or the Wye Valley and revel in the silence.

Pembrokeshire

Penfro

This is fun – idiosyncratic and a tad theatrical, rather than conventional and uniformly stylish. The Lappins' home is an impressive Georgian affair, formerly a ballet school. Judith is warm and friendly; her taste – she's also a WW1 expert – is eclectic verging on the wacky and she minds that guests are comfortable and well-fed. You eat communally at the scrubbed table in the flagged Aga kitchen: tasty dinners, homemade jams and good coffee at breakfast. The garden is big and beautiful so enjoy its conversational terrace. And discuss which of the three very characterful bedrooms will suit you best, plumbing and all!

Open over Christmas.

Rooms	4: 1 double; 1 double, 2 singles sharing bath (let to same party only).
Price	£90. Singles £35-£45.
Meals	Vegetarian packed lunch £6. Pubs/restaurants 3.5 miles.
Closed	Rarely.

Rooms	3: 1 double; 1 double, 1 twin each with separate bath.
Price	£70-£85. Singles from £51.
Meals	Dinner, 3 courses, £20. Packed lunch from £8. Pub 250 yds.
Closed	Rarely.

	Teona Dorrien-Smith
	Upper Red House,
	Llanfihangel-Ystern-Llewern,
	Monmouth,
	Monmouthshire NP25 5HL
Tel	+44 (0)1600 780501
Email	upperredhouse@mac.com
Web	www.upperredhouse.co.uk

	Judith Lappin
	Penfro,
	111 Main Street, Pembroke,
	Pembrokeshire SA71 4DB
Tel	+44 (0)1646 682753
Mobile	+44 (0)7763 856181
Email	info@penfro.co.uk
Web	www.penfro.co.uk

Entry 689 Map 7

Entry 690 Map 6

Pembrokeshire

Pembrokeshire

Cresselly House

Imagine staying at the Georgian mansion of an old country friend – that's what it's like to stay at Cresselly. Step into a sunny square hall with a sweeping stair and the ancestors on the walls. Beeswax and lavender scent the air, cosy bedrooms are as grandly traditional as can be, new bathrooms sparkle and views swoop over the park. Choose to breakfast at the kitchen table, in the dining room or in your room; tuck into a simple supper with Hugh & Co (huge fun) or a gourmet feast à deux. The walking and riding are glorious, and there's amazing stabling for your horse: this is the heartland of the South Pembrokeshire Hunt.

Licensed to hold wedding ceremonies.

Knowles Farm

The Cleddau estuary winds its way around this organic working farm – its lush grasses feed the cows that produce milk for the renowned Rachel's yogurt. Your hosts love the land, are committed to its conservation and let you come and go as you please; picnic in the garden, wander through bluebell woods, discover a pond; dogs like it too. You have your own entrance to old-fashioned, pretty bedrooms with comfortable beds and glorious views. Breakfast and supper are delicious; food is fully organic or very local. If Gini is busy with the farm there are terrific pubs by the river that serve dinner.

Rooms	4: 2 doubles, 2 twins.
Price	£110-£150. Singles £95.
Meals	Supper, 2 courses, £25-£55. Pub 1 mile.
Closed	Rarely.

Rooms	3: 2 doubles; 1 twin with separate bath.
Price	£72-£75. Singles £50.
Meals	Supper from £12. Dinner, 4 courses, £22. (Not in school holidays.) Packed lunch £6. Pub 1.5 miles, restaurant 3 miles.
Closed	Rarely.

	Hugh Harrison-Allen
	Cresselly House,
	Cresselly, Kilgetty,
	Pembrokeshire SA68 0SP
Tel	+44 (0)1646 651992
Email	info@cresselly.com
Web	www.cresselly.com

	Virginia Lort Phillips
	Knowles Farm,
	Lawrenny,
	Pembrokeshire SA68 0PX
Tel	+44 (0)1834 891221
Email	ginilp@lawrenny.org.uk
Web	www.lawrenny.org.uk

Entry 691   Map 6

Entry 692   Map 6

Pembrokeshire

Pentower

Curl up with a cat and watch the ferries – or sometimes a porpoise – coasting to Ireland; French windows open onto the terrace and a glorious vista. Mary and Tony are warm and interesting hosts; their turreted 1898 house has an easy-going atmosphere, quarry tiled floors, decorative fireplaces and an impressive staircase. Spotless bedrooms are light and airy, with large showers; the Tower Room has the views. Wake for a very good full English (or Welsh) breakfast in the tiled dining/sitting room – tuck in while admiring the panoramic view over a bay full of boats. Fishguard is a short stroll, and the stunning coastal path is nearby.

Rooms	2: 1 double, 1 twin/double.
Price	£85-£90. Singles £50.
Meals	Packed lunch £5.
	Pubs/restaurants 500 yds.
Closed	Occasionally.

Tony Jacobs & Mary Geraldine
Casey
Pentower,
Tower Hill, Fishguard,
Pembrokeshire SA65 9LA
Tel   +44 (0)1348 874462
Email   sales@pentower.co.uk
Web   www.pentower.co.uk

Entry 693   Map 6

Pembrokeshire

Cefn-y-Dre Country House

Geoff and Gaye want your stay to go without a hitch, and they're proud of the rich history of their house. Solid, handsome and 500 years old, Cefn-y-Dre is on the fringe of the Pembrokeshire Coast National Park with views to the Preseli Hills. The sitting room is set aside for guests, notable for its striking red chairs used during Prince Charles' investiture in 1969 – quite a talking point! Geoff is a great cook who takes pleasure in using local produce and home-grown veg from the large garden; not so long ago he trained at Ballymaloe. St David's, with its ancient cathedral, is nearby, as are some of Britain's finest beaches.

Licensed premises.

Rooms	3: 1 double, 1 twin/double;
	1 double with separate
	bath/shower.
Price	£79-£99. Singles £50-£70.
Meals	Dinner, 3 courses, £24.50.
	Pubs/restaurants 2 miles.
Closed	Rarely.

Gaye Williams & Geoff Stickler
Cefn-y-Dre Country House,
Fishguard,
Pembrokeshire SA65 9QS
Tel   +44 (0)1348 875663
Email   welcome@cefnydre.co.uk
Web   www.cefnydre.co.uk

Entry 694   Map 6

Powys

Plas Uchaf Country House

Sweep up the drive to this gracious Queen Anne house and marvel at spectacular views over the Tanat Valley. Inside, find a pleasing mix of old and new. Bedrooms with a smart hotel slant have pale carpet or polished old floors, glossy beds and striking wallpapers; you'll feel nicely independent in the garden room. Help yourself from the honesty bar in the cosy book-filled sitting room, from which French windows lead to a garden with reading spots and clucking hens. Chris is easy and chatty and he and Julie are keen cooks; dine well at linen-clad tables in the elegant dining room. Snowdonia National Park beckons.

Powys

The Farm

Lose yourself in the wildlife, from a warm-hearted Welsh Marches B&B. There are just five sheep remaining now (all pets!) and your hosts have hearts of gold. Find fresh flowers on the Welsh dresser, a big dining table with a lovely garden view, breakfasts locally sourced and marmalades, jams and bread homemade. (And special diets easily catered for.) Overlooking the garden – yours to enjoy – are big bedrooms with TVs, clock-radios, tea and coffee making facilities and WiFi; one is on the ground floor in an extension, ideal for the less sprightly. Montgomery and Bishop's Castle, lovely little towns, are a must-see.

Rooms	6: 4 doubles, 1 twin/double; 1 twin with separate bath.		Rooms	3: 2 twins/doubles, 1 double.
Price	£80–£100. Singles £60–£75.		Price	£70–£85. Singles from £40.
Meals	Dinner, 2–3 courses, from £18. Packed lunch from £5. Pub 1.5 miles.		Meals	Dinner from £16. Pubs/restaurants 2 miles.
Closed	Rarely.		Closed	Rarely.

	Chris Brown		Sandra & Alan Jones
	Plas Uchaf Country House,		The Farm,
	Llangedwyn, Oswestry,		Snead, Montgomery,
	Powys SY10 9LD		Powys SY15 6EB
Tel	+44 (0)1691 780588	Tel	+44 (0)1588 620281
Email	info@plasuchaf.com	Email	asj.farmsnead@btconnect.com
Web	www.plasuchaf.com	Web	www.thefarmsnead.co.uk

Entry 695   Map 7

Entry 696   Map 7

Powys

Powys

The Old Vicarage

Come for vast skies, forested hills and quilted fields that stretch for miles. This Victorian vicarage is a super base: smart, welcoming, full of comforts. You get a log fire in a cosy sitting room, a small restaurant with long country views and fancy bedrooms that spoil you all the way. Chef Tim has quite a pedigree, the food is delicious, local suppliers are noted on menus, and much is grown in the garden, where chickens run free. Resist laziness and take to the hills for glorious walking and cycling: the Kerry Ridgeway is on your doorstep as is Powis Castle.

Children over 12 welcome.

The Old Vicarage

A wide hall, deep window sills and expanses of glass have created a light and appealing home. On the edge of the hamlet, this Arts and Crafts house has spectacular views. Pat serves afternoon tea when you arrive, and breakfast is in a snug spot by the wood-burner. Bedrooms are traditional, big and blessed with homemade biscuits, tea trays and flowers; both have views across gardens, woodland and paddocks – there are acres to explore. The veg patch provides for dinner and you can enjoy a sunset drink in the walled garden. Walks are wonderful – Offa's Dyke footpath is close by – and the Hay-on-Wye festival is a 30-minute drive.

Well-behaved dogs by arrangement.

Rooms	4: 2 doubles, 1 twin/double, 1 suite.
Price	£95-£110. Suite £150. Singles £55-£75.
Meals	Dinner, 3 courses, £30. Packed lunch available. Pub 0.75 miles.
Closed	Rarely.

Rooms	2: 1 double; 1 twin with separate bath.
Price	£80-£90. Singles £50-£55.
Meals	Dinner, 3 courses, £22. BYO. Pub 3 miles.
Closed	Rarely.

Tim & Helen Withers
The Old Vicarage,
Dolfor, Newtown,
Powys SY16 4BN
Tel   +44 (0)1686 629051
Mobile   +44 (0)7753 760054
Email   tim@theoldvicaragedolfor.co.uk
Web   www.theoldvicaragedolfor.co.uk

Patricia Birch
The Old Vicarage,
Evancoyd, Presteigne,
Powys LD8 2PA
Tel   +44 (0)1547 560951
Mobile   +44 (0)7903 859012
Email   pat.birch38@gmail.com
Web   www.oldvicaragebandb-welshborder.co.uk

Entry 697   Map 7

Entry 698   Map 7

Powys

The Red Kite Organic B&B

Neal and Juliette delight in reviving the weary in their beautiful, nurturing home where views soar to the Black Mountains and the Brecon Beacons. All is elegant and delightfully understated: find a sitting room with soft colours, jugs of wild flowers, natural linen upholstery, oil paintings and books; on chilly days the wood-burner keeps you cosy and glass doors face that view. Sleep peacefully in elegant bedrooms with a four-poster or French walnut twins, wake to delicious breakfasts: much is organic and it's worth booking dinner. Stride for miles in search of wild ponies and wilderness. Bustling Hay is near.

Rooms	4: 3 doubles, 1 twin.
Price	£90. Singles £70.
Meals	Dinner, 2-3 courses, £20-£25. Pubs/restaurants 1.5 miles.
Closed	Rarely.

Neal Smith & Juliette Fernandes
The Red Kite Organic B&B,
Newchurch,
Kington,
Powys HR5 3QH
Tel   +44 (0)1497 851727
Email   enquiries@theredkite.co.uk
Web   www.theredkite.co.uk

Entry 699   Map 7

Powys

Rhedyn

Come here if you need to remember how to relax. Such an unassuming, little place, but with real character and soul: great comfort too. Find exposed walls in the bedrooms, funky lighting, pocket sprung mattresses, lovely books to read, and calm colours; bathrooms are modern and delightfully quirky. But the real stars of this show are Muiread and Ciaran: warm, enthusiastic and engaging, with a passion for good local food and a desire for more self-sufficiency – pigs and bees are planned next. This is a totally tranquil place, with agreeable walks through the Irfon valley, and bog snorkelling too!

Rooms	3 doubles.
Price	£85. Singles £75.
Meals	Dinner, 3 courses, £27.50. Packed lunch £7.50. Pub/restaurant 1 mile.
Closed	Rarely.

Muiread & Ciaran O'Connell
Rhedyn,
Cilmery,
Builth Wells,
Powys LD2 3LH
Tel   +44 (0)1982 551944
Email   info@rhedynguesthouse.co.uk
Web   www.rhedynguesthouse.co.uk

Entry 700   Map 7

Powys

Trericket Mill Vegetarian Guesthouse

Alistair and Nicky's Georgian watermill is characterful and informal. You eat surrounded by books, beams and the original milling machinery, from a tempting vegetarian menu. Bedrooms are cosy with pine furniture and colourful throws; two are reached via a spiral wooden stair, the third opens to a sunny veranda. Views shoot off towards Radnorshire or sheep-grazed fields... come home to a flagstoned living room with maps, WiFi and wood-burner. Bookish Hay and its festival is a short drive; waterfalls and mountain ranges abound. It's a brilliant base for walkers and mountain bikers – and great value.

Self-catering available in River Cabin.

Rooms	3: 2 doubles, 1 twin.
Price	£68–£78. Singles £48–£58.
Meals	Dinner, 3 courses, £18.75. BYO. Simple supper £8.50. Pub/restaurant 2 miles.
Closed	Christmas & occasionally in winter.

Alistair & Nicky Legge
Trericket Mill Vegetarian Guesthouse,
Erwood, Builth Wells,
Powys LD2 3TQ
Tel   +44 (0)1982 560312
Email   mail@trericket.co.uk
Web   www.trericket.co.uk

Powys

Hafod Y Garreg

A unique opportunity to stay in the oldest house in Wales – a fascinating, 1402 cruck-framed hall house, built for Henry IV as a hunting lodge. Informal Annie and John have filled it with a charming mix of Venetian mirrors, Indian rugs, pewter plates, gorgeous fabrics and oak furniture. Dine by candlelight in the fabulous dining room – maybe pheasant pie with chilli jam and hazelnut mash: delicious. Bedrooms are luxurious and comfortable with Egyptian cotton bed linen. Reach the Grade II*-listed house by a bumpy track across gated fields crowded with chickens, cats... a special, secluded and relaxed place.

Rooms	2 doubles.
Price	£86. Singles from £80.
Meals	Dinner, 3 courses, £25. BYO. Pubs/restaurants 2.5 miles.
Closed	Christmas.

Annie & John McKay
Hafod Y Garreg,
Erwood, Builth Wells,
Powys LD2 3TQ
Tel   +44 (0)1982 560400
Email   john-annie@hafod-y.wanadoo.co.uk
Web   www.hafodygarreg.co.uk

Danyfan Carriage

Emma and Stevie fled London a few years ago and landed in the Brecon Beacons. Sympathetically restored, their railway carriage is from another age; the grand wicker headboard and the burnished walnut wardrobe are welcome additions (so are the tea lights and the Scrabble). This off-grid space comes with its own piping hot shower and compost loo a step away. A wood-burner keeps the bedroom cosy, the bed has mountains of soft pillows, lanterns give a gentle light and two gas rings make cooking a doddle. Emma leaves you a sourdough loaf, milk, tea, coffee and local bacon on arrival... a delicious one-pot supper can be bubbling away too.

Minimum two nights. Book through Sawday's Canopy & Stars online or by phone.

The Old Store House

Unbend here with agreeable books, chattering birds, and Peter, who asks only that you feel at home. Downstairs are a range-warmed kitchen, a sunny conservatory overlooking garden, chickens, ducks and canal, and a charmingly ramshackle sitting room with a wood-burner, sofas and a piano – no babbling TV. Bedrooms are large, light and spotless, with more books, soft goose down, armchairs and bathrooms with views. Breakfast, without haste, on scrambled eggs, local bacon and sausages, blistering coffee. Bliss – but as far from tickety boo as possible. Walk into the hills from the back door.

Self-catering available.

Rooms	Carriage for 2 with separate shower & compost loo.	Rooms	4: 3 doubles, 1 twin.
Price	£80–£100.	Price	£80. Singles £40.
Meals	BYO breakfast (welcome pack provided). Pubs/restaurants within 2 miles.	Meals	Packed lunch £4. Pub/restaurant 0.75 miles.
Closed	Never.	Closed	Rarely.

	Sawday's Canopy & Stars Danyfan Carriage, Danyfan, Cwmgwdi, Brecon, Powys LD3 8LG		Peter Evans The Old Store House, Llanfrynach, Brecon, Powys LD3 7LJ
Tel	+44 (0)1275 395447		
Email	enquiries@canopyandstars.co.uk	Tel	+44 (0)1874 665499
Web	www.canopyandstars.co.uk/ danyfan	Email	oldstorehouse@btconnect.com
		Web	www.theoldstorehouse.co.uk

Entry 703   Map 7

Entry 704   Map 7

Powys

Ty'r Chanter

Warmth, colour, children and activity: this house is fun. Tiggy welcomes you like family; help collect eggs, feed the lambs or the pony, drop your shoes by the fire. The farmhouse and barn are stylishly relaxed; deep sofas, tartan throws, heaps of books, views to the Brecon Beacons and Black Mountains. Bedrooms are soft, simple sanctuaries with Jo Malone bathroom treats. The two children's rooms zing with murals; toys, kids' sitting room, sandpit – child heaven. Walk, fish, canoe, book-browse in Hay or stroll the estate. Homemade cakes, whisky to help yourself to: fine hospitality.

Rooms	2: 1 double; 1 double with separate bath/shower. (Two children's rooms available.)
Price	£95. Singles £55.
Meals	Packed lunch £8. Pub 1 mile.
Closed	Christmas.

Tiggy Pettifer
Ty'r Chanter,
Gliffaes, Crickhowell,
Powys NP8 1RL
Tel   +44 (0)1874 731144
Mobile   +44 (0)7802 387004
Email   tiggy@tyrchanter.com
Web   www.tyrchanter.com

Powys

Llangattock Court

Built in 1690 and mentioned in Pevsner as an 'outstanding example of a country house in this style', this is indeed grand and sits in the middle of the sleepy village, surrounded by a large garden. Both bedrooms are a good size (one has a big French bed and a small shower room) with lovely antiques and a fresh feel; views from one soar across to the Black Mountains. Breakfast in style in the enormous dining room overlooked by framed relatives, stroll through the rose garden, visit a castle or historic house, walk to the local pub for dinner. Morgan is a painter; some of his paintings are on display.

Rooms	2: 1 double, 1 suite for 4 (1 four-poster & 1 twin).
Price	£50–£80. Singles £45.
Meals	Pubs/restaurants within 1 mile.
Closed	Christmas & New Year; 1–2 weeks in October.

Polly Llewellyn
Llangattock Court,
Llangattock,
Crickhowell,
Powys NP8 1PH
Tel   +44 (0)1873 810116
Email   morganllewellyn@btinternet.com
Web   www.llangattockcourt.co.uk

Swansea

Blas Gwyr

Llangennith was once a well-kept secret — now walkers, riders, surfers and beach bunnies of all ages flock. Close to the bustling bay is an extended 1700s cottage with a youthful facelift. All is simple but stylish: bedrooms, two overlooking the road, are modern and matching; bathrooms and wet rooms come with warm floors and fluffy towels. Everything from the bedspread to the breakfast is local: make sure you try the laverbread. After a day at sea, fling wet gear in the drying room and linger over a coffee in the courtyard, or walk to the pub for a sun-kissed pint. Laid-back bliss.

Welsh spoken.

Wrexham

Worthenbury Manor

Welcome to one half of a big country house on the border of Wales and Shropshire. Congenial, generous Ian and Elizabeth look after you wonderfully well. The guest sitting room is warmed by a log fire in winter; the dining room has listed Jacobean panelling. Choose between two comfortable bedrooms, one decorated in Georgian style, one in Jacobean, both with rich drapes, chandeliers, fresh coffee and antique four-posters. Wake refreshed for a beautifully cooked breakfast: local and home-grown produce, home-baked bread and Ian's impressive marmalades; dinner too is a treat. Visit Erddig, Chirk Castle, Powis...

Check directions on booking.

Rooms	4: 1 double, 1 double (with sofabed), 1 twin/double, 1 suite for 2-4.
Price	£110-£120.
Meals	Packed lunch available. Dinner £27.50-£30 (selected weekends). Pub 150 yds.
Closed	Rarely.

Rooms	2: 1 four-poster; 1 four-poster with separate bath.
Price	£80-£90. Singles £45-£60. Additional child £15.
Meals	Dinner, 3 courses, £30. Lunch £18. BYO. Pub/restaurant 5 miles.
Closed	24-28 December.

	Dafydd James
	Blas Gwyr,
	Plenty Farm, Llangennith,
	Swansea SA3 1HU
Tel	+44 (0)1792 386472
Mobile	+44 (0)7974 981156
Email	info@blasgwyr.co.uk
Web	www.blasgwyr.co.uk

	Elizabeth & Ian Taylor
	Worthenbury Manor,
	Worthenbury,
	Wrexham LL13 0AW
Tel	+44 (0)1948 770342
Email	enquiries@worthenburymanor.co.uk
Web	www.worthenburymanor.co.uk

Entry 707   Map 2

Entry 708   Map 7

Alastair
Sawday's

'More than a bed
for the night…'

Britain
France
Ireland
Italy
Portugal
Spain

www.sawdays.co.uk

Self-Catering | B&B | Hotel | Pub | Treehouses, Cabins, Yurts & More

For many years Alastair Sawday Publishing has been 'greening' the business in different ways. Our aim is to reduce our environmental footprint as far as possible and with almost everything we do we have environmental implications in mind. In recognition of our efforts we won a Business Commitment to the Environment Award in 2005, a Queen's Award for Enterprise in the Sustainable Development category in 2006, and the Independent Publishers Guild Environmental Award in 2008.

The buildings

Beautiful as they were, our old offices leaked heat, used electricity to heat water and rooms, flooded spaces with light to illuminate one person, and were not ours to alter.

So in 2005 we created our own eco offices by converting some old barns to create a low-emissions building.

Photo left: Tom Germain
Photo right: Jackie King

Heating and lighting the building, which houses over 30 employees, now produces only 0.28 tonnes of carbon dioxide per year – a reduction of 35%. Not bad when you compare this with the six tonnes emitted by the average UK household. We achieved this through a variety of innovative and energy-saving building techniques, some of which are described below.

Insulation   By laying insulating board 90mm thick immediately under the roof tiles and on the floor, and lining the inside of the building with plastic sheeting, we are now insulated even for Arctic weather, and almost totally air-tight.

Heating   We installed a wood pellet boiler from Austria in order to be largely fossil-fuel free. The heat is conveyed by water to all corners of the building via an underfloor system.

Water   We installed a 6,000-litre tank to collect rainwater from the roofs. This is pumped back, via an ultra-violet filter, to lavatories, shower and basins. There are also two solar thermal panels on the roof providing heat to the one hot-water cylinder.

Lighting   We have a mix of low-energy lighting – task lighting and up lighting – and have installed three sun pipes.

Electricity   Our electricity has long come from the Good Energy Company and is 100% renewable.

Materials Virtually all materials are non-toxic or natural, and our carpets are made from (80%) Herdwick sheep wool from National Trust farms in the Lake District.

Doors and windows Outside doors and new windows are wooden, double-glazed and beautifully constructed in Norway. Old windows have been double-glazed.

More greenery

Besides having a building we are proud of, and which is pretty impressive visually, too, we work in a number of other ways to reduce the company's overall environmental footprint.

- office travel is logged as part of a carbon sequestration programme, and money for compensatory tree planting donated to SCAD in India for a tree-planting and development project

- we avoid flying and take the train for business trips wherever possible
- car sharing and the use of a company pool car are part of company policy, with recycled cooking oil used in one car and LPG in the other
- organic and Fair Trade basic provisions are used in the staff kitchen and organic and/or local food is provided by the company at all in-house events
- green cleaning products are used throughout
- kitchen waste is composted

However, becoming 'green' is a journey and, although we began long before most companies, we realise we still have a long way to go.

The Old Rectory on the Lake, Gwynedd, entry 685

Quick reference indices

Stay all day
Stay all day if you wish.

Quick reference indices

Scotland

Wales

Singles

These places have a single room OR rooms let to single guests for half the double room rate or under.

England

Pet-friendly
Guests' pets can sleep in the bedroom (but not on the bed).

Quick reference indices

Quick reference indices

Harptree Court Treehouse, Somerset, entry 442

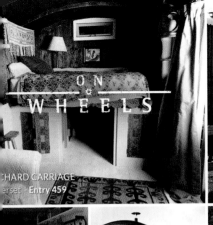

ON WHEELS

CHARD CARRIAGE
...erset - **Entry 459**

THE OLD FORGE
Dorset - **Entry 183**

TY CEFN TREGIB
Carmarthenshire - **Entry 673**

...OT PANTHER
...shire - **Entry 656**

THE SHEPHERD'S RETURN
Sussex - **Entry 503**

UP IN THE TREES

BAGTHORPE TREEHOUSE
Norfolk - **Entry 341**

OUT IN THE WILDERNESS

SECRET CLOUD YURTS
Derbyshire - **Entry 469**

YARLINGTON YURT
Somerset - **Entry 455**

...IGGLY TIN
...pshire - **Entry 242**

SCALES PLATATION
Cumbria - **Entry 82**

RANSOMS
Kent - **Entry 267**

Alastair Sawday has been publishing books for over twenty years, finding Special Places to Stay in Britain and abroad. All our properties are inspected by us and are chosen for their charm and individuality and, now, with seventeen titles to choose from there are plenty of places to explore. You can buy any of our books at a reader discount of 25%* on the RRP.

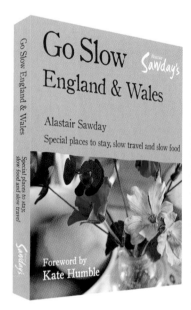
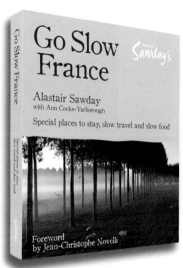

List of titles:	RRP	Discount price
British Bed & Breakfast	£15.99	£11.99
Special Places to Stay in Britain for Garden Lovers	£19.99	£14.99
British Hotels and Inns	£15.99	£11.99
Pubs & Inns of England & Wales	£15.99	£11.99
Venues	£11.99	£8.99
Cotswolds	£9.99	£7.49
Wales	£9.99	£7.49
Dog-friendly Breaks in Britain	£14.99	£11.24
French Bed & Breakfast	£15.99	£11.99
French Self-Catering	£14.99	£9.74
French Châteaux & Hotels	£15.99	£11.99
Italy	£15.99	£11.99
Portugal	£12.99	£9.74
Spain	£15.99	£11.99
India	£11.99	£8.99
Go Slow England & Wales	£19.99	£14.99
Go Slow France	£19.99	£14.99

*postage and packaging is added to each order

How to order:
You can order online at: www.sawdays.co.uk/bookshop/
or call: **+44(0)1275 395431**

423

Photo: The Old Post Office, Dorset, entry 173

SPECIAL PLACES TO EAT & DRINK

Alastair
Sawday's

Pubs

Find handpicked pubs with passion in England & Wales on our website and iPhone app.

Available on the
App Store

Alastair
Sawday's

Special Places to Eat & Drink

Pubs

"Sawday's has never once let us down - invaluable."
Simon Hoggart, The Guardian

We have indexed places under their MAIN postal town. See maps for clear positioning.

Pengwern Country House, Conwy, entry 679

① Gloucestershire

Gloucestershire

Clapton Manor

② Karin and James's 16th-century manor is as all homes should be: loved and lived-in. And, with three-foot-thick walls, rich Persian rugs on flagstoned floors, sit-in fireplaces and stone-mullioned windows, it's gorgeous. The garden, enclosed by old stone walls, is full of birdsong and roses. One bedroom has a secret door leading to a fuchsia-pink bathroom; the other room, smaller, has a Tudor stone fireplace and wonderful garden views. Wellies, dogs, a comfy guest sitting room with lots of books… and breakfast by a vast fireplace: homemade bread, award-winning marmalade and eggs from the hens. A happy, charming family home.

Sherborne Forge

You are in a quiet Cotswolds corner, in your own restored cottage across the garden from the owner's 17th-century house, and overlooking Sherborne Brook. Walk in to a large living space with a high beamed ceiling, comfy sofas, bright rugs, antiques, flowers, books and a dining table and chairs. You have your own small kitchen for toast and tea; Karen brings over a delicious organic breakfast, served on a private terrace on sunny mornings. Your bedroom has pretty fabrics and fine linen; the bathroom has a big tub for long soaks. Fish for trout in the brook, head off for glorious walks and bike rides… this is a sanctuary.

Minimum two nights preferred.

③ Rooms	2: 1 double, 1 twin/double.	
④ Price	£110–£130. Singles from £100.	
⑤ Meals	Pub/restaurants within 15-minute drive.	
⑥ Closed	Rarely.	

Rooms	Cottage: 1 twin/double, sitting room & kitchenette.
Price	£100–£110. Singles £80.
Meals	Pub/restaurant 2.5 miles.
Closed	Rarely.

	Karin & James Bolton
	Clapton Manor,
	Clapton-on-the-Hill,
	Gloucestershire GL54 2LG
Tel	+44 (0)1451 810202
Mobile	+44 (0)7967 144416
Email	bandb@claptonmanor.co.uk
Web	www.claptonmanor.co.uk

	Karen Kelly
	Sherborne Forge,
	Number 1 Sherborne, Cheltenham,
	Gloucestershire GL54 3DW
Tel	+44 (0)1451 844286
Mobile	+44 (0)7796 146130
Email	karen.j.kelly@btinternet.com
Web	www.sherborneforge.co.uk

⑦

⑧ Entry 210   Map 8

Entry 211   Map 8